Progressive Education

ALSO AVAILABLE FROM BLOOMSBURY

The Philosophy of Education: An Introduction, Richard Bailey

Education and Constructions of Childhood, David Blundell

Progressive Education

A critical introduction

JOHN HOWLETT

B L O O M S B U R Y

LONDON • NEW DELHI • NEW YORK • SYDNEY

Bloomsbury Academic

An imprint of Bloomsbury Publishing Plc

50 Bedford Square	1385 Broadway
London	New York
WC1B 3DP	NY 10018
UK	USA

www.bloomsbury.com

Bloomsbury is a registered trade mark of Bloomsbury Publishing Plc

First published 2013

British Library Cataloguing-in-Publication Data
A catalogue record for this book is available from the British Library.

ISBN: PB: 978-1-4411-4172-9
HB: 978-0-8264-4091-4
ePub: 978-1-4411-1051-0
ePDF: 978-1-4411-7758-2

Library of Congress Cataloging-in-Publication Data
Howlett, John.
Progressive education: a critical introduction/John Howlett.
pages cm
Includes bibliographical references and index.
ISBN 978-1-4411-4172-9 – ISBN 978-1-4411-7758-2 – ISBN 978-1-4411-1051-0 –
ISBN 978-0-8264-4091-4 1. Education–Experimental methods. 2. Progressive education.
3. Education–Philosophy. 4. Education–Social aspects. I. Title.
LB1027.3.H69 2013
371.3–dc23
2013015209

Typeset by Deanta Global Publishing Services, Chennai, India
Printed and bound in Great Britain

Contents

Acknowledgements

My foremost debt is to my former PhD supervisor, Philip Gardner, who first sparked my interest in progressive education and its controversies in 2005 and whose erudition, wit and insistence on style have hopefully been (at least partially) vindicated in the current volume. Likewise, thanks are due to Peter Cunningham for his initial suggestions and advice as to the shape and composition of the book at an early stage. Gary McCulloch also provided invaluable comment on the introductory sections. It was during my time at Cambridge that this book was started and the need, as I then saw it, for some sort of generalist book encompassing progressive education. In that regard, I am grateful for all those many students who I taught and supervised and for their never-less-than-useful contributions in discussing the most tangential aspects of obscure progressive texts and for providing me with food for thought as to the focus of certain chapters.

At Keele, within the School of Public Policy and Professional Practice, I have benefitted from the luxury of an understanding and supportive department, all of whom merit thanks. My colleagues there have provided me, often without them knowing it, much to ponder on in relation to debates within contemporary education and the need for those ideas locked away in the past. Of course, this would all have been academic without the original acceptance of the proposal and, in that regard, I must thank Alison Baker, Rosie Pattinson and (latterly) Frances Arnold at Bloomsbury Publishing, for not only commissioning the work but providing continued support, suggestion and assistance, in particular, with the thorny business of proofreading and indexing. I hope the book lives up to their expectations. All errors which remain are, of course, my own. Finally, the biggest thanks must be to my parents for their sustained kindness and support, particularly when living briefly under their roof. I hope this book goes some way to justifying the late nights.

Introduction

The controversy of progressivism

Speaking at Brighton College in 2008, the then Shadow Education Secretary Michael Gove condemned, in a keynote speech, what he saw as 'pupil centred learning' which, in his eyes, had 'dethroned' the teacher. Warming to his theme, Gove continued, 'This misplaced ideology has let down generations of children. It is an approach to education that has been called progressive but in fact is anything but. It privileges temporary relevance over a permanent body of knowledge' (Gove, quoted in *The Guardian*, 9 May 2008). This implicit criticism of teachers and their practices unsurprisingly drew a loud condemnatory response from the teaching unions and the tumult which ensued centred upon precisely the reasons why this 'dethroning' had taken place. Practitioners were keen to argue that this was not a death caused by their own hand but, instead, through the gradual suffocation of their practices inflicted by increased central control on the parts of successive governments, telling them not just what to teach but also how precisely to teach it through headline initiatives such as the Literacy and Numeracy Hours. In addition, Gove's speech raised concerns of a much wider nature than the mere status of the education profession. Was there, in fact, a legitimate distinction to be made, as seemed to be implied, between 'pupil centred learning' and 'progressive education' and was it always equitable to link these philosophies with the failure to impart children with a lasting core of 'permanent' knowledge?

These remonstrations were not though mere knee-jerk reactions to a strategic political sound-bite. They represented instead long-standing disaffection with governmental educational policy from not only those teachers who were required to directly enforce it but those with, for example, stakes in social policy, youth work and childhood studies. Many university academics – whose inclination to dissent, criticize and be hollow prophets in the wilderness is well known – had similarly long made clear where they saw the wider problems for teachers in terms of classroom behaviour, discipline and professional identity. For them, it was through precisely this aforementioned decline in the opportunities for more independent modes of teaching and learning which had stifled the profession's creativity and ability to actively engage young people. The historian Roy Lowe whose fine book, *The Death of Progressive Education: How Teachers Lost Control of the Classroom*, had been published the year before Gove's speech in 2007, concocted a perfect distillation of the increased pessimism felt by many teachers as he charted the incremental increase in those leaving the profession, dissatisfied at government requirements. While the polemical nature of the work undeniably split opinion, it convincingly questioned, contrary to Gove's belief, if in fact in the last 20 years, any such 'pupil centred' methods had existed at all.

Such discontentment also found a more official champion in the 2009 Cambridge Primary Review – one of whose key recommendations was the right of teachers to reclaim the classroom back from 'the personal fiefdom of ministers and their unelected advisors' (Alexander et al. 2009: 2). The then Labour government's systematic and unilateral rejection of the report *in toto* was a clear signal to the teaching profession and their supporters that any future mainstream government was unlikely to ever be supportive of efforts to alter the increasingly inflexible relationship between teachers and the bureaucracy of the educational state. Similarly, in the aftermath of the British 2011 summer riots, many commentators, even those only partially sympathetic to progressive ideas, cited disaffection with school, its seeming lack of relevance, excessive 'credentialization' and the inhering labelling culture of 'success' and 'failure' as contributory factors behind the anger and malaise emanating from the young people spilling out onto the streets.

And yet, it seemed odd that Gove would warn in his speech, in such sweeping, ahistorical terms, of the prevalence of such forms of 'pupil centred' teaching, especially as it had been his party which, controversially, had done most in recent years to centralize educational control and demonize classroom individualism. The National Curriculum, as part of the 1988 Education Reform Act, had devolved power away from the Local Education Authorities into the hands of the Minister of Education and, latterly, the 1992 *Curriculum Organization and Classroom Practice in Primary Schools* report had served actively to discourage enquiry-based learning at the expense of subject-based lessons and whole-class teaching. Both pieces of legislation were seen by many as sounding the death knell of the tacit laissez faire understanding which had been allowed to develop, for the better part of 40 years since 1944, between teachers and policy makers, whereby the state had merely delivered pedagogic and curricular guidance and suggestions and had not actively sought to intervene in the ways in which teachers worked within the classroom.

Appositely, it had been the National Curriculum which had constructed a 'permanent body of knowledge' which, through periodic testing, was to become the basis for the measurement not merely of the individual pupil but of the success or failure of an entire school. Even the Kenneth Clarke-commissioned 'Three Wise Men' Report,[1] also of 1992 which, given the choice of its authors, may have served to induce optimism among the teaching profession ultimately classified the Piagetian view of learning so beloved of an earlier generation of teachers as a 'highly questionable dogma' (Alexander et al. 1992: 1), which served ultimately to reinforce public prejudices regarding the leftist, subversive nature of teaching authorities.

In many ways, however, Gove's speech functioned as a useful piece of *agit prop* as it served to clarify the long-standing, unspoken politicization which existed in relation to progressive education. As Robert Skidelsky (1969) had long ago made clear, it was frequently – although not always exclusively – political affiliation that led to approval or rejection of child-centred approaches. Accordingly, progressive schools were either 'a delinquent's paradise of smoking, swearing, window breaking and free love' or else, 'a society of sages communing with nature, children partaking in games playing, dictating their own curriculum' (Skidelsky 1969: 13). It was, perhaps, no surprise therefore that the high point of British state-sanctioned progressivism contained in the Plowden Report[2] coincided with the decriminalization of homosexuality and capital punishment, the legalization of abortion and a more general social permissiveness under the 1960s Labour government of Harold Wilson. Similarly, the implementation of more state-directed, centralized initiatives designed to encourage and foster competition among institutions was a legacy of the radical, neo-liberal Thatcher government and her dynamic Secretaries of State, Keith Joseph and Kenneth Baker – both advocates of choice, selection and market forces within education.

Yet, for all of the protestations of the teaching unions and the academics, was Gove right? Had reports of the death of progressive methods in schools and classrooms been, in recent times, exaggerated? Many right wing commentaries and pressure groups thought not. The Campaign for Real Education,[3] for example, continues to lay the enduring failings of the British education system at the door of the progressives who, through 'the integration of subjects, the elimination of content, the introduction of cross-curricular themes, the replacement of RE by Personal, Social and Health Education . . . . have reinforced progressivism on a national scale' (CRE webpage). Furthermore, prominent critics such as Melanie Philips (1996) have sought to link what they perceive as the moral breakdown of society and the developing 'crisis in childhood' with a continuing progressive agenda propagated in schools, which seeks to endow children with concepts such as choice and freedom. Such concepts, she argues, are not suitable for children who are neither intellectually nor morally ready to understand and engage with them and, furthermore, the methods of transmission are frequently indicative of 'lazy' teaching and parenting. Far from merely questioning whether such methods provide the best possible education for the young child, those such as Phillips regard the progressive agenda as inherently subversive and indicative of the underlying shift in social attitudes, which has removed traditional forms of discipline and structure from children's lives. Crucially, in light of the intimate and complex relationship historically enjoyed between the Church and the State, the decline in church attendance and ecclesiastical authority has been seen as one of the catalysts for allowing such laxity to develop. Such developments can be seen too in light of the reduction in importance of the daily act of collective worship, once a long-established part of the school day.

This broad range of concerns has certainly been substantiated by a range of longitudinal objective academic studies – from that of Graham Vulliamy and Rosemary Webb (1993) onwards – which have clearly shown not only the ways in which governmental intentions have been subtly misshapen and altered by those at various levels of the decision-making process, but also how teachers themselves, at a more micro-level, have continued to instigate and instruct, depending upon their prior beliefs and practices. Teachers have thus served as agents of 'subversion', both knowingly and unknowingly, in relation to their pre-designated agendas and objectives. Even within the earlier investigations by Ashton et al. (1975), it was found that the three most popular aims of teachers within education were that children should be happy, cheerful and well balanced, that they should enjoy school work and find satisfaction in their achievements and, most crucially, that they, as individuals, should be encouraged to develop in their own ways.

As will be seen throughout the course of the following narrative, there is much within the many strands of progressivism which accords with these pupil-centred aims. Indeed, at the risk of overt generalization, it would be fair to suggest that, in general, teachers themselves tend to be individually more disposed towards wanting a higher degree of professional autonomy. This, after all, was the great battle of the teaching profession over the course of the twentieth century as it strived for an equal, self-regulating footing such as that enjoyed by medicine and law. By its very nature, such a mindset (which arguably still prevails) allowed for the diffusion of attitudes more conducive to freedom of learning and, consequently, child-centred approaches to teaching within the classroom. Such findings and attitudes would therefore seem to have defied many of the more pessimistic predictions of the advocates of progressive education!

To further compound the misery of the 'traditionalists', under successive recent New Labour governments, there were even conscious moves back towards more child-centred approaches. In keeping with Tony Blair's strategy of adapting old and established socialist ideas to fit into the contemporary world, influential educationalists such as Peter Silcock (1999) demonstrated that it was indeed feasible to incorporate progressive approaches within the context of a more pragmatic belief system. Although in practice, the Blair government, with its flagship 'academy' policy and desire to persuade the private sector to involve itself with education, was content ideologically to extend the legacy of the previous Conservative administration, actual classroom practice and policy was constructed more through a tacit acknowledgement of the importance of pupil voice. 'Creativity', in particular, became a key watchword, with initiatives such as Creative Partnerships, piloted in 2002 and expanded over the decade, seeking to not merely develop every individual child's creativity through writing, drama, dance and the like but also to foster ideologies of social inclusion through twinning areas of deprivation with the local cultural sector. While such initiatives hinted in their rhetoric at the communal ideas of John Dewey, so were children encouraged to be 'questioning, making connections, inventing and reinventing' (Creative Partnerships 2007). In this, there was more than a whiff of the radical critical pedagogy movement whose practitioners sought to develop individual autonomy and free-thinking in the school setting.

Furthermore, within the context of the wider world, international societies devoted to preserving the ideas of Maria Montessori and Rudolf Steiner have continued to thrive, and significant numbers of their schools are to be found in the United Kingdom, coexisting, it seems, quite happily alongside their neighbours while still offering the range of National Curriculum subjects and high attainment levels among their pupils. To further reflect more shifts to the progressive wing, recent Labour governments even saw such schools as worthy of financial rewards and tacit acknowledgement, which perhaps served to rubberstamp, if not an acceptance, than at least a recognition that such alternative viewpoints were legitimate and able to be contained under the umbrella of 'the state'.

Contradictions in progressivism

These interchanges serve to highlight the broad unmistakeable dichotomy between, on the one hand, the Conservative establishment, which has traditionally favoured teacher-directed learning and a more rigid 'names, dates and places' curricula driven by standards, and, on the other, those such as Roy Lowe and the late Brian Simon on the left, who have agitated for more progressive methods and increased attention to be paid to the pupil voice. Michael Gove, himself a Conservative, upon assuming the mantle of Secretary of State, quickly promoted an agenda popularly dubbed as 'back to the future', reflecting as it did an unashamedly conventional approach to the curriculum with an emphasis upon discipline, examinations, values and a traditional form of curriculum, including compulsory language learning, calculus (long since considered obsolete) and history, driven by a sense of 'English narrative'.

However, this stark left/right polarization, while opportune, obscures some of the more subtle complexities associated with progressivism for, in the educational world, things are rarely so conveniently demarcated. In 2010, Anthony Seldon, headmaster of the prestigious Wellington College, produced in conjunction with the Centre for Policy Studies, a pamphlet entitled *An End to Factory Schools*, which set about recommending to schools and ministers the pursuit of 'holistic learning' strategies, all the while simultaneously critiquing the existing education system as encapsulating a 'narrow vision of education', which equated, in Seldon's words, to little more than 'the apogee of Fordism gone mad' (Seldon 2010: 16). The invocation of controversial American psychologist Howard Gardner and his contentious theory of multiple intelligences was used by Seldon to further bolster an argument carrying a withering analysis of existing state schools and the system in which they operate, where the sole determinant of success is the passing of limited examinations in the context of a 'factory curriculum':

> While this is still controversial, it is surely common sense to recognize that students – and indeed all individuals – do have a variety of different intelligences; and
>
> that education should be directed towards drawing these out, rather than focusing exclusively on academic intelligence. (Ibid., 30)

Significant too was Seldon's call for subjects to be interrelated ('Interconnections between subjects need to be highlighted to students for a full understanding of the world'), for learning to be related to aspects of the real world, for schools to be freer from the confines of the state and for more ethereal concepts, such as joy and happiness, to be fostered in the classroom.

These claims were startling for two reasons. First, that Anthony Seldon – himself a Tory and headmaster of one of the most distinguished of public schools – was seen to be disabusing the rigid academic ethos upon which such privately funded schools were founded[4] and, second, that the state sector schools which Seldon cited as perpetuating a limited curriculum and a production-line approach to learning appeared to be the very ones derided by Gove and others for having continually advocated 'progressive methods'. There seemed therefore to be a degree of incongruity and confusion about not merely whether progressive methods are being practised, but what in fact they consist, or consisted, of.

It would of course be a mistake to see Seldon – or indeed any of the headmasters of the other public schools who have removed themselves as far as possible from centralized state control – as dyed in the wool progressives. They are not. Seldon's pamphlet was quick to condemn aspects of the Plowden Report and it is difficult not to associate schools whose fees equate to close to the average working salary with a perpetuation of the concept of a privileged elite. However, in many ways, attempts by fee-paying institutions, and their often charismatic and free-thinking headmasters, of which Seldon is undoubtedly one, to attach themselves to alternative forms of learning is nothing new. History offers us parallels; nearly a century ago, a raft of 'experimental' privately funded schools emerged under the aegis of the 'New Education Fellowship' – an all-encompassing term designed to reflect a shared ethos among many progressive educational thinkers who themselves, like Seldon, were dissatisfied with the more unattractive aspects of the state education system. Many of these schools were for the children of the intelligentsia but, nevertheless, their adherence to a curriculum based on relevance, more tolerant discipline, encouragement of the arts and crafts and a reliance upon the new science of psychology to justify their practices made it clear that radical schooling techniques were not always to be for those – the underprivileged and the delinquent – who, it may have been felt, had most need of them.

Given therefore the evident ambiguity and haziness which exists in relation to the debates surrounding progressivism, the term itself is clearly at risk of becoming open to exploitation and abuse by a number of parties with conflicting and potentially subversive aims. Lip service has been frequently paid by policy makers and teaching representatives to progressive notions in relation to the curriculum and learning strategies; yet, as Sol Cohen (1999) has implicitly pointed out, it is a fallacy to accept such essentially political statements as equating to genuine progressive advocacy as they may represent little more than an infiltration of mainstream discourse and, in and of themselves, do not necessarily indicate the existence of 'progressivism'. For Cohen, what defines progressivism is more the existence of its practices at the micro-level of the classroom by individual practitioners rather than what happens to be being said politically at a particular point in time.

Historians and progressivism

Scholarly writings concerning progressive education are themselves comparatively recent. While America has proven an honourable exception in giving long-standing recognition to the academic study of education – and historians of education like Lawrence Cremin have been feted at a national level for their work – the history of education in Britain as an historical sub-discipline has only begun to gain widespread academic acceptance within the past four decades, with the first edition of the flagship journal *History of Education* only being published as recently as 1972. In part, as William Richardson (1999) has shown, such developments were indicative of a wider trend towards the professionalization of the role of the academic, given currency by the rapid expansion in the number of higher education institutions during the period in question. During that time, writings in the history of education began to migrate from basic narratives constructed solely for the benefit of trainee teachers within teacher training colleges and instead towards scholarly investigations whose readership was intended to be a more directly intellectual audience attached to burgeoning university departments. Nevertheless, despite the ever expanding number of individuals who self-define as historians of education, it is, arguably, only Asa Briggs and Brian Simon who have, even now, achieved a level of recognition outside of their immediate field – the former even then, perhaps, more in his capacity as the official historian of the BBC and through his seminal contributions to social history.

Its relative novelty notwithstanding, the abiding problem the history of education has faced in its battle for a more pervasive reception stems from its 'strategic location in relation to three broad areas of study: education, history and the social sciences' (McCulloch 2011: 4). The subject, even today, finds itself in a state of flux between the relative disciplinary pulls of 'education studies' and 'history' with respected figures within the fields often aligning themselves in one, both or neither of the two camps. While the intimate interface with philosophical and sociological ideas in the context of interdisciplinary studies has undoubtedly contributed to its many strengths – and countless leading historians of education such as Philip Gardner (2010), Ian Grosvenor and Martin Lawn (2001 and 2005) and Kevin Brehony (2001) have developed highly nuanced methodological approaches – it has also led, regrettably, to the ostracizing of the discipline in relation to its more well-established brethren, notably political, constitutional and military historians who often see it as, at best, social science masquerading as history. This cleavage is reflected in the number of historians of education employed within university faculties of education rather than history.

It was, however, the writings of the historian W. A. C. Stewart – the *doyen* of progressive educational scholarship – in conjunction initially with his partner W. P. McCann that can be considered as the first modern (by which, I mean the last 40 or so years), large-scale attempt at providing sweeping historical narratives charting the emergence and development of the *progressive* educational movement. In their two seminal works – *The Educational Innovators* and *Progressives and Radicals in English Education* – of 1968 and 1972, respectively, Stewart and McCann not only made educational history the subject of astute and cerebral historical exploration but also unwittingly set the tone for the *paradigmatic ways* in which subsequent educational historians would approach the study of the substantive area. In particular, the Stewart and McCann 'approach' appeared to be, in the first instance, vague in relation to its terminology – Stewart himself admitted to using the terms 'progressive', 'experimental' and 'radical' almost interchangeably throughout – and often, thinkers and educators were conjoined together with seemingly little or no similarities in their actual practices. Susan Isaacs and A. S. Neill, for example, were subject to a joint book chapter despite having little in common with one another. As a consequence, such ambiguity led, second, to the de facto association of progressivism with some form of temporally free-floating criteria, which corresponded more to the authors' unique teleological conception as opposed necessarily to evidencing progressive practices themselves.

In another of the key pioneering discussions on the subject of progressivism, Robert Skidelsky (1969) associated the term with 'the history of the progressive school movement' (Skidelsky 1969: 13). Again, while one could convincingly argue that such a decision as to what schools are worthy of the title 'progressive' is based on a selection which is arbitrary – the author talked of 'the successive stages of progressive foundations' (Ibid) – the overwhelming implication, as with Stewart, was that the historian could 'measure' progressivism over time solely by reference to how practices differed from their precursors and antecedents.

In many ways, these approaches unconsciously echoed the theoretical ideas of the American philosopher A. O. Lovejoy who, in his seminal work, *Essays in the History of Ideas* (1948), perpetrated the notion of the 'unit idea', which was his attempt to explain the existence of long-standing and perennial historical ideas which have pervaded the course of human history. For Lovejoy, such ideas, while capable of being reconfigured at different moments, remained relatively unchanged throughout the course of time. Lovejoy used the analogy of an atom to represent these units of thought which cluster together to form a whole and which float freely through time with an existence independent from individual beings. The human input into the changing nature of these 'units of thought' (in this case, progressivism) is therefore, after that fashion, much downplayed. As a result, the concept of progressivism came ultimately to be seen as existing in an independent temporal space substantially divorced from individual writers of the past. As a result, the only thinkers worthy of study were those whose progressivism could be shown to be, in some sense, 'stronger' than those who had gone before. Nor was such a teleology unique to those narratives concerned with educational history; 'Whig' histories of this kind characterized by advancement, progress and an unwitting reification of a concept above and beyond its constituent individual parts were a feature of much early historical writing which took its lead from the theorist Leopold von Ranke.

Perhaps these initial trends were explicable in educational terms by the frequent overlap which existed between historians and philosophers of education, both of whom – in differing ways and for different reasons – saw progressivism as a topic worthy of their academic study and attention. Much of this latter body of literature – for example, key works by Robin Barrow (1978) and John Darling (1994) – sought instead merely to evaluate the ideas of educational thinkers in successive historical vacuums without recourse necessarily to locating them within their very specific historical, social and cultural contexts. As philosophers, that was of course their prerogative, and their striking analyses were none the less potent for it. In more recent times, however, educational historians have begun to move away from the former, linear style of writing so characteristic of early narratives and to engage more with progressive educators at the more immediate level of texts, contexts and networks of thought.

In part, this move has been facilitated, as Gary McCulloch (2011) has convincingly demonstrated, by the increasing awareness and sophistication shown in relation to fresh approaches in methodological thinking, for example, through the work of the former Cambridge Regius Professor of History, Quentin Skinner. Skinner's work (1969 and 1988) offers, in many ways, a direct repudiation of Lovejoy as for Skinner, meaning is to be sought, found and obtained in the reading of texts and the meaning of those texts as it appeared to those *at the time of writing*. Skinner has long been quite rightly classified as an intentionalist historian for whom the primary criterion for evaluating the meanings of historical statements resides with the intended meaning which the author possessed in the issuing of it. This is ascertained through understanding the sense and reference of the terms, vocabulary and language being utilized by the author and by gaining a comprehension of what an author was actually *doing* in the issuing of the utterance – warning, threatening or promising, for example. Much ink has been spilt among historians of ideas debating Skinner's theories from those – for example, Kari Palonen (2003) – who are genuinely supportive of his approach to those such as Alun Munslow (1997) and Keith Jenkins (2003), who have been actively hostile to his, and indeed, any historical claims which posit an understanding of 'Truth'. There have even been theorists such as Mark Bevir (1999) who have managed to retain an ambiguity concerning Skinner – admitting the benefit of uncovering authorial intention but only in the ways that an author's meaning was apprehended by subsequent critical audiences and not by his contemporary readership.

It has not been the case that educational historians have concerned themselves directly with these debates; yet, Skinner is one of a number of thinkers – the French post-structuralists Michel Foucault and Paul Ricoeur would be others – who have themselves begun to be better understood, apprehended and utilized by modern historians of education. Such desire has stemmed both intellectually from the aspiration to novelty in apprehending textual and ideological meaning in a way distinct from that of earlier writers, and pragmatically as well, with methodological approaches now considered central to the framing of research proposals by academic funding councils. More generally, inspired perhaps by contact, collaboration and discourse from appended social scientific disciplines, historians of education have sought to nullify and blunt the incremental charges levelled by postmodernists that the historical enterprise itself is an epistemological non-starter by providing a greater transparency in relation to their practices. As Philip Gardner (2010) has made clear, this has been a welcome move as many 'mainstream' historians still suffer from the polarizing effects of truth and interpretation, claiming access to the former, yet still, erroneously, acknowledging the limitations of the latter. Some historians in the field – notably Ian Grosvenor, Martin Lawn and Kate Rousmaniere (1999) – have even sought to incorporate the visual into their narrative writings using a range of images to answer the 'silences' which reside in the historical archive. Likewise, the lenses of feminism, discourse analysis and postcolonialism have also been used to underpin historical writings to re-think and reinterpret the views we hold of the educational past.

All of which has meant that the emphasis in educational history now tends to be at the granular level – that is to say, upon individual educators, the texts they produced, the practices they inspired and, more globally, the networks of thought and influence that have emerged between them. This has been reflected in the large number of scholarly articles in important journals – not merely *History of Education* but also its sister publications, the *Researcher*, *Pedagogica Historica* and *History of Education Quarterly* – which have sought to explicate, investigate and, in some cases, rediscover 'forgotten' and lost educators and schools of the past, or else, begin to re-evaluate key educational writings in light of recent trends developments and moves in education. This process has undoubtedly been aided by institutions such as the London Institute of Education and the many repositories housed in American universities which have systematically acquired and catalogued papers and collections relating to a range of important educational thinkers.

Current concerns

In any book of this type, there is always an inevitable element of omission and selection for which I make no apologies. Some writers and educators may be afforded too much space, some too little. The relative importance of an individual or the scope of their influence will always, of course, be subject to personal judgement. There may even be questions raised as to whether some of those figures discussed here are 'progressive' or 'child centred' at all.

I would contend that the latter judgement is 'presentist', short-sighted and guilty of prolepsis for all educators here were considered innovative and ground-breaking in their own time, often at the expense of their reputation and it is surely the context of the time which is the most important – we come back once more to Skinner! Nevertheless, in their own way, such discussions ensure the discipline's vitality and maintain, at the very least, a continued reading of educational texts, all of which have something to say, even if that something is not to taste.

As an example of where I have consciously selected, there is intentionally little reference made throughout to the education systems of the Far East despite those cultures' burgeoning interests in progressivism and the noteworthy attempts by scholars, in particular Yoko Yamasaki (2010), to trace the contribution made by progressive ideas to the post-war modernization of (in her case) Japan's schooling systems. However, this omission is not made out of any sense of denigration but is designed to reflect the immediate aims of the book, the courses it may serve and the fact that those pertinent archives may be geographically distant and not available in translation.

Further to those more instrumental reasons, the fact remains that many countries outside of the Western sphere of influence were borrowing from long-established historical ideas and precedents. Robin Alexander (2000) in his global survey of education identified three distinct dominating educational traditions – the Anglo-American, the European and the Indian – and, in progressive terms, one could argue analogously for an Anglo-American strand of progressivism and a European model, both of which have been taken as the blueprint for much of the burgeoning progressivist industry elsewhere. In the case of Japan, much of the spur towards attributes such as lifelong learning and a more varied curriculum arose out of anxiety over their place in the global marketplace. Equally, although not perhaps fitting into these or indeed *any* model, A. S. Neill's Summerhill School has been of both enormous concern and interest in the global context (particularly Asia) and this will be discussed in the relevant chapter.

This is not of course to suggest that those educators and thinkers either not referred to in the text or who have been afforded little space are, in any sense, less worthy of study and less important to what one could refer to as the 'progressive tradition'. Indeed, historians of education from the doctoral level upwards have long gained significant currency by resurrecting, rediscovering and making explicit the unique contribution of progressive educators of all hues. Often, this has involved individual teachers working within single institutions or those seeking, more modestly, to influence policy solely at the local and regional level. There has been a strong tradition of this in England with, for example, men such as Henry Morris espousing very forward thinking notions within the contexts of the formerly autonomous Local Education Authorities.

However, I would contend that while such individuals were undoubtedly innovative in their practice, their influence was not only confined to the level of single schools and classes of children but that their work was responding and perhaps subconsciously aping ideas established in a corpus of 'key works' within the discipline.

Thomas Carlyle (1888) talked of the Great Men of the past whose decisions and skill placed an indelible stamp on history and made a decisive impact on the orientation of the world. While Carlyle may have been discussing those of the stature of Muhammad, Shakespeare and Napoleon, the same contention could equally apply to the history of education; we *know* the importance of, for example, Rousseau, Dewey and Froebel even if we do not, on occasion, know exactly why. There is perhaps something reassuring about seeing history as evolving through the actions of easily identifiable men and women; understanding their lives, characters, motivations and flaws may indeed help us 'uncover something about [our] true nature' (Carlyle 1888: 2). Such a lens also puts history into a linear narrative, which is not only easily apprehensible but reflects the way in which our own lives are lived and mapped out through time.

Nevertheless, such a view fails to take full account of the *contexts* in which such individuals were operating. We have mentioned one context – the linguistic – which is the basis of the work of Quentin Skinner but there is also the social, the economic and the intellectual. Such consideration has been the basis for the repudiation of Carlyle from, among others, Herbert Spencer (1996) and William James (1897) who argued for men, no matter how 'great' they may seem, as being products of their environments and whose actions reciprocally both *determine* and are *determined by* the time in which they live. These concerns echo the now in-vogue 'structuration theory' of the prominent sociologist Anthony Giddens who has argued powerfully in support of a sociological middle ground – social actors are situated but not clueless. We are both grounded in a social reality, yet are also capable of shaping it.

As a result, the structure of this book has, I hope in a meaningful albeit modest way, attempted to combine both elements by studying the 'key thinkers' (Elton's Great Men, to which we may now add Women) of progressive education but doing so within the context of broader overarching themes. While in each chapter, the focus is broadly chronological, I have tried to indicate how the individuals discussed relate to one another, to those elsewhere and to the more broad intellectual frameworks in which they were operating and to which they were responding. It is important to view progressivism as comprised of individuals and their texts and practices but also to recognize that they were reacting to very different sets of contextual events and conditions, which led to their producing innovative and singular philosophies of education.

As has been alluded to earlier, the history of education is now a burgeoning scholastic discipline and while it may find itself often appended with the social sciences, there is a large body of explicitly *historical* literature in books, journals, monographs and theses which seeks to make sense of all aspects of the educational past. Progressivism, maybe given its attraction through connotations of daring and insurgence, is no exception, with scholars and academics forging respected and successful careers studying it both philosophically and biographically. While this book is intended as an introduction to some of the key thinkers and themes, it is hoped that a flavour of this large body of work and the key debates which have inevitably arisen become apparent. To that end, there are 'key' and 'further' readings listed at the end of each chapter as well as a large bibliography, which the interested reader should endeavour to consult. I would also urge that while the themes of the book are demarcated here for the place of convenience, the reader should recognize the key interconnectedness between them and begin to draw their own associations and opinions. It is only by seeing history in this three-dimensional, as opposed to linear, way that it is possible to truly open one's mind and understand the complexities and relationships of the past as so many in this book would surely have wished.

Notes

1 The Three Wise Men referred to were Chris Woodhead, later HM Chief Inspector of Schools and head of Ofsted; Jim Rose, later to produce the David Blunkett-commissioned Rose Report and himself to head the 2005 Primary Curriculum Review and, perhaps surprisingly, given his later contributions to the Cambridge Primary Review, Robin Alexander.

2 Published in 1967, the Plowden Report (named after its chairman, Bridget Plowden) was the unofficial name for the report of the Central Advisory Council for Education into primary education in England and became famous for its recommendation of radical, child-centred approaches to education, including the importance of play, smaller class sizes, suspicion over intelligence testing and a reduction in the number of examinations.

3 Founded in 1987 by 14 parents and teachers, the CRE is a pressure group concerned with falling standards in education and seeks to return to higher standards and increased parental choice.

4 In a recent article in the *Daily Telegraph* newspaper (19 May 2011), Seldon also admitted to practising and encouraging yoga and breathing exercises in his school.

1

Pioneering Notions and Practices

Introduction

Where to begin with progressive education? Indeed, where to begin with education itself? These are undoubtedly questions with no easy and forthcoming answers. In her recent edited book on the major educational thinkers, for example, Joy Palmer (2001) saw fit to include brief biographical pieces on characters as far back in time as Confucius, Christ and Plato. This seems justifiable, given that each had some concern with children and the condition we know of today as 'childhood'. Indeed, Plato may well have been the first to not only set down a systematic and organized educational programme but also the earliest to devote time to thinking about what the purpose of education should be and the ways it should allow for children to be later integrated into society.

Nevertheless, Plato's system was, to modern sensibilities, unashamedly elitist and designed to educate only the very best students, who would go on to rule and 'govern' his ideal state. Likewise, Christ, Confucius and other early (religious) figures may have been great teachers but not solely of children. It is only in the contemporary sense that we use the term to refer to those practising in school-based settings; such places, as we recognize them today, simply did not exist then. Indeed, for centuries, the concept of the child, more generally, was one totally divorced from our modern-day understanding. One does not have to fully agree with the contention of Phillipe Aries (1962) that childhood before the early modern period did not exist, to at least recognize that the role and purpose of the child was of an altogether different flavour. There were no schools to speak of, most children were expected to work as soon as they were able and the forms of legalistic protection and guardianship given to minors, which we now take for granted, would have been unrecognizable. The law made less of a distinction between child and adult – children were often tried in adult courts – and society as a whole reflected this, with dress, manners and habits being less closely demarcated, a point which was fundamental to Aries' contention. These attitudes permeated through all classes of people; although granted minorities and protectorates, even royal princes had to ascend the throne, regardless of their age.[1]

This was all to change though with the emergence of the 'modern' era and the currents of enlightened thinking which went alongside it. It is from this transformative period, for example, that the first modern systems of public education emerged in Germany under the watchful eye of Martin Luther, designed to promote his particular brand of Christian faith in more tolerant settings and with a view to allowing individual comprehension of the Bible – one of the cornerstones of Protestantism. More though than mere education, the move from the late medieval period into the early modern represented a seminal epoch in human history. Often, as in the case of science and the discoveries of Galileo and Copernicus, this led to challenges to established, centuries-old doctrine, dogma and belief, which were being gradually (and sometimes, reluctantly) overturned with seemingly irrevocable proof gained through the acquisition of carefully acquired systematic evidence. In literature, the works of William Shakespeare and others oversaw the emergence of established Western canonical writing while, in philosophy, thinkers began to grapple with new ways of considering reason and knowledge – approaches which began with the interrogation of the *self* and an individual's place within the world at large.

Although impossible to firmly date, Emily Grosholz (1991) is surely right to signify the common consensus in identifying the Frenchman Rene Descartes and his seminal *Meditations* as being at the heart of this latter process and as representing the start of the Western traditions of philosophy and metaphysics to which we today are the inheritors. In particular, the significance of Descartes stemmed from the ways in which he sought to question what we, as thinking subjects in the world, could and, indeed, could not know. The scepticism which he outlines in the first *Meditation* asks why he should trust his senses, given that they can, for example, in the state of dreaming, be apparently deceived. Given therefore the obvious potential for fallibility, can we ever 'know' the world, as it appears to us externally, in a meaningful way? How do we know we are not being deceived at all times by a universal deceiver? If so, is the only thing we can know with any certainty an awareness of ourselves in the world? From these simple claims, rejoinders and postulates, Descartes thus began the whole discipline of 'modern' philosophy which, ever since, has taken as one of its starting points the querying of particular absolutist claims towards knowledge and how one can ever truthfully claim to 'know' anything at all. Indeed, despite what some may think, we are still in some respects no closer to answering any of these questions today – a worthy testament to Descartes' unique genius.

The implications for what Descartes was proposing were profound, for his ideas served to throw into doubt, more broadly, questions over what constituted valid knowledge about the world. Did this merely mean received wisdom as handed down through the customary channels of the Church and Law and the ruling Monarch or was it possible to doubt this traditional fallibility? What could be the limits of human understanding? Descartes was to answer these queries in his influential work, thereby positing a wholly radical view of understanding, which drastically opposed the long-established Aristotelian notion that knowledge came directly from the senses and that mental states merely accorded with accurate representations of the physical world. In so doing, Descartes, inadvertently, began to provide ammunition for those looking to query and question not only the limits of 'Authority' but also the veracity of claims on the blind acceptance of truth merely as a result of direct sensory experience.

Perversely, Descartes himself was not a rebel in the traditional sense. As A. C. Grayling (2005) has shown in his fine biography, he had a strong Catholic faith, which led him to argue for the existence of a benevolent God who would not allow for systematic sensual deception, still less create a universal deceiver employed to carry it out. Ultimately, Descartes came to accept the world as it essentially was and, more or less, as he perceived it in the waking state. Nevertheless, the section of his book carrying this argument is comparatively weak as the argument put forward was somewhat tautological and was easily dismissed by many of his critics who were prepared to be more dubious and less willing to circumvent the earlier questions merely by recourse to an omnipotent deity.[2] While Descartes himself may have been unwilling to accept the full implications of his work, others read his claims more critically and begun to be increasingly sceptical and challenging about notions of truth in all its forms. While this did not mean circumventing exiting social and political orders, it certainly allowed for a more open mind to be attached to investigations relating both to science and epistemology.

It may seem odd to include reference to Descartes' work in a book dealing with progressive education as he had little connection with education, either directly through practice or indirectly through his writings. However, his significance in this context stems less from what he did or said and more from what he *represents*, for he serves to contextualize and exemplify the important and significant changes that were occurring at this time, specifically in relation to knowledge and the emerging dichotomy between mind and body and the subsequent effects that was to have on the way intelligence, learning and consciousness were perceived. The world was changing and with it so were certain basic assumptions about humankind, including, inexorably, those relating to children. Indeed, it was ultimately to be the man who so vigorously opposed Descartes philosophically – John Locke – who was to be the first to posit fresh and original concerns about early childhood, many of which stemmed from his emergent theories of knowledge, understanding and political liberty. Nevertheless, Locke's own work did not itself originate in an intellectual vacuum and it is therefore important to initially explore aspects of that changing landscape, particularly as they were delineated by the very first modern theorists of childhood. It is to the most central of those figures that the chapter now turns.

Comenius and the changing nature of education

In considering the development of progressivism in this early period, our attention cannot solely be upon texts, ideas, schools and practices for, as has been indicated, recognized patterns of instruction and education are dependent upon attitudes towards childhood that were, simply, not prevalent and widespread before this 'modern' period. To believe in the value of education as a concept, it is first necessary to recognize and acknowledge that children themselves are identifiably different from adults in terms of their mental, intellectual and physical levels of development. Understandably, the latter of these categories was more straightforward to recognize than the others as it was clear that children were dissimilar to adults in terms of their size and strength. To that extent therefore, labour, work and household tasks were divided up according to physical capability, often to the detriment of the child. Explaining how children and adults differed in the other two cerebral facets was then, without the benefit of modern psychology, an impossible task. Not having any way of demarcating adults and children, pre-early-modern assumptions collapsed the two categories to the extent that children were considered (at least, to our sensibilities) 'little adults', with all the attendant responsibilities and expectations which that entailed. These considerations were at the heart of Phillipe Aries' pioneering theory and although it is possible to dispute his thesis and the limited evidence he submitted to support it, it is not unrealistic to suppose that children were viewed under a much different aspect and guise than they are today.

However, while such attitudes remained broadly enshrined in familial and legalistic structures, there were those who had begun to recognize the more subtle differences between children and adults, particularly as they developed mentally. With this recognition went, therefore, the need to provide children with some form of proper specialist, directed education and, commensurately, teaching materials which could better facilitate their learning within these settings. One of the most prominent among these figures was the Czech-Moravian, John Amos Comenius (1592–1679), who has been considered as the 'father of modern education', and given his contribution to the development of universal systems of schooling and the practical basics of education, such a claim may not be as overstated as it sounds. As Jean Piaget (1993) has pointed out, 'Thinkers and philosophers, from Montaigne and Rabelais to Descartes and Leibniz, had [likewise] made profound remarks about education, but only as corollaries to their main ideas . . . .Comenius [was] the first to conceive a full-scale science of education' (Piaget 1993: 173–4).

In many ways, therefore, what Descartes was to modern philosophy and Francis Bacon to science, Comenius embodied in education, evidencing the idea that this was a time in which new developments from other disciplines had resultant effects on distant and seemingly unrelated cognate areas. When these contexts enmeshed themselves within education, it resulted in the gradual transformation of the conception and understanding of childhood – a factor which was to impact upon the work of Comenius. In addition to his support for more universal forms of schooling, Comenius was also among the first to adumbrate what we could consider today as a 'modern' curriculum – one drawing upon new facets of thinking about the world which were so much a feature of the time in which he lived. Comenius's desire for children to study 'real things' – by which he effectively meant science – reflected the growing number of ways in which scientific humanism was beginning to discern laws and theories designed to explain the mechanisms by which the world operated and functioned. Descartes himself had been seminal in that regard as his particular brand of philosophical rationalism had sought to discern a priori physical laws which could be used to distinguish why processes occurred as they did and the basic facets of causality.

Comenius' understanding of education, however, went far beyond merely explaining programmatically what he envisaged as a desirable set of subjects to be studied. For him, education was intrinsically tied to the greater good of society; his educational philosophy which he christened *pan sophism* was based upon the notion that 'universal knowledge would cultivate a love of wisdom that could overcome national and religious hatreds and ultimately lead to peace' (Harmon and Jones 2005: 37). His understanding of society was therefore one which was organic and, in itself, educative – in other words, capable of 'teaching all things to all men' (Comenius 1989: 36) and from all points of view. In that sense, Comenius is equally important for the way in which he refused to view education merely as something instrumental, which was to be apportioned according to reasons of primitive utility – that is, given only to those who would most readily need it. For him – as for many later progressive thinkers – education was to be tied to a particular teleology that was couched in an early utopian discourse. Knowledge bred wisdom which, in turn, developed global harmony. In keeping with this democratic spirit, Comenius was also among the first to advocate universal education and the teaching of all children regardless of ability or social class, which was in keeping with his metaphor of the sun which 'lights and warms the whole earth at once' and 'gives light to all things with the same rays' (Comenius, cited in King 2003: 343). It was thus the moral as much as the social imperative of society to ensure that their population was educated and allowed access to the liberating power of knowledge.

In light of this, it is unsurprising to note that much of Comenius's life was spent organizing schools in various countries across Europe, both in his homeland and also in Holland, Sweden and England – countries whose histories were subject to sporadic and internecine bouts of conflict, at least one of which (the First English Civil War of 1642) forced him to flee his home. This was not perhaps coincidence for it was from his later residence in Amsterdam that he spent much time ruminating upon the possibility of bringing together all strands and disciplines of knowledge, which would constitute the basis of a programme of re-education for man such as would provide a blueprint for future periods of world peace.[3] This re-education was to form part of a more general reorientation of science, religion and politics in human society, which carried with it grand overtones, very much in keeping with Comenius's membership of various secret societies and his desire to keep hidden and covert these final manuscripts.

Although this *pan sophism* and its articulation was driven by education, the grand scope of these late writings forbade any detailed attempt to delineate how this would take place beyond its ultimate purpose of providing for a more benevolent state of humanity. Nevertheless, for the historian of education, there is much in Comenius' other earlier writings which do demonstrate a carefully considered and nuanced understanding of the child's needs and the way that a teacher could attend to them. In their own way, these were really the first sophisticated attempts to divine and set down ways of effectively teaching children subjects that were thought to be challenging, such as the acquisition of foreign languages. By so doing, Comenius was demonstrating early articulations of progressive tenets which would be more clearly defined later on by other theorists, many of whom took some form of influence and inspiration from these initial writings. The first of these important texts was *Janua linguarum reserata* (*The Gate of Tongues, Unlocked*), published in 1631, the second was a significant introduction to that first book, while the third, *Orbis sensualium pictus* (*The World in Pictures*), was a picture book (the first of its kind) designed to teach Latin through the contextualizing of phrases and words in relation to images and informal expositions. Attempting to make subjects of direct interest and repositioning learning in more informal and relevant contexts is, to this day, a key plank of educational practice, particularly in the learning of languages that demand 'real-life' situations. This was also to be an important strand in many of Comenius's educational pronouncements. It may seem tenuous to link the learning of a 'dead' language such as Latin to educational progressivism, yet the principles evinced by Comenius, particularly given the lack of insights he would have had into the mechanisms by which children learn, stand (albeit in a modified form) as relevantly today as they did then.

It is, perhaps, though in his *Didactica Magna* (*Great Didactic*), published in 1649, where Comenius's actual all-embracing educational philosophy comes to the fore, for it was here that he departed from specific teaching techniques, beginning instead to consider placing those methods within the context of a much wider societal viewpoint. We have noted how he believed the destiny of society and the world to be intertwined with education, and under that aspect, much of the book (difficult as it is) reads in a grand and magisterial style. This is perhaps a characteristic of the time in which it was written where – on the cusp of modernity and the discoveries which that would bring – optimism and grand designs prevailed. The education system seen as desirable by Comenius was one whose different gradations and tiers corresponded 'to suit the capacity of the pupil, which increases naturally with study and age' (Ibid). Thus, recognizing the subtleties inherent within childhood, Comenius advocated four 'stages' of learning, whose defining characteristics were the types of subjects children should study. Although Comenius's prescription covered 'traditional' subjects, it did so with the implicit understanding that children's abilities to learn were bound by the limitations of age; they would, for example, only initially learn their own language before graduating to Latin and grammar when they were considered able to do so. Such a system accorded with his stated educational principles that learning must proceed 'from the general to the particular; from what is easy to what is difficult' (Ibid).

These concepts somewhat crudely pre-figure much of the later understanding of children and the codification by educational psychologists of stages of learning and cognitive development and the need for a differentiated curriculum to reflect that. As Rudolph and Cohen state, 'Only by building understanding of what his senses contact, will the child be ready for the symbolic learning that will come in time' (Rudolph and Cohen 1964: 9–10). In the same vein, Comenius's educational structures are closely aligned to modern scholastic frameworks with breaks and transfers at appropriate ages. Comenius thus recognized that there should not be a simplistic homogenous universality to education but that children at different ages required different forms and modes of learning. The learning which took place was to be done in a variety of settings, such as the external world and a university, and so, Comenius was one of the first to properly consider education as not being bound and restricted to a particular locale. It is possible indeed to contend that he was the first to significantly differentiate between education and *learning*, the latter of which was a de-institutionalized form of the other. Through the publications and dissemination of such ideas, he undoubtedly added to the discourse and intellectual considerations as to how the child and the adult were both conceptualized and demarcated.

These are hugely important points, for they illustrate how Comenius developed a very early understanding of the naturalistic child – an idea which was to be central to almost all manifestations of later progressivism but particularly those thinkers working under the broad umbrella of Romanticism, which is explored in the following chapter. In the *Great Didactic*, this manifested in two ways. First, he was keen to emphasize the importance which the role of nature had to play in shaping a child's education as it provided a welcome antidote to the stuffiness of the classroom and a more appropriate setting for learning about the world at large. Although Comenius was not seeking to impute the outdoors with connotations of mysticism and the divine as, for example, we find in the later work of Friedrich Froebel, it nevertheless well illustrated the consideration of learning as something beyond the classroom and the need for alternative places to learn.

Second, and somewhat less literally, naturalism referred to the way in which Comenius tapped into and articulated the latent impulses for learning inherent within children. Learning, he contended, should not be seen as a chore and something to be endured but as a joyful and pleasant activity for children. To that end, we can observe why he developed a curriculum which based itself around interactivity with words and images being used to buttress each other and subjects such as singing being part of the course of study. As Darling and Nordenbo tell us, 'Nature everywhere [was] considered an example for all aspects of teaching: for its phases, progression, manner and matter. For what Nature writes in capital letters is written in Man in small letters' (Darling and Nordenbo 2003: 289).

In thus re-conceptualizing the view of the child, Comenius was endowing it with a greater and more unique range of sensitivity, feeling and emotion, which correspondingly informed his pronouncements on the curriculum. Although not a self-directed curriculum as many progressives were later to advocate – the role of a skilled and humane teacher-as-guide was more than central – Comenius believed that learning should be a matter of enjoyment for the child and they should have at least some interest in their studies. While it would be irresponsible, perhaps, to refer to Comenius as the first 'progressive', his influence in educational terms cannot be overstated. While this manifested in practical ways through his work in setting up schools and systems of education across Europe, he was also the first to begin to formulate a theory of education driven by nature, which referred both to the individual nature of the child and to the nature inherent within the external world. This was undoubtedly influential upon many of the later Romantics whose concerns were likewise driven by both a common humanity shared with children and the conviction that learning was not merely something which should take place in restricted settings. Although many of his ideas concerning learning can be considered crude by today's standards, Comenius' primitive understandings betray the enduring progressive quest for both a refined science of teaching and the search for a differentiated curriculum that could cater for the needs of individual children.

John Locke – The progressive pioneer?

Today, John Locke's (1634–1702) reputation as a thinker of the front rank cannot be overstated. His *Two Treatises of Government* (1689) were seminal in defining modern neo-Liberal (and American) politics with their adherence to minimal state interference and the role of government envisaged as the protection of private property and transaction. Similarly, his *Essays on Human Understanding* (1690) began the line of enquiry known as empiricism, which was to be juxtaposed with Cartesian rationalism over the course of the coming centuries. This was to act at a broader level in defining a particularly British response to the continental faction which took Descartes and Leibniz as their rationalist prophets. Nevertheless, it is Locke's modestly titled tract, *Some Thoughts Concerning Education* (1693), which is of most importance to the historian of education and progressivism chiefly, as we shall explore, because of its particular concerns over the state of childhood and the desirability of a wider and more diverse curriculum. While he clearly shared some of the same concerns as Comenius, Locke's work cannot really be classified as its extension. First, Locke's educational writing overlaid itself with his own sophisticated political and philosophical theory which was of a very different hue to the more ethereal pacifism of his Czech counterpart. Second, each had his own particular slant on the purpose of the virtues to be cultivated by the school. As the philosopher Alexander Meiklejohn (2006) puts it, 'Comenius finds the school driving at three goals – learning, virtue and piety. Locke has four purposes– virtue, wisdom, breeding and learning' (Meiklejohn 2006: 27–8). For Meiklejohn, both Comenius and Locke 'set the stage for a far more profound and complicated educational and political philosopher of the eighteenth century – Jean Jacques Rousseau' (Nelson 2001: 238). Although it would be perhaps unfair to crudely place educational figures in a hierarchy (and can one ever delineate levels of profundity?), such rhetoric serves to illustrate an important point – which is that both Comenius and Locke can be identified as playing significant roles in prefiguring the later work of Rousseau, the man often characterized by historians of education as the 'first progressive'. Meiklejohn is surely correct therefore in appreciating that the emphasis upon community, as laid down by Comenius, and the quasi-competition, outlined by Locke, came together in a particularly productive way in the various tracts of Rousseau whose ideas will be more fully considered in the next chapter.

In seeking to therefore assess more specifically the importance of Locke to progressive education, we can see in the judgements of some writers, such as Puckett and Difilly (2003), a desire to promote him to the very front rank of thinkers and to occupy a de facto position as one of the first major figures in this particular pedagogic tradition. Such a claim nevertheless jars slightly when set against our contemporary understanding of what this term actually entails – hands on classroom practice, individualized learning, childhood empathy and so on. For Locke, what mattered more was not the interests of the child per se – a key facet of child centred education – but the adult that they would ultimately become. This is a subtle distinction but one that is important to remember when thinking about his work. Likewise, much of Locke's educational writing concerned the home and not the school, and where Locke did refer to 'schools', he meant private boarding schools which allowed for the separation of family and child and, by today's standards of thinking, were relatively Spartan regimes.

Authors such as Puckett and Difilly – and they are but representative – are nonetheless right to single out Locke as his pioneering work was among the first to explicate many of the gradually changing attitudes towards childhood and, specifically, certain programmes of study that were emerging in (particularly) England at that time. This significance has been elaborated by the not inconsequential body of scholarship, for example, key works by James Axtell (1968) and Nathan Tarcov (1984), which has sought to accord due status to Locke's educational writing and the way in which it chimes with his more well-known philosophical and political writings. In that respect, perhaps the term 'proto-progressive' is more appropriate in this context as it hints at the significance that Locke himself was later to have while still recognizing that his work was rooted in a time vastly different from that of many of the later writers considered in this narrative, particularly in relation to the knowledge of children which was available to him.

To support this claim to originality, one can identify at once in Locke a humane approach to educating the child, which was far removed from many of the actions of his contemporaries.[4] While other children at the time suffered regular punishment doled out unthinkingly by their elders, Locke (perhaps unsurprising, given he was a qualified physician) was pivotal in drawing attention to the need for a physically, as well as mentally, healthy child. Parts of his *Thoughts* read like a medical manual, and although his prescriptions are today outdated and little more than dressed up old wives tales, they do serve to reinforce the importance he ascribed to caring for the physical needs and well-being of the child. In that spirit, Locke's educational work is very consciously addressing parents and therefore personalizing the nature of childcare and the welfare of children. This was novel in that it was starting to recognize the closeness that families and children must enjoy in order to provide for all aspects of their upbringing. This personalized understanding contrasted with, for example, the vision of Thomas Hobbes, where education was only to occur through the benign influence of a distant sovereign.

Given the later emphasis placed by Romantics like Johann Pestalozzi and Froebel upon the importance of the family as a unit of love and compassion, this 'softer' approach of Locke is clearly of significance. Although, as Nicholas Orme (2001) has powerfully argued, early attitudes toward childhood were not as stark and uncaring as some historians of education may believe, and many families exhibited great sympathy towards their children, Locke was the first to significantly draw the important link between education, health and the child's welfare. As Neil Postman (1996) has further pointed out, it was the emergence of printing which facilitated the production and mass dissemination of texts (such as Locke's *Thoughts*), which were one key aspect in subtly shifting the balance in favour of the child and leading some to begin to review their needs and general treatment.

In conjunction with this aspect of childcare went doubts as to the suitability of the prevailing curriculum which those children who did receive an education were subject to. As is often the case with 'pioneering' educational texts, Locke's work contained distilled elements of a number of key ideas which were finding some form of peripheral currency elsewhere. From an earlier generation, the polymath Francis Bacon, as one example, had challenged the superiority and necessity of the study of the classics at the expense of science, of which Bacon himself was a pioneer. Equally, many liberal-thinking families were beginning to consider the virtues of a practical education for their sons and daughters rather than the more esoteric and traditional patterns of learning (usually involving Latin and Greek), which were the norm for so many young children at that time. Indeed, it was to be one such family – the Clarkes of Chipley in the English county of Somerset – whose letters to Locke and his subsequent replies were to form the basis of *Thoughts* which he published only after much reluctance and consternation.[5]

As a caveat to that point, it must be pointed out that many of these families were aristocratic or in the higher echelons of society, and that for the vast majority of children, any opportunities for even the most basic of education were necessarily limited. Locke himself did not indeed consider that his published thoughts were, or should be, directly applicable to the majority of children. For him, a gentleman such as Clarke was obligated to have his child schooled at home under the auspices of a private tutor, and anyway, Locke's commitments to mass education were, as Peter Gay (1998) points out, ambivalent at best. For some, therefore, Locke's somewhat bourgeois outlook colours our consideration of him as a reforming character, and in many respects, he clearly does not easily fit into the role of a 'progressive' educator.

Further to that, as shall be explored later with Rousseau's *Emile*, such a home environment was naturally very conducive to the promulgation of his innovating ideas, avoiding as it did the inherent problems associated with mass schooling – such as large class sizes and rowdy discipline, which would have been the experience of the many in either the elite public schools or the voluntary efforts of the churches. In that respect, then, it is worth remembering that Locke's educational writing was not seeking to advocate overturning the existing educational structures such as they were or to suggest that his 'thoughts' should become recommendations towards an institutionalized norm. To read his work is to enter seemingly therefore into a privileged world of pseudo-correspondence between men of kindred spirits and intellect. Such high mindedness must not however preclude Locke's considerations from being historically important as they represented a new and emerging view about the state of childhood.

As was to be the case later with Rousseau and John Dewey, Locke's educational writing is inseparable from his broader theories concerning the nature of knowledge and understanding, and so, anyone wishing to comprehend Locke's theory of education must be at least partially cognisant with his other key works. Notable among these are his *Essays Concerning Human Understanding* (1689) which sought to explain how the human mind comprehends information and makes sense of the world. As was alluded to earlier on, this work stood in opposition to the theories of Descartes as Locke was more certain of the ability of the human senses to discern knowledge and information about the real world directly through experience. His educational theory in this context can therefore be seen as reflecting, in an important way, broader developments and intellectual currents of thought and knowledge during this period. Such currents were, as Patrick Dillon (2006) and others have argued, at the centre of the development of the 'modern' understanding of the world and this is certainly true in relation to the changing view of childhood as reflected in both art and – in this case – text.

While, therefore, one could contend that Locke is not a progressive in any real sense, his significance to this narrative lies in the particular way in which he addressed directly certain themes and strands of education that were later to form a key part of the child-centred discourse. Although crude by contemporary standards, and betraying the lack of insight into children's minds afforded to us through modern psychological developments, his early pronouncements set the scene for many of the later forecasts which would come to be seen as representative of innovative educational approaches.

The most important of these emanated from his strikingly original view that children themselves were individuals with, potentially, a range of different interests at their disposal. This was in sharp contrast to those who saw the category of 'childhood' as relatively homogenous and unproblematic and which was reflected in teaching methods which relied upon uniform instruction and rote learning, often of particular texts, such as the Bible. In challenging this view, Locke was drawing upon his earlier writing for he had famously posited, in his *Essays*, that humans were born with a mind akin to a blank slate (*tabula rasa*). This therefore meant that an individual's experiences were formed both empirically and directly through their sense perceptions and imprinted via action and observation. More specifically, this occurred through the 'association of ideas' which was Locke's term for explaining how human beings (and especially, children) made sense of complex concepts which were often mixtures and combinations of simple ideas. These complex concepts were what the philosopher David Hume was to later refer as 'contiguity in time and place' and 'cause and effect' which served to define categories of thought by which humans understood and apprehended the world around them.

The prevailing idea that knowledge and morality were innate to the human mind was thus jettisoned. By extension, therefore, if the child had – at birth – a blank slate for a mind, there was potentially a whole variety of ways in which that could be 'etched in' and completed. The latent potential for individuality was thus adumbrated in a rigorous and philosophical way. Indeed, for Locke to think otherwise would have involved a repudiation of his whole contention! This then gave implicit recognition to the fact that it was education and not other factors which were the determinants of an individual's character and make-up. As Locke put it, 'I think I may say that of all the men we meet with, nine parts of ten are what they are, good or evil, useful or not, by their education' (Locke 1693: 2). This served as a justification for a curriculum that was rational, relevant and sensible as to pervert the developing child with unproven trivia, unnecessary knowledge and poor teaching that was, at best, timewasting and, at worst, dangerous as it risked filling the child's head with disturbing thoughts and images. Locke himself made this point when cautioning against the 'foolish maid' who convinces a young child of the existence of 'goblins and spectres' (Ibid., 285), who the child would forever associate with the darkness. What was the need to patronize children with fairy stories?

Unable to dispense with God, Locke believed that each child had therefore been created with a unique character – 'God has stampt certain Characters upon Mens Minds, which, like their Shapes, may perhaps be a little mended; but ca hardly be totally alter'd, and transformed into the contrary' (Ibid., 66). The role of the educator became one whose duty was to respond to the individual enquiries of the child and direct them in whatever path seemed to accord with their intellectual satisfaction. Once more, we can infer from the tone of Locke's writing his particular social viewpoint; while validating individuality, it was destined to be an individuality propagated by single tutors to young boys of affluent families and not as the dawning of an era of radical education for the many!

Nevertheless, given Locke's ascribed belief in individuality, there is little in *Thoughts* which concerns itself with the development of a prescribed curriculum and he clearly thought it was more important to instruct tutors and parents to develop the child's *ways* of thinking as much as filling them up with pre-determined knowledge. This is the equivalent of what educationalists today would call 'critical thinking skills' which transfer both across subject area and, it would appear, time. In common with many later progressive thinkers, Locke also attached great importance to the notion of curricula relevance, with subjects such as Ancient Greek seen as serving little purpose. They were, for Locke, certainly a particularly poor substitute to learning the native language – a contention he shared with Comenius. Likewise, subjects such as drawing, practical work and (what a novelty!) science were seen as providing skills which would equip children for later life. While in reality, this did not lead to any mass interest and involvement with vocational learning, Locke's concerns with directing learning towards the interest of the child – albeit with one eye on their development into adulthood – was a clear example of his proto-progressive philosophy.

Locke was also influential not merely for his understanding of the child's intellectual needs but also their welfare. He was vociferous in condemning the beating of children which was a regular practice of the time and which went hand in hand with a common deep-seated belief in Original Sin. Aside from the humanitarian aspect of this, Locke appeared to be rejecting the idea that children can only be encouraged to work by external forces such as the threat of pain or the bribe of pleasure. Instead, the key driver behind a child's education must be those impulses which stem from within the child themselves, and so, his educational plan was one designed to foster an enquiring and active mind which would demonstrate the inherent curiosity within a young learner. This could not be achieved, he argued, by the imposition of harsh punishment. Again, this related – beyond its basic compassion – to his brand of empiricism, which was predicated upon the idea that the expansion of the mind and acquisition of knowledge was through its direct attainment by the senses. An often neglected part of Locke's writing indeed concerns these medical aspects of a child's upbringing and the way to foster the development of that intellect through the maintenance of a healthy body. Perhaps this general disregard is attributable to the slightly quaint and unsophisticated advice he proffers – the prevention of colds and chills through regular bathing of the feet and the wearing of thin shoes, for example! While the association of a healthy mind with an equally healthy body was not unique to Locke, he was perhaps the first to readily incorporate such ideas into a grander theory of liberalized education.

Such a point is important to stress as it indicates how Locke's ideas go beyond merely attempting to develop and liberate the child intellectually. Indeed, it serves to emphasize that what was so ground-breaking about his writing was that it sought to develop a system of education, and all the connotations which that term entails, rather than mere instruction. This is a subtle yet important distinction to be made and one which becomes more apparent towards the end of this key work as Locke starts to migrate from theories of mind to those of the body. The traditional association of education was with schooling in a very clearly-defined pedagogic setting to the extent that all other factors – home life, cleanliness, morality – were excluded. Locke's educational writing, however, did not associate education purely with the acquisition of knowledge via didactic habit. To that extent, what Locke seeks to describe is *upbringing* and, as Nathan Tarcov (1984) is at pains to stress, this equated closely to Locke's views about the fundamental entitlements human beings had to basic levels of freedom. While Tarcov's important discussion is complex and detailed, it does stress the key virtues – civility, justice, courage and the like – which Locke saw as necessary for the child to cultivate. Indeed, these characteristics were more highly prized by Locke than learning; although the latter receives very detailed treatment in the *Thoughts* (nearly 50 pages of text), it is clearly subordinate to the acquiring of those particular qualities and characteristics. Even where learning is explicitly discussed, its motive was to spring from 'the pleasure of knowing things' (Locke, Ibid., 178) and not for any prior purpose or sense of utility. Knowledge for its own sake and enjoyment, particularly that which sprung from the child's innate curiosity, was to be a key mantra of many progressive thinkers in later generations. Almost exactly pre-figuring Rousseau, Locke also argued stringently for the learning of a 'manual trade' (Ibid., 201) which served to give students both a useful skill and contributed more broadly to their good health.

This discussion of the curriculum, in many ways, does however embody many of the contradictions inherent within Locke's educational work. Although much of what he said was novel – the cultivation of virtues at the expense of knowledge and so on – his was an education explicitly designed for 'a Man or Gentleman' (Ibid., 135) and this returns us once more to the world of the enlightened middle class and Locke's prime audience. Although keen to stress the values of learning the native tongue and modern languages, he recommended the learning of Latin as 'absolutely necessary to a *Gentleman*' (Ibid., 164, italics added). Borne of a similar contention so, seemingly, was an activity such as horse riding, which was 'of use to a Gentleman both in Peace and War' (Ibid., 198). We can therefore see at once why Locke's works are considered problematic; on the one hand, they betray evidence of new and emergent attitudes towards children which celebrated individuality and a curriculum which certainly had about it aspects of novelty. On the other hand, this was counterbalanced by its bourgeois and somewhat middle-class character with access to this new curriculum restricted only to a privileged few. This perhaps explains why Locke's ideas have not always been openly acknowledged by others in the progressive tradition despite many of their foundational principles and, at the very least, sentiments being found within his pages.

Coda: Beyond the Enlightenment

Nearly 70 years separated the publication of Locke's *Thoughts* (1693) from that of Rousseau's *Emile* (1762). While the latter is often considered the first explicitly 'progressive' educational work, there is little doubt as to the importance of its predecessor. Although there have been certain similarities emphasized implicitly above between the two authors – and these are worthy of articulation – there are as well clear points of educational divergence between them which perhaps, at a broader level, serves to delineate the differences between the rationalism of the Enlightenment and the later, more subjective emotionalism of the Romantic period. Notable among these was Locke's stress upon the importance of *nurture* through the acquisition of habit and the subjugation of the child's natural impulses in favour of the development of adult-imposed virtues. Although Locke therefore took the inherent rationality of the child to mean that it was possible for parents to converse with their children in a mature and respectful way – 'The sooner you treat him [the child] as a man, the sooner he will become one' (Locke, Ibid., 95) – it nevertheless was an esteem built around the sublimation of innate childish character. These more natural and native impulses were to be at the heart (as we shall see in the next chapter) of the later Romantic movement and shaped much of the discourse of, in particular, Rousseau, who critiqued Locke's stress upon learning by habit as, '[giving] an egg to have a cow' (Rousseau 1979: 103). Ultimately, Locke reflects this prejudicing of reason (nurture) over natural instinct (nature). 'Reason' for the Romantics carried with it connotations of outside interference devoid of the spontaneous generation of feeling which children were supposed to exhibit. Rousseau himself provided a withering critique of individuals who followed their reason over the impulses of their heart. While Locke was therefore providing an environment of respect in which the child could develop, it was clearly limited to the growth of certain desirable virtues and characteristics.

The habits cultivated by Locke's child were of course to be put to a particular use, which was the governance and management of the state in which these values of reason and rationality would allow for the freedom's being seen as desirable to flourish. Although his was an education for the aspirant bourgeoisie, Locke himself undoubtedly wanted to democratize learning, knowledge and basic rights throughout society. In the later Romantic movement (and for Rousseau, in particular), we see an ambivalent relationship between the education of the self and how that was to accord with the shaping of a future society. Was education to be directed towards the community at large or was it solely concerned with developing personal worth, self-expression and of being an end in itself? As we shall explore in the following chapter, the purposes behind Rousseau's education system are themselves a matter of scholarly debate and exemplify this teleological issue.

Given then the particular orientation of Locke's educational views, it is perhaps unsurprising to find that those early schools who drew to varying degrees upon his discourse were themselves keen to extend notions of the child's freedom. One powerful example of this was John Gilpin's Cheam School (he became headmaster in 1752) which stood in close proximity to London. Although a member of the ruling British aristocracy, Gilpin's school perfectly reflected the transformative, pre-modern period in which it was conceived, betraying the residing tension between innovation and tradition. Gilpin is certainly to be credited for attempting to incorporate elements of early progressive thinking into the daily practices of his establishment. He involved his students in devising their own discipline system, encouraged the learning of practical skills such as gardening and business techniques, and instilled in his charges a sense of community service. Like Locke, he had a particular disdain for dead languages, arguing instead for children to first gain proficiency in their native tongue. Similarly, he provided a wide range of extra-curricular activities for the boys under his tutelage, including sports, drama, the keeping of animals, the tending of gardens and the running of the school shop. This was in conjunction with the broad curriculum offered, which included drawing and dancing. In a similar vein, the work of the Irishman David Manson in introducing play and amusement into his school (also in 1752) sat alongside novel attempts at self-government by delineating pupils in an approximate order of both rank and hierarchy. Manson's initiatives, in particular, drew largely upon the work of Comenius as he sought to make lessons, 'more interesting and more loosely related to life by the introduction of games based on farming, medicine, war, politics, and so on . . .' (Stewart 1972: 9–10).

For all of their initiatives, however, both headmasters found themselves drawing upon the more rigid strictures and elements of Locke's educational theory. Gilpin, in particular, took in pupils who were expected to become 'landholders, tradesmen and public officers' (Gilpin 1879: 127), who it is possible to associate with Locke's glorified gentry and who were destined to play a significant role in the mechanisms of state governance. Likewise, Cheam's gardening lessons involved the cultivation of personal strips of land designed, in principle, to promote an understanding of economic entitlement as much as the particular workings of horticulture. Such entitlement again was at the heart of Locke's theory which argued for the sole right to possession of personal property. Both schools also stressed a basic respect for discipline and order, which was seen as providing the conditions for the most basic form of liberty.

Although, as W. A. C. Stewart (1972) has pointed out, neither Gilpin nor Manson was to leave a long-lasting legacy or any form of codified educational programme; theirs were systems which did not draw upon continental developments. Rather, their novelty lay in providing deliberate counteractions to the very specific problems of schools at that particular time, which were frequently traditional in both their curriculum and their systems of discipline and punishment. Although not drawing explicitly upon the principles of the Enlightenment, their schools represent pertinent examples of early institutions which sought to affect some of the changes in attitudes which had been developed through the works of both Locke and Comenius. With the publication of Rousseau's *Emile* in 1762, a seismic shift in the educational paradigm undoubtedly took place, yet it was not one without earlier precedent – the novel's many references to John Locke are one obvious testament to that. In reconsidering both the value of the child's education and the way that they should be taught, early writers of the sort described here undoubtedly provided a platform for the more far-reaching and influential ideas of later generations which were to take these basic concepts in new directions and which were driven by advancements in epistemological and ontological understanding simply not widely available to 'pre-modern' thinkers.

Notes

1 Henry VI of England, for example, became King at the age of nine months.
2 Descartes here fell back upon a variation of the ontological argument which is that if one has an idea of God in one's mind, then that must imply that God exists.
3 With a working title of the *General Consultation on an Improvement of all Things Human*, the finished manuscript for Comenius's masterwork was only re-discovered and re-printed in full in the twentieth century.

4 And not merely his contemporaries; John Wesley, born two years after Locke's death, was to promulgate a very 'harsh' view of childhood parodied by Samuel Butler in his epic poem *Hudibras*: 'Love is a boy by poets stil'd/ Then spare the rod and spoil the child'.

5 The book was actually expanded several times before Locke's death and was published anonymously more due to Locke's reticent personality than because of the 'radical' nature of the text.

Key reading

John Locke, *Some Thoughts Concerning Education* (London: A. and J. Churchill, 1693).

Jan Amos Comenius, *Didactica Magna (Great Didactic)* (Göteborg: Daidalos, 1989).

Further reading

Philippe Aries, *Centuries of Childhood: A Social History of Family Life* (New York: Vintage Books, 1962).

Nathan Tarcov, *Locke's Education for Liberty* (Chicago: University of Chicago Press, 1984).

2

Romanticism

Introduction – Rousseau, the man at the crossroads

Is it wrong to begin with Jean Jacques Rousseau (1712–78)? This may seem an erroneous question to pose, given that we have already encountered several of his forebears who one could classify, broadly speaking, as 'progressives', yet it is an incontrovertible fact that, as the Introduction made clear, many of the dominant narratives and writings in the history and philosophy of education – for example, those of Robin Barrow (1978), John Darling (1994) and Blenkin and Kelly (1981) – have consistently taken Rousseau as the teleological starting point and founding father of the progressive education movement. At the very least, many writers have held him up to be the first significant figure of this particular line, discounting in the process the offerings of Locke and Comenius. Such has been the regard for Rousseau's contribution that John Darling – himself no great advocate of child-centred ideas – felt able to paraphrase the philosopher Alfred Whitehead in considering 'modern educational theory [to be] a series of footnotes to Rousseau' (Darling 1994: 17).

In many ways, this sense of importance emanates from the seemingly insubordinate connotation his name still seems to carry. As the film critic David Denby anecdotally remarked, 'I threw a tomato at Ronald Reagan once. I threw a tomato at Reagan while under the influence of Jean-Jacques Rousseau. I may not have acknowledged this influence at the time, but it existed nonetheless' (Denby 1996: 278). While it is his interventions in education that concern this narrative, Denby's tale is nevertheless apt, for in many ways, Rousseau has been encouraging the throwing of tomatoes at figures of authority – namely teachers and the educational establishment – ever since, and his commitment to a particular form of liberty of both the citizen and the child has chimed across the centuries.

The natures of these bold claims are, as shall be seen, somewhat open to contention not exclusively because of Rousseau's precedents and antecedents but also because there was much to his educational philosophy that was not, in a modern or indeed perhaps contemporary sense, progressive. Unlike many of the other major radical educators, Rousseau never ran a school, taught as we would understand it and had scant regard for childhood, placing his own five children in foundling homes on the probably quite correct assumption that they would be better looked after there than with him. As his biographers have made clear, he was tragically beset with depression and mental collapse, yet his life and the events within it – unlike that of other major philosophers, for example, Locke and Kant whose biographies are singularly less tumultuous – relate demonstrably to his own particular philosophy, which is at once talismanic, inspirational and confused, his ideology having been seen as variously foreshadowing both that of the French Revolution and of Nazi Germany. Even a critic as hostile to progressivism as Robin Barrow writes that Rousseau falls into a category of educationist who does not 'propose tinkering with the educational system as it is . . . [he proposed] blowing the system as is it to pieces' (Barrow 1978: 1).

The work on which Rousseau's educational notoriety rests is *Emile* (1762), a fictionalized account of a young boy – the 'Emile' of the title – being raised and educated by a tutor. It is the only work Rousseau published that was explicitly concerned with education, and so, any attempt to discuss his contribution to progressivism must inevitably draw heavily upon it. Stylistically, it is one of the earliest and best known examples of a bildungsroman, that is to say, a novel which takes as its subject the physical and mental development of its protagonist and, as a text, it is among the most widely read and cited in the progressive canon.

It is, however, impossible to properly discuss *Emile* without first briefly contextualizing it in relation to Rousseau's better known work, the *Social Contract*, published in the same year and intellectually entwined with its educational counterpart. This work, containing along with the *Communist Manifesto* perhaps the single most famous opening line in philosophical history ('Man is born free but everywhere he is in chains'), sought to address the question as to how humans should best govern their affairs, given that they were now part of civilization and that it was no longer possible for them to return to a state of nature. The 'state of nature' in this context referred to the philosophical device as utilized most famously by Thomas Hobbes of describing the hypothetical human condition prior to the formation of communities and civilization. Contrary to the popular perception of Rousseau, his particular concept of 'natural man' was not one endowed with innate goodness; he was instead merely self-sufficient (*amour de soi*) with instincts of self-preservation and reason. Over time, Rousseau argued, aspects of the civilized world, including the development of the arts and sciences which sprung from impulses of idleness and luxury, had corrupted man into a state of pride and vanity, encouraging selfishness and pleasure in others' pain (*amour propre*).

As a result, the only form of organization which properly fostered individual happiness and freedom was through the joining together of humans into a civil society and sublimation to a 'general will'. Freedom was therefore to be equated with becoming a part of the group's sovereign body and acting in accordance with this 'general will' – 'Everything you conceive, everything you contemplate, will be good, great and elevated, sublime, if it accords with the general and common interest' (Diderot quoted in Mason and Wokler 2001: 20). For those who refused to conform, they were to be, in Rousseau's unfortunate and much quoted phrase, 'forced to be free'. In order to ensure a continued acceptance and abeyance of this 'general will', Rousseau acknowledged that there would have to be the right societal conditions in place. In part, these resulted from the alleviation of poverty and the limitation of excessive wealth but, more importantly, what was needed was the development of an education system which produced young men (women, unfortunately, had a very different place in Rousseau's thinking) who could distinguish between individual desires and acquiescence to the 'general will'.

The questions Rousseau poses in *Emile* are therefore, fundamentally, how should a child born into the utopia he envisages in the *Social Contract* be reared and educated? Furthermore, what sort of education should provide the framework for the emergence of a more 'natural man'? It has long been a matter of debate among scholars as to whether, in fact, *Emile* was designed to produce a 'civil man', through a breaking and rebuilding of the individual's human nature to fit into Rousseau's democratic political system, or whether it was designed to produce a 'natural man' – that is, an idealized expression of something innate to human nature. While this debate is outside the remit of this book, what *is* worth noting is that Rousseau hoped to indicate in *Emile* where aspects of modern civilization had gone wrong and to therefore try and explain the origins of human vice and misery.

For all the pitfalls of interpretation, *Emile* certainly stands at the crossroads of the two dominant intellectual paradigms of the eighteenth century – the Enlightenment and Romanticism – acknowledging the former while setting an intellectual trend and precedent for the latter. As John Darling (1994) makes it clear, one of the key contextual influences on *Emile* was the growth of science and the increased belief in rationalist philosophy. Rousseau himself, from the late 1740s, was closely associated with *Les Philosophes*, a loose band of French intellectuals centred upon Voltaire and Diderot, who sought to comprehend society, morality, the penal system and religious belief through the principles and application of reason. Very much contrary to earlier medieval precepts which accepted 'truth' by virtue of it emanating from an 'authority' (frequently the Church), philosophers such as Descartes and Leibniz were invoked, as we saw in the previous chapter, in questioning what knowledge one could acquire from one's senses and to equate the acquisition of truth with observation and experiment. In this respect, aspects of *Emile* echo this belief as the young boy is encouraged to find things out for himself through empirical observation and self-discovery. In one noted example, Emile ascertains the position of a kite by mere observation of its shadow demonstrating how, *a posteriori*, reason could be used to apprehend and ascertain the scientific laws of the world. This view of the gradual process of self-discovery is summed up by Rousseau in a key passage:

> Without question, one gets clearer and far surer notions of the things one learns in this way by oneself than of those one gets from another's teachings. One's reason does not get accustomed to a servile submission to authority; furthermore, we make ourselves more ingenious at finding relations, connecting ideas, and inventing instructions than we do when, accepting all of these things as they are given to us, we let our minds slump into difference – like the body of a man who, always clothed, shod, and waited on by his servants and drawn to his horses, finally loses the strength and will of is limbs. (Rousseau 1979: 176)

While this process of self-education on the part of the child may be tortuous, Rousseau is at pains to suggest that it was perhaps the only way to prevent mental and intellectual weakness and thus subside into a state of idleness and vice. Such a system, however, had little place for the imagination which came to be central to later Romantic thought through its associations with creative power, imagery and the formation rather than mere apprehension of reality. For Rousseau, imagination in the child led, potentially, to the danger of him imagining things which may later distort his character – a problem he identified in his own upbringing – and so, he discouraged its development.[1]

However, while *Emile* is inevitably underpinned philosophically by aspects of its historical and intellectual contexts, it is impossible to ignore the suggestion that the book also seems to be a direct critique of many of the social consequences of the Enlightenment, thereby directly foreshadowing many of the later attributes of Romanticism, in particular, the idealized view of the child. Rousseau was undoubtedly the first educator to embrace a wholly naturalistic view of education and system of learning which took place in the surroundings of Nature and the natural world. For him – unlike, say Comenius – this was not just a matter of convenience or well-being; nature represented, as it did for a later generation of English Romantics, in particular, William Wordsworth, a moral guide and stood in direct opposition to the increasing industrialization and urbanization of the age whose by-products – cities – were seen as centres of immorality, squalor and vice.

In describing, in general terms, what he believed childhood to be, Rousseau coined the phrase, 'the age of gaiety' (Ibid., 79) and it is difficult for us to believe that such an utterance was not written without a sense of irony, based upon his knowledge of the sorts of injustices and cruelties being propagated towards children at the time within urban factories and schools. While it has been frequently pointed out by scholars that Rousseau did not beget, or indeed ever use, the term 'noble savage' (and, in fact, saw nothing 'noble' about the state of nature whatsoever), it is the case that many of the subsequent notions in *Emile* seem to relate to a far more simplistic way of living. For example, Rousseau states that initially Emile's vocabulary should be restricted and constitute merely a 'few ideas' (Ibid., 74). It is hard therefore not to equate this with the more simple and straightforward existence of the French peasantry with whose lives Rousseau would doubtless have been familiar and the author himself draws an explicit comparison between peasants and 'city people' (Ibid). Although it is easy to overemphasize the rusticity in Rousseau (and Emile's education is by no means confined to the simplistic), one can see how the virtues and skills emphasized by Rousseau are comparable to an idealized, 'primitive' form of existence.

Rousseau's educational philosophy

To the modern reader, *Emile* comes across clearly as one of the more readable of the 'key texts' within the history of progressivism. It suffers neither from great obscurantism or complexity of construction (although not of ideas) and revels in what Peter Jimack (1983) refers to as Rousseau's 'striking, lapidary phrase which would compel the attention of his readers and move their hearts, even when it meant, as it often did, an exaggeration of his thought' (Jimack 1983: 46). Divided up into five books, the text tracks the chronological development, through various stages, of Emile and his growth into adulthood and eventual autonomy. Perhaps most striking about this arrangement is the way in which it seems to crudely pre-figure many of the psychological theories of the twentieth century which saw human development as traceable through distinct, observable stages, be they cognitive, psychosexual or biological, for example, those of adolescence and puberty. This is a clear example as to how many of the themes and issues addressed by Rousseau can be seen, often tangentially, to be played out in succeeding educational schemes.

At a very basic level, *Emile* is notable for the emphasis it places upon the health and *well-being* of the child. This is explicit, in particular, in the first essay of the book covering zero to two years which, despite opening with a striking declamation that echoes the *Social Contract* ('Everything is good as it leaves the hands of the Author of things; everything degenerates in the hands of man' (Rousseau, Ibid., 37)), concerns itself chiefly with proffering advice to prospective parents over the supposed evils of swaddling and wet nursing. The swaddling of babies – which involved wrapping them in very constrictive material in order to restrict or 'swaddle' their movement – was a common enough practice at the time and was carried out for religious as much as for practical reasons, Christ himself having been swaddled, according to the Gospel of Luke. Similarly, the practice of wet nursing, primarily undertaken by the upper classes, was seen as neglectful towards the newborn child and done purely for self-interest, mothers hoping it would bestow upon them a more rapid return to pregnancy.

In critiquing both practices, Rousseau was demonstrating quite dramatically a view of childhood very much at odds with his contemporaries. In particular, he seemed to be placing great emphasis upon the roles and responsibility of adults to provide the right kind of environment in which children must be raised while also subtly demarcating the intrinsic differences between children and adults. The historian of childhood, Philippe Aries (1962), in fact, cites *Emile* as the key text in affecting the transformation of the general perception of childhood and the child, which occurred from the seventeenth century onwards and which was alluded to in the previous chapter. While the 'Aries thesis' has been contended, most notably in recent times by Nicholas Orme (2001) and Steven Ozment (2001), it does not preclude Rousseau's writing from being anything other than pioneering in this respect.

It was, in addition, in this first book that Rousseau's concept of 'negative education' emerges for the first time. Defined by Rousseau, negative education begins when 'man's first natural movements . . . measure himself against everything surrounding him and [to] experience in each object he perceives all the qualities which can be sensed and relate to him' (Ibid., 125). Here, again, emerges another common misunderstanding; Rousseau does not advocate a completely laissez faire approach to education, as many have believed. Emile is taught how to use language, how to look after himself, the use of cutlery and so on. It is, however, the capacities, readiness and aptitude of the child (his 'nature') that determines the rate of his progress. He is not allowed, for example, to hear words which he cannot pronounce and, therefore, understand. Similarly, he is not placed into social situations until he is deemed to be able to cope with the relationships required. This idea of progressing only when the child is considered ready is, again, one central to later progressive thought, and as we shall see, found in the designs and systems of Montessori and Froebel, to name but two.

To this end, Emile's education was entrusted to the mysterious tutor figure (Jean-Jacques), whose task was to provide not merely supervision of the child but also to act as an indistinct moral guide. Nevertheless, despite the acquiring of certain aforementioned skills, the tutor appears almost redundant as Emile learns ostensibly by the consequences of his actions. Radically, this involved no imposition of rules, regulations or patterns of behaviour into the young child's head. At times, this approach seems to take on a slightly farcical nature as, for example, when Rousseau argues that even when Emile injures himself through his own actions, the tutor must not comfort the upset boy as it would be the equivalent of thwarting and contradicting his natural desires. This can be seen as perfectly illustrative of the point made earlier in relation to Rousseau's position at the intersection of the two intellectual paradigms. Although Emile is learning solely through the products of his own experiences (the Enlightenment-empiricist precept), the form and type of these experiences must spring from the innate impulses and knowledge of the child whose desires, Rousseau contends, should not be thwarted by the tutor. A key plank of progressive and Romantic thinking lay in recognizing the innate value of the wisdom of the child and Rousseau, in his own idiosyncratic way, articulated that position by placing an onus and a responsibility upon the young boy to engage in his own purposeful activity unencumbered by adult interference.

As Emile's early physical and mental education was solely restricted to self-discovery through his own experiences in the context of his immediate environment, his moral education was likewise limited to simple experiments and demonstrations with the tutor. As befitting 'negative education', Emile's earliest moral lessons arose from the first principle that 'Our first duties are to ourselves; our primary sentiments are centred on ourselves' (Ibid., 97). In that spirit, an experiment takes place concerning the planting of Emile's beans on the land belonging to his neighbour, Robert, who himself is acting in collusion with the tutor. Despite initial success in planting his crops, Emile finds one day that they have been torn up by Robert as they were found to be damaging his own plants. Emile thus learns, through it must be reiterated the process of self-discovery and realization, that in the same way he felt wronged on seeing his crops damaged, so must he recognize that his unthinking behaviour angered his neighbour. Thus, Emile is inducted into the idea of reciprocity in regard to social relations and is led to develop an understanding of the role and place of others, based on a primitive notion of utility.

It is a curious, and some may say quirky, fact of Rousseau's work that Emile is prohibited from reading books for the majority of his boyhood. On this point, Rousseau seems quite explicit – 'At twelve Emile will hardly know what a book is' (Ibid., 116). Even the tried and tested device of basic moralizing – the children's fable – was rejected, in a curious piece of circular thinking, due to the child's lack of experience in recognizing any apparent moral message. It was only in the third stage of Emile's development (12–15 years) that he is allowed to read Daniel Defoe's *Robinson Crusoe*, presumably on account of its themes of isolation and self-sufficiency away from civilization. While Rousseau abrogates the use of book learning, he is however very keen for Emile to learn a trade – a useful skill as opposed to an aesthetic one: 'I prefer that he be a shoemaker to a poet, that he pave highways to making porcelain flowers' (Ibid., 197). In part, such desire stemmed from Rousseau's conviction that there was an increasing, emergent fragility in the existing social order and that while the aristocratic nobility and the bonds of the *ancien regime* may lose their currency, there would always be a need in society for those with practical trades and skills and acquiring them when young would act as an insurance policy for the future – 'there is no decency without utility' (Ibid).

Rousseau's implications here are prescient as the eighteenth century, within which his life was contained, was a period of radical transformation and not merely in relation to the disruption of existing social orders through tumultuous events such as the French Revolution. The onset of mass industrialization and the comparative decline in authority of the Protestant and Catholic Churches betrayed an increase in national tensions that had not seemed possible, given the relative tranquillity that had existed back in 1700. While this particular aspect has not always been seen by historians of education as one of the central features of Emile's upbringing, it is important to recognize that the concept of arts and crafts and skills generally were to play an important part in future progressive philosophy, notably in many of the schools associated with the New Education Fellowship, and is a continuing matter of mainstream educational debate today when questions of *what* to teach and the skills a society needs are very much to the fore. Indeed, the development of such skills seemed to fit with later conceptions of Rousseau as the originator of a form of education inclined towards the outdoors and nature. While this is a dubious inference of Rousseau's intentions, and there were distinct elements of cosmopolitanism to Emile's education, *Emile* was nevertheless an influential text for many of those setting up institutions with 'worthwhile' pursuits at their heart.

The acquisition of knowledge such as the learning of a trade takes place during the period which sees Emile confined to a simple coexistence with his tutor, with little knowledge beyond his immediate confines. It is only in the third book of the novel that, for the first time, the boy is introduced to the wider environment. Very much in keeping with the tentative education offered to Emile to that point, his experiences even here are limited and still very much grounded in the principles of self-discovery and immediate sense experience. In his studies of geography, for example, Rousseau advocates beginning with the town in which the boy lives 'so that he will at least know what you are talking to him about' (Ibid., 168). Similarly, in the sciences, explanation was to be found, still, by innate curiosity rather than by any understanding of complex theory – 'I have already said that purely speculative knowledge is hardly suitable for children . . . always begin with the phenomena most common and most accessible to the senses' (Ibid., 177). Because his imagination had yet to be sufficiently cultivated, Emile had no ulterior desires beyond responding to immediate situations in which he found himself, and at the climax of the third book, his intellectual development was considered by Rousseau to be almost complete. By the end of this stage, Emile was 'laborious, temperate, patient, firm and full of courage. His imagination is in no way inflamed and never enlarges dangers' (Ibid., 208). While he has only been, generally speaking, in his own company, it was for this reason that Emile's character had yet to develop the flaws that Rousseau saw in those not privy to his educational system; he was ostensibly passive with no inclination to harm others.

The fourth stage of his development (which represents the ages of 15–20 and is the most lengthy and complicated of the essays in the novel) signals the end of the 'education from afar' and Emile is thus integrated gradually into the community and society at large. Central to this important part of the text is the question of emotion. As we have noted, Emile's development at this stage had been deliberately restricted by the tutor and his task was now to ensure that the *amour de soi* – self-love which Rousseau believed was the 'principal instrument[s] of our preservation' (Ibid., 212) – was not turned into *amour propre* which emerged, within those not educated as Emile has been, through direct personal comparisons of happiness, wealth and well-being, which lead to the emergence of unfulfilled desires. To this end, Emile was encouraged to be happy and confident in himself, aided by his lack of imagination, which meant he could not imagine and therefore desire something 'better', while also recognizing the suffering of others through his developed empathy. Crucially, this process involved restricting his contact with women and it is only toward the end of the book that Emile meets his future wife Sophie, although we again see evidence of the created and artificial environment as even she emerges as a product of the tutor's manipulation. Emile, although having been consulted on what he considers desirable female virtues, is once more systematically deceived into believing that Sophie was his own choice while she had, in fact, been carefully vetted and selected in advance!

It is in this context of the 'wider world', however – which Emile now explores – that slowly a more elaborated programme of study is permitted; he travels to a city, his tastes are cultivated, he learns manners and sophistication and we see his studies in history and literature increasing. Emile as a young man is now considered fit to be able to read history objectively and its works serve to show him the reality behind the 'civilized' world with its vanity and selfishness. Under normal conditions, Rousseau argues, people do not see these falsehoods but that is because their learning and study has taken place within that corrupt society and 'because we already contain within ourselves the passions and the prejudices which fill history and the lives of men'

(Ibid., 241). As in so many other philosophical meta-narratives and their respective truth claims, for example, postmodernism, Marxism and feminism, it seems that the tutor figure (Rousseau) has not himself been corrupted by civilization and can adopt a convenient standpoint of objectivity over and above the world within which he seems to be operating.

Rousseau also stresses at this point in his work the kinds of moral virtues Emile will have acquired as a result of his carefully structured and guided education. His entire moral sense rests on the base of reason, not intuition or emotion, and this, combined with nature and a limited autonomy, serves to produce an ethical conscience and Rousseau suggests that 'Eighteen years of assiduous care have had as their only object the preservation of a sound judgement and a healthy heart' (Ibid). Because of Emile's isolation from 'civilized' society, this impulse has not been oppressed as it would otherwise have been. This moral sense ultimately leads Emile to be fitted for a life of public service, in part through his reading of the *Social Contract*, a fact which has been the basis for those speculating that Rousseau's intent was on producing a 'civil man' rather than cultivating a 'natural man'. Certainly, it is possible to draw parallels with Plato's *Republic*, which Rousseau himself called 'the most beautiful educational treatise ever written' (Ibid., 40) and the attempts in that earlier book to re-make individuals by de-naturing them of, among other things, the arts and the sciences. In the same way that Plato abrogated the learning of 'degrading' art forms, such as poetry, which did not correspond to his concept of Ideal Forms, so Rousseau was actively hostile to those aspects of education that allowed for the development of the negative virtues of humanity. Remorseless hostility and suspicion of certain art forms, in particular, were one of the key similarities both of these great philosophers propagated.

Rousseau's limitations

Bizarrely, given its much feted status as a 'classic' and seminal piece of educational writing, it is unclear if Rousseau intended his book to be taken literally as a guide on how to raise children. As Matthew Simpson (2006) points out, as distinct from his many other, even those insignificant, writings, Rousseau never explained his motives for writing *Emile* and it is doubtful anyway if his friends and acquaintances would have taken his advice seriously, given the somewhat negligent treatment afforded to his own children! Certainly, *Emile* reads as much like a philosophical treatise as a novel; its themes are clearly allegorical and it could be argued that its *raison d'être* was less about an ideal education system and more to demonstrate a notable Romantic precept, which was that of the innate goodness of man. In that respect, as Simpson also elaborates, *Emile* is similar in outlook to Rousseau's earlier *Second Discourse* (1754), which was an explanation as to how man's innate goodness has been altered and corrupted by the knowledge he had acquired over time. *Emile* further demonstrates this by providing a system of education that, instead, allows man's natural goodness to thrive. In other words, Emile's happiness, educational voyage and ultimate acquisition of virtue are mere by-products emanating from a philosophical and theological defence. *Emile* serves therefore as a metaphor not so much for the child as for Man and should perhaps be read in that spirit.

Nevertheless, for all of its moralizing and profundity, there are aspects of *Emile* that are troubling to the reader and seem to be set against the general, more permissive tone of 'progressive' education. Perhaps the most obvious of these is Rousseau's attitude to women which appears, to modern sensibilities, chauvinistic. Certainly, as shall be explored in the succeeding chapter, this was a central bone of contention of Mary Wollstonecraft's. However, it must not be assumed, as is commonly the case – though not of course by Wollstonecraft, who understood *Emile* all too well – that Rousseau was advocating, *not* educating women. In the little-read fifth book of the novel, Rousseau is at pains to stress that Sophie (Emile's wife) is also to be educated along much the same lines as her husband – lines which emphasize the development of her reason in a created environment at the expense of imagination, thereby allowing for the creation of a natural *woman*. Yet – in a novel departure – the elaborated education she has been given is for one purpose:

> the whole education of women ought to relate to men. To please men, to be useful to them, to make herself loved and honoured by them, to raise them when young, to care for them when grown, to counsel them, to console them, to make their lives agreeable and sweet – these are the duties of women at all times. (Ibid., 365)

While Rousseau later, possibly anticipating the criticism to be had from his vehement views on gender, clouds the issue by suggesting the best women are ultimately in control of their men, the sense and implication of his meaning and the role of women in his ideal society is quite explicit.

More significant problems arise when one considers the extent to which Rousseau's child is actually *free*. For all of his rhetoric, discussion and usage of the term 'freedom', and his reputation as a purveyor of liberty, it should be clear that Rousseau's Emile grows up in an environment designed, manipulated and controlled entirely by the tutor. While the tutor pays close and considerate attention to the activities of the growing child, this is not solely to approve of them. Rousseau clearly distinguishes between activities and behaviour which are favourable to development and those which are not.

Many subsequent progressive educators – A. S. Neill and Homer Lane are two significant examples – argued that whatever activities and behaviour children end up espousing is irrelevant, provided that they are 'approved' of by the adult. Neill, for example, famously did not restrain his daughter from destroying his beloved piano while Lane agreed to join in with children if they were engaged in the vandalism of his school. This is clearly not the case with Rousseau's tutor who does not encourage behaviour that conflicts with the ideals he himself has set out in advance.

The sort of freedom given to Emile would therefore appear to be a form of negative freedom – freedom *from* rather than freedom *to*. In this case, the freedom enjoyed by the boy could be argued to be that from the harmful temptations and commands of a corrupted civilization and not freedom to pursue innate child-like desires. Despite Rousseau's call that 'Everything is good as it leaves the hands of the Author of things' (Ibid., 37) and the overtones this powerful statement carries in relation to natural goodness and wisdom, it seems that Emile is not trusted fully to engage in activities of his own choosing without the prior consent of the tutor. Such contradictions become apparent when Rousseau demands that the tutor intervene to stop Emile harming himself when 'carelessly exposed on high places or alone near fire, or dangerous weapons [are] left in his reach' (Ibid., 78). Although an eminently sensible piece of advice, it does little to answer the fundamental question as to the level of freedom Rousseau is ultimately affording the young child. How does this adult involvement reconcile itself with his trumpeting of freedom of action for the young boy and the need to learn from his mistakes? The restrictions posed on entering into wider society also means Rousseau fails to sufficiently address how it is that Emile is able to integrate into the company of others and what he comprehends his role within society to be. At best, one can argue that Emile's social relations are based on the principle of social reciprocity and the recognition of the need for others with different types of skills and abilities but this is hardly perhaps to do justice to the complexities inherent within societal structures or the social aspects which arise from a child's everyday schooling.

These are all powerful considerations and do nothing to ease the puzzlement many still feel when reading Rousseau's work. Nevertheless, such considerations are perhaps to take *Emile* too literally as an educational text and not as a critique of the value systems of the society in which Rousseau was living, particularly the growing wealth and power of the middle-class bourgeoisie whose attitudes towards child-rearing were seen as complacent. Rousseau may well therefore have been attempting to raise awareness, through the context of a thought experiment, of some of the less desirable aspects of civilization and to suggest that individual moral control and guidance were important if one were to be fulfilled in that particular social setting. Quite what *educational* lessons Rousseau wanted the reader to take, we may never know, yet the text's multifaceted nature remains a lasting testament to its author's own unique genius.

Rousseau's Heirs – The Lunar Society

Whatever Rousseau's intentions may have been in writing *Emile*, even within his own lifetime, his ideas began to generate interest and find advocates who were quite willing to embrace them literally as well as metaphorically. Perhaps it was only natural, given his connection with the Midlands (on the invitation of David Hume, Rousseau and his mistress had stayed with businessman Richard Davenport in Staffordshire in 1766), that it was members of the Lunar Society[2] who were among the first to consciously and deliberately experiment with Rousseauian notions of child-rearing. As Jenny Uglow (2002) has made clear in her magisterial study of this group, while it was an unconvinced Erasmus Darwin who first met Rousseau pontificating to himself, as legend had it, in a garden cave, it was left to two of the group's younger members, Richard Lovell Edgeworth (1744–1817) and Thomas Day (1748–89), to more fully apprehend the significance and possibilities of his ideas. Edgeworth, although best known for his daughter Maria and their astonishing joint collaboration, *Practical Education*, was the first to tentatively embrace naturalistic techniques by letting his son go barefoot and wear loose-fitting clothing. By the age of seven, he was 'bold, free, fearless, generous' (Edgeworth 1820: 179) and it led Edgeworth to take a conscious interest in the lives of his children, to the point of making detailed observations and notes on their patterns of behaviour. It was these developments that marked the start of his lifelong interest in child-rearing, which was to have, as shall be discussed in the next chapter, significant effects for the history of progressivism.

Although giving such freedoms to his young family amounted to little worse than well-meaning eccentricity on Edgeworth's part, Day's attempt to procure the perfect wife for himself by commandeering two orphans and moulding them under a Rousseauian scheme smacked of both social engineering and monumental moral disregard. In the event, the two girls appropriated by Day – named for his purposes Lucretia and Sabrina Sydney – were soon taken to France where, in the context of an isolated, uncorrupted environment, they were to be subject only to his control and educated as Emile had been, at a distance from the civilized world. A combination of disease, inability to speak the native language, behavioural difficulties and capsized boats persuaded an exhausted Day to return to England, convinced of his own and perhaps Rousseau's failure. This was hardly surprising in retrospect, given Day's own eccentricities; to teach his potential wife the necessary virtues of Stoicism and resolve, he had applied molten candle wax to her arm! Edgeworth too had also discovered concurrent difficulties, writing of his son, 'he was disposed not to obey' and of having developed an 'invincible dislike to control' (Ibid).

While Day's faith may have been shaken, it had not altogether evaporated, and in 1780, he set out to write a work that combined aspects of Rousseau's philosophy with the budding Romantic notion of sensibility.[3] Couched in the form of a children's story, The History of Sandford and Merton, whose plot concerned the relations between the protagonists of the title, demonstrated Day's partial abandonment and disaffection with Rousseau's system of education. In Day's new setting, book learning was reinstated as a key concept and the boys both lived in the real world from the start of their education, thereby sacrificing at a stroke a central tenet of Emile. Likewise, the book itself – at least the original version prior to a succession of abridgements – was episodically structured and contained elements of stories Day himself had procured and so was less concerned with elaborating any sense of child development as it was with the telling of rollicking good yarns. However, despite these departures, as for Rousseau, Day's explicit concern – as voiced by Mr Barlow, the book's equivalent to Emile's tutor – was with how to instruct boys to live happily in a self-interested world. It was these utopian concerns that therefore provided a key link with Emile and led to Day developing a system of education centred on the needs of the individual child.

Ultimately, the motives behind the boys' education which involved learning to read, a variety of practical tasks and engaging in a series of adventures, was to ensure their behaviour in the world was benevolent towards others as 'it is his [a boys] duty to do it, because every benevolent person feels the greatest pleasure in doing good, and even because it is in his own interest to make as many friends as possible' (Day 1783: 121). In keeping with Rousseau's sense of reciprocity within the context of social relations and the need to be forward thinking, the justification given for friendship was as a safety net in case of a change in the boys circumstances, whereby 'he may have occasion for the compassion of those who are infinitely below him' (Ibid). There was much then in Day's work which seemed to draw explicitly upon the earlier ideas of Rousseau and scholars such as F. J. Darton (1982) have convincingly argued for Sandford as being a deliberate attempt to promulgate these ideas to British children in the form of readable fiction. While hard to gauge, the influence of this work is difficult to overestimate. First published in 1783, reprinted in 1786 and then again in 1789, by 1870, it had gone through over 140 editions. Although well-liked for its rambunctious sense of fun and boys own tales, its consistent popularity into the Victorian era did much to shape their sentimental, pseudo-Evangelical attitudes to children and childhood. While these did not, usually, become embodied in progressive educational practices and discourse, they nevertheless contributed to a changing view of childhood, which led ultimately to the repudiation of such evils as child labour and concerns over children's well-being.

Pestalozzi – the first Romantic

Despite Day's attempts, which have the air of a social experiment rather than of a systematic philosophy to them, the real heirs to Rousseau lay in the continent. This was understandable perhaps as the ideas and implications of Romanticism were to find their most genuine expression in the geography of Central Europe. We know, for example, even from the English literary tradition, the indebtedness of Coleridge to Germanic philosophy while Byron and Shelley are more associated with their European wanderings as they are of being *English* poets – both dying in Greece and Italy, respectively. The two key educators therefore who emerged from this tradition were Johann Pestalozzi (1746–1827) and Friedrich Froebel (1782–1852), both of whom were central figures in the development of a very particular European progressive tradition, which drew upon common ideological tenets and themes, in particular, the development of the concept of the naturalistic child and a quasi-spiritual approach to child rearing.

While the latter has been more extensively written about by historians of education (due, in part, to the continuing worldwide popularity of his kindergarten movement), Pestalozzi has been less well documented. The last full-scale biography of him to appear in English was that of Kate Silber in 1960 and while scholars such as Daniel Troehler have laboured splendidly on the Herculean task of attempting to edit and reproduce his huge corpus of published writings, these and much of the associated scholarship tend to be confined to the German-speaking world. As Michel Soetard (1994) makes it clear, 'Pestalozzi is very often mentioned, but very rarely read and both his work and his thought are still very little known' (Soetard 1994: 297).

This is a tragic oversight because Pestalozzi, aside from in his early years embodying the Rousseauian peasant archetype, was the first to act as a truly rounded progressive pedagogue combining an educational philosophy with both innovative practice and a genuine love of children. The famous painting currently hanging in Basel by Konrad Grob where Pestalozzi is seen holding the hand of a child while another clambers on his back is ample evidence of his natural empathy for the young. All of this occurred against a continuing personal backdrop of perpetual poverty and financial concern. Imbued initially with the same national republican spirit as Rousseau, Pestalozzi's early inclinations were agrarian; his interest in farming stemmed from his Romantic conviction that a more simplistic, agricultural lifestyle was less susceptible to the immorality and vice of urban living. It was, in fact, while working as a farmer that he opened his first short-lived educational institution for the rural poor in 1772. Although his early life contained several such failed attempts at running schools like this, it is through his work, first, at the convent community at Stans where he attempted to provide a more comprehensive system of schooling for the poor and, later, at his Institutes at Burghdof and Yverdon (it was relocated in 1805) that his subsequent didactic reputation has since rested.

Unlike Rousseau, whose educational progressive reputation rests exclusively on a single work, Pestalozzi's writings are voluminous, cover a 45-year period in his life, and in common with many other major educationalists, document ideological evolution and occasional repudiation of earlier beliefs, making it perhaps more difficult to establish a central 'corpus' of ideas. As Lewis Anderson (1931) puts it, 'One will search in vain in the writings of Pestalozzi for any complete and unified system of educational theory' (Anderson 1931: 1). This may partially explain why his work has remained relatively unapproached by scholars; yet, of all of the followers of Rousseau, he was the one who best (and first) attempted to wrestle with the difficulties of *Emile* and, through this engagement, delineate some form of mass educational system.

Pestalozzi's writings are couched in a deeply pessimistic view of human nature; he regarded man as naturally antisocial and selfish and saw education as the device by which humans could be socialized, integrated and properly prepared for work. Such convictions stemmed from his bitter experiences of the European crop failure of 1771–72 and his first-hand observance of the poverty and fragmentation of rural workers linked to their lack of education and basic skills. All the same, unlike Rousseau, whose own philosophy seemed to be based upon a societal pretext of 'make-do-and-mend', Pestalozzi believed that with the right system of education, it was possible to solve the wider problems of civilized society and make that society fair and equitable for all. He was convinced that schools, such as they were, were driven by the curriculum and not by the needs of the students. This was exacerbated by harsh, didactic teaching methods. As Anderson, again, puts it,

> The idea which throughout his life served as the mainspring for his activities was that, for the oppressed poor, the road to the fullness of life, and hence to happiness, lay through the promotion, through true education, of the natural development of the mental and physical powers of individuals, hitherto, neglected or misdirected. (Ibid., 3)

Pestalozzi, at times, made equally grand claims for the importance of his own work, believing that he could, 'neutralize the most oppressive consequences of the evils of the feudal system and of the factory system through renewed effort for the education of the people' (Pestalozzi as cited in Ibid., 101). Much of this conviction can be found in the most important and complex of his early works, the *Nachsforschungen* (the *Inquiry*), published in 1791, in which he boldly attempted to divine and synthesize a middle path between the nature of man and the state of society.

For Pestalozzi, many of the problems with the latter stemmed from abuses of power, selfishness and egoism of the political rulers. Unlike Rousseau though, whose education system, as has been shown, was designed to cater for (in practice, if not in theory) the literate elites of society, the Pestalozzian viewpoint was wholly democratic and universal. Pestalozzi wrote of his objectives in a 1774 diary entry as being 'to join together what Rousseau had rent asunder'. Rather than advocating taking children out of society to be raised and educated, Pestalozzi saw the family and especially the mother as crucial to a child's development. As he himself wrote in *Address to the House* (1818), 'It is indisputable that in the living-room of every household are united the fundamental means for the true education of mankind' (Pestalozzi as cited in Anderson, 143). Perhaps he was all too aware of the habits of families who passed their children's education over to tutors (was he thinking of Emile?) or else threw their children into work as soon as they were able, thereby failing to build up crucial familial bonds. For Pestalozzi, parental love, such as it was, was one determinant towards ensuring an individual could make moral choices throughout his life.

In Pestalozzi's terms, this love was displayed by refusing to view education as a universal instrument through which individuals would be socialized (to use the Durkheimian term) into a 'better' or more perfect society. Pestalozzi preferred that individual children recognized in themselves something which was unique and who could therefore derive something creative from their instincts. As in Rousseau, we see Pestalozzi using a characteristically Romantic *organic discourse* in comparing the development of the child to a plant and suggesting that the child's education must match his ability to apprehend what he is being taught:

> Man, imitate the action of great nature which from the seed of even the largest tree pushes at first but an imperceptible shoot; but then by a further imperceptible growth which progresses smoothly every hour and every day unfolds the young trunk, and finally the smallest twigs from which will hang the ephemeral leaves. (Pestalozzi as cited in Heafford 1967: 44)

In this way, and by these processes, the school's social order created itself from the aggregate desires and interests of the pupils. In all senses, this was truly progressive!

It was in 1798 that Pestalozzi received his first proper opportunity to put such abstracted theories into practice. His native Switzerland had been sucked into Napoleon's Revolutionary Wars with the upshot that the government was centralized, a new constitution put in place and the Helvetic Republic created. In the process, the village of Stans had been destroyed and Pestalozzi was thereby granted permission to open an institution to care for the orphaned and war-ravaged children. While it only lasted for a period of seven months, its impact on his thinking was significant, and his subsequent major works, particularly his novel/parable *How Gertrude Teaches her Children*, as well as his institutes at Burghdof and Yverdon, were all constant developments of a 'Pestalozzi Method' worked out in Stans. The term 'Method' in this context is perhaps misleading, for it implies, as it did latterly for Froebel and Montessori, that there was something unique by way of materials for children to work with or new teaching techniques to apprehend. Visitors to his institutes were, in these respects, to be disappointed, for the originality of Pestalozzi's 'Method' lay within its spirit and, more specifically, the individual spirits of the children under his tutelage.

In a letter to a friend in 1807, Pestalozzi distilled quite presciently the three identifiable stages of his education system. The first was the emphasis upon family life and the catering for the child's basic needs and desires. This was promulgated by the central role he gave, as we have mentioned, to the mother or, in the case of the orphans at Stans, himself as educator. These figures had the responsibility for mediating between those desires of the child and the demands which society placed on the child, and so, had the power to enliven or deaden the child's own sense of autonomy. The second stage sought to encourage children to demonstrate the charitable and loving impulses which had been fostered within them at the first stage. The third and final stage involved children reflecting on those impulses in order to gain a deeper appreciation of what moral action actually was. Such a process Pestalozzi referred to as *Menschenbildung* (the formation of man), which was his attempt to tie knowledge and understanding to moral action.

As for Rousseau, these concerns emanated from a prevailing dissatisfaction with existing political regimes and social structures. In particular, the appropriation of high levels of taxation by the conquering French convinced Pestalozzi that, whatever their hue and standpoint, all such political regimes were dominated and driven by some form of tangible immorality. This is very much reflected in his emphasis on the mother in the domestic sphere, rather than the political leaders in the public, as being at the vanguard of moral example. In another letter, Pestalozzi wrote, 'I'm not a Zuricher, I'm not a Swiss anymore. We don't have a fatherland anymore. Let us stay human beings and not forget the concerns of mankind until our death' (Pestalozzi, quoted in Trohler 2001: 73). Whereas Rousseau's instruction contained evident ambiguity as to the role Emile would play in the future society, Pestalozzi was clear that this was too narrow a vision and that education was necessary in order for there to be some form of divine and global unity among individuals of all nations.

How Pestalozzi thought educationalists could achieve this global integration in practice was by examining the separate roles played by three constituent body components – the head, heart and hand – which were used as metaphors for direct educational action. The head was to be used for reflection on the world, the heart to respond to the demands of other men and civilization, while the hand was responsible for forging a life that best reconciled the two disparate pulls of self and society. The role of the teacher, Pestalozzi stressed, was to keep these three components in equilibrium. Teachers were thereby encouraged not to categorize subjects merely as 'intellectual', 'technical' or 'physical' but to attempt to introduce elements of all into their subject lessons. For example, PE classes would focus upon not merely games playing but the intellectual and physical demands fostered by such activity. Similarly, mathematics would involve not merely theoretical calculations but would be linked to examples within real life and other areas of the curriculum where numeracy was required, in other words, integration of discreet subject areas was encouraged. This was itself to be a recurring characteristic of later progressive schools. Pestalozzi was at pains to stress, however, that the search for this balance was never fully completed and was a continuing, dynamic and evolving process and at any particular point in time, one element may be in ascendancy over the others. It was the job of the educator, he contended, to balance these three components according to the needs of the child. It may be no exaggeration to state that Pestalozzi was the first educator to conclude that teaching was not solely about imparting knowledge but of training the faculties needed for understanding.

In terms of the lessons he organized, Pestalozzi, perhaps unsurprisingly, rejected 'word-knowledge' and concentrated upon the development of *Anschauung* which, as William Kilpatrick (1951) has stressed, concerned itself with observation and reflection upon objects. In keeping with the Romantic precepts of Rousseau, and presumably as much to do with utilizing the beauty of the Swiss surroundings, Pestalozzi was keen to emphasize that such observation was best undertaken in the context of the natural world – 'Let our child out into nature, teach him on the hill tops and in the valleys . . . Let him be taught by nature' (Pestalozzi, in Hayward 1905: 29). Nature thus represented not merely a source of happiness for children through its integral beauty, but also of knowledge as it provided an ordered example and environment through which children could learn. This learning took the form of sketching of landscapes, observations of plants, country walks, interacting with farm animals and so on. The feeling and 'sense' of objects preceded the apprehension of specific details. In its way, this was emotion over reason, which was characteristic of the move away from Rationalism towards Romanticism.

In the same way, Pestalozzi applied his concept of *Anschauung* to children's morality. What was the point, he argued, of learning by heart catechisms or passages of the Bible when their meaning could not be understood by the child? Far better, he believed, for morality to be demonstrated by practical parental and motherly example. Learning had to therefore be a process which entailed emotional involvement and investment rather than mere recitation.

Like other early progressives, Pestalozzi saw the multifarious attributes of his system as being not merely ones in which children were schooled but also that they laid down certain fundamental precepts which could underpin wider communities and societies. From the time of Stans onwards, Pestalozzi created such communities which catered for not merely the desires of individuals but also for the general well-being of the group. Often, this expressed itself in concrete action; Pestalozzi himself remarked favourably on the destitute children of Stans generously accommodating those new arrivals who themselves were even poorer. He envisaged education as having a crucial role to play in the spread of democratic ideals and the setting of social example which related demonstrably to his 'global' vision.

One of the perversities in considering Pestalozzi is that while his name and writings have been largely forgotten today in his own time, his work and ideas were both extremely popular and widely revered. In part, this stemmed from its themes chiming with, and perhaps contributing to, the later cultural *zeitgeist* of German Romanticism and Idealism, which his 'Method', based more on nurturing of the spirit rather than novel didactics, seemed to embrace. Institutes were founded in his name across Europe and, in the immediate aftermath of the publication of *Gertrude*, a plethora of critical literature emerged. Visitors to Yverdon included the philosophers and educators Froebel, Fichte and Humboldt. Recent scholarship has also demonstrated how Pestalozzi's ideas were exported to America by both William Maclure, which culminated in the New Harmony community in Indiana (as shall be discussed later in relation to Robert Owen) and, more indirectly, in the development of the Oswego Method (which will also be discussed later in its North American context).

What was most distinctive about Pestalozzi's work, and why it received so much contemporary attention, was its pioneering attempt to bridge together the two poles of theory and practice. Not for him the philosophical and theoretical abstractions and musings of a Rousseau or a Locke. However, it was to be the contradictions embedded in a philosophy that was at once method-based, and yet, simultaneously desirous of individual autonomy that was to lead to the decline of Pestalozzi's aspirations. Specifically, it was a quarrel with the Yverdon clergyman and Pestalozzi's closest collaborator, Niederer, which facilitated the collapse of the institute. Niederer, seeking to systematize the ideas of his colleague, ended up, in Pestalozzi's eyes, usurping the very principle of freedom upon which the ideas themselves rested. In the day-to-day running of the school, Niederer's focus upon teaching the lessons of 'freedom' from a Christian viewpoint neglected the freedom fundamental to Pestalozzi – that of the children and their developing autonomy. Consequently, Pestalozzi lost control of his staff and, refusing to compromise his fundamental principles, closed down the institute and devoted the rest of his life to philosophical contemplation.

Emergent from this last period of his life came Pestalozzi's educational political will and testament – the *Schwanengesang* (*Swan Song*). Dictated to his son and published two months prior to his death, this last, final, great work is a part-autobiography and part-reflection upon a life of educational theorizing. And yet, bizarrely, for the modern-day reader, of which there have been too few, it is a frustrating book precisely because it fails to reconcile this disparity that had accounted, in part, for the dissolution of his educational projects. Freedom and autonomy, after all, could not be achieved if the educator's work was based upon a theoretical and abstract *modus operandi*. The *Swan Song*, if anything, was a clarion call to the teacher to adapt themselves to new circumstances, develop fresh techniques and strategies, provided they were imbued 'in truth and in love' and carried out in the name of autonomy. Such powerful sentiments not only meant that it was now desirable for the progressives to act on the individual nature of the child but also that, from now on, the art of teaching could be considered more scientifically, given the emergent dialectic, reflexive and occasionally precarious relationship between theory and practice. Nearly 200 years later, we are still searching for this balance – a true swan song for Pestalozzi indeed!

Friedrich Froebel and German Idealism

Yet, while Pestalozzi was educating children to fit into a better world, others were beginning to consider if the notion of an 'actual' world, independent of our own minds, was misplaced and misguided. This movement, one of the cornerstones of Romanticism, known as Idealism was the most direct philosophical reaction to that point against the predominant views of the Enlightenment. If the world, after all, is created by human minds and imagination, what is the role and place of an omnipotent, divine Creator? Throughout the Enlightenment, even scientific discoveries and hard metaphysics had not shaken this implacable faith in God. As Alexander Pope wryly put it in a proposed epitaph, 'Nature and nature's laws lay hid in Night./ God said, "Let Newton be!" and all was light'. Idealism can therefore be seen as the first genuine challenge to the old order, its influence perhaps evidenced by an increasing tendency towards secularization, or at least, reluctance to recognize God as something other than transcendent. As Peter Weston (1998) has pointed out,

> the major philosophical issue of the period [therefore] became analysis of the relation between a self-conscious and autonomous "subject" and the external world of Nature as mere "object". Is the "self" part of nature or apart from it? What is the self that reflects on selfhood? Is the world an aspect of mind, constructed by mind? Is intellectual freedom an illusion? How can knowledge be possible and what is it? What is the origin and justification of moral values? (Weston 1998: 4)

These questions were the main concern, in particular, of the German Idealists, whose search for the unity of subject and object, mind and matter was not merely to shape modern thought but also to play a key role in redefining an important aspect of educational progressivism. This group, and it is never easy to demarcate in historical terms, of whom Kant is often considered the *eminence grise*, believed that what was knowable was only the way objects appear to us as perceiving subjects and not due to any inherent qualities of the objects 'in themselves'. All we could ever know therefore were the products of our own minds. Such a belief system owed much to the work of George Berkeley and his famous 1710 *Treatise Concerning the Principles of Human Knowledge* which put forward the idea that the external world consisted not of physical matter but of ideas, held cogently together at all times by the perception of God. Nevertheless, for Kant, there was a realm of reality (the *noumenal* realm) that consisted of things in themselves, which differed from the *phenomenal* realm which constituted things as they could be perceived. Our senses, therefore, were a limitation upon our perception as they could only operate within the aspects of what Kant referred to as 'categories of understanding' – space, time and so on. Biology acted as a limiting factor on our knowing and understanding.

This cleavage between appearance and reality was therefore at the heart of the Idealist project and its subsequent followers were, for the most part, playing variations on Kant's theme. Johann Fichte, for example, dismissed the idea of there being a thing in itself, arguing that any images and representations were merely products of our own ego. Friedrich Schelling, by contrast, argued that the properties of the internal mind corresponded exactly with that which is external to the mind, while Friedrich Schleiermacher believed that the internal and the external were both brought together under the aspect of God.

Nevertheless, despite their differing hues, this remarkable body of men converged in an epic constellation at the University of Jena, which was rapidly becoming one of Europe's intellectual vanguards. Fichte was a professor there from 1794 to 1799, before being unceremoniously booted out for, characteristically, radical sympathies. He overlapped by a year with Schelling (professor between 1798 and 1820) who, in turn, served alongside the great Georg Hegel between 1801 and 1807. What a crucible! And into this melting pot of intellectual ferment stepped a 17-year-old student who was to produce one of the of the most famous and wide ranging doctrines of progressive educational thought – Friedrich Froebel.

Of all of the concepts and ideas discussed in this book, perhaps the kindergarten, literally translated as 'child's garden', is the one most well known to the layman. Its widespread denomination, global exportation and use in commonplace vernacular in referring to the pre- or early school years have had a tendency to obscure its very specific historical roots and systematic methods of learning. As Norman Brosterman (1997) has additionally shown, the kindergarten philosophy and its concerns with geometry have influenced those whose work has not been at all educational, for example, the architectural and artistic masterpieces of Frank Lloyd Wright and Paul Klee. It is also to Froebel that educational vocabulary owes the term 'child centred', appearing as it does in the introductory section to his great masterpiece, *The Education of Man* (1826).

As is to be expected from such a dominating figure, the literature relating to Froebel is extensive; several, albeit now slightly aged, biographies are available, while the more recent work of Joachim Liebschner (1991 and 1992) and Evelyn Lawrence (1952) successfully charts the growth and dissemination of Froebel's ideas in a more global context and indicates the reverence with which his ideas are still held by practitioners today. The work of Kevin Brehony – himself a Froebel Professor at the University of Roehampton and a tireless champion of the man himself – in overseeing a six-volume reprint of Froebel's major works and those of the English Froebel Movement is also deserving of special mention and is symptomatic of the continuing interest and fascination Froebel's work holds among not merely the academic community but also those with only a passing interest in education. As is also the case with Pestalozzi, much of the best secondary literature on Froebel – for example, the various works of Helmut Heiland (1990 and 1998) – is sadly available only in German.

Such posthumous educational recognition seems all the more surprising, given that Froebel's goal in joining the University of Jena was initially more prosaic; he intended to study the sciences of mathematics and botany with a view to pursuing his career as a forester. The direct impact of these Idealists upon such a tender mind can only be speculated upon and has been traditionally deemed relatively insignificant, given his relative social naiveté at the time and the fact that his university career ended in ignominious imprisonment. Yet, Froebel could not have helped, one feels, becoming immersed in the revolutionary atmosphere and fervour surrounding the small German town.

Certainly, we know that around the time of his leaving, following his father's death, he was reading widely in the fields of literature and philosophy, including key works by Schelling and Goethe. Crucially, what many of these writers were trying to attain – as was the case in other seemingly disparate disciplines, for example, through the increasingly bombastic style of the 'Germanic tradition' symphony or in the developing understanding of the ways that the few known elements made up complex compounds in nature – was a *unified* system of thought encompassing God, nature and Man. Hegel referred to this big concept as the 'Will' or 'Absolute Spirit'.

One significant current underlying much of this search was the idea of *Naturphilosophie* (Philosophy of Nature) which was an omnibus term used to express complex Idealist investigations into the 'structure' of nature. Standing in contrast to the earlier, established work of Francis Bacon and Isaac Newton who saw mathematics and empiricist methodology at the heart of nature and science, Idealists posited that the world/nature couplet was a manifestation of a basic, common force or impulse (that certain of the Romantics equated with God) and that far from our senses imposing a cloud upon our perception, as Kant had argued, human reason allowed some degree of communion and participation in the divine, thereby allowing us to comprehend its totality.[4] Nature was seen as consisting of opposites – forces, substances, elements – which could combine and be reconstituted to form new forces and phenomena through reference to a single underlying force. While such metaphysical speculation may sound vague and hazy, it must be noted that it had a huge impact in not merely shaping investigations into the natural sciences, but also on Froebel's educational beliefs. He betrayed this influence in the opening paragraph of the *Education of Man* (1826):

> in all things there lives and reigns an eternal law . . . This all-controlling law is necessarily based on an all-pervading, energetic, living, self-conscious and hence eternal unity . . . This unity is God. All things have come from the Divine unity, from God and have their origin in the Divine unity, in God alone. (Froebel 1892: 1)

For all that his university days taught him, Froebel's most directly formative educational experiences stemmed not from the metaphysics of Jena but from his prolonged visits (1805 and 1808–10) to Yverdon to observe, at close quarters, Pestalozzi's system. While he regarded the Swiss as the master and took very much an apprentice role at Yverdon, Froebel was ultimately to diverge from his mentor, rarely mentioning him in his later work or letters, and considering those divergences provides us with a sensible platform with which to begin to consider the wider implications of Froebel's complex ideas. Superficially, both with their concerns over 'natural laws' of development, the role that nature should play in the learning process and their shared objections to learning by words and repetition over example, there are obvious similarities. Froebel, however, believed Pestalozzi did not go far enough; for him, mere observation and discussion of objects (the *Anschauung*) did not develop the child's full potential. That was only achieved, Froebel contended, through the process of self-discovery and self-realization – concepts that not only went beyond the theories of his forebears but established one of the key tenets of progressivism that has endured to the present day. In relation to learning through nature, for example, it was not merely enough to tramp across fields discussing what you saw. Froebel's students were encouraged to explore rivers, draw maps, farm land, look after animals and thereby achieve some kind of closer union with nature. In that sense, Froebel's was a far more 'hands on' Romanticism than that of both his contemporaries and forebears.

Similarly, the mother figure, which Pestalozzi saw as the lightening rod for moral example, was not seen by Froebel as automatically being endowed with the requisite innate skills to care for pre-school children. In his letters to the Duchess of Schwarzburg-Rudolstadt, he proposed Sunday meetings between parents and teachers, implying not merely that parents should be reflecting upon educational techniques but also that there was something specialist about the role of the teacher. As we shall see, the instruction of teachers through training colleges was central to Froebelianism and, again, this ethos has permeated through our own age, with much attention garnered on specialist educational preparation.

In many ways then, Froebel's educational philosophy is the most purely 'Romantic' in the progressive canon. He believed that human beings and, of course, children were essentially creative beings who achieved self-fulfilment through the completion of productive tasks which would thereby allow communion with God. Moreover, in much the same way that Wordsworth was to famously contend that the 'child is father of the man', the Idealists believed that at birth all of what one was to become was already present both materially and spiritually. Schooling therefore became a matter of providing the right environment for the child to 'grow', be nurtured and develop. Note once more the organic metaphors which were so much a staple of Romantic and, particularly, Froebel's writing.

Froebel's early life, involving spells of teaching and writing in Germany and Switzerland, has been well charted by historians and biographers and it is therefore not necessary to replicate it here. Earlier writings (including the five Keilhau pamphlets, the *Education of Man* and his various journals) laid down many of his key ideas often in very dense, philosophically circuitous, almost obscurantist prose which can be problematic for the modern-day reader unfamiliar with, or unsympathetic to, the particular contextual nuances of German Romanticism. Writing clearly did not come as naturally to this great communicator as speech and empathy! Nevertheless, to uncover the principles at work, it is perhaps simplest to examine how they were put into practice at the first kindergarten, founded at Bad Blankenberg in 1837. It would not be stretching a point to suggest that had Froebel died in this year, he would have only merited a trifling footnote in accounts of progressivism, indicating the huge impact and importance of his later work and the setting up of these pioneering schools.

The very term kindergarten was, in fact, applied by Froebel retrospectively and sought to conceptualize, in a phrase, an institution dedicated to that particular notion of self – self-discovery, self-learning, self-activity and self-cultivation. The pedagogic methods by which the young children were to cultivate these particular values were through Froebel's famous gifts and occupations. Today, these amount, even among his followers, to little more than kitsch classroom bijoux but they are of central historical importance as they represented early practical attempts to not merely occupy and engage children (and the teacher) but also to concretize the Idealist notion of unity in the context of an educational system. Gifts represented universal aspects of the external world and while they themselves consisted of nothing more than yarn balls, wooden blocks, tablets and cubes, the idea that, 'each object given must condition the one which follows' (Froebel 1897: 174) expressed the hope that they could allow a child to develop at his own self-directed pace, allowing them to gain mastery of their own world by acting directly on it. There was a gradual evolution, for example, of exploring solid shapes in two dimensions to three and of moving from concrete to abstract representations.

Such progress accorded with Froebel's belief that children developed, emotionally and physically, in discrete phases – most obviously, early (birth to eight) and later childhood. His work was almost exclusively concerned with the former group and the idea that children were not capable at this stage of learning effectively other than on things within their 'own world' was, like many other progressive theories, a direct reaction against prevailing educational orthodoxy. The simplicity of such an idea belies its legacy; even today, educationalists still think of (approximately) eight years as an appropriate age to signal a division between the 'primary' and 'middle' years or 'lower' primary and 'upper' primary years of schooling.

Having thus acquired sensual and tactile skills, Froebel's child was now in a position to demonstrate its competence in the occupations – practical tasks such as weaving, paper-folding and wood cutting, which were designed to coordinate the mind and body in unity. Each of these activities was, again, harmonized to fit in with the particular point of the child's development. Unlike, for example, Rousseau's system, it was to be down to the child themselves to determine their own pace of learning and not through a set of pre-designated external criteria imposed by a teacher. In addition, Froebel's kindergartens, quite literally, embodied their name with gardens attached to the school where the children were encouraged to tend plants and preserve nature. The links between such activities, Romanticism and theories of Divine Unity need hardly be reiterated. Cooperation – another form of unity! – rather than competition was the aim.

These big ideas are hugely significant when one examines the consideration Froebel gave to the concept of *play*. Much progressive thought – and arguably, contemporary popular perception – centres on the idea that play is an activity through which children can, and do, learn through the application of their senses. Play should not be thought of as reasoned, purposeful or structured. Rather, it should be spontaneous and free and this is something Froebel realized and encouraged. For him, play was not merely an activity designed to develop physical characteristics and attributes but that it had as well an *educational* and latterly *symbolic* dimension attached to it. In reading the explanations and instructions attached to the gifts and occupations, the pedagogic value he ascribed to play becomes evident. While Froebel's published writings oscillate in terms of the amount of freedom, as one example, to allow children when playing with sets of bricks, he never deviated from the central precept that children can only play with materials with which they are familiar and that these must be constantly changed and refreshed to form a united whole.

As Joachim Liebschner (1992) has charted, in the last two years of his life, Froebel began making important statements on the value of play as being not merely of value for individual children but as symbolizing something greater within the context of society. He cites as evidence Froebel's notes relating to the 1850 Children, Youth and Folk Festival at Altenstein. It was in these, Froebel argued, that the developmental growth phases we undergo as humans are replicated in the various historical epochs of society but that we are not always willing or able to grasp the demands and – in Hegel's terms – the *zeitgeist* of the age.[5] As Liebschner further explains, 'Festivals, such as the one held at Altenstein (but also family festivals, birthdays etc.,) [were] the perfect vehicle for making the "character of our time" conscious' (Liebschner 1992: 56). Typically, such festivals were held atop hills in the countryside and involved children and adults standing in symbolic circles, dancing, singing and playing and coming to a realization of the Divine Unity of things. Individual freedom, nature, joy and celebration thus combined, with play as the catalyst, to enable participants to understand both the function of the festival and the realities of the age. Equating play with freedom of both body and consciousness in this wholly new way worried many – the Prussian government, for one – and yet, it remains at the very heart of Froebel's ideology and reflects the way in which play was at the heart of his kindergarten philosophy.

Froebel and women

No account of Froebel in a progressive context would be complete without a deliberation of the ways in which he opened up the profession of teaching to women. Romanticism, generally, was seen as a movement which welcomed emancipation and celebrated the ideal of equality, and Froebel's thinking was no exception. While the specific contribution of his female disciples in spreading his gospel will be explored in the next chapter, it should be noted here that his interest in promoting women more generally to the profession of teaching emerged primarily from his preoccupation with the role of the mother. As has been eluded, Froebel saw the role of the mother as not merely one of eschewing vice and demonstrating morality but as having a vital part to play in correctly developing the unity of the child. For Froebel, the processes of education began from birth, and so, these relationships were crucial and explain why much writing on Froebel has stemmed from early years practitioners.

This deification of the feminine is most evident in *The Mother Songs*, published in 1844, which, alongside *The Education of Man*, can be considered his most famous work. These *Songs* were a collection of songs, images and stories designed to be read by mothers to their children, with each child then expressing his or her own thoughts, emotions and responses via a set of actions or finger-games. Much like his gifts, these stories and songs to the modern mind are twee, the illustrations not always clear and Froebel's instructions and justification are, typically, convoluted. However, such limitations belie the deep educational principles at work; this was not merely an attempt to strengthen the bonds between mother and child and act physically on the world to improve comprehension. Instead, the exercises Froebel developed and elaborated were intended to move the child away from merely having an awareness of things as they are to things as they might have been. In true Idealist spirit, the case was made for mentally turning objects into images, images into symbols and the symbolic as constituting the spiritual whole of the world. Individuality and freedom for the child were central and it was the child's own personal responses to each story and song which aligned the course of their guidance. It is little wonder Froebel regarded this work as the pinnacle of his written achievement, describing it as recording, 'the most important aspects of my educational theory' (Froebel 1879: 1).

Nevertheless, despite the popularity of the *Mother Songs* and their emphasis upon maternalism, teaching more generally in Prussia at the time, especially within the universities, remained a solidly male preserve. We know that Froebel tried in vain to woo government ministers and school inspectors round to his way of thinking which sought parity between the genders, but he was met with consistent ridicule and rebuttal which pushed him into his own initiatives. He therefore turned, late in his life, to the training of women as kindergarten teachers in 1849 in Liebenstein, and quickly attracted to his ranks the Baroness Martha von Marenholtz-Bulow who was to prove in the forthcoming years to be his most ardent and energetic promoter. Her work, alongside Froebel's other followers, shall be picked up in the succeeding chapter. We know that lessons must have been close, for Froebel ended up marrying one of his students, Luise Levin, in one of those frequent events whereby much younger women (often admirers) are attracted as much to the beguiling presence of a charismatic genius than to anything necessarily physical, for example, in the second marriages of the authors Thomas Hardy and T. S. Eliot.

It must be stressed, however, that while Froebel's legacy in regard to the entry of women to the teaching profession was substantial, it was never his intention, as was thought by hostile contemporary authorities, to spearhead a woman's 'movement' and campaign for greater gender parity. Typically, Froebel's insistence on the 'other half of humanity' becoming involved in child-rearing was to ensure a complete and total unity in a child's life – male and female in harmony. Still, the positive association held to this day of women being allied with the care of young children owes much to Froebel and his attempts to promote all that was 'good' about the virtues of womanhood.

Froebel's great educational philosophy is not, of course, without its critics. We may have cause, for example, in a more modern secular climate, to question Froebel's belief system and its overt reliance on God as underpinning an eternal material and spiritual universe. More pertinently, as Herbert Bowen (1893) queried in one of the key early considerations of Froebel's impact, is it not problematic to begin to use artificial objects to represent aspects of human nature which are innate anyway to our beings? Can such intrinsics ever be satisfactorily and successfully replicated at a physical level? Such metaphysical speculation certainly begins to explain why there has been selectivity in interpreting Froebel's principles – some educators preferring to focus on his transcendentalism, others being solely concerned with its relationship to actual classroom practice.

Furthermore, William Marsden (1997) has seen little to commend Froebel as a 'progressive' in the modern sense as 'his pedagogy's long-term bent was to deny key progressive principles held dear in a later period, namely, cherishing present experience for its own sake, and promoting autonomous thought' (Marsden 1997: 225). Yet, as the author is quick to make it clear, this does not itself amount to a sufficient critique of Froebel or his ideas which were seen as both radical and progressive in their day and held dear a profound love of children. If anything, as Marsden clearly shows, it instead points 'to the omission of this contradiction in the dissemination of his ideas, ideas that legitimated a subsequent version of progressive primary theory and practice' (Ibid). These contradictions will become more apparent in subsequent chapters when exploring the legacies of the early progressives.

The last stirrings of Romanticism

Froebel died in 1852 – appropriate in every sense, as the period/movement known as Romanticism is generally thought to have ended in 1850. By the end of that year, most of its major protagonists from different fields and generations – Wordsworth, Chopin, Mendelssohn, Byron, Paganini – were dead, while the after-effects and reprisals of the 1848 revolutions indicated that Europe was not, to paraphrase the historian A. J. P. Taylor, ready, or indeed capable, of turning towards the climate of liberty. Significantly, 1844 had seen the emergence of *The Vestiges of the Natural History of Creation* while the first publication of Darwin's *On the Origin of Species* was only nine years away. However, in this key period, thoughts in the conceptualization and understanding of children and childhood had been immense; it was only in 1748 that John Wesley had opened his Kingswood school with its own peculiar brand of rote learning, scripture and attempts to 'break the will' of the child and to ensure its conformity to the norms and values of its parents who, *ipso facto*, were best conditioned to know what a child needed and needed to know. In referring to *Emile*, Wesley called it, 'the most empty, silly, injudicious thing that ever a self-conceited infidel wrote' (Wesley, 1993: 284). This was clearly Wesley venting his anger at what he saw was Rousseau's error in supposing that a child was born anything other than inherently sinful. This constituted a flawed assumption as Rousseau's position, at best, was that humans were born neutrally – not perhaps the selfish creatures of the world of Thomas Hobbes but certainly not the symbols of innocence which the Romantics (Pestalozzi and Froebel) envisaged. *Amour de soi* was a device, after all, of self-preservation.

In considering this question, the social historian Lawrence Stone (1977) identified four categories of thought and views of childhood adopted by educationalists and parents in this period – the Wesleyan view, the Lockean view that the child was a *tabula rasa* who learns by direct experience of the world, the biological view that the child's character was determined at birth, and finally, the view that the child was born innocent and corrupted by society (Rousseau). Such categories were, of course, retrospectively imposed and while they represented a convenient way of demarcating viewpoints and allocating thinkers into various camps, it perhaps obscured some of the inhering educational complexities. *Emile*, for example, may have argued for education 'from afar', yet the boy learnt through direct experience with the world. Similarly, Froebel's child is clearly an innocent, yet learns through tactile experimentation. The same problems of characterization and demarcation, as Alan Richardson (1998) reminds us, apply to an examination of a broader range of Romantic texts:

> There was . . . no one dominant "Romantic" image of the child: literary representations of children during this era range from Wordsworth's "best

philosopher" and Lamb's dream children to the over-indulged Middleton brats in Austen's *Sense and Sensibility* and the barely sentient, drooling "varlet" of Joanna Baillie's "A Mother to her Waking Infant. (Richardson 1994: 9)

However what *is* certain is that for the first time in recorded history, childhood was becoming considered as a phase of life to be celebrated rather than endured. Even under Rousseau's quirky strictures, the child was still recognized as something unique and 'apart' from adults. This was not, of course, a viewpoint that gained immediate widespread currency; it must be remembered that large, state-run, national systems of schooling were either distinctly embryonic or else not in existence at this time, and so, educational innovation, under the aegis and ideological steam of Romanticism, was by default confined to a few willing individuals. As the historian Andy Green (1990) has brilliantly shown, the rise of mass schooling and educational initiatives tended to be synonymous and attributable to the development and emergence of the nation state (Italy in 1860, Germany in 1870) or else facilitated by an overturning of the existing political and social order (America, for example, in the 1860s). Even where the state had taken on some educational provision, for example, in Switzerland, we have seen how progressive writings and texts seemed to be a direct reaction against traditional didactic teaching methods. Often, these problems were factored out to explain and account for more widespread malaises afflicting society.

It would, of course, to be a mistake to only equate this period exclusively with Rousseau, Pestalozzi and Froebel. Romantic artists of all hues took children seriously. In music, for example, exquisite miniatures by Schumann (*Scenes from Childhood*) and Mendelssohn brilliantly evoked the innocence and purity of childhood, tinged with the wistful longing and nostalgia of the adult. The poet Samuel Taylor Coleridge, in discussing his utopian Pantisocracy movement with fellow writer Robert Southey, spoke of a shared desire to educate their children under a communal Rousseauian system in the context of nature and under the influence of a more progressive 'curriculum'. William Wordsworth in the *Prelude* offered a *sotto voce* critique of rational education for making a 'dwarf man' out of one born a 'Mighty Prophet'. William Blake in his *Songs of Innocence and Experience*, likewise, offered oblique reference to education in his critique of schools as institutions preserving compliance as much as perhaps to their practices ('The little ones spend their day/In sighing and dismay'). As we shall see in the next chapter, the writer Mary Wollstonecraft was unique in formulating not merely a proto-feminist approach to society and education's place in it but also the utilization of progressive methods in an educational setting. In painting, the art historian Anne Higonett (1998) has made a strong case that from the work of Joshua Reynolds onwards, artists increasingly came to portray aspects of vulnerability and innocence in their representations of children rather than merely accentuating certain 'adult' characteristics, for example, burgeoning sexuality or willingness to labour.

However – Wollstonecraft aside – none of those other figures could be characterized in any way, shape or form as an educationalist or an educational thinker. One man that does need special consideration in that regard is the Prussian Wilhelm von Humboldt (1767–1835), for he, more than anyone, can be seen to be responsible for engraining aspects of Romantic and progressive thought into systems of mass education and for developing a coherent antithetical response to the more formal aspects of schooling at a time where mechanistic forms of learning were still *de rigueur* in existing institutions.

In every sense a late 'Renaissance Man', Humboldt's life encompassed philosophy, education, politics and the military and it is difficult in the corpus of works and fragments he left us to provide a brief summation of either his enduring beliefs or lasting ideals as he touched so brilliantly and fleetingly upon many fields. His educational theory is no exception, being scattered and fragmented across a range of manuscripts. However, although many of his views have come to us as the product of scholarly inference, they are important not merely for their philosophical contributions as regards language and learning practice but also for the underlying ideas which gave outward expression to the development and establishment of certain progressive (or more accurately, perhaps, 'liberal') practices within a national educational context. Unlike many of his German contemporaries – Kant, Hegel and Fichte – education was not merely a tangential aspect of his ontological project to be mused upon almost at leisure or else having its principles inferred from a philosophical premise.

While not in the same mould as Pestalozzi or Froebel – that is to say, a practising educator – in his briefly held role of Prussian Head of Education, Humboldt reformed his nation's education system based upon the noble ideal of free and universal provision. His crowning, concrete achievement was the foundation of the University of Berlin in 1810 – an institution which combined aspects of both teaching and research and which was to prove a template and model for other European universities and one of the hotbeds for radical, Germanic, Idealist thought. In relation to progressivism, Humboldt's contribution was to instil into the Prussian system a pioneering view of childhood foregrounded by a particular European aspect of thought. Humboldt's outlook was of a middle path between the ideas of Locke and Rousseau; education and learning were neither an imposition upon a blank mind nor did they derive from any aspect of 'innate' nature. His development of the concept of *bildung* (almost impossible to translate but 'spiritual formation' is closest) was an attempt to explain that the singularity and unique nature of man stemmed from an awareness that what he will learn is only that which is homogenous to his inner form. Humboldt thus rejected the idea that there were educational 'laws', based upon generalizations about the human condition, which could be applied to pedagogy. As such, he argued, *cultivation* rather than instruction should be the primary strategy for education and this became reflected, in particular, in many of the emerging European universities which stressed open-minded critical thinking. All experience, rather than just that designated as important by virtue of its academic standing, was considered important in the development of a rounded and reasoned education.

The process of *bildung* therefore not only inculcated a progressive humanism at the expense of more traditional methods into Continental educational systems but officially designated the idea that an individual's education, character formation and discovery of their potential can and must take place outside of a rigid, state-sanctioned curriculum. We know from his biography that Humboldt had visited and drawn inspiration from Pestalozzi and there is something of that man's conception of the mother figure in the criteria that Humboldt set out in regard to teacher training. Under Humboldt's system, empathy, warmth, knowledge of children, social conscience and understanding of *Bildung* were to be prized ahead of substantive knowledge or proven academic learning. Again, this sowed the seeds of the discipline and study of 'pedagogy' which still today occupies an important place in many European universities where understanding of child development and a broad liberal education is considered more valuable than subject-specific knowledge.

Humboldt's progressive credentials are perhaps strained when one notes that the cultivation of *Bildung* resided for him in the 'great arts' of poetry and the theatre and he himself frequently commented that his purpose was to 'inoculate the Germans with the Greek spirit'. This hardly seems the manifesto of an educational revolutionary and it would be difficult to equate him with the other progressives of his time, given the nature of his writings which are speculative, philosophical and gathered together retrospectively. Yet, while Humboldt's curricular concerns may have been 'conservative' and his work diffuse, the concept of *Bildung* can be seen as not merely echoing many of the past educational precepts of the early Romantics but as foreshadowing many of the later developments in the field, such as the concepts of lifelong learning, the development of social attributes and moves towards periods of personal reflection on the parts of children. Humboldt's belief was that individual development was commensurate with more general social improvement, with societies aspiring to higher conditions through the models of education which he proposed. This was to be largely apparent in Europe where the ideas of Romanticism took root most deeply and inculcated more enlightened views about childhood, even if these were not explicitly ascribed to individual thinkers. The ideas, and more importantly the spirit, of Rousseau, Pestalozzi and the German Idealists were thus channelled through the sorts of virtues Humboldt sought to justify both ontologically and epistemologically, and this perhaps explains why they continued to have currency well into the succeeding century.

Notes

1 It is worth noting that an aspect of Romantic thinking was its association with the macabre as much as with beauty. *Christabel*, *Frankenstein* and *The Monk* are pertinent examples of texts which shaped the 'Gothic' in modern literature.

2 The Lunar Society – so called because they met on the night of the full moon – were a learnt society of intellectuals, industrialists and scientists from the Midlands who met regularly to discuss new ideas, concepts and ideas. The most prominent figures in the group were considered to be Erasmus Darwin, Matthew Boulton, Josiah Wedgwood and James Watt.

3 This concept is more fully explained and elaborated in the following chapter.

4 Shelley in his brilliant *A Defence of Poetry* (1819) argued that it was through the medium of poetry that this was achieved: 'Poetry lifts the veil from the hidden beauty of the world, and makes familiar objects be as if they were not familiar . . .'

5 This is remarkably similar to later recapitulation theories developed by Granville Stanley Hall and Charles Darwin, who compared the phases of children's growth with the processes of democratic civilization and evolution, respectively.

Key reading

Jean-Jacques Rousseau, *Emile or On Education*, translated by Allen Bloom (New York: Basic Books, 1979).
Friedrich Froebel, *The Education of Man*, translated from the German and annotated by W. N. Hailmann (New York: D. Appleton & Company, 1892).

Further reading

Matthew Simpson, *Rousseau: A Guide for the Perplexed* (United Kingdom: Continuum International Publishing Group, 2006).
John Darling, *Child-Centred Education and its Critics* (London: Paul Chapman Publishing, 1994).
Jenny Uglow, *The Lunar Men: The Friends Who Made the Future 1730–1810* (London: Faber and Faber, 2002).

3

Gender

Introduction

It would certainly not be a mere token sop to the women's movement to suggest that they have not always been sufficiently or faithfully represented in many of the past narratives relating to progressive education. Often, these histories – some of them written well before the onset of the recent slew of feminist criticism and thought – were male-dominated and guilty of a particularly 'masculinist' form of writing, downplaying and relegating the role that women played in the development of educational theory and practice. Often, this involved characterizing them as 'wives, sisters, followers, assistants and believers; rarely as leaders, ideologues, founders, or policy makers' (Hilton and Hirsch 2000: 1). This seems all the more inexplicable, given the continued rise in the number of women within the teaching profession and common associations with the virtues of 'womanhood' and the nurturing of the child. While such neglect did not generally include larger, more recent figures such as Susan Isaacs or Maria Montessori whose achievements have been more readily recognized, there was a traditional disregard of those earlier, pioneering women who did so much to revolutionize educational practice. In that respect, education studies reflect writing on the other arts where female writers from earlier generations – Mary Robinson, Charlotte Smith and Felicia Hemans from the Romantic period, for example – are only more recently beginning to be seen rightly as the equal to their more famous male counterparts.

Nevertheless, in the last 20 years, a host of noteworthy scholars such as Mary Hilton, Jane McDermid, Pam Hirsch, Kathryn Gleadle and Jane Martin have sought dynamically to redress this balance by re-examining and reinterpreting the role played by women in the educational sphere in light, not merely of new archival material, but also of increasing mainstream acceptance among the academic community of histories pertaining to under-represented body politicks – women, ethnic minorities, the working class and so on. Such writers have emerged from a variety of traditions, including literary criticism and philosophy, and it has not always been the case that they have identified themselves as either historians or, where they have, as necessarily sympathetic to progressive ideas. This is perhaps explained through the subjects of their research; of the many women who were historically attracted into the teaching profession within the state or private sectors, most were not themselves advocates of progressive ideas. Popular perceptions of British schools are redolent of images and caricatures of shrill, punitive school mistresses extolling the 3Rs as much as they are of donnish men peering disparagingly over the top of their pince nez. Such caricatures, as is usually the case, carry elements of truth. Even women as ground-breaking as the children's authors Sarah Trimmer and Hannah More, both heavily involved in educating the poorer classes of society at a time when it was deeply unfashionable to do so, leant heavily upon religious instruction and the stern rhetoric of deliverance and damnation.

There is therefore an important distinction to be made between those women who were pioneering by mere virtue of their gender and those who, in addition, were also progressive in their educational practices. Inevitably perhaps, there is an overlap between these two aspects. As Hilton and Hirsch put it, 'the liberalization of the concomitant establishment of better and higher education for girls and women remain intertwined in progressive ideology' (Ibid., 16). This chapter therefore will attempt to elaborate upon this tight-knit relationship through a discussion of pioneering female educators – those women who, either independently or through acting as conduits and disciples for men such as Froebel, not only contributed to the development of the 'progressive tradition' but were instrumental in its global exportation.

Mary Wollstonecraft – The original feminist?

Perhaps the most logical starting point in any discussion concerning women and progressive education is with the ideas of Mary Wollstonecraft (1759–97), not merely because of her overwhelming importance and contribution to this particular tradition, and more generally, the women's movement but also because she provided a direct antidote to some of the more noxious ideas of her near-contemporary, Rousseau. To attempt any full-scale reappraisal of Wollstonecraft's achievement would be well beyond the scope of this particular book and, as much as any other progressive educator, there already exists an enormous amount of secondary literature devoted to her life and intellectual achievement. Such literature is political (Claudia Johnson and Virginia Sapiro), feminist (Maria Falco), literary (Mary Poovey) and biographical

(Lyndall Gordon, Claire Tomalin) which reflects both the breadth and scope of Wollstonecraft's writing and is indicative of how it has garnered attention from scholars working in a wide range of cognate disciplines. Perhaps this is unsurprising, given her acknowledged and iconic status as the academic ancestor of modern feminist thought, compounded by her tragically early death and seemingly tempestuous private life.

It is indeed difficult to define her philosophy succinctly as, like all great intellectuals, her thoughts and standpoints were constantly evolving. Her writings betray clear evidence of a shifting and increasingly radicalized perspective; one can readily contrast, for example, her early middle-class conduct book, *Thoughts on the Education of Daughters* (1787), which described the desired attributes and characteristics of young girls, with her last, unfinished and posthumously published novel, *Maria: or, the Wrongs of Woman* (1798), which carried a withering critique of marriage and placed great emphasis upon women's latent sexuality as a device for empowerment. Certainly, to label her merely an 'educator' is the equivalent of pigeonholing Marx as an 'economist' – correct to a point but tags that fail to do justice to their more global, all-encompassing brands of philosophy in which (respectively) education and economics, while central, do not represent the totality. However, given the glut of writing in existence, and the compass of this narrative, it is to her educational aspects and their progressive nature that we will turn.

Any attempt to examine her progressivism should be gleaned initially through a close textual reading of her most well-known work, *Vindication of the Rights of Woman* (1792), and also by probing the practices in both her Newington Green school, which she founded with her sisters and close friend Fanny Blood, and her subsequent work as governess to the Dublin-based King household. *Vindication* itself emerged against the bloody background of the French Revolution and a series of debates – the so-called 'Revolution Controversy' – which ignited in England as writers and critics began to come to terms with the full implications of the momentous and tumultuous events across the Channel. As Wordsworth found bliss to be alive, passions were simultaneously poured out in a series of books and pamphlets, which indicated a polarization among the English intelligentsia. On the one hand, the radical publisher Joseph Johnson's social circle of Thomas Paine, William Godwin, the oft-neglected preacher Richard Price and Mary Wollstonecraft wrote dazzling defences of individual liberty, freedom and anarchy, while, on the other, Edmund Burke's *Reflections on the Revolution in France* (1790) provided an equally brilliant, staunch justification for the aristocratic principle arguing that it was against the foundational ethics of civilization for citizens to overthrow elected governments. A surprising bestseller, it completed its author's apostatic and ideological break from his former Whig allies such as Charles James Fox – a move some found hard to ever forget.

Vindication, however, was not simply another response to Burke or indeed the unravelling political situation. Indeed, one of the reasons why the work has, at times, a haphazard feel, full of breathless prose is that its concerns were far more immediate, conceived as it was as an explicit and direct response to a statement made by the leading French politician Talleyrand in relation to the foundation of a new French education system. While claiming to be directly inspired by the Enlightenment ideas of progress, Talleyrand's declaration to the French National Assembly seemed anything other than forward thinking:

> Let us bring up women, not to aspire to advantages which the Constitution denies them, but to know and appreciate those which it guarantees them . . . Men are destined to live on the stage of the world. A public education suits them: it early places before their eyes all the scenes of life: only the proportions are different. The paternal home is better for the education of women; they have less need to learn to deal with the interests of others, than to accustom themselves to a calm and secluded life. (Talleyrand 1791, reprinted in Wollstonecraft 1792)

The ideas of the Enlightenment were certainly not anathema to Wollstonecraft. In many ways, she was a true daughter of the movement and its ideals and her philosophy fundamentally celebrated the idea of natural, God-given rights which were based on the principles and foundation of rationality and reason. Nevertheless, she argued strongly that prevailing contemporary prejudice, such as that espoused by Talleyrand and from an earlier period, Rousseau, did not allow women to share in this male-dominated realm – reason and rationality were deemed the sole intellectual preserve of men with no apparent logical justification. How indeed could one know women were *not* capable of judicious thought, given that they had never been allowed the opportunity to demonstrate otherwise? If they were, Wollstonecraft argued, then surely it must be to the benefit of society en masse that they are educated and their thought allowed to flourish as, in her famous phrase, 'meek wives are, in general, foolish mothers' (Wollstonecraft 1792: 346) and it was ultimately women who shouldered the lion's share of educating the children of the nation in their roles as school mistresses, teachers and governesses. In a particularly powerful passage, she alluded to these inherent dangers of not educating women:

> It is plain from the history of all nations, that women cannot be confined to merely domestic pursuits, for they will not fulfil family duties, unless their minds take a wider range, and whilst they are kept in ignorance they become in the same proportion the slaves of pleasure as they are the

slaves of man. Nor can they be shut out of great enterprises, though the narrowness of their minds often make them mar, what they are unable to comprehend. (Ibid., 402)

The tone of this passage, as throughout the work more generally, is carefully reasoned and almost appeasing, betraying her reluctance to antagonize her readership which would have been overwhelmingly male.[1]

Part of Wollstonecraft's intention in *Vindication* was, therefore, to argue carefully and systematically that women had to be allowed to be educated in much the same way as men had been through the mental exercise of their reason. Earlier conduct book writers[2] such as James Fordyce and John Gregory, although well meaning, in attempting to preserve what they saw as womanly virtues, had inadvertently ended up legitimizing the supplication of women by encouraging such qualities as reticence, modesty, compliance and piety. Fordyce's *Sermons to Young Women* (1765) had proven particularly popular for its notable elevation of the concept of honourable love which was referred to as 'that great preservative of purity, that powerful softener of the fiercest spirit . . .' (Fordyce, 1765: 24) More infuriating for Wollstonecraft had been Rousseau's text *Emile* which although, as we shall see, eliciting much of her sympathy in relation to the educational schemes and methods outlined, was distasteful in its glorified pimping of women to be mere playthings and serving male delectation and amusement – a courtly version of Fordyce's drawing room.

That is not to say though that she wrote *for* her sex. Indeed, the tone of much of the *Vindication* would suggest that she was in fact very anti-woman. As one scholar succinctly puts it, 'Few writers of her day were as critical of women as she was' (Tomaselli 1995: xxvi). Wollstonecraft's ire was directed at women as they were, particularly those from middle-class backgrounds, who were most susceptible to, 'false-refinement, immorality and vanity' (Wollstonecraft, op., cit., 5) and who were effectively 'bought' by their husbands in much the same manner as aristocratic women lusted after titles, estates and assets. In a perverse extension of this position, she thus appeared envious of the poor who would never suffer the consequences of the lure of riches – 'Happy is it when people have the cares of life to struggle with; for these struggles prevent their becoming a prey to enervating vices, merely from idleness!' (Ibid., 116)

Much of this was associated, in Wollstonecraft's eyes, with the development of sensibility which, broadly defined, was the extension of emotional empathy and understanding from one human being to another. Although feelings of this type had hitherto been seen as feminine, the writings of Burke and others, which encouraged and elicited a more emotionally active and direct response to nature and the cultivation of the sublime, had led to a masculinization of the aesthetic, which risked rendering redundant even this traditional womanly role. While not abrogating any loss of emotion, Wollstonecraft was therefore concerned that women who were prey to their feelings more than their reason risked being 'blown about by every momentary gust of feeling' (Ibid., 129), thereby losing the ability to think rationally. Such claims have led some feminist critics such as Cora Kaplan (1986) to suggest that Wollstonecraft was, in some ways, 'de-sexing' women by choosing to rob them of sexual desires and impulses in order that they not be bound to men through superfluous emotional bonds. This is evidenced by Wollstonecraft's comments in the *Vindication* concerning relationships between men and women and her advice to prospective partners to 'calmly let passion subside into friendship' (Ibid., 269), warning that 'love and friendship cannot subsist in the same bosom' (Ibid., 160).

However, while a detailed and extended treatment of these ideas is not warranted here and has already been much covered by scholars, they do have to be sufficiently understood and outlined as they underpin Wollstonecraft's views on education as set out in Chapter 12 of the *Vindication*, within the chapter entitled 'On national education'. She is implicitly very critical, in the chapters proceeding, of many of the existing theories and ideologies relating to education and readily critiques and lambasts teachers, school masters, governesses and conduct book writers for creating, preserving and justifying the gender inequalities of society. Rousseau, in particular, was singled out for his ideas relating to the education of Emile's companion, Sophie. Wollstonecraft's scathing, heartfelt attack (Chapter 5, Section 1) goes beyond the merely ideological as she links his writing with what she considers to be not merely defects within his own character but, more deeply, to those of French society more generally, where 'the art of pleasing was only to extract the grossness of vice' (Ibid., 179). It would be a common mistake to consider Wollstonecraft as the first woman to critique Rousseau and Mary Trouille (1997) has shown that there had been various earlier published challenges in France to the education suggested for Sophie. Nevertheless, Wollstonecraft's pioneering position stemmed from her desire to link restrictions on the education of women with a more nuanced and sophisticated argument pertaining to civil rights which emerged out of natural rights.

Yet, while her opprobrium was aimed primarily at Rousseau's gendered prejudice, it is evident that she was generally sympathetic to his ideas regarding the need for new ways of bringing up and teaching children, moving beyond the didactic habits of contemporary schooling. It is this, as much as her striving for educational equality, which gives much of her brilliant writing an underlying progressive flavour. In a passage targeting the public schools, for instance, Wollstonecraft attacks the notion that what constitutes a 'good' education is purely that which seeks to raise the level of the intellect. For her, as for later progressives, such assumptions meant that 'the health and morals

of a number have been sacrificed' (Ibid., 372) and the development of the
mental and aesthetic attributes were as important to her as the intellectual.
The characteristics associated with the wealthy, such as vice, decadence and
the power to exploit, were precisely those that allowed for the subjugation
of certain women – referred to memorably by Wollstonecraft as 'toys' and
'spaniels' – who were susceptible to the superficialities of charms and trinkets.
The development of bad manners and habits stemmed, she argued, from
strict same-sex systems of schooling and education which, at the time, were
considered the societal norm.[3]

Wollstonecraft's 'plan' therefore for a national, government-sponsored
system of schooling was based around the pioneering premise that boys and
girls be educated together. This itself is a subsequently long-held progressive
trait. While these plans as set down in the *Vindication* are sketchy, and
nowhere as detailed as other writers in this field, Wollstonecraft suggested
initially educating the children of the rich and the poor together with a view
to breaking down distinctions of rank and class. The school itself was to be
set in large enough grounds to allow children to exercise and take gymnastics
while teaching was to be a combination of traditional methods, as befitting
subjects such as botany, mechanics and astronomy, and a more informal
conversational style which suited more discursive subjects such as history,
politics or philosophy. Understandably, Wollstonecraft was loathe to advocate
a differentiated curriculum and was keen that women and girls should study
elements of anatomy and medicine – subjects traditionally thought outside
their intellectual range – in order to not merely 'guard against the errors of
ignorance' (Ibid., 410) but also to allow them to be rational, sensible and
proficient nurses of their children, parents and husbands.

This last assertion all too readily highlights a limitation in Wollstonecraft's
educational thinking of which it is important to be aware. While she was
clearly sympathetic to the need for a universal system of schooling for all
children, *Vindication* indicates a set of values which constrain Wollstonecraft
from offering solutions that would be considered subversive of the moral and
(possibly) the political, order. In charting Wollstonecraft's evolving thought,
Gary Kelly (1992) refers to her as that most damnable and puzzling creation,
a 'professional middle-class revolutionary' (Kelly 1992: 134) whose appeals
to the values of virtue and reason betrayed a sensible and genteel approach
to revolt more in keeping with the parlour than the barricades. In her plans
for education, for example, while wanting children to be schooled together
between the ages of five and nine, she planned a later programme of streaming
according to intellectual ability and, by implication, career destination. The
more intelligent children – and tellingly those with sufficient capital – were
destined for an academic education, while the rest were to train in the trades.
As Kelly succinctly puts it, 'This system preserve[d] both class and gender

distinctions, while aiming for the *embourgeoisement* of children of all classes' (Ibid). The fold that she therefore chose to bring women into was one in which the middle-class typology as to what constituted an 'academic' and 'successful' student and career still lingered.

Nevertheless, to critique her or indeed any early progressive on these grounds may be considered somewhat presentist and retrospective, especially given that many of the more radical ideas concerning the restructuring of society – socialism, Marxism and the like – had yet to emerge in their modern recognized form. Such critiques also fall apart when one considers how, during her teaching experiences, she readily embraced and implemented progressive teaching approaches, even prior to her commencing her writing career. Her initial experience of running a school originated in Newington Green when she was 25, having accepted an invitation from a Mrs Burgh to take over the teaching within the establishment which Burgh's late husband had founded. In many ways, the school represented all that was antithetical to progressive approaches:

> Burgh held that a girl should know just enough arithmetic to do household accounts, and just enough geography to converse with her husband and his friends. Boys were generally trained to block tenderness as a form of weakness. The only emotion Burgh encouraged was patriotism. (Gordon 2005: 43)

Wollstonecraft, though, was already beginning to identify the problems inherent within a curriculum which constrained boys and, more significantly, girls – 'I am sick of hearing of the sublimity of Milton, the elegance and harmony of Pope and the original, untaught genius of Shakespeare' (Wollstonecraft 1787: 52). These words, coming two years later in *Thoughts Concerning the Education of Daughters*, offer an insight into the tangible problems Wollstonecraft had encountered from contemporary teachers entrenched in their views and epitomized by the intransigent Burgh. Nevertheless, we know from her most recent biographer that beyond merely recognizing the problems, Wollstonecraft had also been quick to implement solutions:

> Mary Wollstonecraft ran her school along entirely different and what were then innovative lines: she had a maternal attentiveness to the physical as well as mental needs of a child; she was committed to wholesome food; and her methods were flexible . . .She did believe in moral discipline, but not in the first place as a set of rules to be enforced . . . (Gordon, op. cit. 45)

Central to her viewpoint – a lesson undoubtedly gleaned from her understanding of Rousseau – was that each child was an individual and had to be allowed to develop their own voice and character. She valued the principle of naturalism, that is, pupils developing under the aegis and steam of their own interests and passions rather than the imposition of any external, 'objective' criteria from an adult or teacher. In addition, she held very dear the importance of the mother and the home in playing a central role not merely in educating the child intellectually but, more importantly, caring for them physically. Like Rousseau, Wollstonecraft objected strongly to the practice of wet-nursing, believing that the first form of learning began with a child's mouth upon the maternal breast. Such parental neglect manifested itself too in the sending of young girls away from the home to be schooled in the country – a common enough practice among the middle and upper classes at the time, including, as Claire Tomalin (2000) points out, the young Jane Austen. Was there really such a difference, Wollstonecraft argued, between this practice and the spartan and harsh regimes of the boys' public schools and their avowed mission to discourage 'femininity' among their boys?

With the shadow of Burgh and the orthodox teaching establishment hanging over her, Wollstonecraft found it difficult to fully implement the types of progressive, forward-thinking teaching approaches she may have preferred. Opportunity though came a short time later when she was entrusted with being governess to the King children, daughters of the aristocratic Kingsborough family in Ireland. We are fortunate in that while carrying out her duties, Wollstonecraft found time to pen *Original Stories from Real Life* (1788), an education book for girls, which undoubtedly reflected elements of her continuing practices with the children, a fact corroborated by later statements made by Margaret King, the eldest of the King girls[4] and from what we know of the King household prior to the new governess.

To the historian of education today, it is a revealing work not least as it uses the cloak of fiction as a device, perhaps inadvertently, to cleverly disguise a radical educational philosophy. The book provides, like the later *Vindication*, an implicit critique of the educational methods of the day as the two young protagonists – Mary and Caroline – are identified at the outset as flawed due to the inadequacies of their previous schooling. These girls had been brought up by servants to possess 'every prejudice that the vulgar casually instill' (Wollstonecraft 1788: vi–viii), that is, vanity, conceit, pride and a lack of feeling – characteristics we know Wollstonecraft opposed being associated, in her eyes, with a singular lack of emotion or empathy. One may also casually notice, again, the association Wollstonecraft makes with inadequate education and those of a lower social standing.

To that end, the character of Mrs Mason, who serves as the new governess and tutor to the young girls (undoubtedly drawn from Wollstonecraft's own experiences), seeks to overturn the existing character flaws, through embarking on a programme of education which embraces novel and progressive techniques and ploys. Indeed, the explicit purpose of Mrs Mason/the author is, 'to cure those faults by reason, which ought never to have taken root in the infant mind' (Ibid., 33). In particular, she explicitly seeks to cultivate friendship and devotion rather than greed and avarice, emotion and compassion rather than prejudice and bigotry. Much of her educational work occurs in the outdoors; Mrs Mason takes the girls for morning strolls in the woods where the girls are made to observe the cruel behaviour of boys towards animals and birds and they see first-hand the unfortunate lives of the downtrodden peasantry with such names as Crazy Robin and Sailor Jack who are found to be ostracized by society.

In literary terms, getting these characters to tell their stories in flashbacks is somewhat clunky and the final conversion of Mary is a too easy *deus ex machina* – 'I wish to be a woman, said Mary, and to be like Mrs. Mason . . .' (Ibid., 47). Similarly, the rapt attention of the girls towards the outlandish tales, in the first place, is scarcely believable nor is their sudden desire, having previously acquired many 'paltry ornaments', to wish to suddenly give them away on the basis of the tales of their unfortunate interlocutors. Nevertheless, to critique the book from such a stylistic viewpoint is to somewhat miss its major purpose. The message within is allegorical – testament to Wollstonecraft's democratic ideals and is clearly no less powerful for its bluntness. Even in an early work such as this, we can see how Wollstonecraft was developing the notion that feelings could themselves be liberating in eliciting profound emotional responses. In much the same way that Mary and Caroline develop empathy for the birds and tramps of the rural surrounds and acquire a desire to help them, so later on would Wollstonecraft ascribe such feelings as necessary for the more general emancipation of women. These emanated, ultimately, from God and the text does contain much of what Jonathan Wordsworth has referred to as 'moral earnestness' (Wordsworth 1994). Its piety and dedication to the doctrine of moral improvement can seem, for the modern, secular reader, slightly excessive and overdone though it is by no means alone in that regard.[5] It is almost certain, however, that the kinds of practices described occurred with the King children – all of whom were to grow up to be independent and free-thinking spirits. Margaret, in particular, was always quick to ascribe such traits and habits of mind to the formative influence exerted by Wollstonecraft and her conviction in challenging widely held educational notions.

Anna Letitia Barbauld and the Palgrave Academy

In making any assessment though of Wollstonecraft's progressive educational importance, it is necessary to remember – and given the esteem in which she is rightly held, this can prove problematic – that her ideas did not originate in an ideological vacuum. She was, quite simply, not the first woman to consider the distant prospect of equality – educational and otherwise – and possible measures to achieve it. Earlier individuals such as Catherine Macaulay and Elizabeth Montagu, for example, had provided active demonstrations of the role individual women could play in forming part of the intelligentsia of society. Nevertheless, their views regarding education accorded with Wollstonecraft's only in so far as they conceived of it as having to involve an element of rationality. For them, the purposes of such an education were hardly revolutionary; their equality was designed to halt, as they saw it, the seemingly inexorable decline of society into one full of misery and vice. As one of the leading historians of female education, Mary Hilton rightly states that the Bluestocking case rested on the simple assumption that 'Virtuous, educated and physically strong wives, mothers and sisters would produce and preserve virtuous families' (Hilton 2007: 69).

What was therefore being promoted by these writers was educational equality through the cultivation of reason and moral necessity in order to develop and maintain virtues of dignity and restraint which accorded with a society in harmony. In the sense that these ideas were not associated with aspects of educational and individual freedom, one can legitimately argue that they were not progressive. Macaulay herself, in offering a characteristically brilliant philosophical defence of her position, argued for the existence of 'one rule of right for the conduct of all rational beings' (Macaulay 1790: 201) and this moral imperative was used as her basis for an educational curriculum which, while promoting equality, was also both limiting, prescriptive and conservative.

Far more relevant, in our context, therefore is the work and ideas of Anna Letitia Barbauld (1743–1825) who, in both pre- and post-dating Wollstonecraft's life, has been singularly identified by Mary Hilton as being the originator of progressive pedagogy, at least in relation to its development by women. Hilton makes explicit the point, noted here in previous chapters, that the traditional association of progressive education with an innocent, Romantic child and its crude contrast among historians of education with the unprogressive, original sin-laden Puritan child can be construed as anachronistic and overtly simplistic and she uses Barbauld as an exemplar of an earlier form of liberal dissent which was beginning to recharacterize the position of the child more in line with later progressive and Romantic archetypes.

Barbauld herself was an extraordinary 'woman of letters' whose output consisted of poetry (for which she is today best known), political tracts, essays and children's works. Throughout all of these works, however, education is an underlying and often explicit theme and her essays *On Education* and *On Prejudice* (1773) act as dazzling crystallizations not merely of her own position but also as an embodiment of the liberal Dissenting tradition more generally.

Like Rousseau's *Emile*, many of her writings which involve education are as much moral and philosophical treatises as they are guides as to how to rear a child.

Barbauld's significance in the history of progressive education lies heavily in the fact that she was one of the first female progressive pedagogues to put her ideas into practice within the context of her own educational establishment – in this case, the Palgrave Academy in the English county of Suffolk. In the 11 years between 1774 and 1785 in which the school was open, it provided a legitimate and radical alternative to the rigid schooling methods and practices of the day which were more concerned with 'enforcing student discipline and study habits by flogging and other brutal methods (as in the military), reproducing class tyranny in the "fagging" system, and allowing students to pick up all the expensive and feckless vice of a self-centred social elite' (McCarthy 2008: 170).

Located very much in the tradition of the dissenting academies,[6] the Palgrave school reneged on the teaching of traditional subjects such as Greek and Latin in favour of more practical subjects and, somewhat unfashionably at the time, the natural sciences. Much of the literature the pupils studied was modern, a direct reaction to the unapproachable and obtuse Classical canon which blighted, according to Barbauld, many children's school experiences. Her own teaching approaches were based upon making subjects memorable for her students at the expense of the staid, dogmatic approaches of memorization and rote-learning. Even where Latin was studied at Palgrave, 'It was always Barbauld's belief that one should learn a language for the practical, pleasurable and ethical purposes of reading, not in order to join a social elite' (Ibid., 176). The idea that subjects were to be studied for their intrinsic enjoyment rather than for any pre-designated social purpose was to be central to later progressive thought.

One of the notable features of the Palgrave Academy, which has been widely acknowledged by many commentators, was its status as one of the earliest examples of a school with truly democratic leanings. In contrast to Rousseau and his 'education from afar' which forbade the child from taking any part in the world for a significant period of time, Barbauld's conception of citizenship, which was fundamental to her educational theories, revolved around individuals making outwardly positive contributions to democracy and democratic living. In order to nurture that precept, Palgrave was designed to be an example of society 'writ small'. These ideals were, in part, reflected in the school's initial membership and intake from the local area. While not selecting exclusively from the working class (it was not perhaps *that* democratic!), the school did successfully integrate children from a range of diffident backgrounds, with the offspring of the aristocracy rubbing shoulders with those as radical as Joseph Priestley.

In many ways, therefore, the school can be seen as proffering an answer to one of the key areas of the Enlightenment debate which sought to reconcile the onward march of rational progress with the shape of society and the character and education of its future citizens. Rousseau had offered one answer, Wollstonecraft another. Barbauld though, undoubtedly under the influence of her French husband Rochemont, believed that the role of a good citizen was constructed not through mere passivity but by being actively of direct benefit to others. This was especially the case among the wealthy whom, she argued, had an even greater moral imperative to 'consider [themeselves] as under a strict moral obligation to pay off this great debt [to the society that has conferred riches upon them] by every attention to the interests of the community which leisure, an enlightened mind, and a command of property, can enable [them] to give (Barbauld, quoted in Maccarthy, op., cit., 171).

In light of this, the organization and arrangement of the school became of paramount importance. As an embryonic community, the pupils, in their roles as active citizens, had certain rights and were bound in a close-knit organizational structure under the elected senior figure, called a captain. The captain had the responsibility to oversee school discipline, to preserve 'honorable practice' and to act as an example of the school at its finest. While this carried similarities with the role of the head boys at the elite public schools, corporal punishment at Palgrave was banned (a common-enough progressive precept), with a system of fines being instilled in its place. Boys were not subject to Flashman-style beatings and the school seems to have been run along harmonious and orderly lines. What evidence exists of justice being meted out suggests students themselves participated in the 'trying' of their peers, which seemed to foreshadow similar attempts at 'student democracy' in British progressive schools in the twentieth century which, likewise, were seeking to act as a direct antidote to the more rigid systems of prevailing state and private education.

Attempts to foster this community and civic spirit were not, of course, unique to Palgrave; the long-established boarding-house structure of public schools such as Eton and Harrow, along with their encouragement of service to the Nation and Empire can be legitimately used as an historical parallel. Nevertheless, the basic understanding as to the composition of that spirit surely differed. For Barbauld, and her democratically infused writing, public schools engendered arrogance, social superiority and a belief in the necessity of military-style ceremony which was designed to prepare young boys for their roles in the maintenance and governance of an Empire – itself associated with subjugation and exploitation. At Palgrave, the aim was instead to integrate young children into a social and moral membership, bound by a progressive moral code, which was to serve as an exemplar and benchmark for future societies.

While teaching at Palgrave, Barbauld published two important books – *Early Lessons for Childhood* (1778) and *Hymns in Prose* (1781) – which provide the historian with the most tangible evidence of the broader theories underpinning her esoteric educational practices. Both works betray a clear debt to the earlier investigations of the English philosopher William Paley (1743–1805). Sadly, today he is little known and read other than among students of philosophy and his reputation rests far lower than that of John Locke or David Hume. This is surprising as his *Principles of Moral and Political Philosophy* (1785) was long considered a key text of the Enlightenment period. To refer to Mary Hilton once more, '[his] work reflected the subtle shift that was taking place in the theological understanding of nature and the forces of evil, through presenting a picture of a more dynamic world' (Hilton, op. cit., 96). Barbauld's not inconsiderable debt to Paley stemmed primarily from his deployment and understanding of the term *happiness*. For Paley, happiness arose not from our senses and their immediate gratification but from good health, habits and contentment. Much of Paley's writing and, for that matter, Barbauld's rested therefore on the existence of a Divine Creator (God) whose benevolence, care and love was to be observed in the beauty of nature and the natural world. In an oft-quoted passage, which could be considered an instruction to her students, Barbauld extols the wonders of the natural world in an almost Wordsworthian declamation:

> Come, let us walk abroad, let us talk of the works of God . . . Take up a handful of the sand; number the grains of it; tell them one by one into your lap. Try if you can count the blades of grass in the field, or the leaves on the trees. You cannot count them, they are innumerable . . . Every plant hath a single inhabitant . . . Who causeth them to grow every where . . . and giveth them colours and smells, and spreadeth out their transparent leaves? Lo, these are part of his works; and a little portion of his wonders. There is little need that I should tell you of God, for everything speaks of Him. (Barbauld 2001: 250)

Sentiments like this run the gauntlet of pantheism and it is unsurprising why Barbauld is now considered a significant progenitor of the Romantic movement. In educational terms, the idea of the divine in 'nature' has also been identified, as we have seen, with the writings and practices of both Froebel and Pestalozzi. Indeed, reverence and awe at nature and God's works occur so frequently in the contemporaneous literature that it would be easy to lump together Barbauld with other Romantic thinkers but one must be careful not to overemphasize such comparisons. While Paley's/Barbauld's Deity was essentially benevolent and awe-inspiring, it was, nevertheless, a transcendent rather than imminent being, which Paley justified by recourse to old, established teleological arguments and watchmaker analogies. This was not the eternal, floating spirit being, literally, conceived of by those metaphysical alchemists in Germany! Nevertheless, whatever its origin, through an admiration of his benevolence, individuals were destined to find contentment and happiness and these undoubtedly were the virtues encouraged and facilitated by Barbauld in her school. In that respect, perhaps the aims of Barbauld were not too dissimilar to those of the kindergarten after all.

Contrasting pedagogues

In much the same way that it is problematic and facile (albeit conveniently so) to group thinkers together under the broad banner of an intellectual movement such as Romanticism or Modernism, it is equally incorrect to lump together all female thinkers purely on the basis of their gender. It is usually the case that historians and writers like to group artists and thinkers together, whereby they themselves prefer to emphasize their differences. Certainly, when examining Barbauld in relation to Wollstonecraft, it is important to be aware of this conflict. In disparaging, as we have seen, Fordyce and Rousseau, Wollstonecraft in a lengthy footnote within *Vindication* also took to task Barbauld herself for one of her early poems which compared the beauty of flowers to the beauty of women.[7] While the poem's charm cannot be denied, Wollstonecraft believed such phraseology approximated to the language commonly used by men, thereby carrying denigrating and platitudonous overtones. Likewise, her emphasis upon reason and the corresponding suspicion of sensibility ran contrary to Barbauld's belief in the sublime and the power of direct emotional response. Considering the 16-year age gap and her more sensitive temperament, one imagines it must have been difficult at times for Barbauld to take such rebuttals from her younger contemporary.

Furthermore, in contrast to Wollstonecraft who seemed far more comfortable with the educational precepts laid down by Rousseau, his conception of the 'natural' man left to his own devices and educated outside of civilization without recourse to texts and traditional learning methods did not sit easily with Barbauld. While Rousseau was attempting to educate his child according to the precepts of reason, Barbauld preferred to support the desirability and rationality of an education whose outcome was to produce a child whose opinions were not mere reflections of a 'perfect' parent or tutor. Instead, like the liberal she was, she celebrated diversity and freedom – 'Do not expect the mind of your son to resemble yours . . . He was formed, like you, to use his own judgment, and he claims the high privilege of his nature' (Ibid., 343). Clearly not for her the suspension of belief which legitimized Rousseau's systematic deception of the young boy!

We must not, though, go too far in emphasizing either the differences or the personal antagonism between the two women. First, it must be remembered that they almost certainly would have met in person in the amicable setting of Joseph Johnson's rooms or dining table and we have no written records of any hostilities or fierce intellectual disagreements. Second, as Barbauld scholar and her foremost biographer, William McCarthy, points out in his definitive study, there are clear cases in some of her later writings where Barbauld sought to engage directly with the sentiments expressed in the *Vindication*. One such example stems from a posthumously published poem entitled 'The Rights of Woman' in which she declaims, in rhetoric worthy of Wollstonecraft herself, 'Yes, injured Woman! rise, assert thy right!/Woman! too long degraded, scorned, opprest' (Ibid., 130). More evidence is to be found in *Remarks on Public Worship* (1792), which attempted to disprove Wollstonecraft's notion that women had been too reluctant to engage in political study and discourse. Barbauld could clearly point to herself as one who had studied politics and sought, quietly and without clamour, to effect (she hoped) microcosmic change through her Palgrave Academy. Therefore, while Wollstonecraft's more abrasive statements, particularly those disparaging to women, may have met with disapproval, Barbauld's frequent staunch defences of the place of women in society and the need for a greater form of equality for all undoubtedly resonated with the other's statements.

A family dynasty – Maria Edgeworth and *Practical Education*

Maria Edgeworth (1767–1849) is unique in that she was the only one of our female progressive thinkers to emerge directly from an upbringing that sought to practise the kinds of educational philosophy and regimen she herself was to later espouse. As was alluded to in the previous chapter, she was the daughter of the Lunar Society's Richard Lovell and, given the enormity of her contribution to both the women's movement and progressive education, it is strange to note why she has not received the same level of critical and scholarly attention as her contemporary 'rivals' such as Jane Austen, George Elliott or Mary Wollstonecraft.

A notable exception in that regard has been the work of Marilyn Butler who, as well as writing perhaps the best single volume biography of Edgeworth in modern times, has recently overseen the appearance of the first collected edition of her complete works since the nineteenth century. Coming in 12 volumes, these monumental tomes reveal anew the startling quantity and breadth of Edgeworth's writing, including her four Irish novels which were among the first 'regional' novels in English, her moral tales, her comedies of manners as well as her pedagogical and non-pedagogical tales and lessons for children which act as a precursor to her magnum opus, *Practical Education* (1798). Given the sheer scale of her writing, it can therefore be problematic and daunting for the historian to distil in a concise manner the essence of her progressivism which was but one facet of her extraordinary output.

For all of her multifarious writing, education was nonetheless certainly in Edgeworth's blood. Her father and his second wife, Honora, had paid close attention to their children's upbringing, noting their patterns of behaviour, observing them at play and inscribing their findings in detailed notebooks. While Richard, through his Lunar Society and latterly Irish school board connections, is well known, it would be a mistake, especially in a chapter considering women, to overlook the contribution made by his wife. In the Appendix to *Practical Education*, she is acknowledged as being the Edgeworth who first sought to record the conduct and actions of her children, believing that 'the art of education should be considered as an experimental science, and that many authors of great abilities had mistaken their road by following theory instead of practice' (Edgeworth 1996: 324). Education was not for her to be a matter of dogma but an organic entity, constantly adapting its practices towards a child's direct and practical needs. These ideas are epitomized in Honora's own writing, particularly in her best known work, also confusingly entitled *Practical Education*. Although not a significant work in the progressive canon (it is little read today), many of its ideas foreshadow, albeit in far less depth and with less sophistication, much of what was to later emerge in her stepdaughters identically titled volume specifically through Honora's exploration of the most productive ways to interact with children.

While Maria herself was the only one of the many Edgeworth children not to have been substantially educated at home, having been sent away to be schooled, upon her return, with almost two cricket teams worth of siblings around her, she had myriad opportunities to partake in and, latterly, observe at close quarters the effects that Richard Lovell's tolerant and proto-progressive outlook had upon their learning and development.[8] Perhaps as a result of their earlier encounters with Rousseau and the enthusiasm of their father, education was of central importance to the Edgeworth family en masse. Susan Manley (2003) describes a typical domestic scene:

The family method was to allocate the youngest children to an older sister or adult. All would gather round the big table at Edgeworthstown House, talking, reading and writing, the smallest children playing round the table, the older ones reading alongside their allocated adult, who would make sure that every word and idea was understood. (Manley 2003: ix)

In that rarefied and conducive atmosphere in which Richard oversaw and Honora recorded, Maria was encouraged to put together educational story books which, while moralistic in tone, began to successfully evoke the world of the child from its own perspective rather than merely approximating it from that of the adult. Her ability to not merely be sympathetic to children but to actually understand how they themselves thought and experienced the world was to come to full fruition in the unique collaboration between Maria and her father, which produced, in 1798, her most magisterial tome, *Practical Education*. It would not be stretching a point to concede this as the most brilliant and, arguably, the most forward-looking 'how to' guide in rearing young children ever written and one of the cornerstones of progressive educational and child-rearing literature. The issue of collaboration between the Edgeworths, while on the surface seemingly inconsequential, is a thorny one. In the preface, Maria Edgeworth acknowledged the endeavours of both her father, half-brother and the physician Thomas Beddoes for their contributions and, according to Marilyn Butler (1972), 'Although Maria did more than half the writing, the technical chapters were by Edgeworth himself' (Butler 1972: 169). It seems, however, from personal correspondence that the family regarded this as 'her work' and it was exclusively Maria who appropriated and used the earlier findings of Honora, which ended up forming the basis for the substantive sections of the book. It was, after all, only posthumously that Richard Lovell Edgeworth became increasingly associated with the work itself, the subsequent success of Maria's later educational works perhaps giving the impression that she had been, even then, the driving force. Scholars, have thus sought to debate the influence (malign or otherwise) that he exerted upon the work and writing of his daughter, extrapolating outward to enlarge his contribution to Maria's career more generally.

At around 750 pages in length, and divided into two volumes, even today *Practical Education* is a daunting read, made more so perhaps by the frightening number of disparate pedagogical topics the Edgeworths sought to discuss from acquired virtues such as obedience and vanity to children's temperaments to the role of books, grammar and chemistry in the context of a general curriculum. The range of their observations and the ability to unify these seemingly unrelated elements into a grand theory with a clear textual structure is, frankly, remarkable. The first third of the book deals with the training of pre-school children in terms of morals and habit formation, the middle pages tackle the ways to teach a range of different subjects (grammar, geography, chemistry and the like) while the last section attempts to account for the range of attributes education should seek to cultivate, including judgement and imagination.

For all of its variety, the text is not, however, by any means insurmountable, particularly given the pithy and memorable quality of its prose. Its seminal status stems precisely from its unique combination of practical examples drawn from many years of trial and error, scientific application which used many of the most advanced theoretical frameworks and, finally, a genuine desire to understand the needs of children in order that they may be better educated. This was part of a deliberate and provocative move away even from those as radical as Rousseau, whose system, while clearly 'practical' in the sense of being capable of being re-enacted, was seen as too reliant on philosophy and metaphysics at the expense of genuine feeling and understanding. The intellectual circles in which the Edgeworths moved (notably among those pioneering geniuses of the Lunar Society) undoubtedly contributed to the work being inflected with aspects of theory and developments that were happening further afield in Europe and on the Continent and so, its fame and impact were to go far beyond the domestic setting. The historian Brian Simon (1960) has even made the case that it represented the first ever attempt to systematize and justify the idea of 'discovery' in education – a concept so central to later progressive discourse.

For Edgeworth, such a process did not consist of working in artificial environments with toys such as dolls which were merely imitative of real life. Instead, as the text makes it clear, children were to be given paper, scissors and glue and encouraged to create their own shapes, patterns and objects in whatever configuration they saw fit. Edgeworth thus was following the earlier precepts of John Locke in seeking to explicitly validate and offer approval to children's individual lines of enquiry, no matter how insignificant they may have seemed. A critical aspect of her methodology was not in patronizing or disdaining the opinions of the young but instead valuing them as valid, potential avenues for exploration, discovery and dialogue. This latter adjective is most apt as, for both Edgeworths, the term 'dialogue' embraced not merely talking *at* but listening *to* children who were themselves in the process of searching and groping for truth, be that scientific, moral or otherwise. Much of *Practical Education* is therefore devoted to stressing the importance of children, 'exercis[ing] their invention upon all subjects' (Edgeworth 2003:421) which encompassed both the arts and the sciences in an unhindered orgy of self-discovery. We have direct evidence of this in practice from the notebooks and records Honora made of the Edgeworth children's own discussions, some of which were reproduced as an appendix to Volume Two of the original text and from parts of Richard's *Memoir*, a section of which was devoted to a retelling of the methods he used in bringing up his own children.

In proffering acceptance of young people's opinions, Edgeworth was implicitly, and in the text, explicitly, clearly encouraging children to challenge authority and received wisdom. One particularly striking example, often cited by those wishing to validate her progressive credentials, occurs in a discussion of geography textbooks which, according to Edgeworth, proffered generalized, stereotypical and nasty caricatures of individual nations and ethnicities which must not be blindly accepted by the reader. Frequently, such textbooks imposed the authors' own, 'moral reflections and easy explanations of political events' (Ibid., 202) on their young readers, which in turn lead to them developing prejudices and a skewed historical sense. It was only in allowing children's thinking to be liberated through question, discussion and argument that a true understanding could be reached – 'When the young reader pauses to think, allow him time to think, and suffer him to question the assertions which he meets with in books with freedom' (Ibid). Of course, for all of Edgeworth' pains to stress that there should therefore be no imposition of adult belief systems upon a child, in practice, this was impossible to achieve – the mere fact of demanding they challenge such orthodox received wisdom on the grounds of its potential falsehood was a loaded judgement in itself! Nevertheless, Edgeworth's belief in the necessity of encouraging children to think the unthinkable and be allowed to express those opinions without fear of contradiction, correction or reprisal drives hard to the core of all progressive ideologies.

Ultimately, the real value of such strategies lay in their celebration of individuality. This was not merely reflected in permitting all children to express their thoughts and responses freely but also by ensuring that such responses were not to be measured against those of their peers – that is to say, a foregoing of competition and a focus instead upon individual attainment. Edgeworth clearly conceived of learning as being an enjoyable pursuit for the child and thus it was undertaken in the form of experiment, trial and error, discussion and observation. In that regard, as another leading Edgeworth scholar Mitzi Myers (1994 and 1995) has pointed out, her work echoes the practices and culture of the Lunar Society – of which her father was a key figure – in terms of its emphasis upon intellectual discussion, problem solving, the sharing of knowledge and theories, observation and a sense of cultivating the scientifically bizarre in the name of experiment. Furthermore, Myers sees Edgeworth's writing as being in the same vein as Mary Wollstonecraft's in that it too posed a challenge to that line of thinking stemming from Edmund Burke, which emphasized the concepts of tradition, precedent and, ultimately, moral order. Such virtues for Burke were to be cultivated and developed through the 'right' sort of schooling. It should be apparent that such conformity was most definitely not part of Edgeworth's plan! Burke too, no doubt, would have baulked at the idea that children should be actively seeking after their own answers rather than being informed directly by the authority of adults whose wisdom and claims to truth were informed by both their seniority and direct experience of the many processes of 'civilization'.

This type of criticism relating to progressive pedagogy, founded upon the assumption that it is adults and not children who know best what and how to learn, is one with a long historical shelf life. Even today, respected commentators continue to attribute the breakdown of societies' moral values to the rise of 'democratic' and 'progressive' teaching methods. By contrast, there continue to remain many, following the presumptions of thinkers like Edgeworth, who hold true to the idea that children know far more about the world than is commonly recognized and that, with the right guidance, they themselves can be, in modern terms, self-directed learners. In Edgeworth's case, much of this was tied to a particular conception of citizenship which saw the necessity of children, as future citizens, being active agents in the shaping of an enlightened (though not necessarily an Enlightenment!) society.

Unlike Wollstonecraft, who conceived of God given 'natural' rights and, after a fashion, Barbauld with her pantheistic wonderings, *Practical Education* is different in that it is very obviously *not* a religious work. It does not invoke or mention God, or utilize any of the then common euphemisms such as Deity or Creator. For some historians, this omission has been seen as a direct riposte by the Edgeworths to the problems of sectarian Ireland which had been aroused by long-running feuds between the Protestants and Catholics. Whether a politically conscious decision or not, their rhetoric seemed a natural extension of the case to encourage children to challenge commonly-held assumptions and beliefs and to take nothing for granted – even, it would seem, God. Undoubtedly, a bold move it was, however, this religious neglect that was used as a critical stick by which to beat the Edgeworths and a succession of poor reviews undoubtedly contributed to the continued ostracizing of Maria Edgeworth as a major educational figure and perhaps explains, until recently, her continuing place upon progressivism's periphery.

Nor was it merely the case that she was seen as a misguided heathen – some contemporaries went as far as to suggest that her particular scheme of education and her reluctance not to bow to pressure to observe religious doctrine risked endangering and undermining the very moral fabric of society. Sarah Trimmer, the well-respected children's author, wrote drastically of, 'a conspiracy against Christianity and all social order . . . endeavoring to infect the minds of the rising generation, through the medium of *Books of Education* and *Children's Books* . . . .the true centre of education should be religion' (Trimmer 1802, vols. 1, 2). Similarly, in a damning review of Richard Lovell Edgeworth's *Memoirs*, John Wilson Croker in the influential *Quarterly* journal lambasted him for being a pagan and cast Maria as his willing disciple. Aiming squarely at the Edgeworth educational project Croker thundered, 'Why is there no mention of piety, of gratitude to God, of confidence in a savior . . .' (Croker, July 1820: XXIII.544).

Such attacks which set out explicitly to derail and vilify the Edgeworth's progressive venture, undoubtedly contributed to the relative neglect experienced domestically by *Practical Education* in the aftermath of its publication. While the book's enormous effect on the continent, mostly among those who were attempting to set up progressive establishments, will become clearer in the context of succeeding chapters, its impact closer to home was, at best, limited. Part of this, as Marilyn Butler (1972) has astutely observed, was down to the timing of its publication; by 1798, most of the Lunar Society were dead, Joseph Priestley had fled to America and their ideas and dreams of progress were becoming increasingly forgotten and passé. It was only in the twentieth century, following the emergence of the history of education as a discipline and the increasing mainstream acceptance of progressive ideas, that the full significance of *Practical Education* in England came to be realized. The assessment therefore of the historian Alice Paterson in declaring it 'the most important work on general pedagogy to appear in this country between Locke's *Thoughts* in 1693 and that of Herbert Spencer's *Essay on Education* in 1861' (Paterson 1914: v–vi) represents the general modern historical consensus in acknowledging the work of Edgeworth as being seminal in contributing to the progressive educational narrative.

The impression given thus far to the reader is, however, marginally one-sided. While it is true that *Practical Education* was seen in some quarters as a 'dangerous' text and far too radical for mass consumption, this did not prevent Edgeworth's other pedagogic works such as her *Popular Tales* and *Early Lessons* being well-received and widely acclaimed in their day. There is no single reason for this. Perhaps the absence of her father's name from the front cover helped. Maybe the later publication dates (1804 and 1801, respectively) when the sting had been taken out of various radical impulses contributed. More so perhaps, the presentation and stylization of the works was important. These were not vast, demanding books full of radical theorizing and provocation. Instead, although published by the radical publisher Joseph Johnson thereby initiating an earlier link to Wollstonecraft, they were promoted very much as texts for general moral improvement and the public good. Indeed, as Elizabeth Eger (2003) has observed, the structure of *Early Lessons* owed an enormous debt to the earlier and very popular *Lessons for Children* by Anna Barbauld published nearly a quarter of a century earlier which have been previously referred to. In that sense then, they fitted comfortably into a relatively established tradition of moralistic writing aimed at 'improving' children through recourse to moral example and desirable virtues. Like Barbauld, the gentility of the subject matter and its presentation in the form of innocent children's stories and narratives would perhaps suggest that the sentiments expressed therein were equally mawkish but this is far from the case. Eger herself refers to the *Lessons* as 'a *revolutionary* educational text-book' (Eger 2003:xv, italics added) and given such scholarly assessments, it would thus be fair to consider these works as vibrant companions, especially when attempting to appraise and review Edgeworth's contribution to progressive doctrine.

The raison d'être of these books was, as Edgeworth made clear, not to yoke readers to a particular educational schema but 'to exercise the powers of attention, observation, reasoning, and invention, rather than to teach any one science, or to make any advance upon first principles' (Edgeworth, 1825: vi). While her *Tales* represent the more 'literary' aspect of her output, it is to her *Early Lessons* that the historian of education should gravitate in order to better understand her particular pedagogic viewpoint. Alluded to within the previous quotation is the exploratory and ephemeral nature of these works. As Marilyn Butler (1972) once more points out, 'All Maria's early tales for children are quite unlike the 1780 *Practical Education*, which comes into the category of an educational tool, not primarily a story' (Butler 1972: 158). Unlike Wollstonecraft's efforts within the same genre, Edgeworth's works betray little maudlin sentimentality; the tone instead tends to be emotive and evoking of sympathy towards particular characters and situations, which were designed in themselves to provide an education for the growing child. Although perhaps no longer relevant to the needs of contemporary adolescents and their parents, it is the principles behind these works which mark them out as particularly distinctive. Some of the material was undoubtedly drawn from the ideas and observations of her father and there is much in the stories which reflect his egalitarian and progressive spirit. In particular, as Emily Lawless summarizes, 'They are stories for children, written, not from above, but . . . from the point of view of those to whom they were addressed' (Lawless 1904: 51). In that sense, like *Practical Education*, Edgeworth here demonstrates her profound empathy for the experiences of childhood which was particularly important as these *Early Lessons* were written with an intended audience of parents who wished to follow a more progressive programme of education. Although today these books are little read – and Edgeworth was never the most sophisticated of fictional stylists – they nevertheless serve to reinforce the impression of her as one of the most important early progressive thinkers and among the first to truly empathize with the experience and perceptions of childhood.

It should be thus far clear that Wollstonecraft, Barbauld and, to a lesser extent, Edgeworth were concerned not merely with developing innovative ways of teaching and understanding young children but also with using education as part of a socially ameliorating device by which equality, both in gender – and to a lesser degree – in class, could be achieved. This is evident from the range of writings calling for equal education of girls and boys and the more challenging, politicized writings of Barbauld and (particularly) Edgeworth. Although less 'gendered' in her writing, Edgeworth along with her father had a strong social conscience which emerges more in the liberating tones of her 'Irish' novels which offered a fresh and radical take on a long-standing political problem, in this case, the religious discontent within Ireland.

When considering progressive women as a category, however, it must not be assumed that all were seeking to utilize educational practice in this way. For some, there was a clear binary line between, on the one hand, the use of radical education as a device for a more general political purpose and, on the other, promotion and demonstration of innovative educational techniques and philosophies not necessarily tied to those political concerns. Many of these women emanated from the aristocracy, titled classes, bourgeoisie and intelligentsia whose values, almost by default, were those of the socially conservative. Indeed, it was still comparatively rare to find teachers drawn from the working classes. One important manifestation therefore of this dissemination was in relation to the rapid spread of the kindergarten concept and, given its palpable global appeal, it is now worthy of consideration at some length.

Froebelian women – England

It was perhaps inevitable that it would be Prussian (latterly German) women who would have the greatest impact upon the progressive stage, exporting radical educational philosophies to far-flung corners of the globe. The previous chapter touched briefly upon the importance of Friedrich Froebel and his nephew Carl in seeking to elevate the status of German women and womanhood by enabling them to use their unique maternal gifts in the public sphere. Theirs was not however a feminist crusade; Froebel's appreciation of women lay in the idealization of their unique feminine traits rather than in any desire to seek to empower them politically. For Froebel, such characteristics were to be equated with an almost divine-like quality, emphasized in the intimate activities described in the *Mother Songs* or through the exchange of his cherished symbolic gifts. The first of these gifts (the sphere), for example, was intended by Froebel to be given *by* the mother *to* the child, symbolizing not merely the closeness of their maternal bond but also the awakening of the latent conscience of the child – as Liebschner (1992) is at pains to stress this object provoked the whole world of self-activity for the child. Crucially, it was always the mother whom Froebel referred back to time and again in his writings as being the individual with the appropriate sensitivities and understanding best suited to rearing the young.

Beyond ideological conviction, there were many advantages for women, particularly in Germany, in becoming kindergarten teachers. Theirs was a respected position within the local community (far more so than was the case in England) and ensured a level of economic independence not usually given to women in other professions. In addition, the emphasis upon women using skills and knowledge to aid their children was undoubtedly empowering and appealed broadly to the more leisured members of the intelligentsia. Training was done, initially, within working kindergartens which allowed for a form of apostolic succession with senior figures such as the Baroness von Bulow passing on their wisdom and expertise directly to those who came to visit and study. Two such women who came under her spell and were key members of this particular community were the sisters Margarethe and Bertha Meyer (latterly Schurz and Ronge) who had been among Froebel's last pupils. Having initially opened kindergartens in Germany, Berthe Ronge and her husband set up the first such establishment in England in Tavistock Place, London in 1851 and its success preceded to not only attract over her sister to teach but also Baroness Bulow herself on one of her extensive propaganda tours.

This move effectively marked the beginning of English Froebelianism and the foothold established by the kindergartens was to prove important in offering a legitimate challenge to more rigid methods of teaching. While, as Evelyn Lawrence (1952) has pointed out, the reasons for the relative success of the spread of Froebel's ideas in England owed much to the previous philanthropic work done by men such as Robert Owen (see Chapter 7 of this book), the continual interrogation of the ideas of Rousseau by the Lunar Society and the patronage of major literary figures such as Charles Dickens, without question, the main force behind the spread and dissemination of the kindergarten concept was the result of the tireless work of women.

It was, for example, a result of a series of seminal articles written by Emily Shirreff in the *Education Journal* which laid the groundwork for the first meetings of the London Kindergarten Association, one of a number of groups dedicated to promoting and safeguarding the kindergarten name. Shirreff also achieved distinction in becoming President of the English Froebel Society between 1875 and 1897 and, surrounded by a predominantly female committee, engaging in attempting to coerce the state into adopting Froebel's ideas and beliefs within the context of mainstream English education. Evelyn Lawrence (1952) and latterly Kevin Brehony (2001) have charted these developments and, while these were difficult years for the Froebelians with constant infighting and frequent lack of progress, with the gradual introduction of government grants to aid schools and H. A. L. Fisher's Education Act of 1918 which allowed Local Education Authorities to provide for nursery schools, dissemination of this progressive ideal ultimately moved a stage closer. Some of these early nursery schools, such as those set up by the McMillan sisters, were run along kindergarten lines and owed much to Froebel's earlier ideas.

Any close reading of the aforementioned historical narratives will likewise indicate the large numbers of women involved in these developments at both the micro- and macro-levels. The guiding text for many kindergarten teachers was undoubtedly Johann and Berthe Ronge's *Practical Guide to the English Kindergarten* (1884) which, as the historian Kevin Brehony (2000 and 2006) has suggested, impacted strongly on the development of English Froebelianism. As Brehony is also at pains to point out, although the Ronges identified in their book 30 such establishments, anyone at the time could open a school and call it a kindergarten, and so, in real terms, that number may have been many more with schools originating outside the 'formal' channels of the Froebel Society. Many of these early practitioners were also doubly conscious of their position as female pioneers and there is evidence of a large number of 'first wave feminists' contributing to the debates and discourses of these Froebelian groups.

The desire to thereby emancipate women and girls through education and the democratic appeal and spirit of the kindergarten coalesced together in key educator networks which emerged within the nascent Kindergarten Association founded in 1874. This comprised individuals from a number of different countries, thus emphasizing the international and cross-border appeal of Froebel's ideas. Although the development of English education and progressivism was subject to a plurality of influences over time, including the later experiments of Montessori and Steiner, the kindergarten idea proved resilient and pervasive and much of this can be attributed to the strong foundations laid by these powerful early women. Many of the cornerstones of the kindergarten ideal such as play, creativity and a strong feminine presence continue to inform mainstream educational debate today and stand as a testament to their attempts to influence and shape the orientation of the curriculum in a distinctively novel way. Aspects of this influence will be addressed in Chapter 5, which explores the pioneering New Education Fellowship movement.

Froebelian women – The United States

With Berthe busy conquering England, her sister Margarethe had moved on with her husband to the United States where, in Watertown, Wisconsin, she developed the first transatlantic kindergarten at the behest of local parents who saw how successfully its philosophy had been in preparing children for the upcoming rigours of elementary school life. Such was its success – made possible by Margharethe's tireless championing – the Watertown kindergarten served as a model for others in years to come and continued until the First World War, when it was closed down for its continued use of the Germanic language. Even today, Watertown serves as a site of pilgrimage for all aspiring Froebelians. Sadly though, Margarethe was not to enjoy the fruits of her success; as Hannah Swart (1967) recounts in her biography, she died at the tragically young age of 43 in 1876 following the birth of her third child. Dogged by ill health her entire life, she was therefore robbed of the chance to observe her great legacy – the rapid spread of the kindergarten idea across America, commonly attributed to two extraordinary women, Elizabeth Peabody (1804–94) and Susan Blow (1843–1916).

It was perhaps not surprising that Peabody – who, if not in looks, then certainly in demeanour, bore resemblance to Whistler's iconic Puritan mother – would have been drawn to the kindergarten philosophy. In her early years, she had worked as an assistant teacher to Amos Alcott whose pedagogical principles she was to summarize in her first book, *Record of a School* (1835), her still very readable and absorbing account from which many subsequent historians have drawn, including this author as will be seen in Chapter 6. In addition, Peabody was the business manager of the *Dial* – a journal devoted to the spread of the Transcendentalist message of Ralph Waldo Emerson and his followers. Drawing upon the lessons of Kant, their rejection of empirical principles in favour of the divinity of experience owed much to German Idealism which, as we have observed, had been of central importance to the work of Froebel. In 1860, following a visit to Margarethe Meyer's school, Peabody set up her first kindergarten-type establishment in America and, through both her practice and editorship of the *Kindergarten Messenger* journal, was prominent in establishing its principles throughout the United States. The number of kindergartens, particularly within the east and upper Midwest, rose from a dozen in 1874 to nearly 4,000 20 years later!

These numbers verge on the unthinkable, yet these were the days of the emergence of the common school movement of Horace Mann and the growing belief that universal schooling was essential to the creation of 'good' citizens and the alleviation of poverty. Having therefore decided collectively that it was wrong to restrict education merely to the wealthy, in 1852, Massachusetts became the first state to pass a compulsory school attendance law, followed by the state of New York a year later. Coupled with the need to reconstruct a nation after the trauma of the Civil War, it therefore became a matter of federal persuasion to convince those in authority that the society's changing needs were best met by an adoption of the kindergarten system. Such a message was undoubtedly channelled through the European refugee intelligentsia which had settled in New England following the 1848 revolutionary upheavals.

Through the efforts of champions such as Elizabeth Harrison in Chicago and Eliza Blaker in Indianapolis, the 'kindergarten concept' thus became engrained within the emerging nation's discourse and vocabulary. As Evelyn Weber (1969) has demonstrated, the kindergarten movement frequently overlapped with wider collective concerns as the move from private philosophy to public practice delineated much of what was positive about American social welfare programs throughout the course of the century. This was especially the case in relation to the settlement scheme undertaken in Chicago and its nearby kindergarten under the stewardship of Alice Putnam.[9] The rapid growth was additionally fuelled by the re-discovery and fresh editions of Froebel's original texts for a new generation. The author Josephine Jarvis was prominent in translating many of his published and unpublished writings into English, with Peabody herself contributing a Preface to the *Education of Man*.

Nevertheless, it would be a mistake to equate the speed with which such ideas spread with homogeneity and general acceptance. The extension of the kindergarten movement in America was neither systematic, uniform or, in any sense, ideal. It was a perverse twist of fate that led to many of the distortions, attacks and false interpretations of Froebel's work coming from those who claimed to revere him – friends, adherents and disciples – rather than those who may naturally have been expected to have been more hostile. Jarvis's own translations had, sadly, much to do with that. Overwhelmingly popular, they were nevertheless prone to distort the liberal essence of Froebel's intentions, preferring to insert her own particular conception of Victorian values and spinsterhood. Her explanation of the most straightforward of concepts appeared at times convoluted and she was as liable to promulgate her own interpretations as attempting to decode Froebel's original textual intentions. This was notable in her translation and discussion of the Snail Game which was devised initially by Froebel simply as an activity to allow for the transition of pupils from the outdoors into the classroom after an extended period of activity. In the hands of Jarvis, however, this simple playground game took on a more symbolic and ritualistic meaning, an interpretation latterly condemned by Froebel scholars. Given the frequency with which Froebel's philosophy imbued even the most basic of children's games with multiple layers and levels of meaning, to make such an assumption may appear understandable and even excusable, yet it serves to highlight the recurring difficulties a writer as complex, diffuse and ambiguous as Froebel posed for those who were seeking to interpret and offer authoritative commentary upon his work.

These difficulties become magnified when practitioners began moving beyond textual interpretation to exploring how his ideas were to be put into practice in the classroom. Such was the magnitude of ideological difference that a schism emerged within the American Froebelian movement between those who favoured child-centred approaches and those whose preference was for more teacher-directed activity. At the heart of the affray was Susan Blow, an obstinate, abstruse and ultimately brilliant woman whose own lifelong dogmatic adherence to Froebel's ideas alienated and outraged potential supporters. In taking de facto control of the group who sought to interpret his ideas symbolically, Blow was in opposition to those more child-centred theorists who, through the general labelling common to historians of education, have come to acquire the nomenclature of the 'Progressives'. This perhaps throws into question the legitimacy of including Blow in this account; yet, in a narrative exploring the spread of kindergarten ideas and more specifically the contribution of *women*, her distinctive involvement cannot be overlooked, not least as it highlights the problems faced in attempting to reduce educational philosophical ideas to an exact 'science of teaching'.

Without question, the most intellectual of the 'American kindergarten women' Blow was born in St Louis (a city with which she grew to become indelibly associated) to a middle-class and affluent family which allowed her, from a young age, to pursue her own intellectual interests. While at school, she had read J. H. Stirling's classic account *The Secret of Hegel*, the power of which led to the kindling of her lifelong passion for Hegel's dense Idealistic philosophy. Following an invitation to Europe in 1870, Blow, like Peabody before her, sought out the famous Froebel kindergartens which seemed to be a physical embodiment of the Hegelian principles of which she was now convinced offered self-evident truths about the nature of humanity. Upon her return to the United States and in direct consultation with William Torrey Harris (the Superintendent of St Louis Public Schools), she opened her first public kindergarten – the celebrated Des Peres School in Carondelet, St Louis. While the school was undoubtedly novel in orientation compared to its contemporaries (in relation to its classroom layout, décor and structure), a first-hand newspaper report of the time unwittingly hinted at some of the issues which were latterly to prove so divisive:

> Literally, it is a children['s] garden, and the purpose is to direct the child's mind under six years of age into preliminary grooves of order, cleanliness, obedience, a desire for information, and to combine with these the more prominent idea of object teaching. (St Louis Republican, February 1875)

We can see immediately from this brief snippet the particular and distinctive interpretation of Froebel's ideas which was to lead to later disagreements. The notion of a teacher being 'prominent' in 'directing' children and fitting them into 'grooves' has implications which seem to run counter to the child at the centre of his own world as associated with Froebel's original methods. Likewise, values of 'obedience' and 'cleanliness' seem antithetical to the spontaneous activities which children in the kindergartens were encouraged to carry out.

Nevertheless, doctrinal differences were in the future. St Louis was very much Blow's patch, and, within a decade, every state public school had an attached kindergarten which made it a model for the nation. More so perhaps than Peabody, whose distinctive contribution was more ideological, Blow was tireless in her efforts to promote the new idea. A training college for prospective teachers was founded in 1874 and we know from her own accounts that she combined teaching in the morning with training in the evenings. Two of her most famous students were the young Elizabeth Harrison and Laura Fisher who themselves were to play a crucial part in the spreading of the kindergarten ideal.

Combining two occupations – teaching and training – inevitably took its toll on even Blow's iron constitution and she retired in 1884 to spend the rest of her life writing and lecturing on the kindergarten movement. Later works such as *Letter to a Mother on the Philosophy of Froebel* (1899) and *Symbolic Education: a Commentary on Froebel's Mother Play* (1895) may sound little more than glorified synopses but, in fact, they provided a range of penetrating insights and marked out a very distinct interpretation of Froebel's legacy. Her last (and most enduring work), *Educational Issues in the Kindergarten* (1908), attempted to provide some rounded cohesion to her thought and can be seen as a summation of her creed. It is therefore to this book that the modern reader should turn to first to begin to understand Blow's distinctive take on Froebel's beliefs.

It is clear that her championing of the kindergarten concept stemmed more from its inherent intellectual and academic benefits than from any purpose of social reform. Reference has already been made to William Torrey Harris and it was he who not only edited the aforementioned *Letters to a Mother* but who shared with Blow an understanding that the kindergartens should nurture educational achievement rather than emotional advancement. Underpinning their considerations was the belief in the 'Hegelian dialectic' and its possible conjoinment with Froebelian principles. Hegel's teleology (which is among the complex ever written) posited the idea that the end point of human freedom was to be obtained through a complete awareness of self, mediated by the existence of institutions. For Hegel, the Prussian state in which he lived was the perfect embodiment of this form of conscious awareness and Harris and Blow sought after this fashion to appropriate education as 'the process through which the individual is led to attain his freedom' (Harris, Twentieth Annual Report, 41).

Education – as the instrument of the state, church and civil society – was therefore the tool by which individuals were trained to understand their place in society. While this notion sounds innately conservative, it was predicated upon the assumption of 'freedom' as being broadly equated with a fuller understanding of social structures and strictures and a guiding of the child away from their primitive self. Harris's education programme was therefore centred upon embracing 'only such matters as have a general theoretical bearing on the world in which the pupil lives' (Cremin 1961: 18). In reality, this involved self-activity but only within the context of a range of subjects – mathematics, literature, grammar and the like – which Harris saw as allowing for that process of self-estrangement which was in keeping with his Hegelian beliefs in seeking to connect the individual with larger social structures.

Ultimately, these formalistic approaches to learning and dogmatic adherence to a particular conception of Froebelianism conspired to characterize Harris and Blow as reactionaries whose primary agenda was with individual mental development rather than social change. As the kindergarten movement underwent a process of fragmentation, it was to be younger female members of this group, such as Alice Putnam and Anna Bryan, who began to adopt Froebel's ideas to the needs of urban children and who embraced freer forms of play at the expense of the more rigid adaptation of the kindergarten ideas espoused by their illustrious forebears. This need to adapt the learning process to the shifting requirements of American children was heightened by the rise of child psychology which began to appropriate the language and practices of more child-centred approaches to schooling and learning. On the eve of the First World War and the International Kindergarten Union's Committee of Nineteen whose reports were published as *The Kindergarten* (1913), the separation between Blow and her younger colleagues became terminal and the kindergarten concept in that particular form was dead. While Blow had clearly succeeded in raising an awareness of the kindergarten ideology to the level of national consciousness, increasingly such ideas bound up with calls for social change and democratic living. Chapter 6 of this book will take this American context further and explore the developments of American education in the light of these changes.

Nevertheless, while her practices may have been seen as constrictive within the context of the emerging nation, along with her counterparts in England, Susan Blow provided a powerful example of the influence that large numbers of women were beginning to exert over progressive educational policy and practice – particularly, in this case, the kindergarten movement. Although their stories are only now coming to be told (aided by the work of the increasing numbers of educational scholars), they represent powerful exemplars of the historical importance of women in education and particularly the ways in which the progressive movement has owed them, to this day, a considerable debt.

Notes

1 It is a common misconception that Wollstonecraft was unpopular and vilified in her own time. In fact, it was only with the publication of William Godwin's memoir after her death detailing her love affairs and bastard child (Fanny Imlay) that her reputation went into its long decline.

2 The conduct book, as a genre, really found its popularity between c. 1760 and 1820. For the most part, such works described 'correct' virtues and how these could be obtained through systems of education. While some writers, such as Hester Chapone and Catherine Macaulay, argued for women to cultivate their mind though independent programmes of study, many of these conduct books, as Nancy Armstrong (1987) points out, encouraged a very bourgeois conception of the individual.

3 Even today, several of the great public schools – Eton and Harrow, for example – admit only boys. It should also be remembered that women, although permitted to study at both Oxford and Cambridge Universities from 1878 and 1869, could only do so at designated women's colleges and were not allowed to receive full degrees until 1919 and 1948, respectively.

4 Margaret King was an extraordinary woman deserving of a biography in her own right. Settling in Italy, she became one of the first pioneers of preventative medicine, setting up a successful practice as well as writing several didactic works for children. It was in Pisa she made the acquaintance of the Shelley circle, including, in a final irony, Wollstonecraft's daughter, Mary.

5 See, for a point of reference, the sentimentalism within Thomas Day's *History of Sandford and Merton*. As was mentioned in the previous chapter, this book proved abidingly successful throughout the nineteenth century and its underlying theme of education as 'rescue' can be seen to have pervaded many aspects of Victorian teaching.

6 The dissenting academies were those schools and colleges run by dissenters or non-conformists – Quakers, Baptists, Methodists as well as Catholics and Jews. Originating towards the end of the seventeenth century, these schools tended to favour a more modern curriculum, including sciences and modern history. Alongside their emphasis upon knowledge often went a harsher regimen. The reader is directed towards Herbert McLachlan (1931) and Ashley Smith (1954) for still-relevant historical discussions as to their importance.

7 The poem in question was titled 'To a Lady with Some Painted Flowers' and Barbauld's choice of adjectives such as 'sweet' and 'delicate' are capitalized by Wollstonecraft in the footnoted text (page 113) to suggest their inferior, feminine quality.

8 As Susan Manley (2003) points out, 13 of Richard Lovell Edgeworth's 22 children were educated exclusively at home.

9 The settlement scheme, similar in ethos to Toynbee Hall, was an attempt by the American government to deal with the growing problems of urban poverty. Middle class settlement workers – often young and democratically minded – lived cooperatively with their poorly educated neighbours in order to share knowledge, skills and culture. The kindergarten idea – with its emphasis upon holistic development – much appealed to their outlook and Putnam's kindergarten classes took place in Hull House, the most famous of these settlement buildings which had been founded by two women – Jane Addams and Helen Starr.

Key reading

Mary Wollstonecraft, *A Vindication of the Rights of Woman with Strictures on Political and Morl Subjects* (London: Joseph Johnson, 1792).
Maria Edgeworth, *Practical Education in Three Volumes* (New York: Woodstock Books, 1996).
William McCarthy, *Anna Letitia Barbauld: Voice of the Enlightenment* (Baltimore: The Johns Hopkins University Press, 2008).

Further reading

Lyndall Gordon, *Vindication: A Life of Mary Wollstonecraft* (London: Virago, 2005).
Marilyn Butler, *Maria Edgeworth: A Literary Biography* (Oxford: Clarendon Press, 1972).
Michael Shapiro, *Child's Garden: The Kindergarten Movement from Froebel to Dewey* (University Park: Pennsylvania State University Press, 1983).

4

Psychology

Introduction

The relationship between practising educators and those in the psychological profession has long been in a constant state of flux and agitation. At best, seen as useful adjuncts whose theories serve to validate the continuing assessment methods of pupils by teachers (including the diagnosis of children with SEN) and, at worst, as pursuing policies of meddle and muddle while unnecessarily cluttering up the curriculum, the role and purpose of the educational psychologist has, since the discipline's emergence, been subject to frequent questioning, scepticism and outright condemnation. Indeed, it may not be unfair to suggest that few scientists have aroused as much long-standing opprobrium and hostility as those whose business concerns the science of testing or 'psychometrics'. In part, as Adrian Wooldrich (1994) has pointed out, this has been attributable to the fact that much of their work has been centred upon two of the most controversial and acrimonious debates in the educational field – those concerning socio-biology and race and IQ.

In many respects, these issues, while on the surface disparate, are two sides of the very same coin, for they both concern the idea of the latent or otherwise potential of individuals, the 'nature versus nurture' question and the ways therefore in which the inequalities in levels of attainment across society can be calculated, analysed and explained. It has been the contention of many psychologists that it is as a result of parents and genetics rather than opportunity and education which can account for variation in life chances and outcome. Most famously – or perhaps infamously – the *Bell Curve* (1994) by Charles Murray and Richard Hernstein reignited this debate afresh for a new generation by arguing credibly and reasonably not merely for a high percentage of our human intelligence as being hereditary but also for the impossibility of ever being able to successfully manipulate IQ changes through a changing of environment. So much therefore for education compensating for society! Furthermore, stringent claims were made in the book validating the use of intelligence testing and the importance of being able to capture and measure a general intelligence factor – 'g' – which could constitute a fixed and quantifiable measure of intelligence attributable to an individual.

The search for an indicator of general measurable intelligence was, in one sense, nothing new; indeed many supporters of the *Bell Curve*, for example, the Berkeley psychologist Arthur Jensen, had been promulgating (very much against the cultural *zeitgeist*) similar theories back in the 1960s[1] which were intertwined with the then nascent debates about declining educational standards in literacy and numeracy. Later, in light of the hornet's nest stirred up by Murray, 52 academics signed a *Wall Street Journal* petition entitled 'Mainstream Science on Intelligence' which attempted to give a scholastic coherence to the belief in IQ testing. Even then, however, some of those ballotted refused to posit their signature which indicated the bitter polarization still residing in the field. Furthermore, from the British standpoint, the idea of intelligence testing had long underscored the educational climate, finding its best expression in the hugely important Education Act of 1944 which introduced a system of selection at the age of 11 – the so called 'Eleven-plus' examination. Accentuating much of its thinking had been not merely the insight of the foremost psychologist Cyril Burt – a devout believer in mental measurement – but also the headmaster of the prestigious Harrow School, Cyril Norwood, whose earlier Report (1943) into the state of secondary education at the national level was to have a crucial impact on the final shape of the Act. Critically, Norwood conceived of 'selection by psychology' as allowing the classification of knowledge into three discrete forms – mechanical, technical and abstract – which were to be met in three different kinds of school. These were christened the secondary modern, the secondary technical and the grammar into which pupils would be placed depending on which institution best suited their abilities and aptitudes. Such a system broadly accorded with the tripartite model adopted by Plato in his *Republic*, with ancient stratifications representing the plebeians (workers), the auxiliaries (administrators) and the guardians (rulers), respectively. This analogy reflected not only Norwood's own classical upbringing but also served to popularly stereotype believers in selection and testing as elitists committed to the preservation of tradition and hierarchy at the expense of innovation and progress.

It would therefore seem strange in a book exploring the development of progressive education and its thinkers to devote a chapter to its relationship with psychology. After all, progressivism has tended to be broadly antithetical to the ideals of testing and measurement and progressive advocates of all hues have repeatedly refused to characterize knowledge and its importance in such crudely hierarchical and quantifiable terms. This has long been a problem within the English educational mainstream. The 'English disease', diagnosed repeatedly by (among others) the historian Corelli Barnet in his influential tome *The Audit of War* (1987), was a particular term which referred to the common historical antipathy and disparagement felt towards vocational skills and their practitioners. Barnett cites as evidence for this the collapse of the technical school movement and the long, hard-fought battle practical subjects such as engineering faced in achieving recognition at the university level even at the academic hothouses of Oxford and Cambridge.

Similarly, for many progressives, including Rousseau, Froebel and Dewey, the environment provided for a growing child was seen as decisive in allowing them to develop to their full potential – *whatever that potential might be*. Even if, in an Idealist sense, one accepts that at birth we are all what we are destined to be, that prospect still has to be mitigated by the environment, and nowhere are those potentials as clearly delineated as they were later to be by the science of psychometry. Testing and measurement, by their very quantitative nature, also implicitly foster comparison and evaluation and comparative data such as league tables and test scores breed competition and engender rivalry which can, again, be seen to be in contravention of many progressive ideas which have all too often stressed cooperation, equality and fairness.

Nevertheless, it is far too simplistic to pit progressives and psychologists against one another and dichotomize their relationship as this fails to recognize the enormous contribution made by psychological exponents toward the progressive tradition and the global impact more 'scientific' figures such as Maria Montessori and Rudolf Steiner have had on school-based practice. As Adrian Wooldrich (1994) points out, 'Educational psychologists tended to be progressive in their approach to education and meritocratic in their attitudes to the social structure' (Wooldrich 1994: 14). This point is particularly pertinent when one considers the ways in which the established canon of writing on this topic, for example works by Brian Simon (1971) and Stephen Jay Gould (1981), has tended to dismiss out of hand psychometricians as 'reactionary in their politics and traditionalist in their educational thinking' (Ibid., 164). These points of view have proven particularly unhelpful as they have perhaps failed to take full account of the historical contexts in which certain ideas developed and the ways in which these ideas have subsequently enmeshed themselves within the discourses of meritocracy and, in our case, progressivism.

Nor has it ever been simply the case – and this is a common misattribution – that those on the left and right of the political spectrum have always adopted polarized 'pro-' and 'anti-' positions on psychology and testing. Indeed, as Robert Skidelsky (1969) has shown, and we will see in the next chapter, there was significant overlap between the progressive school movement and the discipline of psychology, not least as both parties continually held fast to the notion of the 'self-educating child' capable of making sense of the world around them with a mind more attuned to the understanding of constructs than had previously been thought to have been the case. The recognition of difference debunked the view that children were a homogeneous grouping and instead advocated methods which were attuned to an individual's potential. Likewise, the broad anti-authoritarianism posited by both Sigmund Freud and Carl Jung sat comfortably with those educators such as A. S. Neill who sought in their own way to challenge received wisdom and who frequently invoked such ideas to validate their own particular educational ideologies. In such cases, opposition to repression as perpetrated by parents, schools and the State accorded with Freud's belief in repressed feelings and memories which attached itself to complexes which were frequently sexual in nature.

Such flawed characterizations of the type outlined above have conversely served to pigeonhole and stereotype educational thinkers into particular categories when, often, their ideas are less than straightforward and can provide justifications for alternate and competing viewpoints. The English psychologist Sir Percy Nunn is a good case in point. While an advocate of selective education intended for a sophisticated elite – shades once again of Norwood's Plato – he was also simultaneously desirous of pupils developing in a manner more akin to a performer through them finding their individual expressiveness. In describing generally the duty of the educator, he wrote that the 'ultimate duty is not to let our natures grow untended and disorderly, but to use our creative energies to produce the most shapely individual we can attain' (Nunn 1920: 249). As the philosopher of education John White (1982) puts it, Nunn therefore conceived of the child 'much more like an *artist* than a truth-seeker seeing his life as the expression of his deepest feelings and intuition' (White 1982: 44). These soundings, although rooted in empirical, evidence-based study, nevertheless had much to commend them to progressive ears with their conceptualization of the child as an intuitive being, capable of self-discovery and a creative sense of purpose.

Quite aside from the problems associated with characterization, representation and portrayal, discussions of psychology also involve, inevitably it seems, some degree of scientific theory and substance, habitually quite alien to those in the business of education. Whenever therefore any narrative attempts to examine, no matter how tangentially, the developmental and educational strands of the psychological field, it is impossible to fully divorce its thrust from the complex ideas of Sigmund and Anna Freud and, latterly, Jean Piaget as it was they who laid down many of the foundations from which were to grow the emergent discipline. It is not, however, the purpose of this chapter to explore these psychological ideas in any great depth as these are extensively well-trodden paths and in *Measuring the Mind* (1994) by Adrian Wooldrich, there exists already for the reader a compelling account exploring the singular relationship between ideas, policy and practice. Instead, the focus here shall be more upon the ways in which these ideas have been developed and utilized within the educational context and, more specifically, how they have been adopted and adapted by those thinkers seeking to elaborate their own brand of progressive practice.

While, as has been pointed out, such a discussion could easily encompass many of the schools within what became known as the New Education Fellowship (explored in Chapter 5), it must be noted that that particular relationship was not always explicit and openly acknowledged. Certainly, there was a rapprochement and broad intellectual consensus between both parties but many of the schools themselves tended to go about their daily business unencumbered by the finer points of psychological theory nor indeed were many of the pioneering educators themselves theorists in that realm. In some cases, such as in Bertrand Russell's Beacon Hill School, the institution's aim was not to generate a theory of learning but was instead used as a vehicle for its creators' own radical social ideas. The 'progressive school movement' in the British and European context shall therefore be distinguished from the psychological theories which influenced it and will be considered elsewhere through considering those schools as democratic entities.

There were, of course, notable exceptions to this rule and schools such as Susan Isaacs' Malting House and Maria Montessori's *casa dei bambini* were deliberately set up as institutions where children could be observed analytically and recorded systematically alongside the day-to-day educational operations.[2] This was despite being, particularly in the case of Isaacs, important contributors to the debates within the New Education Fellowship. Given, however, their acknowledged status as 'laboratories' which sought to combine scientific theory and practice, it seems more appropriate to focus on them here, given the intimacy long enjoyed between psychology and scientific methodology. Nevertheless, it is hoped that the overlap between this chapter and the next will become clearer as the narrative progresses.

The origins of 'progressive' psychology – Child Study and Granville Stanley Hall

The origins of psychology's interest in children can be seen to surface in the Child Study movements which emerged in the late Victorian period toward the end of the nineteenth century. These groups often reflected the English attitude towards science – optimistic, industrious, speculative and wholly amateur. Science, as was the case with engineering and natural history, was generally the preserve of the gentleman enthusiast or the gifted autodidact.

Restricted channels existed for the dissemination and publication of findings, and these, such as they were, were frequently open only to a very select group of scientists who had the appropriate membership of organizational bodies. Nevertheless, for all their inherent limitations, the analysis of large groups of children propagated by Child Study – which became more possible when mass schooling became compulsory – and the collation of data allowed information to be gathered, which began to identify and demarcate differences between children according to ability and aptitude. Many of these enquiries were tied to anxieties about the 'condition of the nation', which was not merely embodied in concerns over children's physical health (a cause later to be famously taken up by the McMillan sisters) but also their intellectual well-being.

Further afield in Germany – not traditionally a country beset with amateurism – the British-born William Preyer began to develop theories of child psychology, which drew upon the evolutionary ideas of Charles Darwin, to construct a narrative of child development where instinct and reflex were seen to be overtaken by action. Crucially, Preyer's research stressed the importance of the observation of healthy children for the purposes of science, and through his endeavours, native societies dedicated to Child Study and Child Psychology emerged. Both groups published widely and elicited the support of the teaching profession, a fact not perhaps too unsurprising, given the influence that Froebel's work continued to hold over educational practice in the land of his birth.

Nevertheless, despite these developments chiming with the Germans' long history of elevating pedagogy to the status of an academic discipline, neither their efforts nor those of the comparable British groups ultimately had much to recommend either about schooling or, more pertinently, progressivism. In the case of Britain, the amateurism so redolent of an earlier age soon became superseded by a culture of professionalism not just in education but also in leisure, patterns of work and systems of government. Likewise in Germany, the very different priorities of educators and psychologists, emphasized by the divisions between Wilhelm Lay who favoured school-based research and Ernst Neumann who favoured applied psychology, meant that child study entered into its perennial conflict with the teaching profession, thereby losing its educational slant and alienating its potential target audience. Neither case was therefore satisfactory in seeking to conjoin with education and elaborate progressive tenets.

Perhaps, therefore, a reasonable starting point in that regard should be with a consideration of the role of the American psychologist Granville Stanley Hall (1844–1924). The word 'role' here is carefully chosen as it is wholly improper to refer to him as a traditional 'progressive' in an ideological or practical sense. Indeed, he is often considered in the literature as a pioneer of the 'child study' movement and a man whose reactionary, and at times downright odd, politics cast a shadow over his legitimacy as a forward-thinking educationalist. Despite this, his contributions to both theory and practice, in particular, his belief that education and psychology should be intermeshed with one another, mean that he emerges from the pack as a more significant object of study albeit while sitting uneasily on the periphery of the progressive circle. Nor is this significance merely something appended here in a retrospective fashion. His monumental two-volume work, *Adolescence* (1904), was widely acknowledged by legislators (although, given its density, probably not so widely read!) and was to play a not insignificant role upon the development of governmental policy, particularly through its reconceptualization of the category of the 'child'.

A firm believer in sterilization and eugenics (not, admittedly, especially uncommon at the time) Hall's educational beliefs, of which much has been written, were a curious blend of both the innovative and the heavily didactic. On the one hand, he believed, in the early years, for example, that children should have a curriculum which appealed directly to their interests and, within that, play was seen as having a central role. In a paper given concerning the 'ideal school', Hall argued that reading and writing, 'should be neglected in our system before eight, and previous school work should focus on stories, the study of nature, and education by play and other activities' (Hall 1901, quoted in Kliebard 1986: 41). Conventional subjects traditionally seen as part of a broad curriculum, such as Latin, Greek and geography, were considered by Hall as idle luxuries not worthy of the status habitually afforded to them. Furthermore, Hall's concern and pseudo-obsession over the health and well-being of the child which he shared with other child study pioneers were, as we have noted earlier, influential upon pioneering thinkers as far afield as the Macmillan sisters. So far so progressive.

Nevertheless, many of Hall's related educational frameworks indicated a viewpoint at odds with many of these more child-centred notions. Segregation by gender at the secondary level, as one example, was encouraged by Hall as he was concerned, in terms reminiscent of Nietzsche, with the 'progressive feminization' (Hall 1903) of schools which denied the young access to the 'strong man' whose presence was vital in informing and stabilizing much of their upbringing. Even the earlier call for the centrality of play emanated from his belief that the infant child had limited powers of reasoning and was not yet ready for more arduous forms of learning – a contention that would have sat uncomfortably even with some of his more primitive American forebears such as Amos Bronson Alcott. Given this deterministic conception of children's development, which was indicative of a classic 'stage' model, Hall thus placed great emphasis upon memorization and rote learning for the child at later stages of their development when they were seen as more capable of apprehending what it was exactly they were being taught.

These contradictions were well summed up by the historian Herbert Kliebard (1986) – 'His [Hall's] proposals for reform of the curriculum amounted almost to a denigration of intellect in favour of a sentimentalization of childhood . . .' (Kliebard 1986: 50). This sentimentalization, while wholly commendable and destined to draw sympathy for those campaigning for the rights of children, did not ultimately manifest itself in an individualist philosophy. Hall refused to believe that children could be reduced to distinct entities that went through unique and select passages of learning. Instead, childhood and, particularly, adolescence, were seen in light of what he termed *recapitulation theory* (Hall 1904) which sought to link the stages of child development with equivalent stages in the progress of human civilization. The transformation of human society from a primitive form of existence dependent purely on carnal instinct and self-reliance to a state of being characterized by civilization and democratic structure reflected, for Hall, the growth of the child from an age of infant adolescent turbulence to the more critically aware adult. As Hall put it, 'To understand either the child or the [human] race we must constantly refer to the other' (Hall 1904: 443).

This has more important educational consequences than may first appear for, as John Dewey (1897) was to prophetically point out, the linkage of educational development with that of human society potentially predisposes a differentiated curriculum which would accord with the future needs of that particular community. While, as will be made clear in a later chapter, this has been a critique occasionally levelled at Dewey himself, in Hall's case, such an evaluation is all the more significant, given the unequivocal way in which he sought to associate child development with homo sapien progress.

Belief in the onward march of human civilization and an emphasis upon healthiness led to Hall staunchly advocating for the qualities of rural education which he saw as providing the best circumstances in which to foster 'American' virtues of hard work and discipline. This led him, however, into direct conflict with many in the kindergarten movement who saw his appropriation of the solution to the nation's ills as a snub to their continuing hard work in alleviating the worst of America's urban problems. In addition, the situation was not aided by the personal conflicts between Hall and the kindergarten figurehead, Susan Blow. For all of their many fine qualities, neither was greatly endowed with modesty and their frequent intellectual spats served to symbolize the ideological polls within the 'kindergarten versus child study' debate. In their own ways, these disputes, 'revealed much about the context of nineteenth-century educational reform' (Shapiro 1983: 109).

At heart, their *contretemps* centred predominately on the idea of a 'return to nature'. Was it to be literal in the kindergarten ('child's garden') sense or a sentimental idealization as envisaged by Hall? In 1895, the otherwise academic and somewhat ethereal nature of the debate became publicly visible as, during a summer gathering of 35 educationalists assembled to study the kindergarten movement, Hall's open disparagement of both Froebel and Blow led all but two of the delegates present to walk out in protest. Those remaining, including Anna Bryan and Patty Smith Hill, stayed to plan their own 'ideal scheme' of kindergarten education and, in the process, contributed to the terminal spilt within the kindergarten movement, which has been discussed earlier in the chapter relating to women. It also led many to fundamentally question Hall's relationship to American progressivism and, in many ways, acted as a blow from which his reputation among progressives never truly recovered. Few writing today would credit his pseudo-Nietzschen rhetoric as being 'child centred'!

However, to historians of education, the progressiveness or not of Hall's philosophy is a relatively moot point as it is his contributions in areas slightly further adrift which are worthy of note in the context of this narrative and which justify his place in any discussion of this type. These can be delineated in three ways. First, as has been made clear, he was a key figure in the burgeoning 'child study' movement and was one of the first to fully professionalize the discipline of psychology, making redundant the earlier amateur organizations whose quasi-scientific approaches to examining the child now seemed redolent of a much earlier and backward age. His ways of working were soon to become the norm for those seeking to investigate the ways children behaved and the reasons why. If anyone can be credited with driving the final nail into the coffin of British-style amateurism, it is surely him.

Second, his most celebrated educational achievement – the recognition and development of a theory of adolescence – had profound implications for later conceptions of progressive thought. While Hall's theory has come to be seen as simplistic and superseded in light of more recent scientific and anthropological research, for example, the classic study of Margaret Mead (1928) into Samoan girls which argues that the dominant adolescent behavioural patterns of 'storm and stress' are not universal, it nevertheless provoked urgent responses in relation to the conceptualization and considerations of childhood, particularly during the turbulent early years period.[3] Indirectly, the anxieties of governments at the turn of the century, with adolescence becoming associated with prevailing juvenile delinquency, caused many to begin to make children the focus of their attention and policies by, for example, providing more effective pathways into employment, developing organizations to promote good character and deliberating over more relevant considerations in relation to both skills and the curriculum. This last point is particularly important as, with schools and the raising of the school-leaving age being used as mechanisms by which children were institutionalized and kept out of the debilitating labour market, it meant that the curriculum such as it was had to appeal more directly to their interests.

Finally, Hall's 'laboratory school' allowed for the school setting to be oriented in a wholly unique way as an observational post and 'test bed' for the development of theory. Systematic inspection of children and the minute chronicling of their behaviour were not, in themselves, original and had been undertaken by others such as Richard Lovell Edgeworth and the American psychologist Lightner Witmer. Nevertheless, Hall's vision went beyond mere note taking, for he envisaged a profound intersection of psychology with education, with the former having a prominent role to play in relation to the administration and governance of schools. This was significant as it conceived of the potential for psychologists to begin to act in professional capacities as policy makers and legislators, which had implications in the dissemination of progressive ideology particularly within the British context.

This British circumstance is an important one to consider as it is here in which one can perhaps recognize most obviously the association between psychologists and the acknowledgement, in a formal legislative context, of progressive educational thought and resultant developments of state-sanctioned child-centredness. Indeed, Hall's work was particularly influential as it offered a fresh interpretation on the problems of juvenile delinquency and the backward nature of many of the philanthropic attempts to deal with it – uniformed youth, rational recreation and so on. It also pointed towards the haphazard nature of transfer into the labour market. As such, this chapter shall now take a British focus to illustrate the ways in which psychology and psychological ideas had an impact upon the development of progressivism at a nation-wide level. This shall be explored by examining two official government sponsored publications – the interwar Hadow Reports and the 1967 Plowden Report. While clearly intimately connected to the historical narrative of Britain, anyone with even a passing interest in progressivism would be well served by reading these documents, for they elaborate important precepts which borrow strongly from more global traditions, notably the emergence of sophisticated psychological theory. They are also significant in showing the mechanisms by which progressive ideas can be implanted into the mainstream consciousness and thereby serve as a welcome antidote to occasional cynicism about the stagnant nature of bureaucratic education departments.

Psychology and progressivism joined – The case of Hadow in interwar Britain

Although setting up a system of national elementary schooling in 1870 which was subsequently made compulsory from 1881, the British state had enshrined an arrangement which allowed for a very loose relationship to exist between the governing Board of Education and individual schools, notably those at the lower age group levels. This allowed, as Kevin Brehony (2001) has shown, for the creeping influence of groups such as the Froebelian Society, particularly during the dynamic tenure of Emily Sheriff, to have an impact upon the ways that ever-willing teachers adopted progressive methods within the classroom. The influence, too, of thinkers such as Maria Montessori was, as we shall see later on, equally profound and, although the quality of state education was undoubtedly patchy and many teachers still subscribed to strategies of recitation and rote learning, there were at least opportunities for dynamic and forward-thinking professionals to adopt a range of teaching strategies.

Mainstream psychology, however, was still relatively unenlightened during these early stages, particularly, as Ian Copeland (2002) has made it clear, in relation to those children diagnosed with what are now called Special Educational Needs (SEN). The nascent science was instrumental in framing and constructing a discourse based around such concepts as 'imbecility' and 'retardation' – rudimentary terms which served to justify repressive and occasionally humiliating mechanisms of treatment. This broadly echoed the views held even in relation to those who were not considered as 'suffering' with some form of disorder; it may not have been an individual's fault if they were 'less' intelligent than others but it was not something which could be significantly corrected, adjusted or accounted for. Early progressives may have focused on the activities involved in acquiring knowledge but this did not always mean that the social or quasi-scientific factors which may have limited that process were fully understood. One of the key breakthroughs of the psychological revolution was therefore to give legitimacy to the idea that children themselves develop at different rates with different capabilities and should not be judged according to their position relative to a 'norm'. This naturally entailed entertaining strategies which moved away from whole-class teaching and instead towards personalized programmes of learning. Following from that, would it therefore be possible to educate those children with more mild forms of SEN – autism, schizophrenia and the like – if they were given more help and assistance?

As diagnostic testing became more sophisticated, however, and the discipline of psychology became increasingly refined and professionalized,[4] the influence of certain practitioners began to be felt more keenly, with pupils being seen increasingly as individuals with very specific needs within the context of the classroom. This led to a gradual ramification between psychology, the state and progressive education with webs of mutual influence being ever more keenly felt. One prominent and important example of this emerges in the Hadow Reports – a series of six governmental enquiries chaired by Sir William Henry Hadow between 1923 and 1933 – whose investigations into primary schools were both pioneering and wide-ranging. The best known of the reports, *Psychological Tests of Educable Capacity* (1924) *The Education of the Adolescent* (1926) and *The Primary School* (1931), are, in many respects, the most important for they not only betray exceptionally progressive approaches to learning but they do so underscored by a close intimacy with psychological thought and ideas. Indeed, of the five factors listed by Alan Blyth (1965), which he argued formed the core philosophy of the Hadow Reports, the first two are listed as the growth of developmental psychology and the influence of John Dewey, respectively. Indeed, the 1924 Hadow Report set the tone for the subsequent investigations in concluding its analysis by calling for the Board of Education to 'set up an advisory committee to work in concert with university departments of psychology and other organizations engaged in the work of research' (Hadow 1924: 144).

It was, therefore, this desire to appropriate both psychological expertise, often from within the newly founded university departments, and progressive ideas which so distinguished the Hadow Reports from other official contemporary publications. A good illustration of this prior-established reluctance to engage with advancing ways of thinking which contrasted with the Hadow Reports emerges through a reading of the 1921 Newbolt Report under the chairmanship of the distinguished poet Sir Henry Newbolt. Concerned predominantly with the importance of literature within the school curriculum, the Newbolt Report deployed an analysis which relied upon the concept of 'academic missionaries' – teachers and professors who would enlighten the masses by the promotion of all that was 'best' within the English literary canon. Although the synergy between language development and acquisition and cognitive improvement would appear obvious and ripe for debate within an official and wide-ranging publication, as Giles and Middleton (1995) point out, many of those entrusted with the enlightening educational processes were themselves 'too busy writing belle-lettrist reviews or conducting pseudo-psychological tests about the reading process to worry too much about the needs of the working classes' (Giles and Middleton 1995: 151).

These psychological experiments, even those of an amateur nature, which placed primacy upon individual development, were thus formally neglected in favour of a viewpoint which sought to use education as a device to civilize and maintain the status quo. While its impact was ultimately to be marginal, the Newbolt Report was evidently one step behind in its understanding of the potential utility of the teacher in the development of pupil learning. The difference with Hadow, to labour the point, should be apparent and serves to illustrate the increasing ways, in the interwar years, in which progressive ideas were achieving some kind of recognition and status and coming to supersede more 'conventional' beliefs in education, both in terms of its content and form.

It must be admitted that much of the utilization of psychology within the Hadow Reports was, notably at the committee stage, indirect; the prominent psychologist Cyril Burt did not sit formally on any of the consultative committees and these groups were equally served by a wide body of interested parties, including school teachers, economists and bureaucrats. This should not though be to downplay the role that Burt was to play. He informally proffered much information and advice – much of it in relation to the value of testing and the reorganization of the curriculum – and many of the Hadow Reports are clearly inflected with much of the jargon and approach of the psychologist. This is unsurprising, given the burgeoning community of practice that was evolving, of which Burt was a prominent member, and the scientific discourses it was seeking to promote. Many of these discourses were evident in the content of the Hadow Reports and they therefore gave implicit recognition to scientific developments taking place further afield. Due to their more advanced national educational systems, many of the first sophisticated instruments of testing were, in fact, pioneered within Europe and America. Drawing upon the famous Binet and Simon test during the First World War, for example, the American psychologist Lewis Terman had administered the first mass I.Q. test to American soldiers. Although such investigations were designed predominantly to construct models, figures and graphs relating to large-scale populations at the expense of individual accomplishment (and Hadow was to be broadly antithetical to intelligence testing), various findings and assumptions nevertheless were incorporated into the 650,000 words of the various reports, with a view to putting forward an educational framework justified by the latest advancements in scientific thinking.

This particular intersection was manifest most clearly in relation to the proposals to restructure the existing British education system which Hadow put forward. To that point, schooling in Britain had suffered from a fundamental class-ridden confusion with both elementary and secondary school systems existing in parallel to one another with little curricular coherence or crossover. The barrier to a secondary education for the majority of young people remained, sadly, money. To many, even those whose sympathies were not necessarily progressive, this system entailed a high level of intellectual wastage, with many elementary students effectively 'marking time' prior to their deployment into the unskilled labour market where they would remain in perpetuity.

Contemporary theories of learning though had begun to suggest that the (approximate) age of eleven was a suitable point for some form of scholastic separation and differentiation. One of the key thrusts of the Hadow Reports was therefore to suggest the restructuring of the anachronistic elementary/ secondary school structure into a more streamlined system of primary and secondary with that natural break at 11. In and of itself, such a contention was not obviously progressive; nevertheless, one must be wary of seeing the individual Hadow Reports as discrete entities with little or no connection between each other. Intentionally, there was a continuity of committee members, meaning that the reports formed part of a coherent package of progressive ideas demonstrative of a common ideological agenda. One could, in some respects, refer to this not incorrectly as the 'Hadow period' of progressive thinking in England. Restructuring of education therefore went in parallel to the promulgation of a system of schooling which provided a framework by which children could learn in new innovative ways and with a secondary education being the right of all. As if to demonstrate the ways in which the reports can be shown to be coherent and interconnected, there were detailed proposals for the type of curriculum that pupils within this newly proposed school structure should study.

Indeed, study may in this case be the wrong word, as Hadow's proposal was for a curriculum seen 'in terms of activity and experience rather than of knowledge to be acquired and facts to be stored' (Hadow 1933: 183). This particular phrase – probably the sole thing about Hadow for which even those only casually acquainted with the history of education will be aware – could itself stand as an accurate summation of the whole British progressive movement and approach to learning. In practice, such 'activity' meant teachers encouraging pupils to express their own ideas in writing, using a variety of techniques in assisting in the development of literacy, facilitating children in the act of discovery, utilizing project and topic work and being far more sceptical over the widespread uses of intelligence testing. While it is unsophisticated to suggest any form of direct linkage between Hadow's pronouncements and the rise of psychology – many of the reports' authors were, after all, educationalists – there is little doubt that, at the very least, the reports were responding in a very direct way to the various challenges being posed by the new-fangled science.

For all of their forward-thinking proposals, their wide circulation among policy makers and the broadly sympathetic reception the reports garnered from the intelligentsia and some enlightened teacher training facilities, the impact of Hadow was, at best and, depending upon one's educational persuasion, sadly, rather limited. Even many of its less contentious proposals such as a free secondary education for all took a generation to implement and its progressive ideology has yet, even today, to have been fully incorporated into British educational dogma. Much of this can, of course, be attributed to the global economic situation; the Depression and the 'hungry 30s' was a period characterized by an absence of forward thinking in social reform due to highly restrictive constraints on the public purse. In the words of the poets Robert Graves and Alan Hodge (1940), the 1930s was the equivalent of a 'long weekend' – leisured, lazy and distinctly unproductive – and nowhere was this more keenly felt than in the public sector.

Yet, one must be wary, when discussing education, of attributing these trends solely to the dismal science of economics. After all, the teaching profession of the 1930s was an older demographic reared on the received notions of their more didactic forebears and established institutions such as Empire Day which was widely celebrated in schools. It was only when, as Peter Cunningham and Philip Gardner (2004) have speculated, teachers themselves were forced into improvising pedagogically in adverse war-time conditions that some (though by no means all) began to adopt more informal teaching practices. It is unlikely that they did so, however conscious of the earlier precedents set by the Hadow Reports. Expediency based upon lack of facilities was undoubtedly a bigger incentive to innovate than any ideological conviction! However, latter-day ignorance should not preclude us from underestimating the importance of Hadow. While, on occasion, the reports betray many of the less desirable attitudes of the period, notably in relation to issues of gender, they serve nonetheless as an important historical testimony to the ways in which progressive ideas can be, and were, codified in a formal governmental context. Furthermore, they were important as an intellectual touchstone for later generations of educational thinkers determined to revisit progressive attitudes from an earlier period.

Progressivism in the 1960s – The Plowden Report

If the Hadow Reports can be seen therefore as embodying a powerful example as to where nascent psychology could ramify with educational policy, they were to be followed a little over 30 years later by a more explicit illustration of this particular relationship. In many ways, the Plowden Report – published fittingly enough in the Summer of Love of 1967 – reiterated much of what had been said before. As Bridget, Lady Plowden (chair of the Committee) was to later write, 'we did not invent anything new' (Plowden 1987: 120) and it was only as a consequence of British teachers' continual reluctance to engage with the earlier proposals – in other words, to sacrifice innovation at the expense of conservatism in the classroom – that necessitated the Plowden investigation into primary practice.

The situation in Britain had not been aided either by the post-war introduction of the school selection examination at 11 – perversely constructed out of faith in psychological testing – which led to many teachers falling back into more didactic teaching habits. This became more pronounced, as Brian Simon (1999) has pointed out, as processes of in-school selection began to be introduced at the lower age levels in order to mirror the later discriminating school structure. Nevertheless, Britain in the 1960s, in common with much of the Western world with its heady cocktail and prevalent whiff of social egalitarianism and fairness,[5] had begun to move towards a position of rejecting pupil selection and the flawed, elitist psychology which buttressed it. This was thought to be an age of innovation and change, and so, in the social sense, the timing of the Plowden Report was particularly apposite. It should therefore come as little surprise to learn that from an investigation promulgating progressivism, the heartbeat of Plowden, as it had been for Hadow, were the precepts of learning through discovery, play and self-expression in the classroom. Its very first sentence tells us all we need to know about its main thrust – 'At the heart of the educational process lies the child' (Plowden 1967: 7). It was to be this child-centredness which was at the centre of the report and made it such a powerful advocate of progressive classroom practices.

Far from it being a representative relic of a bygone era, however, the weighty Plowden Report[6] is of fundamental importance today, for not only was it a state-authorized document promoting progressive ideologies but it did so knowingly underscored by the ideas of the Swiss psychologist Jean Piaget whose work on children's cognitive development, as Margaret Donaldson (1978) points out, was very much in vogue within the culture of the 1960s. Kathy Sylva and A. H. Halsey (1987), in discussing this influence, are surely right however to assert that although

> educational psychology had long been associated with a "progressive" stance . . . what was new about *Children and their Primary Schools* [the Plowden Report] was the manner in which it consistently applied these ideas to primary practice, spelling out in detail ways whereby a combination of individual, group, and class work would allow children to be "agents of their own learning". (Sylva and Halsey 1987: 8)

After this fashion, throughout the report, the child is frequently described as a 'Piagetian learner' – that is, one active in exploration and discovery according closely with Piaget's conception of the child as a 'lone scientist' discovering new things through trial and error and carefree experimentation. Plowden itself further elaborated Piaget's particular framework for tracing cognitive development through a series of developmental growth phases which Piaget christened the sensori-motor, intuitive thought, concrete operations and formal operations. While these were fixed in terms of the order in which they occur, *when* they occurred within children varied enormously. As such, each child had to be allowed to grow and develop at their own pace – 'Individual differences between children of the same age are so great that any class, however homogeneous it seems, must always be treated as a body of children needing individual and different attention' (Plowden Report 1967: 25). This developmental stage model delivered a ringing repudiation of the earlier thinking which had supported testing and measurement at fixed ages as rates of intellectual growth and development varied from person to person with some children peaking early and others being 'later developers'. The ways in which this accorded with the 1960s' notions of justice, fairness and equality should be self-evident.

In many ways, the ideas of Piaget which were in-built within Plowden's rhetoric seemed a throwback to earlier and cruder Romantic precepts; Rousseau, as we have encountered, conceived of the young Emile as going through four independent stages of growth, while Froebel's preoccupation with spatial awareness within the context of his special gifts and finger games finds an eerie echo in Plowden's contention that 'a child cannot read without having learnt to discriminate shapes' (Ibid., 18). Many of Plowden's subsequent recommendations regarding practice, including the use of team teaching and the integrated day – a range of activities taking place at the same time – hinted at practices which were therefore designed to impact upon individual children while still allowing for them to be fully interactive within the context of their peers. Plowden also objected to fixed and standardized forms of testing, the psychology for which was considered too rigid and not an 'infallible predictor' (Ibid., 26) of accurately measuring pupil attainment.

The extent to which these recommendations were implemented by classroom teachers and the distinct Plowden ethos disseminated has been a matter of some historical contention; the studies of Deanne Bealing (1972) and Neville Bennett (1987), for example, indicated that the Plowden Report's impact was localized and confined only to particularly forward-thinking areas of the country. Similarly, the ORACLE project of Maurice Galton and Brian Simon[7] and its follow up investigations led its founder to conclude, 'although there had been considerable change in the organizational patterns in the primary schools within that framework the teaching emphasis had hardly changed' (Galton 1987: 85). Nevertheless, such views must be considered in light of the findings of the sociologists Bernstein and Davies who famously referred to Plowden as the 'semi-official ideology of primary education' (Bernstein and Davies 1969: 56) and the testimony of numerous trainee teachers to whom Plowden was recited book, chapter and verse.

Perhaps – as is usually the case in such matters – the truth lies somewhere in the middle and even with increasing state and government interference signified by Prime Minister James Callaghan's famous Ruskin College speech of 1976 and the desire to find a common curriculum, many teachers undoubtedly continued to propagate its virtues with acts of 'defiance' within the classroom. Such acts as they occurred may have been through subversion of official rhetoric, alternative schemes of work being developed or else simply not teaching to the test in the manner required. These strategies are significant as they indicate the ways in which, even within the confines of state-directed education, it has been possible for radical pedagogic ideas and strategies to be deployed within the classroom with a view to subverting official policy and diktat. In some cases – such as the William Tyndale Affair in North London – individual schools became active sites of progressive practice fuelled by a heady mix of Plowden-inspired thought and far left revolutionary politics.[8]

Part of the confusion within the Plowden Report – and the reason, according to Galton, why the spread of such ideas was initially at least not as widespread as was hoped – was the mystified nature of its ideology, emanating from a 'basic confusion about the nature of progressive education' (Galton, op. cit., 91). Within the text, the ideas of Rousseau, Froebel, Montessori, Piaget and Dewey vie for hegemony and are cherry-picked where appropriate so as to meet the needs of Plowden's diverse readership. This perhaps does not indicate confusion in relation to progressivism as a concept per se but more perhaps with those authors of the Plowden Report itself, whose job it was to appeal to a broad demographic of theorists and practitioners. After all, scholars of progressivism have long been all too aware of its differing delineations and strands but in the context of the report, this had serious consequences, and Galton is right to draw attention to these, of conflating thinkers such as Dewey and Rousseau who represent two differing interpretations of progressivism – the one individual and European, the other collective and American. Equally significantly today is the way in which Piaget's theories – like those of any psychologist, it seems! – have been superseded by 'new and improved' understandings of learning and development. Peter Bryant (1984) and the aforementioned Margaret Donaldson were two of the key figures in this particular intellectual dethroning, yet even they were forced to confess that 'if you look at almost any new programme for teaching mathematics or science, there Piaget tangibly is. His work is cited as justification for many of the new methods and for some old ones too' (Bryant 1984: 251).

While this statement is evidently less true today, undoubtedly the significance of Plowden in the context of this chapter stems from its innumerable references and allusions throughout its text to the terms 'psychology', 'psychiatry' and the associated findings of these disciplines. Although this was not new (all educational reports used, out of necessity, some form of valedictory science), in its breadth and scope, the Plowden Report was ground-breaking and remains to this day the largest review ever undertaken of primary education in Britain. In particular, the way in which it welded together psychology and progressivism using the one to buttress the other was quite novel. There may be those today who find it too finely attuned, or too specific, to the context of 1960s Britain to be of much relevance in a clearly very different contemporary educational world. They would, however, surely be wrong as it remains, even now, a testament to the optimism of its founders and temporal origins and the passionately held belief in the liberating power of progressive education.

In many ways, beyond their obvious educational similarities and their receptiveness to new ideas, both Hadow and Plowden were cautious about promulgating a universal and total approach to teaching and learning. Plowden, in particular, cautioned against the use of education being subject to the vagaries of intellectual fashion. Given the paradigmatic shifts that science goes through, with new discoveries repudiating old systems of belief, this seemed eminently sensible and betrayed Plowden's understandings of the way science should be used to buttress rather than lead educational debate. The Hadow Reports too recommended that a range of methods should be used in the gathering of educational data. If therefore one can take anything from these documents – beyond their obvious progressive leanings – it is that it does not serve governments well to impose 'one size fits all' approaches onto educational settings. As a case in point, the recent controversy in Britain over language acquisition and the teaching of phonics stemmed from the results of a single experiment in Scotland, which was not in itself conclusive,[9] and which has led to a particular style of classroom instruction being adopted nationwide. Such strategies undoubtedly do much to stifle individuals whose learning style may not approximate to their peers. Similar has been the basic fundamental adherence in the education system to examinations geared around the ability to write rather than speak. Perhaps this is a result of our residual clinging to a belief in the power of a general intelligence ('g') which is elaborated through rigid forms of assessment, typically involving literacy. What, one wonders, will the successors to Plowden make of that?

The Malting House and Susan Isaacs

The two examples previously discussed well illustrate how psychology increasingly began to interact with progressive practice and led the development of its ideology in new directions, in part, necessitated by that important ramification with the State. This was not coincidental and there are really two identifiable reasons why, in the years separating the Hadow Reports and Plowden, psychology became seen as an increasingly worthwhile and legitimate means of validating educational practice. On the one hand, within the global context, the ideas of such thinkers as Maria Montessori and Rudolf Steiner were seminal in developing educational philosophies based around specific psychological precepts designed to foster children's cognitive and spiritual growth. Theirs was a wide pan-European discourse which had enormous effects globally and was promoted through speaking tours, lectures and discipleship. Their impact shall be examined later. Equally important to consider, however, was the gradual rise of psychological practitioners to positions of authority within existing educational, institutional and governmental frameworks of power. Cyril Burt, for example, not only gave testimony to government committees in the guise of an 'expert witness' (including, as we have seen, those chaired by Henry Hadow) but was also the psychiatrist to the London County Council – then an important and leading barometer of educational opinion and practice. In a similar vein, Percy Nunn was professor of education at London University, while Susan Isaacs (1885–1948) also contributed to the Hadow Committee as well as working tirelessly with Local Education Authorities, subsequently becoming the first head of the Child Development Department at the internationally renowned London Institute of Education.

While such things are impossible to ever properly quantify, it is perhaps Isaacs whom posterity has decreed to be the most noteworthy. This has not been exclusively her doing; Burt's reputation has been beset with allegations of forgery and falsification[10] while Nunn has remained relatively unknown to all but the specialist. However, Isaacs is also significant in her own right as it was she who founded and developed the pioneering Malting House School in Cambridge which served as the model laboratory institution by which children could be subject to scientific study and scrutiny. Furthermore, she was, even among her esteemed peers, considered intellectually meteoric and was chiefly responsible for the popularizing of the psychological theories of both Freuds (Sigmund and Anna) and Melanie Klein within British and European intellectual frameworks. She was clearly a figure who transcended the traditionally parochial context of ivory tower academic Britain and made popular, particularly through her Ursula Wise 'agony aunt' columns, the application of complex psychological theory to the laymen.

Given her substantial achievements, it is therefore strange to consider why her reputation has taken, comparatively, such a long time to become established. Even as recently as 2000, Mary Jane Drummond was forced to concede, 'It is not the least remarkable aspect of [her] unique contribution to educational progress that it remains so under documented by other educationalists' (Drummond 2000: 221). One could attribute this neglect to any number of factors – her gender, the continuing scepticism held towards psychologists or the fact that many key documents, notably the verbatim reports and exchanges between members of the British Psycho-Analytical Society of whom Isaacs was a central figure, have only recently become available. It is this last aspect which is cited by Philip Graham (2008) in his recent large-scale biography as being key to the 'gaps' in our knowledge of Isaacs and her practices. His work and a number of smaller articles in academic journals have however, mercifully, gone some way to righting this prevailing wrong; nevertheless, she is still under-represented in many discussions pertaining to progressivism. Her place in this narrative, however, is assured due both to the pioneering nature of her findings which impacted upon our views of childhood and to the remarkable institution in which these findings were generated, notably the Malting House School.

It may appear odd why the Malting House should be not considered in the next chapter and the wider context of the British Education Fellowship, particularly, given Isaacs' own status within that group and the reputation which the school gained for being at the forefront of the progressive school movement. Unquestionably, the Malting House shared some of its contemporaries' characteristics; it was a play-pen of the liberal intelligentsia and was run, as shall be examined, along very progressive lines with children being allowed to play and roam free in an environment as closely shaped to the natural world as is possible to imagine. Nonetheless, whereas the focus of many of the schools in the Fellowship – and indeed, many progressive schools, more generally – was upon allowing children to be, to a greater or lesser extent, concerned with nothing but their own activities, the Malting House sought to combine this with detailing accurate records and transcriptions of the daily lives of the pupils so as to aid Isaacs in formulating her own theories of child development and learning. In that respect, it was more closely aligned to the earlier work done by Granville Stanley Hall in his 'laboratory' school.

Isaacs' meticulous observations and subsequent reflections led to two substantial publications – *Intellectual Growth in Young Children* (1930) and *Social Development in Young Children* (1933) – which Willem Van de Eycken (1969) has rightly referred to as 'the high water mark in the literature of child development in Britain' (Van de Eycken 1969: 183). Although their dry and difficult style reflects the academic audiences for whom they were intended, these works are still of huge substance today and they are notable for their combination of observational data and Isaacs' analysis of that data on developmental and psychoanalytic lines designed to indicate directions for further study. Although some of their aspects may have been superseded and there remains quaintness to much of the writing, these books were central in changing prevailing attitudes towards children, particularly among the teaching profession whose colleges and training departments of education increasingly introduced psychology to their incumbent members at the expense of more esoteric disciplines such as philosophy. Many of Isaacs's fellow teachers and colleagues, notably Evelyn Lawrence and Dorothy Gardner, themselves became writers, teachers and advocates of progressive methods later in their careers – testament, if nothing else, to Isaacs' own persuasive and powerful personality.

While her books are clearly important in acting as vessels by which Isaacs could distil a distinct educational philosophy, what marks them out as 'progressive' are the conditions in which the formative data itself was gathered. Within the Malting House School, these were delineated by two key factors. First, there was 'an all-round lessening of the degree of inhibition of children's impulses' (Isaacs 1930: 12) and, second, there were few practical limits placed upon their behaviour. As Mary Jane Drummond (2000) so eloquently puts it, 'there was virtually no constraint on the child's verbal expression, their intellectual impulses, their expressions of infantile sexuality, their anal and urethral interests, their feelings, including anger and aggression, their views on everything that happened around them, and their questions' (Drummond, op. cit., 222). As important were the ways in which Isaacs and her trained staff responded to the children's impulses which led to them being active and generally exploratory within the confines of the school. Uniquely – nor unsurprisingly given its role as a 'laboratory' – there was much for the children to be involved with. Isaacs' vivid descriptions reveal an environment more akin to a children's adventure park than a school, with science laboratories, gardens full of animal menageries, aquariums, seesaws and climbing frames. Contemporary fussiness over health and safety would no doubt render many Malting House activities such as climbing on roofs and boiling mercury as too dangerous, yet Isaacs' accounts revel in the freedom afforded to the children and, crucially, the ways in which they were seen to develop from their activities.

When analysing Isaacs's utterances within these works – and indeed, her corpus as a whole – a number of central points become immediately noticeable. First is the way in which much of the child's behaviour is associated with, and ascribed to, functions of the body. We have already seen in the above quotation, a reference to 'anal and urethral' interests and Isaacs, in channelling the ideas of Freud, was indicating an important way in which the discipline of psychology came to recognize the significance of children's' nascent sexual activities and proclivities. Children's sexual behaviour and tendencies, even among many of the earlier progressives, had never before been considered as anything other than physical deviation, and in many examples, such as that of masturbation, it was actively discouraged. The idea of imbuing such behaviour with intellectual as well as physical significance and arguing that it formed part of a natural upbringing was one of the great contributions psychology was to make to the doctrines of progressivism. This was not of course total license; perhaps only A. S. Neill of Summerhill School would have permitted sexual relations among his pupils but Isaacs and her psychological allies doubtless allowed for a more sophisticated understanding of children's emotional and social development through paying lip-service to those features of a child's education that had only previously received tacit acknowledgement.

This point links closely to the second emergent feature of Isaacs' work which was her profound articulation of the breadth of children's range of understanding and enquiry. Much of her writing, especially that relating to her observations of children in the Malting House, was concerned with their play, their games and their liberated exploration, certainly as much as it was with their education. In many respects, those two things served as one and the same thing, for Isaacs held firm to the belief that play was an activity which was not only natural but also educative and was a means, if not *the* means, by which children learnt best to apprehend the natural world. Since Rousseau's *Emile*, play had long been part of the progressive discourse and, increasingly, an established activity within many schools but only with the works of Isaacs and, more importantly, Jean Piaget, was it receiving a form of scientific legitimacy destined to become part of every subsequent government curriculum and review.

Our commonplace assumptions today must not though cloud the significance of these early scientific experiments which were designed to place the child at the heart of their own learning experience. Crucial to this conception of play was the development of 'phantasy' which was Isaacs's particular term for expressing play's more imaginative aspects. Play for her allowed many of the child's emergent feelings and emotions to express themselves through external gesture and motion. It thus had a dual function – to enable interaction with the environment but also to allow children, crudely speaking, to convey their emotional states through a range of activity. In some respects, this reflected the contentions of Froebel, who had argued for a bridging of the gap between the child's internal and external worlds. Although, as we have seen, his articulation was more bound up with metaphysics and Idealism, the comparison remains valid particularly when one considers that permitting the externalizing of individual children's feelings – a precursor to which is surely a slackening of traditional forms of discipline – is an important strand of progressive thought.

Perhaps the two key prerequisites to being a 'successful' educator are love of children, or at least, recognition of the significance of childhood, and an understanding of how they think and act. From the existing testimonies in the historical record such as those of Dorothy Gardner (1969), we know Isaacs had both qualities in abundance and many of her writings such as her pseudonymous 'Ursula Wise' columns were vehicles by which she could deploy her particular affection for young people. Her fundamental beliefs were those in sympathy for what it was like to be a child and her works thus sought to locate its contentions from that perspective. As she writes in the introduction to *Social Development*: 'I was just as ready to record and to study the less attractive aspects of their behavior as the more pleasing. Whatever my aims and preferences as their educator might be' (Isaacs 1933: 19). The success of her writings, the devoted following she acquired and her increasingly enhanced reputation today are testament to her profound ability to articulate the experiences of young children and bestow upon their activity meanings which were both symbolic and spiritual.

In many ways, though, the success of the Malting House School could be seen as illusory as its environment was tailor-made for children's development with an abundance of activities, animals and attentive staff. It was clearly not the raw natural world in which the children of Pestalozzi and Froebel lived and learnt. Likewise, the parents of the children attending represented an amenable demographic; Cambridge then as now was an affluent area, ever receptive to advance and modernization and this was reflected in the forward-thinking nature of those (often university academics) who placed their children within the school's care. As W. A. C. Stewart (1972) points out, 'Isaacs recognized the significance of . . . Dewey's radical and most original practice' (Stewart 1972: 256) and there was something distinctly democratic and liberating about the sort of education provided in her school.

For most families in the country, however, such intellectual indulgence was an impossible luxury as most schools at the time had few of the advantages of the Malting House, being, as they were, relatively run down and ramshackle with few basic amenities. An awareness of this therefore led Isaacs to focus much of her critical attention upon the role of the family – and particularly, the nuclear family – in the rearing of the child. For her, this was as much a moral as an educational crusade; there is a prevalent strand of neo-Romanticism to Isaacs' writing which held fast to the belief that while children may not be as innocent and naïve as originally believed (psychology had proved otherwise!), their development was still vulnerable to potential abuse and deformation, and so, it was vital that parents were informed as to the 'right' sorts of ways to bring up the child. To once more quote Wooldrich:

> The issues at the centre of her thought – the proper upbringing of children, the relationship between health and sickness, the claims of individual will and cultural restraint – all belonged to the moral life; and she hoped to influence as well as to analyse personal conduct. (Wooldrich 1994: 128)

Isaacs' theories held that adults were crucial to mediating the social development of children, and so, her intention in popularizing psychology in her later works was, in part, to educate the population at large as to the importance of their actions and conduct on the developing minds of young children. The term 'super ego' was used to denote the uncompromising need for self-expression demonstrated by the children she had observed. As her biographer Lydia Smith (1985) explains, the adult's role was therefore to 'promote this social development by acting as the good parent, as the positive side of the super ego of the children' (Smith 1985: 107). Given the significance attached to this social development, Isaacs was insistent on nursery education being provided for children as an 'extension of the function of the home' (Isaacs 1952: 31) which could presumably mirror, and potentially compensate for, the work of the family.

In many respects, Isaacs' pronouncements on this subject stand at a critical juncture between, on the one hand, the nursery schools and child clinics of the McMillan sisters and, on the other, the importance of the nuclear family 'unit' that found expression with many in the decade of the 60s. The Plowden

Report, in particular, was to have much to say on the importance of triangulating family, school and community and the long-term value of seeking to involve and educate parents much more in relation to their child's education. While considered by some feminist authors as legitimizing a bourgeois pseudo-patriarchal concept of society in insisting on the vital role played by the mother, such a view fails to apprehend the very liberalizing tone inherent within much of Isaacs' writing. As was set down in practical terms within her school, Isaacs frequently cautioned against suppressing children's instincts and desires, including those of a sexual nature, and argued that to do so would be to risk permanently stunting their growth and development. Like Margaret McMillan, Isaacs' rhetoric often attenuated itself to the 'state of the nation' question, arguing powerfully that if her ideas were neglected, individual children would end up as delinquents rather than as 'useful' members of society, thereby adding to the burdens faced by a society languishing in the depression era.

There is much to Isaacs' progressive philosophy which has endured till date. In particular, as Jenny Willan (2011) has pointed out, her insistence on compulsory nursery education has found expression in recent government initiatives such as the Early Years Foundation Stage (EYFS) and Sure Start which aimed at improving the provision of pre-school education. Part of this involved educating parents on how to build strong parent-child interaction and promote good example. Likewise, her system of recording the behaviour of children in as systematic a way as possible has formed the basis of many subsequent pieces of academic research which, although using more sophisticated methods of recording than the humble stenographer, echo Isaacs' meticulous record keeping and insistence on accuracy. Although much of her output focused, almost exclusively, upon young children, her avowal on the educative value of play, the importance of education as a social as much as intellectual activity and the need to care physically for the child have become integral components of global educational practice. While Isaacs may not have been the first to put these ideas forward, she is perhaps the most shining example as to how progressive practice, psychology and scientific experiment could work together and elaborate a sophisticated educational philosophy underscored by empirically deduced scientific principles.

The European systems – Decroly, Montessori and Steiner

Although the focus of the chapter thus far has been solely Anglo-American, that is to give a distorted picture of events. In truth, the growth of educational psychology, theory and its applications to progressivism owed as much to developments on the continent of Europe where the research of two particular Frenchmen, Edouard Seguin and Jean Marc Gaspard Itard, into mental defects proved particularly significant to those interested in human and, specifically, child development. Their hugely significant work with the mentally disabled and the stunting of their learning capacities was to combine itself with the more traditional Romantic notions of tactility and sensibility to the environment to lead some to begin to formulate what some commentators have called theories of 'scientific pedagogy'. Although never formally adopted as a label by any particular group of individuals, this catch-all term is beneficial to historians as it describes educational philosophies which attempted to bring together both the increasing intellectual understanding of the workings of the mind and ways in which these could manifest and evolve within particular educational settings. In particular, it was an enhanced knowledge of children's motor and cognitive skills which led to re-evaluations of both the expectations and the abilities of children in the classroom. Such theories came to enshrine a belief that children learnt best from direct experience of acting upon the 'real' world, in both its literal and representational form.

Given that much of the pioneering work on retardation involved patients' feelings, emotional developments were seen as equally important as the intellectual. The discipline of psychology was increasingly demonstrating that emotions were not capable of simply being controlled by a teacher and displayed or retracted as appropriate. It was instead becoming all too clear that emotions were infinitely more complex and multilayered than had previously been imagined. They also represented more than just a simple externalizing of immediate feelings of anger, happiness, pleasure and the like. Emotions and behaviour were tied as much to the child's inner and spiritual nature, and so, they were encouraged to be expressed through what Abraham Maslow was to later refer to as 'humanistic psychology' – his way of defining the consciousness of an individual's biological makeup. Through these advances, it was now therefore more and more a part of the educator's role to provide a suitable environment where this was achievable. We have seen in the discussion on Susan Isaacs how this took place in the Malting House School and was referred to by her as 'phantasy', yet such ideas were really part of a much broader and (in relation to Isaacs) initially much earlier framework of educational theory developing in Europe. As proof of this, across the continent institutes were founded – notably in Leipzig, Antwerp and Geneva – and they were dedicated to the exploration of these principles, which reflected the residual *fin de siecle* concerns with interpreting and understanding the depth of human beings' inner psyches.

Such developments were apt, for this was, in the sociologist Ellen Key's (1900) famous phrase, the dawning of the 'century of the child', with psychological developments and concerns allowing for a much greater understanding of emergent cognitive and spiritual pathways. Holistic philosophies of this type encouraged respect and reverence for both the child and its beliefs, and in Maria Montessori (1870–1952), Ovide Decroly (1871–1932) and Rudolf Steiner (1861–1925), we find three personages who best embodied this transition into the modern preoccupation with what one may loosely call, in the broadest sense of that term, 'child care'. All three were at the forefront of a revolution in education which, for progressivism, was vital as it legitimized a move away from older, established educational beliefs which held that children were to be instructed in values which adults and society decreed as necessary, and towards a system which was driven by the child's auto-education and which legislated much more for children's individual, self-directed growth and progress.

For those even at least only partially familiar with the subject, two of these names (Steiner and Montessori) will be recognizable for their educational 'brand' which, to this day, continues to educate huge numbers of children worldwide in schools devoted to paying lip-service to their particular pedagogic systems. As a consequence of this, there is an enormous body of scholarship (alongside their own copious writings) relating to these two figures which considers every conceivable aspect of their thought. While the present narrative will engage only perfunctorily with certain key ideas, and it would be disingenuous to claim that their precepts will be treated here with any novelty, the reader is encouraged to seek out this literature (much of which is listed in the bibliography) in order to better gauge the importance of these concepts for the development of the progressive educational tradition. Nor should we forget the Belgian Decroly who, while today somewhat overshadowed, in his own lifetime acquired hero status, a worldwide reputation and a legacy which only very recently found him placed in the top 100 most influential educationalists of all time.

It is certainly an unlikely triumvirate – Steiner, the flamboyant Austrian attempting to feminize Teutonic manhood; Montessori, the first female engineer and doctor in Italy battling pugnaciously within a man's world and Decroly, the brilliant Belgian psychiatrist who was to probe the minds of children in his laboratory school. It may also appear incongruous to group them together in this fashion and, as shall be teased out, there were crucial differences in their educational viewpoints; yet, all recognized the importance of children as independent learners on paths of development which were capable of being clearly mapped as understanding of the many aspects of the mind became more sophisticated. It was perhaps no coincidence that both Montessori and Decroly had backgrounds in biology as its specific methodologies were to be central in the way that they were applied to the study of children, notably the processes by which the external environment interacted with the child's physiological and psychological growth. Steiner too was to argue strongly for understanding and verifying the spiritual through the ways and means of the rational scientist. Perhaps for this reason all placed an emphasis on combining the creative arts and aesthetics as tools by which to develop intellectual faculties while socialization of their children was encouraged through mixed-age groupings and open play areas.

Above all, though, went the recognition of the need to adapt education and schooling to particular stages of individual human development which accorded with the changing perceptions of childhood, driven in part by scientific advances. In all three thinkers, this is perhaps the strongest area of correlation. Steiner's work, in particular, seems a forerunner of much of Piaget's later suppositions. His Waldorf education system[11] was devised upon an approach which recognized distinct phases of intellectual growth ranging from the basic sensory at a young age to the abstract during adolescence, with the emotional and the artistic emerging somewhere in between. Likewise, the Montessori-designed apparatus and materials were considered sequential with children moving onto different sets in different classrooms as they got older and their motor and sensory skills became more advanced.

Alongside intellectual advances were emerging changing conceptions of the physical status of the child; as was being revealed by the work of the McMillan sisters in England, respect for the sanctity and wellbeing of the child was becoming ever more paramount. It was perhaps no coincidence that much of their work drew heavily, like that of Montessori, upon the research of the French physician Eduard Seguin; not only were his investigations into the handicapped providing greater understanding of the human mind and its applications, but it was also fostering a more tolerant and inclusive response to the full range of human conditions.

One way by which such a response manifested was in the particular 'systems' designed to allow for the growing child's development. The Montessori Method is perhaps the most well known of these, and in the famous aforementioned apparatus which was an integral part of her educational framework, she developed a set of objects (apparatus) and tasks which enabled the child to act very directly upon individual aspects of the real world. As each stage of the apparatus was completed and the educational outcome achieved, the child was allowed to progress to the next. The parallels with Froebel and his 'Gifts' should be apparent and it is perhaps unsurprising why the philosopher of education Jane Roland Martin (1990) has inferred the neo-Romantic aspects of Montessori's work, an observation evidenced by her deeply imbued love of children as to any intellectual preoccupation.

Today, the globalized nature of the Montessori name and franchise and its immense popularity have tended to obscure its very specific historical origins and the derivations of its influence. In that respect, the work of her near contemporary Decroly has tended to be relegated to being that of a 'prop', mentioned only as a member of the supporting cast whose research merely contributed to the inhering achievement of 'La Dolteressa'. In part, this has been down to the relative paucity of English language scholarship; many of the best books, papers and articles on Decroly continue to be in French and difficult to access for the English reader. Although, as Angelo Van Gorp (2006) points out, there has been from some quarters a quiet canonization of Decroly, overall, it seems his global profile today is negatively out of all proportion to the importance of his thinking and the manner in which he pre-dated many of Montessori's key principles. Perhaps unsurprisingly, an exception to this has been his native Belgium where even today 'Decroly schools' and scholastic programmes maintain a high reputation and level of popularity.

'Learning for life' might be an appropriate epithet for Decroly's educational philosophy and it was this which drew the American educator John Dewey into his orbit. Whereas Dewey's interpretation of the term 'life', however, was to be one which was more sociopolitical, Decroly's understanding was biological and driven by the nascent science of child psychology. Part of this 'education for life' process therefore involved preparing the child, as Van Gorp points out, for the modern age 'characterized by industrialization, urbanization, impoverishment, disease and poor hygiene' (Van Gorp, 2006: 42). In its way this was a more visceral appreciation of the real world than the quasi-utopias concocted by other theorists. It was in preparation for such realties that Decroly believed children would encounter increasingly challenging situations, adapt themselves and thereby cognitively develop by solving each stage as it came along.

There was nothing especially doctrinal about Decroly's philosophy; if anything, his progressivism sprung from recognizing the organic needs of the growing child and the acute interrelationship between organisms and their environment. While this sounds rudimentarily scientific, it was very important within the context of education as the idea that children sought this interrelation with their peers meant that they themselves – without recourse to adults – would naturally form groups and worlds of activity independent of external influence. The classroom for Decroly, thus, became the 'world' whereby children could enact these broad biological needs. One can easily apprehend therefore why he believed that everything, including resources, materials and ideologies, should be directed towards the need of the child.

The belief that more state resources should be ploughed into education chimed with the social agenda which lay at the heart of both Decroly's and Montessori's educational viewpoints. This was of particular importance for the former as Belgium had yet to make education compulsory, and so, his writings can be seen as coming at a crucial time in his countries' history where various educational agendas were up for tender. Although not as pronounced as Dewey's programme (which will be explored in a later chapter and recognized as more inherently national in character), it was still seen as important that within liberal democratic societies, not only that the child had rights but that these rights derived from the opportunity to learn spontaneously. This spontaneity was to derive from the child's inherent interest in their learning, hence the need for the school to provide a curriculum that was both constructive and engaging. For Montessori, this emerged through the apparatus which was tailored towards the child's innate need to be tactile and practical with its native environment. Likewise, Decroly, although eschewing physical devices within the school, shared Montessori's concern with understanding the holistic nature of the child and argued that both personality and character formed a 'psychic whole' (Decroly, 1927). It was the school's job to ensure that these were developed together so as not to fragment the rounded business of education. This was evidenced by the curriculum plans Decroly advocated, which were designed to disdain existing systems of learning. According to Francine Dubreucq, children 'would freely choose what subjects to study. Adults would only show them practically useful, technical operations, according to their stages of development. Curriculum planning was thus transferred to the children themselves' (Dubreucq 1993: 263).

It would be fallacious to conjoin Montessori and Decroly inseparably together as there are evident differences in their educational viewpoints. In particular, Decroly's stress upon 'learning through living' (Decroly, cited in Clarepede, 1925, xxvi) which advocated schools being set in natural surroundings so that children could observe the processes of nature and the importance of food and shelter contrasts with Montessori's less organic scholastic rigidity as espoused through her apparatus. Similarly, some, such as Amelie Hamaide (1925), have argued that Montessori's work was unoriginal, artificial and insufficiently global in outlook. Such critiques, which have served to emphasize these differences, have tended though to emerge from those with vested interests in supporting one group over another. Hamaide, as a case in point, was one of Decroly's assistants and taught at his Ermitage School, and so, their desire to appropriate individuality, while understandable, fails to address common points of origin for these differences which are perhaps those of degree and not of kind. Clearly, both thinkers emerged from a scientific background (they were doctors by training) and they were responding directly to a common body of knowledge (Seguin and Jean Gaspard Itard) which took mental development as its starting point.

In many ways, the work of Steiner seems more closely aligned with that of Friedrich Froebel and the kindergarten movement. This is reflected in the more ethereal nature and terminology Steiner's education and its associated writings seem to put forward. In summarizing its distinguishing features, for example, L. Francis Edmunds (1987) argues that it 'embraces a new view of the whole life, in particular, of the human being in his threefold nature of body, soul and spirit, and therefore, also of the successive phases of childhood leading on to adulthood' (Edmunds 1987: 7). This is an important point for it serves to illustrate how, like Montessori, Steiner saw the sequential development of the child as pivotal to his educational view, and thus, there was an intrinsic need for the school and teacher to adapt themselves to the appropriate stage of that development. Following that precept childhood was thus seen as 'the shaping of the instrument for the life of the adult' (Ibid., 13), and so, Steiner's education can be seen as a 'stage' model which sought to develop and promote children onto the path of responsible adulthood.

Nevertheless, although Steiner, like Decroly and Montessori, trained initially in mathematics and the sciences, he afforded a greater prominence in his copious writings to the notions of spirituality and the development of the creative and imaginative child. He argued powerfully for the need for human beings to bring their creative powers to greater fulfilment and for an education that served to free the human spirit and its capacity for emotional empathy. As Roy Wilkinson (1996) points out in his sympathetic treatment, Steiner's education is one which is dedicated to the development of the whole individual (and the range of their faculties) rather than the merely intellectual. Presupposing an assumption of the Divine in nature, much of the Waldorf system of education therefore relies on an understanding that there exists both a physical and a spiritual world which are in a constant state of temporal flux. Eliciting the child's search for the 'self' in the context of this physical world is therefore one of the primary aims of the Steiner school.

Given Steiner's preoccupations, it is possible to see why he has become such a revered figure, particularly among those whose belief systems are more finely attuned to the notions of spirituality – Buddhists, New Age followers and the like.[12] Many of his advocates similarly write extensively about the possibility of utilizing his ideas to solve global problems and he is seen as a pseudo-guru whose 'children' and their more developed level of spiritual awareness are at the vanguard of movements towards world peace and harmony. While, on occasion, his writings betray the quirkier side of such viewpoints – his notion that human civilizations pass through epochs, including Atlantis, has not stood the test of time well – there is much that feels instinctively 'progressive' to his educational writings. In particular, his belief that 'conventional education stifled spiritual growth and led to [the] dead abstract lives and stunted lives' (Lachman 2007: 196) resonates with those who seek to encourage children's creativity and outward expression. Like the earlier Romantics, Steiner believed that the developed spirit could serve to alter the course of the world for the better and he posited the celebration of life through festivals and play.

However, in the context of this chapter, one must be wary of juxtaposing Steiner's spiritualism with the more obviously scientific philosophies of his near contemporaries. It must be remembered that the term 'spiritual science' is frequently one associated with the Steiner-created philosophy of 'anthroposophy' and this seemingly oxymoronic epithet serves to capture the complex ways in which Steiner and his disciples attempted to synthesize the natural sciences' unlocking of the secrets of nature with the development of a higher consciousness. This carries echoes of the earlier Idealist search for *Naturphilosophie* and it is unsurprising to find that the works of Goethe were a key intellectual fixation for Steiner. Much of his life was therefore concerned with developing a philosophy which could adequately combat the poisonous (as he saw them) effects of rampant materialism and, after that fashion, his work has significant social, ethical and religious implications. It is perhaps these which distinguish his achievement from many other progressives; although education was central to his success, and it is his pedagogic writings which are most widely read today, his work concerns itself with attempting to understand the development of the thought, feeling and will of man and the ways in which his growth can lead to a more harmonious configuration of society. This was perhaps an inverse form of psychology as it attempted to probe the spiritual rather than the explicitly cognitive and sought to locate individual development in the context of more macrocosmic concerns. While therefore it would be a mistake to label him a 'child psychologist', his theories of the spiritual and emotional development of the child had much to recommend them to the scientific habit of mind, even if these were overlain with more intrinsically sacred aspects.

The legacy of psychology

If testament were needed as to the lasting impact that psychology has had in relation to progressivism, then one need look no further than the truly global spread of both the Montessori and Steiner schools. According to recent figures, there are over 1,000 Steiner schools across the world, while an enormous 20,000 schools claim some allegiance to the principles of Montessori. Both have thriving societies dedicated to their names which in themselves have become educational 'brands' with even Montessori's apparatus available to buy commercially on the internet! In part, this huge success can be attributed to the efforts made by their champions to actively spread the gospel. Montessori's speaking tours were legendarily well attended by practising teachers and she was frequently feted by the political establishment which perhaps failed to recognize in her benign presence any revolutionary ardor. Equally, John Paull (2011) has cited the importance of Steiner's lectures at Oxford University as being a foundation stone for the British Steiner movement, the enormous impact of which upon the New Education Fellowship will be explored in the next chapter. Like Friederich Froebel and Robert Owen from earlier generations – both of whom in their own way propagated distinct educational 'systems' – Montessori and Steiner (and, to a lesser extent, Decroly) have become deified, acquiring saint-like status and a band of disciples committed to exporting their educational gospel.

Today, however, few of the establishments carrying a progressive name look, at least externally, much different to more conventional schools and, in some cases, these similarities may extend to the classrooms and curricula being put forward inside. Increasingly, ideologies which once stood outside of the mainstream and were considered forward-looking and even subversive are now being integrated within state education systems through either partial or complete governmental funding or else working to the same national testing frameworks as those schools in the 'mainstream'. Undoubtedly, this transition reflects developments in the sciences; aspects of what was once taken as scientific and pedagogic innovation now constitutes orthodoxy and, as Ellen Key prophetically made it clear, our age has been one in which the 'rights' and 'welfare' of the child which were so dear to past progressives have been enshrined in belief and law, through our residual clinging to the romantic view of childhood 'innocence'.

In another respect, though, the adaptation and, in some cases, downright dilution of the original ideas can be strongly attributed to a perennial difficulty facing the historian of education when exploring ideological transmission and this is the problem associated in interpreting texts whose ideas are complex, ethereal and open to multiple-readings.[13] Although this is often considered more challenging with texts written further back in time where authorial intention is more problematic to discern and language more difficult to comprehend, the writings of Steiner and Montessori which combine technical ideas, hypotheses and jargon with an aesthetic appreciation of the child pose unique sets of challenges. Typically, such works liken the quasi-psychological scientific 'method' to educational 'truth', which has often led to staunch dogmatism on the part of those adherents willing to believe wholeheartedly in the educational philosophy espoused and a reification of the ideology to the status of a religion. Given that such theories rest on science, which through its methodologies of verification and falsification ascertains to a condition of 'truth', it is seen as illogical to reject any conclusions postulated in relation to cognitive development, behaviour and systems of education arising from these suppositions. How can 'truth' be wrong? Such intransigence perhaps offers an explanation as to why these ideologies, in particular, have proven so resilient over time.

However, in the last 50 years or so, the foundational psychological principles upon which such ideas rested have become widely debated, contested and, in some quarters, unfashionable. Competing theories, discourses and ideological priorities have served to call into question what were once seen as self-evident truths with, as earlier mentioned, even retrograde ideas concerning intelligence becoming resurrected. The case of the splits in the Montessori movement in the latter half of the twentieth century serves to illustrate this fragility. Although in her lifetime a controlling and dominant personality adopting a 'hands on' and autocratic approach to her education programme, upon her death, fractures emerged between those who took her pronouncements and those of her son and heir apparent Mario, as being the well-spring from which all followers must draw and those instead more willing to adapt her ideas to the emergent context of the twentieth century. The matter came to a head over the business of teachers' certification; in her lifetime, Montessori had given her blessing to the Association Montessori Internationale (founded in 1929 and forever known as the AMI) to be the sole body invested with the power to recognize those qualified as Montessori teachers. Through a complex, lingering (and some would say, hollow) legal battle, however, the American courts decreed that the Montessori name and method was generic and did not represent a particular 'product' which was a trademark of the immediate Montessori family. This decision had a number of important ramifications. In the short term, it opened the flood gates for other practitioners to compete over the use of her system. In 1960, for example, the American Montessori Society (AMS) was founded under the leadership of Nancy Rambuschon on the grounds that the existing Montessori ideology had failed to adapt itself to the American education system. In particular, the AMI advocated using the Montessori Method exactly as laid down in her key published works, notably *The Montessori Method* (1912) which, for many forward-thinking American teachers, was perceived as too restricting as it did not allow the use of any form of external materials in the context of class teaching.

More pertinently, the decision to 'de-corporatize' the Montessori name illustrated the way in which psychological models and theories have had to diversify and adapt themselves in order to maintain their currency in the contemporary context. Steiner schools, for example, while driven by the moral message of their founder, often explicitly jettison some of the more religious aspects of his work, thereby recognizing the more modern secularized climate, which does not see a religious message as a prerequisite for an ethically sound and spiritually whole education. Often, these schools themselves betray evidence of great variety in their location and practices and, with the British Coalition (2010–) government's 'free schools' policy effectively empowering local interest groups with the ability to set up schools if they so wish, 'Steiner education is on the brink of a significant expansion' (quoted in *The Guardian*, 25 May 2012). Montessori schools seem to be following suit; in a brilliant defence of her ideas, the psychologist Angeline Lillard (2005) recognizes the fundamental critiques of progressive education, yet still mounts a vibrant justification for the continued importance of Montessori education today. Promisingly, she argues stringently that the Montessori Method offers a credible alternative to traditional systems of schooling. Boldly, she states that 'The [state] education system should instead draw on scientific study of how children learn' (Lillard 2005: 36) and takes to task those taking their historical cue from W. H. Kilpatrick who have attempted to disparage the science and social presumptions behind Montessori's pioneering work. Clearly, hers is an education attenuated for the twenty first century!

Given the proximity that Steiner, Montessori and Decroly schools now have to the mainstream and, in some cases, how remarkably similar are their practices, it is easy to lose sight of how radical and innovating such ideas actually were at the point of their ideological conception. Each thinker appropriated a particular view of childhood – Decroly the biological, Montessori the cognitive and Steiner the spiritual – which had at its heart, reverence for the child and an inbuilt tacit acceptance for the choices they made. All, in addition, were underpinned by nascent psychological precepts which sought to better understand the developing mind of the child and the key stages it went through on the way to adulthood. While psychology today may concern itself with individual difference through the passing of examinations and their approximations to a societal norm (which, in itself, determines grading), these thinkers equated difference with diversity and as something to be celebrated. While their theories may not sit comfortably with everybody, in that respect, perhaps they still have something to teach us.

Notes

1 Jensen's seminal 1969 article, 'How Much can we Boost IQ and Scholastic Achievement?', published in the *Harvard Educational Review* became one of the most widely cited and debated pieces in the history of intelligence

testing, not least for its suggestion that the discrepancies in IQ between various races was attributable to genetic differences.

2   The advert to which Susan Isaacs responded was written by the school's founder Geoffrey Pike and called explicitly for an educated young woman to 'conduct . . . a piece of scientific work and research'.

3   Hall's understanding of the adolescent period was that it constituted a period of *sturm und drang* (Trans: 'storm and stress'), characterized by emotional turbulence, angst, depth of feeling and the search for a leader. Its characteristics accorded with many of those of protagonists found in the literature of Goethe and Schiller.

4   As an example, the first edition of the *British Journal of Psychology* appeared in 1904 with its educational counterpart emerging in 1931. Both continue to this day.

5   To cite three pertinent British examples – the death penalty was suspended in 1965, homosexuality was decriminalized in 1967 while, in the same year, abortion was made legal for women.

6   The Plowden Report is comprised of two volumes. The first volume (556 pages) is the Report itself while the second (633 pages) contains the research and surveys which made it possible.

7   The ORACLE (Observational Research and Classroom Learning Evaluation) project conducted between 1975 and 1980 was one of the largest funded studies into teaching and learning in the primary classroom.

8   Having been taken over in 1974 by two left wing teachers, Terry Ellis and Brian Haddow, the William Tyndale School became, briefly, a *cause celebre* for its promulgation of extreme progressive practices and political extremism. It was only after parents began withdrawing their children that its fate was decided.

9   The 'Clackmannanshire' experiment pioneered from 1997 suggested that, in the teaching of phonics, the synthetic (as opposed to the analytic) method worked better in improving reading levels. Critics have argued that it is mechanistic and, more importantly, may not suit all reading styles.

10   Accusations regarding the falsification of data stem from both Burt's official biographer Leslie Hearnshaw and various subsequent articles arguing that he fabricated elements of his research and even invented collaborators. Although defended by some, including Arthur Jensen, who argued that Burt's research findings are nevertheless accurate, the truth is still unknown and the scandal undoubtedly contributed more generally to the tarnishing of the discipline of mental measurement.

11   This name derives from the Waldorf-Astoria cigarette company in Stuttgart, the employees of which were the first to send their children to a Steiner school in 1919.

12   Steiner's most recent biographer Gary Lachman (himself a former rock musician in the band Blondie) memorably recounts his conversion to Steiner while working in a Los Angeles New Age bookshop.

13   As will be shown, this has proven particularly problematic in the key works of John Dewey.

Key reading

Adrian Wooldrich, *Measuring the Mind: Education and Psychology in England, c.1860-c.1990* (Cambridge: Cambridge University Press, 1994).

Maria Montessori, *The Montessori Method: Scientific Pedagogy as Applied to Child Education in 'the Children's Houses',* translated from the Italian by Anne E. George, with an introduction by Professor Henry W. Holmes (London: William Heinemann, 1912).

Susan Isaacs, *Intellectual Growth in Young Children* (London: Routledge & Kegan Paul, 1930).

Susan Isaacs, *Social Development in Young Children* (London: Routledge & Kegan Paul, 1933).

Further reading

Philip Graham, *Susan Isaacs: A Life Freeing the Minds of Children* (United Kingdom: Karnac Books, 2008).

L. Francis Edmunds, *Rudolf Steiner Education: The Waldorf School* (London: Rudolf Steiner Press, 1987).

Plowden Report, *Report of the Central Advisory Council For Education (England) into Primary Education in England* (London: HMSO, 1967).

5

Democracy: The New Education Fellowship

Introduction

Britain has long been a prisoner of its own history, and if anything can be identified as being at the root of this incarceration, it is, as George Orwell famously pointed out, *class*. The continuing British fascination with class has both amused and envied in equal measure. Evidence abounds of other nations consciously (and even unconsciously) aping its eccentricities and quirks through accent, dress, affectation and manner while, conversely, there have been those who have regarded the class obsession with disdain – at best an idiosyncratic trait of a somewhat pompous people whose seeming geographical insignificance was disproportionate to the global weight she was allowed to distribute and carry through her Empire.

Whatever the contemporaneous perceptions, however, and regardless of the truth and veracity of such claims, what is without question are the ways in which the long-standing nationwide attachment to a rigid class system with its inbuilt deference to symbolism and ritual was used by many to legitimate rabid inequality. *Laissez faire*, in every sense, prevailed. To do otherwise was, for some, to disrupt the natural order and harmony as laid down by God. Napoleon pithily, and probably apocryphally, sneered that England was a nation of shopkeepers and his jibe, while misplaced within its context, served as an appropriate metaphor for the then national character – avuncular and welcoming, yet equally parochial, plodding and reserved. Britain simply did not 'do' revolution, upheaval and turmoil; even in 1848 when the rest of Europe was on the brink of turning towards something infinitely more glorious and enlightened, she remained unaffected, save for the last damp flings of the

Chartist movement. Deference, stoicism and a healthy streak of working-class conservatism were very much in the blood.

Change in Britain therefore was very slow; a series of Reform Bills in 1832, 1867 and 1885 provided welcome progress but by the beginning of the twentieth century, women and, still, a significant number of men (those without property), were disenfranchised, dislocated and cast adrift from having any stake in the country. It was to take a global conflict in the form of the First World War to go some way towards righting this particular wrong with recognition on the part of policymakers – acquiescing to embody the national conscience – of individual sacrifice and heroism. With the subsequent promise of a 'Land Fit for Heroes', nascent welfare reforms and the continuing pressure of the various suffragette and suffragist societies, one can therefore identify the first two decades of the twentieth century as being those in which modern, recognizable social and political structures emerged.

These events mirrored trends happening at a more global level. Undoubtedly, this was an era of great uncertainty – a point implied by the historian Eric Hobsbawm who chose to title his history of the modern period *The Age of Extremes* (1994). International cooperation was therefore seen as a mechanism by which potential conflicts could be nipped in the bud, disagreements smoothed over and economies restored through reciprocal arrangements regarding trade and commerce. As a consequence, the League of Nations, whose remit was pan-global, was set up in 1919 and a succession of treaties and pacts held true to the ideals of non-aggression and diplomacy.[1]

These notions of expanding international democracy and, particularly, the increasing emphasis upon international collaboration were equally manifest through the means of education, specifically via the organization known as the New Education Fellowship. Although, as we shall see, a catch-all term which covered an assorted array of practitioners, thinkers, educators and classroom practices, its importance as a unifying body for progressive educators across the globe to exchange ideas and engage in ideological and pedagogical debates cannot be overstated. Although 'membership' was free and open to all, this was not an informal, peripatetic group; there were designated and formalized channels in place for contact and communication, of which the most important was the *New Era* journal. Its very title reflected much of the spirit in which the Fellowship acted for their pioneering ethos and was designed to be at once forward-looking, progressive and impelled by visions of global utopia.

As Kevin Brehony (2004) has also shown, great importance was attached to the periodic conferences hosted under the New Education Fellowship umbrella during the 1920s until the eve of the Second World War. The historian R. J. W. Selleck states how such gatherings 'became important means for the interchange of ideas and gave prestige and solidarity to the progressive cause' (Selleck 1972: 46). In the same way, then, that democracy and democratic patterns of thinking were becoming engrained into more wider aspects of society and political channels, so was that being replicated within the context of education with, particularly, a new breed of progressive educators and their writings consciously drawing upon the egalitarian aspects of its past historical narrative to designate a new vision of child-centred education for a changing world.

The New Education Fellowship

When discussing the New Education Fellowship as a collective entity, one should be wary of divorcing it from contemporary thinkers discussed elsewhere; Montessori, for example, was a key figure within the group and her ideas provoked much debate as, perhaps unsurprisingly, did the pronouncements further afield of John Dewey. Likewise, the work done in England by Susan Isaacs and her psychological colleagues was seen as particularly important and the Malting House School would have to be considered one of the flagship Fellowship establishments. As one example of this overlap, it was perhaps no coincidence that the birth and initial promotion of the Association Montessori Internationale (the global society devoted to promoting Montessori's ideas) took place as part of the Fifth International Conference of the New Education Fellowship. This fact should also serve to illustrate that this was a time of great ideological and fraternal fluidity in which different clusters of thinkers migrated, overlapped and entered, on occasion, into onerous and heated debates out of all proportion to the minutiae and details of the educational doctrine and policy which they were discussing. Despite these occasional deviations, however, much of this antagonism was contained under the umbrella of the Fellowship, one of whose major concerns was the spread of, at a general level, progressive ideas which were, more specifically, underpinned by notions of democracy in relation both to the structure of the school and the freedoms afforded to the individuals within them.

The spider at the centre of this particular web was the remarkable figure of Beatrice Ensor who, as the founder and first editor of the *New Era*, was to play a pivotal role both in advancing the international agenda and quoracy of the Fellowship and also through her ceaseless championing of radical education more generally. Counting among her close friends the educational firebrand A. S. Neill, the psychologist Carl Jung and the novelist H. G. Wells, she served to bring together those in a range of disparate fields and disciplines, thereby giving an intellectual hegemonic legitimacy to the fount of emergent progressive ideas.[2] This was important as it helped wed education and educational strategies to political, literary, scientific and philosophical aspirations built upon creating a 'better world'. In its own way, this carried with it an element of novelty; although educators like Robert Owen had previously talked of building new societies, social experiments of the sort carried out in his New Lanark settlement tended to be confined to the microcosmic level of the individual village. Likewise, that ultimate revolutionary Karl Marx had devoted less than a couple of sentences in his copious writings to the role that education should play in his communist utopia. It is even more unlikely he ever ruminated to any substantial degree on the ways in which young children were to learn.

What makes this period so vital therefore was the way in which many progressive educators articulated political positions often couched in the discourse of 'advancement' in which schooling was to play a major role. As we shall see, this did not always translate into facilitating a child's engagement with the wider world – some of the Fellowship schools were positively insular in outlook – yet undoubtedly their progenitors were convinced that their products would go out and change society for the better. A sense of the wide-ranging conception Ensor held of her role is evidenced by her address to the 1937 International New Education Fellowship Conference in Australia:

> The Fellowship has purposefully refrained from formulating any dogma in the field of education. It has not even urged the advisability of any particular form of school room procedure, recognizing that new education is primarily a thing of spirit, the fruits of which are new relationships between child and teacher, and between child and child, new attitudes towards learning, towards authority, and one might also say between life itself. (Ensor 1938: 97)

Such rhetoric should perhaps clarify why, as Kevin Manton (2001) has so brilliantly described, there were close ideological links between the doctrines of socialism and late nineteenth-century thinkers from whom the Fellowship was to draw inspiration. The poets and social thinkers Edward Carpenter and William Morris and the political reformer Sidney Webb are excellent examples of intellectuals whose utopian socialist visions were driven by an ideological (though not in any sense carefully thought out) commitment to the role education should play in the liberation of young minds. Carpenter, as a case in point, argued powerfully that the knowledge acquired by pupils through books bore little physical and philosophical resemblance to the world at large and schools were therefore contributing to the corrupting and injurious effects of modern civilization. As Manton puts it, 'While socialists were not necessarily critical of [the] teachers for implementing the curriculum allotted to them, this view of knowledge and the proposed style of education it engendered set out a whole new paradigm of both curriculum and methodology . . .' (Manton 2001: 57).

Written into the language of socialism was the need for education to not reinforce existing social structures but instead to seek to overturn and replace them with, if possible, commensurate changes in pedagogic practice. Why should any systems which reinforced social inequality be maintained if they were complicit in this unequal provision? It is important therefore to be aware that many of those subsequently working under the auspices of the Fellowship naturally gravitated ideologically to the left and one can certainly identify it as a movement which broadly opposed more conservative notions of rote learning and memorization.

It was not always, of course, the case that there was exclusive support from the left for progressive educational doctrines. In seeking to combat the lack of opportunity afforded to the working class to gain a good education, some socialists preferred instead to focus upon reforming existing bureaucratic structures and amending precipitous legislation rather than agitating for any innovative methods of teaching. Such fights were frequently undertaken in the parliamentary ring through attempting to democratize control of school boards and, where possible, providing genuine equality of opportunity within existing structures through the increase in 'free places' at the expense of fees. Indeed, some on the left were actively hostile to any new-fangled science of child-centredness for they argued that it failed to provide working class children with the intellectual tools and abilities to compete with those who had the traditional advantages of money and networks of connections. 'Hard' facts and 'real' knowledge were thus preferred by some in order to fight and compete with those privileged children at their own game. Such ideological splits on the left were manifested in their fragmented opposition to the 1902 Education Bill which had been proposed by a Tory government and which sought to maintain a relatively conservative hegemony of both church and state. In explaining how 'the Fabians supported the act, the SDF [Social Democratic Federation] opposed it and the ILP [Independent Labour Party] were perhaps indifferent to it' (Ibid., 179), Manton once more captures something of the general confusion in relation to the differing points of view concerning education. Nevertheless, this fact should not disabuse us of the notion that the heartland of support for the New Education Fellowship was from those aligned with the political left who desired the more liberalizing effects progressive education could bring.

Origins and ideologies of the Fellowship

It is perhaps unnecessary here to recount in any great detail the internecine squabbling which led immediately up to the formation of the New Education Fellowship. To successfully uncover its origins, and to understand perhaps more accurately the ways in which it sought to incorporate emerging notions of democracy, it is better perhaps to locate it in relation to two longer term trends which had developed within the preceding years and which were to form the twin prongs upon which the organization was to rest. First, one can identify the influence of the Theosophist Fraternity, which drew as its inspiration from the work of Rudolf Steiner whose ideas have been traced already. Beatrice Ensor was the secretary to this particular group and, in fact, had started the *New Era* journal predominantly as a vehicle to export Steiner-inspired ideas related to spiritual growth. Furthermore, she, on behalf of the Society, had founded a school called St Christopher, dominated both by Theosophist ideals and by notions of self-government. The parochial nature of the Theosophist Fraternity – St Christopher was very much an English institution – meant though that it was soon subsumed within the more cosmopolitan outlook of the Fellowship. Strands of Steiner's thinking, however, continued to permeate many of the nascent practices of the emerging schools. We have seen the ways in which the Waldorf-Steiner schools spread globally[3] and this, coupled with Steiner's lecture tours and copious writings, ensured that he was to remain a point of ideological reference and interest for many working within progressive education at this particular time. The very term 'Fellowship' even carries with it mystical and spiritual connotations and the elevation of educational method to the status of a faith had much in common with the more otherworldly preoccupations of those devotees of Steiner.

More importantly for our purposes, however, and the second of the more significant strands to feed into the Fellowship, was the New Education Movement which was a term coined to describe the first British child-centred schools in the late nineteenth and early twentieth centuries. Once more, terminology can be problematic; the New Education Movement is referred to in some works, for example that of Robert Skidelsky (1969), as the New *School* Movement which, he posits, encompassed both Britain and Europe. Furthermore, he argues cogently for the spread of such progressive schools in three distinct phases; the first being at the turn of the century, the second in the period after the First World War and the third during the 1930s. Although an orderly way of considering the progressive school dissemination, this 'three stage' thesis does not allow, as we have mentioned before, for the inherent ideological and temporal untidiness that inevitably results when the historian attempts to delineate and pinpoint the origin and spread of ideas.

Nonetheless, although there may seem to be elements of terminological uncertainty within the literature, what many of these schools had in common was a concern for democracy. This did not just relate to democratic forms of self-government (although that was important) but also by being equitable through recourse to co-education and a co-curricula, by children cooperating through the work they undertook and by being allowed where possible to follow and pursue their own individualized interests. The most well known of these schools, which we will mention later, were Abbotsholme (founded in 1889 by Cecil Reddie), Bedales (founded in 1893 by J. H. Badley), Gordonstoun (founded in 1934 by Kurt Hahn) and Summerhill (initially founded in 1921 by A. S. Neill). These schools, while representative of the ideological thrust of the burgeoning interest in new educational ideas, were only the tip of the proverbial progressive iceberg. A cursory glance through the copious archives of the London Institute of Education, for example, reveals important collections relating to Lucy (Winnie) Nicolls and Isabel Fry, both of whom founded experimental schools based on the ideas of fraternity and brotherhood. Likewise, the American Homer Lane, recently subject to a fine (2005) biography by Judith Stinton, founded his school, the Little Commonwealth, in the English county of Dorset where pupils had 'joint responsibility for the regulation of their lives by the laws and judicial machinery organized and developed by themselves' (Lane 1928: 189). In fact, by 1922, the *New Era* was listing 23 such establishments, with some, such as the Russell's Beacon Hill and William Curry's Dartington Hall, yet to be founded.

Nor should a discussion of this type be solely confined to the narrow shores of England; there were many such institutions arising throughout Europe at the time, for example Salem School in Germany founded in 1920 and which exemplified the increasingly international nature of the Fellowship's membership and governance. While this pan-Continental spread is explicable in light of the advances made by Montessori, Steiner and Decroly in understanding the ways that children learnt and apprehended the world around them, it is also pertinent to remember that much was attributable to the exportation overseas of this peculiarly British 'phenomenon'. As the historians W. A. C. Stewart and W. P. McCann (1968) and W. F. Connell (1980) have illustrated, the example of Cecil Reddie's Abbotsholme School provides a powerful exemplar of this ideological exchange. In this particular case, Reddie's ideas were brought to Germany by Hermann Lietz who established the *Landerziehungsheim* or country boarding schools with an emphasis placed upon arts and crafts and sports and far less upon the traditional patterns of rote learning and memorization. On occasion, these models worked the other way; the Scottish school Gordonstoun, for example, was founded by Lietz's friend Kurt Hahn and embodied a similar ethos of hard games playing and rugged masculinity.[4]

Interestingly, Lietz himself was, politically, on the right and, in the images and records we have of these Germanic country schools with their physical pursuits, gymnastics and drill, there clearly exists something distinctly Teutonic. Such 'back to the land' activities, the emphasis upon fitness and physical prowess and the enthusiasm by which young boys were encouraged to pursue games were later appropriated and invoked by the Nazi Party as one strand of their propaganda campaigns. In preferring to develop and emphasize the body at the expense of the mind, Lietz had unwittingly provided a pseudo-Nietzschen model which resonated with the Nazi's particular conception of the *volk* and its Aryan inhabitants. No better example could thus be drawn to show the overlapping complexities which exist in relation to progressivism (however loosely defined) and politics! Further to that, the inhabitants of such schools tended to be those children of the intelligentsia and the *avant garde* and not necessarily the artisan children who may have benefited most from the sorts of education being provided – a pattern that was generally to be replicated across both Europe and Britain. Indeed, as we shall see, many of the English progressive schools attracted wealthy parents as the education they offered was sold as a viable and more liberal alternative to the elite public schools (Eton, Harrow, Winchester and the like) whose harsh regimes were not perhaps to everyone's taste.

As well as locating the Fellowship and its democratic concerns geographically, it should also be conceptualized in terms of *time*. If one, for example, stretches to include the period leading up to the Second World War as Robert Skidelsky (1969) suggests, then a whole catalogue of 'minor' progressives emerge, who would each merit discussion on their own terms and within the contexts of their own schools.[5] While any detailed cataloguing is outside the remit and scope of this chapter, such awareness serves to indicate not merely the popularity that these new progressive ideas were gaining and the ways in which they were sustained over time but also the heterogeneity of the movement as a whole which was not limited to one area, time or place. Equally, recognizing the longitudinal dimension allows the historian the ability to trace the ways in which, ideologically, the character of the Fellowship schools changed over time. Two things, in particular, emerge which hint at these changes in character. The first is the gradual incorporation of a libertarian philosophy into the communal patterns of living. While the early schools were founded on a sense of community, only after the First World War did they start to give freer reign to the pupil's natural instincts which meant, in practical terms, leaving them alone to discover what interested them rather than imposing order upon the day and the curriculum. While this had been on the agenda of the early schools, there were subtle shifts in character to encourage the development of permissive legislation, of which Summerhill was perhaps the most obvious, although not perhaps the most characteristic, example.

The second shift in ethos came with the later progressive schools such as Gordonstoun which sought to conceive of education as being something 'not only outside the classroom but outside the school community itself, into the world of real problems' (Skidelsky 1969: 22). This chimes with much of the culture of the later Plowden Report (discussed in the previous chapter) which sought to triangulate education with the community and its overtones of social justice. Intrinsically, of course, such notions are not inherently progressive (and in many respects, Gordonstoun is, and was, condemnatory of 'soft' permissiveness) but in this particular context, they are noteworthy in demonstrating how 'democracy' came to be conceptualized not merely as embodied within classroom and school structures but as representing something more global and as an outside political agency.

Drawing, somewhat inevitably, upon the work of John Dewey, many of these later schools saw it as their duty to turn out pupils who were themselves imbued with a civic and community spirit and a willingness to serve. This would be down not merely to a sense of cultivated public obligation but also through the development of the imagination and character which the performance of such civic tasks inevitably entailed. As W. A. C. Stewart (1972) has pointed out, many of these schools tended to be somewhat serious places with such duties recognized as an intrinsic part of the curriculum. Likewise, although organized religion and its attendant values tended to be spurned, these were not locations of a moral free for all with little or no regard for the feelings of others. Indeed, it was hoped that educating boys and girls together and promoting co-education would *reduce* the possibility of sexual attraction.

These notions of service, and high-minded weightiness were undoubtedly reflected, at least in the United Kingdom, within many of the more private and elite institutions where boys were expected to be leaders and administrators of the still British Empire.[6] This serves to reiterate the point that many of the so called 'progressive' schools of the Fellowship often held much in common with their more illustrious forebears, notably a civic spirit, the outdoors and hard games playing. Cecil Reddie and J. H. Badley had themselves begun with the intentions of altering and reforming the public school system so it is not surprising to see many of their changes as stemming from direct revolts against certain long established practices.

It should, of course, be also evident that, frequently, the ends to which these pursuits were being put were very different. In the private schools, which almost exclusively tended to be conservative in outlook and desirous of preserving the status quo, service was couched in the discourse of servitude to the 'greater good' of Empire, Monarch and Country and team games were designed to engender that ethic through rugged cooperation and gentlemanly fair play. While drawing on this model, those Fellowship schools that were descended from their illustrious ancestors tended to consider service not out of necessary compulsion but as stemming from children's innate impulses to help each other and, by extension, the community as a whole. While competitive games playing may have been anathema to many of these institutions, one notable feature was to be activities – building projects, farming and the like – which allowed for collaboration between students and the chance for them to engage in meaningful work.

Differing intentions aside, however, drawing such historical comparisons remains pertinent for it serves to illustrate the middle-class nature of many of the Fellowship schools which were providing a progressive and alternative substitute (albeit often at a cost) for more 'traditional' forms of education as practised in ancient centres of learning. This is not to provide a critique of the movement but merely serves to delineate the essential features and characteristics of many (though by no means all) of the schools which emerged during this fertile period. Much of this was down to the early pioneers such as Badley and Hahn who were themselves direct products of the sorts of education to which they sought to provide some form of mild antidote.[7] Even later on, there was seemingly no disparity between espousing left wing socialist politics and being a member of the reflective bourgeois intelligentsia!

The forgotten progressive – Edmond Holmes

In seeking to chart the origins of the New Education Fellowship, one key figure of whom it is important to be aware is the Irish-born English School Inspector Edmond Holmes (1850–1936) who, more than anyone, can be identified as being the critical figure in its formation and who was to act as the first point of unity for the development of a recognizable and coherent ideology. In many ways, Holmes represents, and was an advocate of, all of the traditions discussed above. Educated (typically!) at the prestigious Merchant Taylor's School and Oxford University, Holmes was intellectually at ease with Steiner's quasi-spiritual educational philosophy while professionally, in his capacity as Chief Inspector for Elementary Schools, he was in close proximity to many of the emerging institutions and schools which themselves were drawing upon the new ideas from the continent and, more pertinently, those who were not. The vast majority of schools Holmes observed – controlled, funded and run by the State – undoubtedly fell into this latter category.

Unusually, and somewhat scandalously for a figure of such importance, the existing literature on Holmes is virtually non-existent. While his name recurs within many of the narrative educational histories of the period, it is frequently tangentially and, even then, only to characterize him somewhat vaguely as a 'prop' whose progressive utterances served to inspire other later and more radical thinkers. Unsurprisingly, given this neglect, there is little for the historian of education in the way of secondary biographical or critical literature about Holmes. Only a perfunctory work by Chris Shute (1998) and an earlier bibliographic article (1983) by Peter Gordon have taken him as the sole focus of their published research endeavours. Even a work as definitive and engaging as that of W. A. C. Stewart (1972) has only three references to Holmes in nearly 500 pages of discussion pertaining to the 'progressives and radicals' in English education.

And yet, Holmes himself was a remarkable man and far more notable, influential and sympathetic than many others who have long been part of the established progressive canon. A dreamy poet (and acquaintance of W. B. Yeats), philosopher, literary critic, spiritualist and religious scholar, he had a remarkably broad hinterland and it would be mistaken to think of him solely as one whose focus was exclusively educational. This expansive range of intellectual interests is reflected in Selleck's point that, 'Those who knew Holmes thought him as much a poet as an inspector and probably he was as much philosopher as poet' (Selleck 1972: 25). Holmes' philosophical position converged, at varying points of his life, upon both Idealism and Pantheism, and so, much of his work, like that of Steiner with whom he could perhaps be compared, sought to marry his ethereal concerns with the physical realities of the everyday world. One important aspect of this existence, clearly, was education and Holmes was to draw upon his extensive experiences as a Chief Inspector of Schools to adumbrate a philosophy encompassing his understanding of both spirituality and its place within the school curriculum.

This intellectual assortment is most apparent within the pages of his seminal work, *What is and What Might Be* (1911), which served as a key text for those later members of the Fellowship whose concerns were very much with the sort of utopian vision imagined by Holmes. A. S. Neill, Caldwell Cook, Norman MacMunn and Beatrice Ensor, all paid written tribute to Holmes' book and for acting a pioneer in speaking up about the limited and, indeed, limiting education being afforded to the mass of school children within state elementary schools. Such was the interest in Holmes' book that by 1917, it had gone through eight impressions. This perhaps makes it all the more unexpected, given the importance ascribed to him by his contemporaries, why he has received such little critical recognition today. Perhaps the difficulty lies in ultimately pinning Holmes down to one particular field. To understand the enormity of his achievements, it would be necessary to mark out, and have an understanding of, his substantive work in philosophy, education and spirituality and then be able to weave together the overlapping threads – a skill perhaps beyond all but the specialist within those areas. It is however his achievements as an educationalist which most concern this narrative.

As a school inspector himself of some distinction, Holmes' criticism of the elementary education system was as much an attack on his professional colleagues and acquaintances as was it on 'the establishment'. *What is* therefore carries with it a courageous and pioneering spirit in more than one sense and his achievement surely seems all the greater, given that his was the clearest articulation of the problems facing English education at that point – notably, a leaden-footed failure to apprehend the significance of new technologies and theories of learning.[8] As its title might suggest, the book is divided into two parts, the first attacking the 'Blind, passive, literal, unintelligent obedience' (Holmes 1911: 43) of Western education – the 'what is' of the title - and the second suggesting 'what might be' through his descriptions of a school he calls 'Utopia' run by a teacher named 'Egeria'. In actuality, Holmes based his narrative upon the school run by a woman called Harriet Finlay-Johnston, a noted dramatic educator, at Sompting in Sussex.

Given its mystical and spiritual dimension, and its underlying pantheism, there is much within *What is* that harks back to the writings of the earlier Romantics, particularly Rousseau and Froebel. As was the case with his illustrious forebears, freedom was central to Holmes' educational viewpoint and Part 1 of the book is spent in a sustained and withering critique of what he terms 'mechanical obedience' which, as Galton, Simon and Croall (1980) make clear, manifested itself in the nineteenth century through military drill, compliance and learning by rote under the implicit threat of some form of punishment. These ritualistic elements of school life would undoubtedly have been seen by Holmes on an almost daily basis through his inspections and were, for him, the source of all that was 'wrong' with education at that time.

For Holmes, though, freedom was not merely a political or democratic conceit and its advocacy was not limited solely to the presence or absence of physical and mental constraints within the setting of the school environment. Instead, Holmes' use of the term 'freedom' was one saturated with connotations of both mysticism and spirituality. He referred, for example, to the ideal and freest form of education as being one in which children were placed upon 'the path of self-realization' (Ibid., 235) and it is this theme which concerns the second and more important half of his magnum opus. This section of the book, detailing Holmes' solution to the generic problems of Western education, was to that point unique in English progressive educational writings as it was the first articulation of a viewpoint which sought to combine the philosophical traditions of what could broadly be called East and West. It also reflected one of the most significant attempts to date in importing aspects of Continental Idealism into the English educational tradition. As Peter Gordon and John White (1979) have persuasively shown, the influence of Idealist philosophers like T. H. Green and F. H. Bradley upon educational reforms was profound and in viewing humans both as social beings and ones whose individualism was to be celebrated and valued, the Idealists provided much for a forward thinker like Holmes to use in support of his educational position. Similarly, the Idealist emphasis upon spiritual unity sits relatively easily with aspects of Eastern mysticism where the spirit rather than the body serve as the controlling force.

Betraying an enduring allegiance to spirituality, 'self-realization' in the context of *What is* referred not merely to the processes of education by which mental aptitudes could be developed but also to the achievement of spiritual 'salvation'. This was equated by Holmes, as we have mentioned, with forms of emancipation and freedom – perhaps indeed, the ultimate form of freedom. Once emancipated, children could learn to expect, and live, a life of love in its very richest sense. There is something quasi-Buddhist in the way Holmes associated freedom not only with the body but also with the mind. This is made clear from the descriptions of the fictional Utopia school which placed a significant emphasis upon describing the ways in which children simultaneously developed spiritually and physically. The notion of a life lived in contentment, happiness and security was one that was to be central to much of the New Education Fellowship's thinking and discourse. Indeed, much of the later promotion of their endeavours was reliant precisely upon promoting an image of the child as contented, carefree and as developing in a range of different ways, every one unique to the particular journey of each individual child. The *New Era* journal – which serves the historian as a lightening rod of progressive educational currents and trends – periodically carried a series of articles and vignettes betraying these ideals. A search of its pages reveals, for example articles dedicated to the pleasure of manual work and labour, opportunities afforded by individual artistic expression and even the educative value of holidays!

Drawing from the wellspring generated by the importance ascribed to 'salvation', many of Holmes' utterances within his book are therefore contingent upon the notion of growth – both physical and spiritual. Like Froebel, Holmes saw the child as evolving and growing from a particular spiritual source, in this case, the inevitability of the soul developing from an inner core of spiritual energy. Crucially, this spiritual energy was conceived of as being divine in origin and destination which carries echoes of the *naturphilosphie* of the German Idealists and their search for a universal system underpinning all organic life. Given its celestial source and a conviction that one was equipped from birth with an 'essence' which was to constitute all one would be, Holmes therefore believed that it was a redundant and ultimately self-defeating exercise to instruct the child within this process of growth and that what pedagogic guidance there was should take a passive form. Instead of command or authority, activities undertaken by the child derived from latent impulses or (to use Holmes' term) *instincts* within the soul which make for 'the expansion and elevation of the child's nature' (Ibid., 164). Holmes delineated these instincts clearly as communicative, dramatic, artistic, musical, inquisitive and constructive.

By suggesting that children, whose natures are innate, seek to expand and elevate their beings through a range of functions both performative and intellectual, Holmes' writing provides an important link between two important historical ages. On the one hand, he takes a very Romantic approach in seeing the child as innately wise and realistic; on the other hand, he also provides an important link with the well-traced developments in later psychological theory which attested to children as being self-directed learners. Holmes therefore forms an important bridge between two seemingly disparate ideological and methodological poles and approaches and it is evident how he provides a significant connection to subsequent thinkers in the Fellowship who themselves drew both upon psychological theory and notions of individuality in constructing their nascent theories and educational experiments.

Indeed, Holmes' ideas seem to resonate strongly in our own age not only with the pervading progressive precept of children having within them an innate ability to learn and apprehend aspects of the world but also with later understandings of intelligence. These more recent models of intelligence, specifically those of Richard Sternberg and Howard Gardner, have a remarkably broad conception as to its constitution and, they argue, these categories are not solely defined in relation to mental measurement and performance. Gardner, for example, talks of musical, artistic and visual-spatial intelligences and he refuses to view intelligent activity as merely problem solving and the application of logic. Such theories are inherently democratic as they seek to recognize and accredit – as did Holmes – the value of all purposeful and instinctive childhood activity which can manifest in a range of forms. It is unsurprising why some commentators have sought to equate Gardner's theories with the range of attributes fostered by Waldorf Steiner schools.

For Holmes, however, such impulses towards creativity and socialization were best embodied in a particular attribute of childhood – 'These instincts manifest themselves in various ways, but chiefly in the direction that they give to that very serious occupation of young children which we call play' (Ibid., 170). *Play* therefore formed another factor which became central to Holmes' philosophy and he sought in his work to outline the purpose of schools as being institutions whereby play and its associated activities were to be taken seriously for it was through play that the true nature of the child was both revealed and personified. Indeed, the spontaneous spirit evoked when a child engages in play was one which Holmes desired to see present throughout the school as a whole. This is apparent from the lessons developed by Egeria which, like those of Pestalozzi and Froebel, took place within the context of the local landscape and, in its broadest spiritual sense, Nature which was incorporated into a range of activities through walks, exploration, sketching and folk song.

The key concepts laid down by Holmes – play, spirit, an organically growing child and the like – were all ones which were to reverberate strongly with those such as Beatrice Ensor who were to be the heartbeat of the later Fellowship and, when it suited their purpose, to identify themselves as disciples of

Holmes. Furthermore, Holmes touched upon a key issue at the heart of many progressive ideologies, notably the purpose to which the sort of education proposed within Utopia should be deployed. This was of importance for the New Education Fellowship, as its wide discursive remit and membership meant that political and social debates became bound up with questions concerning the governance of education. Could it be an instrument for cooperation across Continents and, by so doing, could it contribute to and reflect the moves towards pan-global unity and collaboration which were happening at the supra-national level?

Surprisingly, perhaps, despite the widespread sharing of ideas and osmotic diffusion of practice, several of the leading thinkers in the group did not conceive of education as having a political role to play. A. S. Neill, as one example, was to famously write that the sole value of his Summerhill School was to provide a 'little happiness to some few children' while Bertrand and Dora Russell's Beacon Hill School was set up quite intentionally as a non-political statement, far distant from its founder's typical dispositions. In that respect, Holmes' educational ideals corresponded with much of that rhetoric. While evidently aware of models of education which today we would call both socially controlling ('education is useful . . . to keep the "lower orders" in their places' (Ibid., 230)) and instrumental, Holmes' view of education was conceived as one which developed simply 'good' people, free of the demoralizing cares and concerns of mass society.

Although that in itself may seem a somewhat insipid manifesto and the term 'good' could be endlessly contested, Holmes – in keeping with his Buddhist sympathies – saw pure goodness as an unobtainable end and something therefore to be continually striven for. The purpose of education for him was to provide a setting, by default, isolated from the outside world, whereby children could develop 'activity, versatility, imaginative sympathy, a large and free outlook, self-forgetfulness, charm of manner [and] joy of heart' (Ibid., 231) – attributes which were to stand them in good stead on the path to 'goodness'. To achieve such goodness would be to achieve an inward tranquillity and harmony, the possession of which would enable individuals to have reached a desirable spiritual state, thus enabling them to live in the fullest sense. All other considerations, including the acquisition of skills, career, employment, one's position in society or salary, were secondary to the living of a spiritually rich and contented life.

It was probably the case that Holmes did not see such ideals as being incommensurable with the gainful finding of employment and, if anything, his desire to not specifically address the notion of utility reflects his innate social conservatism. His well-heeled educational background meant he had no great desire to overturn the existing social order through education. In the sense of every individual obtaining spiritual freedom regardless of the job they did, one could argue this was Marx without the Marxism; a spiritual rather than a political democracy. After that fashion, there is perhaps a spirit of appeasement in Holmes' closing proclamation to the penultimate chapter:

> Nor are Egeria's ex-pupils less efficient as labourers or domestic servants because they are interested in good literature, in Nature-study, in acting, or because they can still dance the Morris Dances and sing the Folk Songs which they learned in school. (Ibid., 234)

Such statements clearly indicate that Holmes' concern with children's spirituality was not predicated upon engaging them in a political or social struggle. While some may have argued that the one was not possible without the other, Holmes' belief in the distant possibility of a spiritual awakening and tranquillity seemingly stood independent of these wider concerns and served to exemplify not merely the optimistic and utopian flights of fancy common among the Fellowship educators but also the occasionally insular and inward-looking nature of some of the earlier schools. It is to the practices of these schools themselves that the chapter now turns.

Inside the Fellowship schools – Ideals and principles

Thanks to the status and wide circulation afforded to *What is*, many of Holmes' precepts became incorporated – after one fashion or another – within the various progressive schools which emerged and developed over the early twentieth century. As was mentioned earlier, this was by no sense an homogenous grouping and the New Education Fellowship encompassed schools whose aims were as diverse as looking after working-class children (the Caldecott Community), war orphans (Tiptree Hall started by Norman MacMunn), a school based around the ideas of nature (the Forest School) and the early pioneering schools (Bedales and Abbotsholme) whose mission was to reform the worst excesses of the private sector and, specifically, the uniquely British public schools. Part of the joy of exploring this movement comes therefore in examining the wonderfully idiosyncratic figures who helmed many of these institutions, each of whom, in their own right, is worthy of more lengthy treatment. Cecil Reddie, for example, argued that boys should see each other naked as much as possible, that indoor toilets were as source of evil and that the weather could control moral conduct!

While life history is not to be the focus here, the reader is nevertheless directed towards the lively accounts of Robert Skidelsky (1969) and W. A. C. Stewart (1972) and the myriad of recent smaller journal articles which have provided informative and entertaining discussions of a number of these men and women. Understanding the human motivation and impetus behind these schools is often as enlightening as exploring their working educational philosophies and the intricacies of their practices. This is not to suggest, of course, that this was a movement whose concerns were parochial and its protagonists narrow-minded; it should already be clear how the idealizations of Pestalozzi and Froebel impacted upon the thought and practice of the group's membership and there was a clear exchange of ideas which percolated between Britain and Europe and vice versa. W. A. C. Stewart (1972), for one, has emphasized the spread and dissemination of a particularly British progressive ethos across the Continent.

However, perhaps the most direct influence on many of these schools came through the aforementioned work of Holmes, not merely for its temporal proximity but because one can clearly observe a number of key features which can be convincingly brought together as general themes by which to convey something of the overall substance of this myriad of schools developing at this time. Underpinning many of their ideals were the tenets of Romanticism and Idealism which had inflected much of Holmes' own writings particularly, as we have noted, the democratizing effects of child-centredness and the deification of the individual. After that fashion, what marked many of these schools out as distinctive was their preference for artistic creativity over the rational intellect and for allowing free rein of the imagination instead of a designated programme or pattern of learning. Following Rousseau (who was also an important influence), many of these schools held dear to the belief in the innate 'good' of the child and that it was only the corrupting effects of civilization (and that included parents and other schools) which served to deviate them from their natural righteous path.

In keeping with the rusticity inherent within the Romantic cultural project there was an anti-industrial feel to the atmospheres of many of the schools and this echoed an aspect of the intellectual spirit of the age at large where concern reigned over the contaminating effects of newly emergent cities. In England, the writer and artist William Morris campaigned for a return to 'traditional' arts and crafts while simultaneously publishing mock heroic poetic romances which celebrated old fashioned virtues of nobility and chivalry. Elsewhere, many others in a range of disparate art forms emphasized the nation's pastoral qualities through the collection and preservation of traditional folk songs and the setting up of artistic communities in deliberately rural, isolated settings. Wordsworth and, particularly, Walt Whitman were (once more) the guiding lights in seeking to reject certain of the unappealing traits of Modernity.

Nor was this an exclusively British phenomenon. Further afield, in Germany, the *Wandervogel* (Wandering Birds) was founded in 1901 by groups of disaffected youths and intellectuals as an explicit stance against rising industrialization. Their activities which included camping, the singing of folk songs, the learning of traditional dances and reading of epic poetry clearly owed much to the earlier festivals overseen by Froebel. Nevertheless, for all of their mysticism, such gatherings still served to convey that particular strand of Teutonic outdoor spirit which allowed for freedom and a sense of adventure among its participants. Beatrice Ensor was one of their keenest admirers and even that old curmudgeon A. S. Neill, himself not wholly in tune perhaps with the more masculine side of their activities and too inclined to view such horse play as repressed Freudian symbols, set down a grudging admiration for their pioneering activities.

In many ways, this anti-industrial sentiment inflected countless practices within the Fellowship's progressive schools. Many of the schools were keen to stress, for example, that work should not take place simply within the confines of the classroom. Instead, children were actively encouraged to engage in communal work and activity in the outdoors by repairing buildings, constructing huts and new facilities and partaking in honest manly toil. These activities carried rural and agricultural overtones, and frequently, the schools themselves had attached farms which provided opportunities for both manual work and practical demonstration and example through, for example, the milking of cows. Given, too, that many of these schools saw themselves as self-sufficient communities, the opportunity to encourage cooperation in shared activities must surely not have gone unnoticed and tied in with much of the widely accepted spirit of communal living.

The nature of this outdoor work meant an ambivalent attitude emerged in relation to school uniforms. This was not solely, of course, about practicality; uniforms symbolized conformity and more traditional school attire involving shirts and ties seemed Victorian, bourgeois and just a mite too respectable. Abbotsholme and Gordonstoun were two of the first schools to suggest that children wear shorts and open neck shirts, while Dartington Hall was even more relaxed, stressing the individuality and personal choice of each child. It was hoped that these beliefs would encourage the emergence of the 'natural' child who was not shaped or moulded by any particular aspect of civilization. Although non-uniform establishments are more common today, the lack of uniform in those earlier schools was hugely symbolic for it represented an attachment to the ideas of individual difference and taste and seemed a direct repudiation of one of the key aspects of British (and state-sanctioned) schooling, which tended to foster formal homogeneity at the expense of difference.

In allowing children to engage in what were considered by some to be less academically rigorous pursuits, schools in the Fellowship were betraying an adherence to the psychological ideas of those such as Susan Isaacs and latterly Jean Piaget who had 'proven' that children had the ability to be more self-educating than was ever previously realized. Isaacs, as the previous chapter has alluded, made substantial advances in exploring children's cognitive development and it was as a result of this kind of research that a distinction emerged between the teaching of children and the process of getting them to think. It had been a prior standard scholastic assumption that groups of children shared comparable potentials of intelligence and that all were capable of learning at a similar pace.

Drawing upon new findings, however, and driven by the prospect of a 'science of teaching', many of the progressive school leaders sought to radically alter their curriculum, which meant abandoning many of the more staple subjects in favour of ones which more readily accorded with 'real' life. J. H. Badley, for example – far more so than his initial mentor Cecil Reddie – was quite prepared to strike out in innovative ways by drawing upon advances in psychology such as those ideas of Montessori and by utilizing such techniques as the Dalton Plan which allowed for more individualized work schemes to be drawn up. Following that, teaching often took place by practical example and was aided by the natural surrounds many of these institutions enjoyed. The school farm, for example, was versatile in being a resource for both biological study and outdoor manual activity. Nor could the value of this physical work be overstated in teaching children, often without their realizing, skills in related cognate subjects such as mathematics and engineering. This form of learning was also, as we shall see, characteristic of John Dewey and was widely practiced in his schools in America.

Making subjects more suited to the child's own interests meant also that each pupil could be accommodated at their own pace and their learning could be matched to the rate of their intellectual progress. We have seen, through the case of Maria Montessori, how the idea of developmental and cognitive growth phases was an important driver behind the formulation of her specialized Apparatus. If, therefore, one believed that children developed at different rates, it logically followed that the school would have to adapt its curriculum to accommodate that range of differences. Many schools thereby started to adjust themselves to the idea that differing learning capacities meant that a greater range of activities had to be made available. Edward Thring, headmaster of the prestigious Uppingham School, famously believed that in every cohort, 'Every boy could do *something* well. It was the duty of the school to discover what this "something" was' (quoted in Newsome 1961: 221). Much of this adaptation was through the abandoning of old didactic methods and habits of teaching such as rote learning and memorization and – particularly, later on – attempting to use innovative ideas, for example, those which came to be known as the 'integrated day' and 'team teaching' whereby groups of teachers oversaw a wider range of activities among the classes which were themselves frequently mixed by age. In these ways, many of these schools thus sought to challenge accepted viewpoints concerning not merely assumptions about pupil performance but the transmission of knowledge itself and the role of the teacher. In this new world, it was not sufficient for the teacher to merely be a passive distributor of information; instead, they were to be a facilitator by enabling children to find out what interested them and to guide them on their individual paths with the minimum of interference.

The anxieties of many of the Fellowship schools were not purely scholastic though; as has been made clear, education was but one part of their agenda and this was intertwined with a range of social concerns, and in these, one finds reflected the most direct attacks on the inherited traditions of elite forms of private education – a system seen by many of the pioneering headmasters as riddled with privilege, abuse and inequality. In particular, the stern systems of discipline and lack of co-education seemed to them to be out of tune with many of the evolving psychological ideas and theories of childhood which were becoming more widely established. These included not only more scientific enterprises but also those ideas of Margaret McMillan (discussed in Chapter 7) which had focused more upon the physical well-being and health of the child. One particular bone of contention remained the traditional prefect system – control and maintenance of school discipline by older pupils – which was seen as arbitrary and which was not based on any form of meritocratic selection to justify why certain individuals held the whip hand over others. Power residing in the hands of a privileged elite was seen as fundamentally undemocratic and disenfranchising for the majority of students. It is perhaps no surprise that the book which did most to draw attention to this issue – the novel *Tom Brown's Schooldays* (1857) by Thomas Hughes – was drawn from the author's own experiences at Rugby School and its rigid prefect system (a creation of the headmaster Thomas Arnold). The popularity of the novel ensured it did much to illustrate to a wide audience the climate of fear which pervaded the public schools and which the Fellowship and certain of its members sought to overthrow.

In a direct retaliation against this, certain schools therefore introduced the concept of 'self-government' which encouraged full pupil participation in the running of the school. Perhaps the best known of these was to be found in A. S. Neill's Summerhill where, even today, the School's 'Council' is a truly democratic body with pupils and teachers each having an equal voice in the decision-making process. The same was also true to varying degrees at schools such Dartington Hall, King Alfred School and Kilquhanity, the latter of which drew significant inspiration from Summerhill. Such initiatives served to not merely diffuse and devolve responsibility but also to instill in young children the values of cooperation and, crucially, democracy. While these schools may not have been consciously attempting to ape the patterns of society (which, in the early part of the century, could hardly be described as in any way representative), there remained a residual sense that it was irrational to not allow children to express themselves at school as, at best, it was a poor preparation for adulthood and, at worst, it served to further repress and inhibit the child's natural desires to be sociable. Given how much psychology was coming to inform educationalists of the value of social activity – again, the work of Susan Isaacs was pertinent – it seemed only right that children should be encouraged to partake in shared activities together.

Such considerations also impacted upon many of these schools as they began to adopt, or at least consider, the possibility of co-education. While in some cases seen as a direct reaction against the prevailing homosexuality of the single-sex public schools, educating boys and girls together was seen as furthering democracy by reflecting the real-world setting in the confines of the school. In their Beacon Hill school, for example, the Russells promised 'complete frankness on anatomical and physiological facts of sex, marriage, parenthood and the bodily functions' (quoted in Gorham 2006: 47) with a view to advancing the course of social betterment. Given, after all, that life was co-educational, why should schools not reflect that in their own membership? Although wary of encouraging sexual liaisons and the need to be totally honest on answering children's sexual questions – and debates about co-education perennially returned to these problems – many felt that such settings actually stunted such desires and impulses and that 'the coeducational ideal was that of comrades rather than sexual partners' (Skidelsky 1969: 46). Although Freudian psychology was built around interrelated constructs of sexuality, it nevertheless talked extensively about repression and, for those who were willing to tentatively embrace his theories, co-education provided an important way of manifesting both equality and a 'proper' upbringing free of lies, awkwardness and half-truths.

Adherence to a viewpoint which rejected taboos and suppression also meant questioning the necessity for corporal punishment and beating – a fine exemplar of Freudian theory in action. Freud had held that to remove the symptoms of a problem, one first had to locate the cause. Mere beating failed to do that as it did not attempt to identify why children misbehaved as they did which, Freud argued, stemmed from the complexes developed in childhood. For many of the Fellowship thinkers, these causes may have been lack of love or parental affection. Further to that, corporal punishment simply did not 'fit' with many of their received notions of peace, democracy and non-violence. By rejecting corporal punishment and sterner systems of discipline, the Fellowship schools were repudiating the need for an institution whose authority derived solely from force which, in itself, represented something which was fundamentally anti-democratic.

It should thus be clear from the discussion above that while the schools of the Fellowship varied in their intentions and practices, broadly speaking, they all held dear to a core set of beliefs which centred around the liberation of the child and the need for their freedoms to be valued in the context of more democratic structures through the abolition of punishment, constraint and restriction. Whether for economic and ideological reasons, or else that their specific concerns ceased to be important in the modern world, some of these (often the smaller) schools no longer exist or have been moulded into a form unrecognizable today. By contrast, the more significant of the Fellowship establishments are currently going strong; Bedales continues to produce alumni who excel in a range of creative and artistic fields (including the model Sophie Dahl and singer Lily Allen), Gordonstoun is still emphasizing civic manliness through cold showers, morning runs and a range of outdoor initiatives, including its *de rigueur* classes in seamanship while Abbotsholme even now holds dear to the global perspectives of its founder through its diverse and cosmopolitan pupil composition.

These institutions have however maintained their private status with commensurately high fees and so they have retained their reputations as playgrounds for the liberal intelligentsia or else stamping grounds for those parents who desire a curriculum for their children whose virtues go beyond those celebrated in the state sector. Perhaps this has been born out of necessity; Maurice Galton has long commented on the British educational establishment's reluctance to fully embrace creativity as anything other than an 'optional extra' and that, coupled with the inherent advantages a boarding school provides, means that such establishments can promote themselves as something beyond a 'good' school, defined solely by successful examination results. There is clearly an appeal there to those who recognize the value of extra-curricular 'trimmings' and can afford to pay for them.

Much of what these schools stood for at the time of their founding – aversion to punishment, the pupil voice and even outdoor activity – have, of course, become subsumed into standard sets of scholastic assumptions. R. J. W. Selleck (1972), among others, has argued that by as early as 1939, many of the 'radical' opinions put forward by the progressives 'had captured the allegiance of the opinion-makers' (Selleck 1972: 156) and 'had become the intellectual orthodoxy' (Ibid). This was particularly the case in relation to those who stressed the importance of the good health and welfare of the child who was increasingly seen as bound up with the future of the nation – a contention held in various forms to this day. These schools have thus become more broadly diluted in their radical ideology with perhaps less now to differentiate them from their peers who themselves may be co-educational, non-uniform and with older pupils mentoring the young. However, there stands one school whose philosophy is still as radical as the day on which it was founded and whose predilection to cock a snook at the educational (and indeed any!) establishment is equally strong today. It is therefore the radical

Summerhill School and its iconic founder A. S. Neill that this chapter now seeks to explore.

The iconoclasts – A. S. Neill and Homer Lane

A. S. Neill (1883–1973) is, for many, the ultimate progressive. In a book concerning nearly 300 years of progressive educationalists, even today his name is distinct from the rest. As a person, he is regarded as either a secular saint – education's equivalent of Mother Teresa – or an irresponsible old fool full of redundant windbaggery whose key works are nothing more than simplistic homespun wisdom dressed up in the cloak of profundity. As Louise Bates Ames (1970) makes abundantly clear, 'A. S. Neill is so dreadfully opinionated. Everything for him is black or white' (Ames 1970: 65). Whether therefore one sees his educational viewpoint as demonstrating great and reflective love of children or else naively imputing them with wisdom beyond their years and thus caricaturing the malign effects of 'evil' adults once more depends upon one's prior moral, social and ethical standpoints. His creed represents a touchstone for those looking for a model of rearing children *in extremis*. His philosophy is individualistic, iconoclastic and, ultimately, impossible to ignore for those with even the vaguest interest in education. His books, particularly *Summerhill* (1968), which compiled many of his most significant thoughts on education, continue to sell well, attract scholarly interest and are on the reading list of many a university course. It seems the 'Neill phenomenon' is here to stay regardless of what the detractors may think.

Tucked away in the leafy rural county of Suffolk, Summerhill School, which Neill founded in 1921, has a claim to being the most famous educational institution in the world and it has generated more interest and imitators across the globe than any other such establishment. Characterized in the media and among the general public as the 'school without rules' and a haven of 'all play and no work', these descriptors serve to infuriate the scholar for not only are they inaccurate (Summerhill, in fact, has many rules, which are continually reworked), they also serve to denigrate an institution whose longevity, whether one agrees with the Summerhill ethos or not, surely indicates that there is *something* contingent about the school which warrants more than arrant dismissal.

The academic community has been seemingly polarized in its assessment as was demonstrated by a fascinating collection of essays brought together in Neill's lifetime entitled *Summerhill: for and against* (1970). Here, the school was variously described by Fred Hechinger as 'a model for mass education . . . one of the world's most powerful ideas' (Hechinger 1970: 38) and by Max Rafferty as a 'cross between a beer garden and a boiler factory . . . a caricature of education' (Rafferty, 1970: 24). Polarity indeed! Even in 1999, with the well-documented court case brought by the British school establishment as a result of a scathing inspection report, Summerhill survived against the odds, indicating that even in an increasingly conformist educational world, there were still those who could legitimately challenge authority, retain educational autonomy and act as a pocket of resistance in the face of adversity.[9] Oh, how Neill would have smiled at that!

And yet, who, or perhaps more pertinently, *what* was A. S. Neill? Answering this question is in itself problematic for a number of reasons and not only for the opprobrium often heaped upon the man himself. First, he was the author of more than 20 books and this means that distilling the essence of his educational philosophy can prove difficult, particularly given the very pithy, direct and aphoristic quality of his writing. This is further compounded, second, by the *form* Neill, on occasion, employed. Many of his earlier books are in the style of novels centring upon a fictional 'dominie' (the Scottish term for teacher) and can be read as adventure stories and fables as much as works of educational substance. As the historian David Limond puts it, '. . . it is possible to identify Neill's Dominie books as thoroughly problematic' (Limond 1999: 302). Utilizing the license afforded to creators of literature, Neill uses pseudonyms for his characters and the scenes within his books act as symbols and metaphors rather than being actual depictions of events.

This has certainly confused at least one scholar in the field; James Scotland writing in his exhaustive *History of Scottish Education* (1970) failed to recognize that Neill's *A Dominie Dismissed* (1916) was a work of fiction, leading him to make subsequent claims about Neill's life (based on the novel) which were not true. David Limond (1999) has also further observed that these early 'Dominie' books were equally concerned with developing a particular construction of Scottish national identity as much as developing a progressive philosophy. Even in those later works where Neill had abandoned fiction to write more 'standard' educational prose, the pithy and aphoristic nature of his writing style can make it difficult, once again, to bundle everything together into a unified set of principles. Perhaps this explains why it can be complex and overwhelming to distil and apprehend a 'core' series of educational principles. Given the nature of the man and his character, many claims in his books likewise appear unexpected or contradictory. He retained, for example, a lifelong support for private education (the maintenance of which allowed Summerhill to retain its protected status) and his statements regarding homosexuality jar in the current climate and with his professed 'liberal' viewpoint. Personally, he was kind, diffident and softly spoken, yet his writing could be powerful and, to his detractors, dipped in vitriol.

Finally, as if to further frustrate the historian, there is the lack of any collections of papers available relating to Neill. For other progressives, this is less of a problem – Holmes, for example, can be traced through his Inspection

Reports, and in the case of figures such as Susan Isaacs and Cyril Burt, large archives exist *in situ*.[10] Aside, however, from collections of letters to selected correspondents, there is little in the way of useable material for Neill – a problem recognized by his official biographer Jonathan Croall who talked of the 'unevenness of the oral and written evidence' (Croall 1983: 3) and found himself obliged to rely on Neill's own accounts of his childhood when telling his life. If such issues do not serve to add to the mystique surrounding Neill, they certainly create an air of inscrutability which has perhaps served towards advancing the purpose of his school.

In seeking to trace and explain the phenomena of Neill, it is first important to mention and elaborate the work of one of his close friends and advocates – the educator Homer Lane (1875–1925). As with Edmond Holmes, until Judith Stinton's recent (2005) biography, Lane was a figure languishing in relative obscurity – a footnote worthy only of mention through his relationship with Neill and the later controversy surrounding his educational affairs which included the closure of his school The Little Commonwealth due to allegations of sexual impropriety. It was perhaps for these reasons as much as for his educational and social radicalism that he has remained on the outskirts of academic discourse. In some senses, this neglect is perversely appropriate, for, in many ways, he was himself the Great Outsider. An American running a school in the quintessentially English countryside supported by the largesse of the aristocracy,[11] Lane had a predisposition to shock and antagonize often on purpose and his authorization to his students to vandalize his school and destroy his property could hardly have endeared him to those of a more moderate persuasion. Not that that would have much concerned Lane who had a happy knack of being able to make friends and enemies in equal measure with little care for the consequences. In that respect, Lane and Neill were similar characters as both were persistent, cussed and resilient in pursuing their viewpoints often in the face of bitter public hostility. Indeed, Neill's works suffer on occasion from a hint of demagoguery, historically characteristic of those whose arguments are controversial and divisive.

Underneath their hardened exteriors, however, both had a deep love of children which emerges through a reading of the accounts of their practices at their schools. While day-to-day life at Summerhill has been well traced, for example, in the works of Popenue (1969) and Snitzer (1964), less has been written in relation to Lane. This is partially explainable through the controversial closure of the community but also a result of his pupil demographic which tended to be those categorized as delinquent and who lacked the expertise to record their schooling experiences. Nevertheless, as J. H. Simpson tells us:

> When I have put together all that I can find to say against Lane . . . it remains true that I think of Lane as the man who, more than anyone else whom I

have known among educators, love those among whom he worked with absolute unselfishness, without favour or sentimentality, and made them feel that, whatever the might do, he would still understand their actions and motives, and continue to love them nevertheless. (Simpson 1953: 23–4)

This love of children reflected the way that Lane felt himself to be 'on the side' of the child against the adult and this he proved quite dramatically to one boy by his encouragement towards wanton acts of vandalism in the school. This was done not only to deter future such activities by removing the element of adult disproval but was also designed to demonstrate Lane's intrinsic empathy for troubled children. Did such radical behaviour stem from experiences of his own strictly New England Puritan upbringing and the need to rebel against forms of childhood repression? Psycho-history of this type is notoriously speculative, yet it would seem plausible, particularly given Neill's similarly ascetic and unhappy childhood among the Scottish Calvinists whose first recourse to misbehaving children was also punitive. In Neill's case, this involved the use of the tawse, a rudimentary device for beating children, which was employed with a flagrant disregard for the emotional and physical well-being of the child. Neill's own writing on this in his autobiography, as well as that of his biographers, including Jonathan Croall (1983), indicate the great importance he attached to his early experiences as a child and latterly as a pupil-teacher in these local settings, so maybe it is not an invalid inference to explore those shared biographical contexts.

Certainly, Neill himself believed that his visit to Lane's school was the turning point in his own life and there was clearly an emotional affinity between the two men which extended beyond a shared educational agenda. As Croall tells us, 'Many of Lane's ideas had a profound and lasting effect on Neill, to such an extent that he incorporated them – sometimes down to the precise wording – into his own belief system' (Croall 1983: 85). This influence was also seemingly subliminal. In a 1928 article in the *New Era*, Neill, in reviewing Lane's *Talks to Parents and Teachers*, seemed to form an inadvertent link between the philosophy therein and his own childhood. By analysing Lane's example of an infant's desire to guide its hand to its mouth and the mother's response to it, Neill utilized pseudo-Freudian notions to invoke the dichotomy between activity and creativity represented by the father, and security and possession embodied within the mother. One can certainly draw parallels not merely within his own life, but also with the way in which, later, Summerhill became more associated with fostering such notions as possession rather than inspired creativity – a charge that was to be levied against it by critics over the succeeding years.

Returning to Lane, as its name, richly laden with democratic overtones would suggest, his Little Commonwealth was set up as a community which would allow for the fundamental empowerment of children, with its own constitution and the young inhabitants given the role of citizens and the guardians of the 'state'. As Stinton's account makes it clear, this even led to children being elected for set terms in courts of law with one girl – Ellen Stanley – acting as judge who passed sentence on herself for the misdemeanour of leaving a candle burning dangerously! Indeed, the relationship between Lane and his charges was not that of traditional teacher and learner. As W. David Wills (1964) points out, 'he [now] no longer regarded the community as an institution; he regarded it as a family' (Wills 1964: 138), and in that he shared something of his idol Pestalozzi whose communities at Stans and elsewhere were manifestations of a remarkably similar ethic of self-sufficiency. This was most evident in the stipulation that each individual cottage, and the community as a whole, had to earn enough from its work to be economically viable and be able to support itself.

Nevertheless, unlike Pestalozzi's Stans paupers, the children under Lane's charge were of a particular kind – mostly delinquents with troubled pasts – and his purpose in setting up the institution was less about the deliberate devising of an educational experiment and more about seeking to 'cure' the difficult children through empowerment, admiration and love. What is most novel about the Little Commonwealth therefore is not perhaps any pioneering system of instruction but more the idea that even 'difficult' children can and should be entrusted with some form of responsibility for decision-making. Indeed, it was very likely that few of the children present would have benefited from any system of education which could have been offered. Lane, as was to be the case with Neill, considered the reason why such children had ended up delinquent was not through innate defects of character but a combination of a lack of love and the need to condemn on the parts of their parents, thereby misdirecting the naturally good impulses of the child. Traditional forms of authority and repression needed to be abolished and teachers permitted to allow children to resolve their differences in the classroom – 'Freedom cannot be given . . . it is taken by the children . . . freedom demands the privilege of conscious wrong doing' (Lane 1928: 112). Lane therefore believed that if one could demonstrate these additional qualities to children and show them kindness, then the urge to rebel would be taken away and they could be 'cured' of particular impulses.

Through the rise of the disciplines of social work and childcare, such ideas sound rudimentary today; however, at the time, they were considered revolutionary, in particular, through the trust Lane was prepared to exhibit towards the children under his care. While many tried to question its applicability as a model to be adopted elsewhere, the point remains that Lane's central belief in child approval and attachment to instinct and repressions owed surprisingly little to Freud and far more to his own original and ingenious understanding of childhood. Indeed, delinquent children themselves became held up – including by Kurt Hahn – as symbols of 'good apples gone bad' and evidence of the effects of poor parenting and societies who ceaselessly refused to allow children to be themselves and sought to propagate aspects of repression. Whether as a result of a lack of love, as Neill posited, or else being given insufficient ways to express desire for achievement, in the manner of Hahn, the maladjusted child was therefore frequently hoisted aloft as a *casus belli* against the educational mainstream and a warning to society of the dangers in not educating children properly.

The Little Commonwealth also served as a distinctive exemplar of a key progressive precept dating back to Rousseau, which was that the child was born innately good and that it was only the corrupting effects of civilization – for Lane manifested in the uncaring natures of teachers and parents – which had necessitated changes which ultimately produced the juvenile delinquent. This is not, of course, to suggest that Lane was right, and modern genetic ideas about prevalent predispositions towards crime may count against him, but he is to be at least admired for the courage of his convictions and for acting out his beliefs in the context of an educational and, more importantly, democratic setting.

Although contact between the young Neill and Lane was brief, the latter was to inadvertently play a large part in the shaping of Summerhill School which was seen in later years by many of Lane's disciples as the only true continuation of their mentor's work. As Judith Stinton (2005) has shown, Lane not only convinced Neill that it was possible to implement the 'free' systems of education he had started to imagine into a workable practice but he also introduced Neill to the ideas of Freud whose notions of the Unconscious and Fantasy were, as we shall see, to be assimilated into his later writings. In *A Dominie Dismissed* (1916), written shortly after their first meeting, Neill praised his newly acquired ethic – 'There are two ways in education: Macdonald's[12], with Authority in the shape of School Boards and magistrates and prisons to support him, and mine with the Christ like experiment of Homer Lane to encourage me' (Neill 1916: 53).

By the time of Neill's fourth book, *A Dominie in Doubt* (1921), encouragement had turned to Damascene conversion as, in the introductory dedication, Lane is praised as the man, 'whose first lecture convinced me that I knew nothing about education' (Neill 1921: 5). As Ray Hemmings (1972) mentions, by this stage of his life, Neill had foregone his apprenticeship and was now 'searching out the implications' (Hemmings 1972: 36) of his emerging theory. The most obvious of these perhaps centred upon Lane's concept of 'original virtue' which was the notion that that which is instinctual is good and that which is imposed is bad. As Lane himself wrote, 'Human nature is innately good; the unconscious processes are in no way immoral' (Lane, op. cit., 130). This idea was to form a key element in Neill's own educational writings. As he put it: 'My strong conviction is that the boy is *never in the wrong*. Every case I have handled has been a case of misguided early education' (Neill 1926: 3).

Neill was also to follow Lane's belief that, at weaning, the child finds substitute pleasures that are seen as sinful and is thus forced to retreat from his or herself. Lane believed that this process of retreat could be avoided only if the child is 'allowed to 'grow up' and not be 'brought up'. Morality is spontaneous' (Lane, op. cit., 124). There are resounding echoes too of Lane's philosophy in many of Neill's writings on child-rearing. In outlining his notion of the free child, for example, Neill wrote that 'to impose anything by authority is wrong. The child should not do anything until he comes to the opinion - his own opinion - that it should be done' (Neill 1968: 114). These exemplars, and there are many more, should thereby serve to illustrate to the reader the interaction and overlap between the two men at the levels of both educational and social ideology.

In Lane, then, Neill had found a guiding example of an educator who embodied perfectly his belief in the nature of childhood, which he had been observing and ruminating on through his work as a young teacher at the school in Gretna Green. It is perhaps fitting (although not right) that Lane himself should have been comparatively marginalized since his unfortunate deportation for, along with the psychologist Wilhelm Reich, the great rebel Neill was to be continually attracted to intellectual pariahs and those whose ideas today are characterized by quirky discipleship rather than universal acknowledgement and approval. Reich's theory of 'orgone' energy (ostensibly a form of cosmic libido), for example, has attracted controversy as being the progenitor for free love, while the ideas of Lane have received, as has been mentioned, little scholarly attention. In seeking to therefore answer the question as to the identity of A. S. Neill, one cannot divorce his educational writings from his biography and the huge impact particular individuals were to hold upon his imagination.

The Summerhill ethos and influence

The aspects and traits of Neill's character described above are noticeable in his dealings with the New Education Fellowship with whom his relationship was, at best, ambiguous. While broadly supportive of their efforts to provide, in the loosest sense of the word, an emancipatory form of education, in 1923 the young Neill and the group's de facto leader, Beatrice Ensor, suffered a falling out over an ideological disagreement via an editorial published by Ensor in the *New Era*. Ensor had chosen to heartily and vigorously champion a new form of education developed by the Frenchman, Monsieur Coue, which relied upon the technique of auto-suggestion, which was characterized by being able to will oneself to avoid particular courses of action. Neill, characteristically, railed against this notion not merely for the unsound nature, as he saw it, of the science but also because for him any form of suggestion was dangerous and led to the potential for education to become totalitarian.

While Ensor and her supporters believed that undesirable traits could, through the correct channelling of the mind, be 'willed away', thereby leading to the creation of a utopian society, such a concept sat uneasily with Neill who saw the potential for its misuse. This small academic debate may seem comparatively insignificant today but it is illustrative of a number of important factors. First, Neill's lack of allegiance to any particular group or designation; second, his unerring talent to constantly find himself pushed to the periphery of the mainstream (often by choice) and, most importantly, as Robert Skidelsky (1969) has shown, the emergence of his own libertarian position which declared that 'the instincts of the child are good [and] they must not be moulded, however subtly and understandingly' (Skidelsky 1969: 159).

It is worth noting that at the time of this disagreement Neill had published half a dozen books and was in the process of synthesizing his nascent ideas into a coherent philosophy. These early texts were fictional works and they betray the intrinsic tension found in articulating a clear educational viewpoint within the context of a story-bound narrative. Such was this long intellectual and educational journey that Neill did not fully embrace the 'free for all' ethos with which he is now associated with immediate effect. It was only after his familiarization with the works of Freud and then Wilhelm Reich, with whom he underwent a conversion, that his educational philosophy became fully formulated. As Ray Hemmings (1972) reminds us, 'the change in the form of titles marked a move out of these years of speculative debate to a greater certainty' (Hemmings 1972: 60).

In many ways, *The Problem Child*, first published in 1926, therefore represents the earliest coherent statement of 'Neillian' educational beliefs and was directly responsible for making Neill's name more widely known in educational circles and which lead to his school achieving the level of prominence which it still enjoys today. One of the most apparent ways in which Neill's views were transformed, beyond the obvious indebtedness to Homer Lane, was his increased understanding of psychological theory, drawing particularly upon the work of the theorists mentioned above. This association is made abundantly clear by Jonathan Croall (1983) who argued persuasively for the personal influence that Reich, in particular, was able to countenance, convincing Neill of the significance of the experiences of childhood and the cathartic need to explore their implications. While this was manifested immediately through the early sections of Neill's own autobiography (as well as sessions of Reich's vegetotherapy), it also meant that his later published works focused upon a concept of education which sought to incorporate these larger concepts into a grand 'theory of everything'. Education from now on was to be linked to universal theories of both human behaviour and development and Summerhill School was to be their most definitive manifestation.

It was from Reich's complex theories that Neill originated, particularly, his opposition to sexual oppression which he saw, in his newly acquired widened perspective, as a palpable manifestation of parental and social control. In two of his later and most important works, *The Problem Family* (1948) and *The Free Child* (1953), Neill was keen to stress that many of the previous responses to children's sexuality – including those originating from several progressive educators – had been designed to perpetrate guilt and hatred towards their bodies, leading to despair and unhappiness. Susan Isaacs (1932), for example, had advocated splints as a device to prohibit children from engaging in masturbation, while Neill found Montessori's system to be 'highly intellectual but sadly lacking in emotionalism' (Neill 1921: 145). At Summerhill by contrast, Neill never forbade child nudity and did not discourage genital and/or sex play, believing that it constituted a natural part of a child's upbringing.

The issue of sex is of great interest for not only does it indicate how Neill was continually unafraid to stand against social taboos – and is there anything more taboo than childhood sexuality? – but also the way in which his philosophy was enacted within the context of his school. Neill's interest in sex confirmed his psychological preoccupations with those intangible aspects of a child's mind. Following Freud, many of his writings confirm the importance of latent aspects of the unconscious, particularly within the psyches of young children. Although a detailed exploration of such theory is outside the scope of this narrative, it is enough to note that these concepts underpinned many aspects of his theory relating to moral, sexual and disciplinary instruction. As Neill writes, 'The psychology of the unconscious has shown that most of our actions have a hidden source' (Neill 1968: 220) and so many actions can be ascribed to elements of upbringing and schooling. In the case of delinquents and criminals, Neill was adamant that their impulses sprung from forms of earlier repression often perpetrated by parents, schools and teachers. While such corollaries have been long-established now by classic sociological studies such as those of the Gluecks (1950) and F. Ivan Nye (1958), which indicate the link between criminality and the broken home, Neill's conceptions of freedom and 'un-freedom' were of a much broader hue.

Freedom for Neill sprung from an understanding that the child was capable of self-regulation, which equated with, 'the right of a baby to live freely, without outside authority in things psychic and somatic' (Neill 1953: 42). This entailed not imposing patterns of behaviour or standards of morality upon young children which risked stunting their growth and development. Such repression related to not answering their questions honestly, being unwilling to discuss issues of sexuality (or worse, actively discouraging them) and conforming them into patterns of prohibition. The self-regulated child, by contrast, was free of adult suggestion and imposition and allowed to develop naturally as their own impulses and desires allowed. It should be apparent from these ideas that Neill held true to a particular conception of childhood which went beyond the default Romantic position of an innately good being. Drawing upon the latest psychological theory, Neill believed that the child was not only capable of developing emotionally without guidance but also intellectually, ultimately finding out what interested them and ways of investigating it without recourse to any form of guidance or imposition. While this may vary from individual to individual, Neill was adamant that if a child was unwilling or unable to apprehend, for example, a subject such as mathematics, he should not be made to do so. In countering his doubters who believed children would never therefore actively seek to learn, Neill had faith that children would find out themselves what interested them but that it was only they who were the best judges as to when that should take place. As Neill makes it clear, this idea was strongly linked to the notion that the child was born innately good – 'Self-regulation implies a belief in human nature; a belief that there is not, and never was, original sin' (Ibid).

Within this childhood narrative constructed by Neill, *play* was an absolutely central aspect and the one which Neill used as a vehicle to express his interest in the development of childhood psychological fantasies. Indeed, many of the images we have of Summerhill involve aspects of play within the setting of the school grounds, with children partaking in child-like pursuits such as climbing trees. While these have served to symbolize the happiness and inherent naturalism of the environment, they have also been used as a stick by which to beat the school's ethos, as too often these activities have been dichotomized with academic study to propagate the myth that Neill's educational vision was founded on allowing children to run wild at the expense of 'proper' forms of learning. Nevertheless, as we have previously seen, play was an important plank of progressive thought, particularly among the emergent psychologists such as Jean Piaget who argued for its cognitive developmental significance. Once more, though, Neill goes beyond the 'acceptable' face of progressive thought and this seemingly uncontroversial notion by equating play with the expression of fantasy – a key characteristic of children's unconscious. By this, Neill meant a form of role play whereby children would enact latent impulses in the context of, say, the theatre or the games field or the dormitory. In some respects, this had a therapeutic dimension attached to it as it enabled children to externalize their illusions and release them through the context of activity. Neill, typically, argued that this is was an essential precondition for not merely a healthy condition of childhood but also for the maintenance of social order – 'One could, with some truth, claim that the evils of civilization are due to the fact that no child has ever had enough play' (Ibid., 68). The tone here is pure Neill, yet it serves to illustrate the ways in which he viewed any form of childhood repression – including the disavowal of play – as having consequences far beyond the basic educational setting.

Understandably, much can, and has, been said about Neill but his willingness to combine theory and practice and not to entertain accusations of hypocrisy does him, as even his critics would cede, great credit. Summerhill can be said to be as close a manifestation of Neill's radical philosophy as is possible to imagine. Not for Neill the disjunction between his utterances on education and what took place in the confines of his school! Interestingly, the character of Summerhill and the 'perfect' democracy which it espouses did not formulate along traditional lines. As writers on Summerhill have been quick to point out, the school evolved out of Neill's concern with children who were considered at the time to be 'difficult' or 'problematic' – akin in their way to the delinquents of Lane's Little Commonwealth. Such children were wrongdoers, deviants, thieves and criminals and it was through observation of their behaviour and an enactment of his profound convictions that Neill came to realize what was lacking within *all* educational systems.

Neill believed that behaviour of this type – what he characterized, following Freud, as *neurosis* – emanated from a lack of love and affection from the individual child's upbringing. As such, he saw actions such as stealing, as Skidelsky makes clear, as a 'symbolic stealing of love, the staking out of a claim for love, based on, and justified by, the expectation that the real thing would be denied' (Skidelsky 1969: 165). If motivation stemmed, therefore, from an assumption of parental disproval, then Neill simply approved of the act which confused the child's understanding of reality, leaving the way open for a cure. Many people therefore misunderstood the activity taking place within the school; Neill was not allowing delinquent behaviour merely for its own sake. Instead, he was doing so in order to allow the child to ultimately sublimate such feelings in favour of those which were not destructive and harmful. The distinction between freedom and license was an important one for Neill and recognizing and respecting the rights of other children was seen as a moral prerequisite in many of his writings. Engrained into the Summerhill ethos even today is the right to an upbringing free of adult imposition but only at the expense of recognizing that such freedoms come with a duty to likewise not harm others.

Although these ideas hark back to much earlier Romantic precepts, nowhere are they enacted with as much vigour and with as much ideological conviction as at Summerhill. In their own way, these ideas represent the ultimate expression of democracy – a democracy of the individual where children and their viewpoints are not only respected but also highly prized and valued. It would also be pertinent to stress that democracy in this context was not limited to personal freedom and aspects of Summerhill echoed many of the more traditional notions of self-government found in earlier Fellowship schools. The school itself was – and still is – fully self-governing with decisions being made at general school meetings at which all pupils and staff attend and their voices given equal weighting. The voice of the teacher counts for as much as that of the pupil. These regular meetings serve therefore as a decision-making body which delineates the schools' life and surroundings and which is constructed genuinely through a broad communal consensus. It is also one which affords children total freedom to govern all aspects of their life, including the social. In that sense, both forms of democracy can be seen to coalesce together and, overlain with the conviction of the innate wisdom of children, this could be seen to penetrate to the very heart of Summerhill's unique educational spirit.

There are, of course, inhering problems with Neill's approach which, understandably given its radicalism, go beyond the usual criticisms and accusations hurled at child-centred educators. First, comes a question at the very heart of progressivism generally and that is whether children freed from adults and civilization would resort to savagery and primitive barbarism, as William Golding seemed to posit in his novel *Lord of the Flies*. In many ways, as Neill admitted, the children brought to Summerhill did display such behaviour but, crucially, this was only a result of the discipline imposed upon them from their previous school or home life which had enabled them to develop perversions and anger. For Neill, then, savagery and barbarism in humanity was caused by an abundance of civilization and not seemingly by its lack! As a model for delinquent children, therefore, Summerhill seemed to work for it undoubtedly took away the urges to damage and destroy. This is still the case today where the school acts to successfully remove many of the worst impulses and habits of its more troubled pupils.

However, is this a model upon which one could construct a national education system? Does Neill overemphasize the ability of the child to be a self-directed and guided learner who, above all, wants to ultimately find out what interests him? This is a powerful argument and the degree to which children themselves are capable of understanding concepts such as democracy and freedom is questionable and has been articulated by critics such as Melanie Philips (1996), among others, who see the recent moral breakdown of society as stemming from more relaxed and 'progressive' attitudes to teaching and parenting. Should certain things be kept from children? It is true, of course, that within the confines of Summerhill these concepts and ideas were understood and used responsibly but was that perhaps due to its composition which was both small in number and fee paying?

This is a more important point than may first appear as it taps into an inhering limitation of Neill's educational system. As Neill himself recognized, Summerhill was as much a way of life as a school and despite his pronouncements to the contrary, he did not readily recognize that his education 'should acknowledge any duty to society to ensure that the new generations were trained for its purposes' (Hemmings, op. cit., 173). Concerned as it was with the development of individual children rather than the ways that the child might respond to the outside world meant that Neill's philosophy was only really adumbrated successfully in the context of Summerhill. It also meant that Neill perhaps failed to take account of the way in which children's desires and needs altered as they engaged with the outside world. Indeed, the extent to which Neil failed to engage with this external setting has proven a sticking point for many who accuse him of a naivety and idealism which is not rooted in the world of experience. Is it too simplistic to posit that 'the aim of life is happiness' (Neill, 1968, op. cit., 109) when the world demands that success (not that Neill would ever have countenanced the term!) comes down to passing examinations? It is the classic 'idealist versus pragmatist' debate and there is no easy and forthcoming answer.

Given the success of Summerhill in spawning a host of imitators (which will be further discussed in the Conclusion), there is evidently something to what Neill had to say in relation to pedagogic theory. Nevertheless, perhaps his greatest contribution has not been these educational pronouncements but the unconditional love of children which he both exemplified and demanded. Although he would perhaps have blanched at separating out the educational and the social aspects of his philosophy, it remains true that while few today would actively betray allegiance to his notions of unregulated child freedom, our contemporary assumptions about childhood are underlain by a greater desire to love, to be honest, to include and to approve than was previously the case. We cannot attribute this solely (if at all!) to Neill but undoubtedly he provides a corpus of writing whose basic integrity and humanity must make us question our own assumptions about childhood in a less than clear-cut age.

Notes

1 Some, such as the Kellog Briand Pact, were instigated with the sole purpose of declaring an end to the future use of war as a means of solving international problems.

2 This is evidenced by the range of authors who contributed to the *New Era*. A cursory search of articles reveals offerings from authors such as A. A. Milne and Aldous Huxley, the conductor Adrian Boult, Rabindranath Tagore and the South African leader Jan Smuts. Even the then Prime Minister Ramsay MacDonald promised to 'observe keenly' the activities of the journal!

3 The first Steiner school to open in Britain was Michael Hall, East Sussex in 1925.

4 Perhaps its most famous alumnus was HRH the Prince of Wales (Prince Charles) who memorably described the school as 'Colditz in kilts'.

5 One of the strengths of the history of education as a discipline has been, in recent times, the willingness and capacity of its practitioners to rediscover such figures and make cases for their importance in the progressive narrative.

This has been facilitated by the excellent cataloguing of their materials through collections such as those held in the London Institute.

6 Henry Newbolt's famous 1892 poem *Vitai Lampada* with its famous final line, 'Play up! play up! and play the game!' is a fitting testament to this ethos.

7 Badley was educated at Rugby School and Trinity College, Cambridge while Hahn read Classics at Christ Church, Oxford.

8 This was not the first time that Holmes had upset members of his own profession. Infamously, the Holmes-Morant Circular (in effect, a private written correspondence), also of 1911, called into question the competency of local school inspectors and teachers. There was a storm of protest from both political parties, the local authorities and, most significantly, the National Union of Teachers about the manner of Holmes' offhand denigration of an entire profession. While Robert Morant (the other party within the correspondence) was sidelined, Holmes avoided a similar fate by presciently retiring.

9 The most recent school inspection in 2007 was, however, in all senses, glowing, indicating perhaps a grudging reluctance on the part of the establishment to recognize that Summerhill's distinct culture seems to work at least for the pupils present there.

10 As well as the National Archives in Kew, the London Institute of Education retains a large collection of educational material and serves as a goldmine for scholars working in the field of the history of education.

11 Lane's patrons included the Duchess of Marlborough, who was herself an American but living in England following her marriage to the Duke of Marlborough – cousin to Winston Churchill.

12 MacDonald was Neill's hypothetical School Board Inspector and a representative of educational conformity and officialdom.

Key reading

A. S. Neill, *Summerhill, A Radical Approach to Education* (London: Penguin Books, 1968).
Robert Skidelsky, *English Progressive Schools* (Harmondsworth: Penguin, 1969).

Further reading

Judith Stinton, *A Dorset Utopia: the Little Commonwealth and Homer Lane* (Norwich: Black Dog Books, 2005).
Mark Vaughan, *Summerhill and A.S. Neill* (Maidenhead: Open University Press, 2006).
Edmond Holmes, *What is and What Might Be: A Study of Education in General and Elementary Education in Particular* (London: Constable, 1911).

6

Democracy: Parker, Dewey and the American Tradition

Introduction

In many ways, the twentieth century can be said to have been the *American* century. Although, at the vantage point of the twenty-first, we now take for granted the hegemonic dominance of American culture through its mass of televisual and multimedia exports, it must be remembered that the hunt for a cultural and artistic identity which was to define and characterize the nation was a process which occupied much of the period leading up to the Second World War. Prior to that, American lifestyles, practices and mores were testaments to a lasting pan-European influence. Much of this can be explained by the genealogical heritage of the pioneering settlers but also through the Francophile and Europhile tendencies of many of the early American politicians and nation-forgers such as Benjamin Franklin and Thomas Jefferson. Following in their footsteps, native artists like James McNeill Whistler and Winslow Homer betrayed this tradition in their landscapes and portraits; composers like Edward MacDowell emerged as Lisztian Romantics; Henry Wadsworth Longfellow and Walt Whitman were nascent Victorians while German Idealism, in the form of the kindergartens, pervaded the education system.

The succeeding century, however, was to see the emergence of a recognizably 'American' discourse and cultural achievement. George Gershwin and Leonard Bernstein were set to blend the sounds of jazz with the classical idiom, F. Scott Fitzgerald's *The Great Gatsby* was widely considered the first 'American novel' and defined the era which became known as the Roaring Twenties, poets like Ezra Pound and Wallace Stevens were lionized for their innovative Modernism, celebrities emerged in the figures of Babe Ruth and

Charles Lindbergh while painters like Jackson Pollock and William De Kooning with their energetic artworks forever associated New York with Abstract Expressionism and as being at the vanguard of 'the modern'.

The search for an American identity was not, however, solely forged through the creative arts. Within the more ethereal realm of philosophy, individual writers began to explicate, refine, concretize and develop the very notions upon which the American nation had been originally founded. These values had a long historical gestation as they had been enshrined from the outset in the United States Constitution and the triangulated governmental configuration with its unique form of checks and balances designed to form the most harmonious and fair system of administration and democracy. It was not therefore surprising that these thoughts began, over time, to be transmitted and channelled through those institutions and structures which, in one form or another, impacted upon the lives of all Americans – schools and the education system at large.

In defending the protracted and osmotic nature of the process, Michael Shapiro (1983) quite correctly points out that while initially, many Americans were in agreement about the aims of education, which was seen as a way to provide for the spiritual salvation of the individual, 'there was no consensus about the concepts that defined its methods and content' (Shapiro 1983: 1). Although the earlier ideas of John Locke relating to child psychology were starting to have an impact, as they had done in defining America's *laissez faire* political system, the dominant early religious perspectives of Calvinism and Evangelical Protestantism were crucial in defining educational practice throughout the decades immediately following the Declaration of Independence. While the more forgiving Protestants may have seen the harsh doctrine of 'Original Sin' as theologically and psychologically inadequate and were therefore comfortable in passing the burden of education from God to the mother, it did not stop even their educational regimes being relatively spartan, with habits such as 'obedience' thought of as capable of being learnt as well as any other.

Gradually, though, with the Calvinist's grip on American spirituality beginning to loosen, and writers such as the Hartford Congregational Minister Horace Bushnell advocating the importance of play in relation to spiritual growth, other more progressive philosophies became inculcated and ingrained within educational practices. A particularly popular model was that of the kindergarten and we have already traced its spread and development in the earlier chapter relating to women. Much of its initial influence was undoubtedly affected by the increasing ease with which men and women could now travel to Europe and observe, first-hand, the practices of Froebelian institutions. Occasionally, as in Lydia Marie Child's popular work *The Mothers Book* (1831), this drifted into slightly mawkish sentimentality – mothers not, for example, interfering 'with the influence of the angels' (Child 1832: 1) as their children 'come to [them] from heaven, with their little souls full of innocence and peace' (Ibid). Sugar-coated as such rhetoric seems, even this served to convey the changing spirit that was beginning to permeate thinking about children and young people in America. Gone was the frontier mentality of work and toil, to be replaced, instead, by a subtler appreciation of the significance of the child. In apprehending these lessons and seeking to reject what they perceived as the limitations of a restrictive and dogmatic religious curriculum, many young Americans, drawing upon their first-hand experiences, may have been struck by Friedrich Froebel's own personal religious battles against his father, a devout Lutheran minister, and the troubles of his own rebellious childhood and early youth. Froebel thus embodied the conflict between religious convention and ethereal philosophy which was now coming to America.

Alcott – The American Pestalozzi

One such figure to whom this new display of intellectual fervour appealed was Amos Bronson Alcott (1799–1888), scion of the famous Alcott dynasty[1] and the most significant figure among the early American progressive educators. Like Froebel, with whom he so clearly identified, even before entering the classroom or attempting to formulate any grand educational theory, he had shown himself a rebel by standing against the prevailing orthodoxy and setting his intellectual stall out against what he saw as the theory of innate depravity as purported by the Calvinists. In 1831, he commented, 'Of all the impious doctrines which the dark imagination of man ever conceived, this is the worst' (Alcott in Strickland 1969: 17 cited in Cavitch 2007: 319). Armed with these convictions and a strong working knowledge of Pestalozzi, Alcott therefore became a central figure in the gradual liberalization of the influential New England intelligentsia – a process which drew upon the anecdotal findings and homespun observations of many parents, published extensively in small newspapers and journals, which indicated that children, aside from being able to make far more sense of their surroundings than was originally believed, were increasingly taking a palpable delight in the external world and landscape. It was as a result of these recognitions that infant education was born in America, as schools emerged designed for 'educational experimentation as much as social reform' (Shapiro, op. cit.12).

In many ways, these schools could be considered the forerunners of the later kindergartens and while that parallel would not be invalid, it must be remembered that Alcott's theories drew equally strongly from his earlier classroom experiences as a school master in Connecticut and, in the vein of

Richard Lovell Edgeworth, from the observation of his own children as much as from any external influence. Nevertheless, like the European Romantics, Alcott's ideas also stemmed from a heartfelt sincerity that the role of the educator was to nurture the organic growth of the child rather than channel or lead them in pre-designated directions. His adherence to the value of developing the 'natural' child led many, including the pioneering historian and wonderfully named Ocatavius Frothingham, to dub him the 'American Pestalozzi'. This nurturing that was so much a part of Alcott's system was designed to focus primarily on the emotions and the conscience rather than the intellect as it was affections which, according to Alcott, acted as the, 'powerful spring which puts the young heart in action, and unfolds all its faculties in the sweetest harmony' (Alcott 1830: 8). Significantly, Alcott's theories were to be put into practice at a school in Boston's Masonic Temple which served to embody much of the Transcendentalist philosophy which he espoused.[2]

The kindergarten champion Elizabeth Peabody was his young assistant and it was her subsequent *Record of a School* (1835) which has allowed the historian an intimate access to the workings and practices of Alcott's establishment. Central to its function, the overall configuration of the school including its furnishings and décor was designed to 'address and cultivate the imagination and the heart' (Peabody 2007: 1) of the child. The term 'cultivate' in this context is important as it was through the observation of his own young children that Alcott had developed a theory which divided the infant's growing nature into two crude phases – the animal and the spiritual. According to Alcott, the animal nature of the child was the first to appear and this sought its enjoyment solely through the satiating of its basic appetites and desires. This was then succeeded by the divine or spiritual side of the child which emerged only after the adult had taken it through this process of cultivation via a series of 'conversations'. Peabody recalls: 'On these occasions he [Alcott] conversed with them, and by a series of questions, led them to conclusions themselves upon their moral conduct' (Peabody, Ibid., 7–8).

The educational goal therefore of these 'conversations' was to ensure the conquest of the lower, animal nature by the higher morality. The conversations themselves tended, in that vein, to focus more upon the development of the heart and the imagination rather than merely a filling of the head with unnecessary moral prescription. This can clearly be identified as an example of an early 'progressive' philosophy allowing, as it did, the child direct participation in its own education by ensuring that the impulses for reform and self-recognition came from within and were not imposed externally. Coming as it did alongside the Second Great Awakening in America's history – ostensibly, a migration away from the Calvinism subscribed to by many American Protestant churches – Alcott's work can be seen as developing and rationalizing a much more humane understanding of children and childhood.

Through understanding the significance of the conversations, the similarities and differences between Alcott and his Romantic contemporaries should therefore be evident. Clearly, Alcott did not believe in the idea of innate goodness as, for him, there was a perpetual struggle being waged within the growing child between the more primal animal feelings and their more cerebral moral counterparts, which it was the teacher's job to help the child overcome. The role of the teacher and environment was thus intertwined with the destiny and fate of the child. However, Alcott revelled in the power of the imagination which he attempted to stimulate through his pedagogy and, underpinning his education, was the belief in enabling children to achieve a more heightened and refined spiritual state – something which accorded closely with the Romantic idea of childhood 'purity'. Likewise, his attempts at facilitating this state relied upon the teacher acting as a guide, assisting the child in revealing the true extent of their inner self, which echoes much of the earlier Romantic discourse surrounding the organic growth and development of the child.

The effect of Alcott's schooling experiments and subsequent writings were profound, not least as the reactions they generated, ranging from the devotional to the outraged, sparked many in America to begin to ask searching, fundamental questions concerning the nature of childhood and the desired method and content of education. When, for example, should schooling begin? What was the role of the mother in relation to the teacher? What should be the balance between mental and moral education? In seeking answers to these enquiries, by the time of the Civil War and its aftermath, many Americans, particularly women, as recounted in Chapter 3, had begun to look to the European Continental tradition. Even Alcott, himself more sceptical over European methods, confessed that 'The German Kindergarten or child's garden is attracting attention with us. It is the happiest play teaching ever thought of, and the child's Paradise regained for those who have lost theirs' (Alcott quoted in Shaprio, 1983: 17). Although the kindergarten movement's spread in popularity and the widespread celebration of its ideals during its early years was not to last and was later counterbalanced by the increasingly rigid and dogmatic approaches of its followers and factional splits, it is important here to recognize the ways in which it emerged as one solution to the fundamental questions that were being posed by those such as Alcott.

As had been the case with the practices espoused by Rousseau, many parents began to successfully assimilate Alcott's ideas into their child-rearing, learning to appreciate the value and potential of the child more than had previously been the case. These departures were novel in the ways that they served to introduce a range of new religious and philosophical doctrines and concepts into pedagogical practice. While the roots of American educational Protestantism were, of course, too entrenched for it to be entirely uprooted and sidelined, it had to learn to accommodate itself with other creeds, which were frequently more metaphysical and speculative in their nature. In his own way, Alcott's belief that schools existed to build and develop general traits of character and that this was constituent of an education which was general and not skill-specific mark out this self-taught genius as the pioneer of so many of the perennial traits of American education, not least those relating to progressivism.

The new challenge to the old orthodoxy

If the ideas of Alcott, then, can be said to have been a forerunner to the spread of one particular tradition which has been traced within a previous chapter, by the end of the nineteenth century, one can identify the emergence of another, which arose ostensibly as a reaction against some of the more constraining aspects of individual state's school bureaucracies and the inflexibility and rigidity of their curricula. It was administrators such as William Torrey Harris (previously discussed in the kindergarten context) who bore the brunt of much of this resentment and it was his style of bureaucracy which was especially targeted for the steadfast grip it continued to exert over key areas of the American pedagogic system. In his magisterial study of progressivism, the doyen of American educational historians Lawrence Cremin (1961) cites this period, and the 1890s in particular, as a distinctly revolutionary time for American education in which it truly found its voice and identity. In this 'great decade', works such as William James's *Principles of Psychology* (1890) and his *Talks to Teachers on Psychology* (1899), Francis Parker's *Talks on Pedagogics* (1894) and Edward L. Thorndike's *Animal Intelligence* (1898) were set to usher in a uniquely identifiable and novel blueprint for future American progressivism. This spate of texts went some way to providing important features and characteristics of the American education tradition which, as we shall see, became adapted over the succeeding years by a host of different progressive educators. These works were thus pivotal in moving American education beyond its preoccupation with European theory and practice and into something recognizably as its own.

It would of course be overtly simplistic to conceive of American progressivism as being dominated by two competing idealistic viewpoints – that of Harris and his St Louis supporters and that constituted by the young rebels. As Herbert Kliebard (1986) has pointed out, the complex battle for supremacy over the American curriculum, in fact, encompassed a variety of interest groups whose ideals both overlapped and diverged even, he argues, to the point of rendering the term 'progressive' contradictory, meaningless and drained of any form of unique specificity. But, as even he was forced to acknowledge, there is little question that much of the 1890s reaction was the culmination of a more widespread, long-standing critique propagated by influential academic journals such as the *Forum* which explicitly sought to question the professional and administrative competence and bureaucratic unyieldingness of the nation's schools. Furthermore, theirs was a systematic protest attuned to the more widespread problems of society and its politics, which manifested in the need to oversee urban municipal reform and to provide a more vocational workforce as demanded by the up-and-coming and increasingly daring emerging business community. The aforementioned high-profile Harris was a particular target for their opprobrium. As Cremin makes clear, 'His emphasis [was] on order rather than freedom, on work rather than play, on effort rather than interest, on prescription rather than election, on the regularity, silence, and industry that "preserve and save our civil order"' (Cremin 1961: 20).

Such virtues, though undoubtedly noble, were seen by these younger men as otiose and failing to adapt to the demands of the modern America. Harris's programmes of study, which had become institutionalized across many counties, fostered too much divergence between subject areas, thereby failing to account for the full comprehension of human experience. Likewise, his insistence upon, 'Interest . . . as subordinate to the higher question of the choice of the course of study that will correlate the child with the civilization into which he is born' (Harris 1896: 493) was seen as limiting the potential choice and dynamism of the nation's future. This last point is particularly significant as his avowal of a carefully plotted Hegelian path, which had at its heart Hegel's own concern with tradition, institutions and bureaucracy, was increasingly seen as insufficient within the context of a brash, emerging and vibrant nation state. In respect, therefore, of the fact that the ideas of Hegel were central to Harris's educational vision, the critical response and desire to build upon and move away from his system represented, more broadly, an overturning of the dominant Anglo-European influence in favour of the development of something more distinctively and retrospectively identifiable as American. One could further posit that this was a moving away too from the earlier ideas of Alcott whose innocent and dreamy flights of fancy were being replaced by something altogether more modern drawing on understandings of the mind simply not available in the earlier age.

In the generation of this intellectual riposte, the most significant of the figures to emerge in this period was, without question, John Dewey (1859–1952) who was to himself be best characterized and most indelibly associated with this tradition. There was something Janus-headed about his vision, as it not only looked forward in defiantly rejecting earlier European precedents such as the kindergarten, but it was also retrospective, drawing as it did implicitly upon the pioneering American values of the distant past. Many of these values had emanated from the pen of Thomas Jefferson and Dewey, in one of his more political tracts *The Public and its Problems* (1927), was to later argue that education, at the most fundamental level, was necessary in order to allow the public at large to 'judge' events by making considered, reasoned decisions which would allow for the increase in the overall good of society. While the Jeffersonian conception of democracy was enacted in an age when America was, in all senses, far smaller with multiple and overlapping communities and settlements, Dewy held true to the value of education as a social (and not merely individual) good. He thereby represented an important aspect of emerging American intellectual thought which held that truth was formed in the day-to-day context of the lived social world and was subject to a scrutiny of its contribution and its effects within the community.

It was, furthermore, his belief that many of the problems of the world emanated from a basic lack of democracy – a term, as we shall see, which was central to his thought and which carried for him, and many other thinkers, a whole host of meaning. Although seemingly unproblematic with its overtones of cooperation and conciliation, this has not stopped political philosophers throughout history remarking upon the apparent injustices and legal complexities generated by democracy. Plato, indeed, went as far as to adopt what was, to modern understandings, an anti-democratic position in his *Republic* while all the while claiming that his was a fair and equitable system. One of the running threads therefore throughout American progressive educational history was the way in which democracy came to be understood in this unique context and the extent to which, now, we can consider such systems of schooling to be 'child-centred'.

Given his centrality to American progressive education and, particularly, his unique formulation of the concept of educational 'democracy', this chapter will have unashamedly as its central focus the work and achievement of John Dewey. This emphasis is hardly misplaced or novel and is reflected in many of the standard histories relating to American education where Dewey has been referred to as histories relating to American education, such as those by Lawrence Cremin (1960) and John L. Childs (1956), where Dewey has been eulogized and seen to embody the 'American faith in education'. (Childs, 1956: 105). Such deification, though, causes a problem as the vast shadow cast by Dewey means we are often blind to those others working in his umbra. Quite simply, while he may have been its most articulate exponent, democracy and schooling were not his invention and there are important earlier examples from American history which indicate attempts at conjoining progressive educational methods with democratic ideals.

Perhaps the most celebrated of those past experiments was that carried out by Colonel Francis Parker (1837–1902) who can be seen as an important pioneering figure in this American democratic tradition. Dewey, recognizing this, was to refer to Parker deferentially as 'the father of progressive education' (cited in Cremin, op. cit., 21). However, Parker's reputation rests, unusually, less on his writings than from his development and implementation of a specific educational scheme which he developed at schools in Massachusetts and Chicago, the former of which located in Quincy was to give its name to his famous 'Plan'. Having served briefly as a schoolmaster and as a volunteer in the Union army (hence the soubriquet), he undertook the obligatory tour of Continental Europe through a family inheritance where he became immersed in the philosophies and pedagogies of Germany, France and Switzerland. Upon his return, Parker was appointed by the local school board with a brief to rectify and improve the schooling of the local children who, while competent in the more formal aspects of the curriculum such as grammatical rules and textbook familiarity, were outwardly ill-prepared when writing personal letters, comprehending unseen passages and the general skills of life. Under Parker's stewardship therefore, the set curriculum was abandoned, as was the insistence upon the use of copybooks and readers. Instead, magazines and newspapers were introduced into the classroom, geography was taught via outdoor excursions, spelling techniques were modified so as to be more inductive and subjects such as drawing were initiated to stimulate children's creativity. Subject interrelation, which made meaning more accessible to children, was practised and attempts were made to relate children's learning to aspects of real life.

Given, perhaps, its novelty as much as its success – the pupils stood fourth in their county in respect of arithmetic – the school was soon overrun by the national media, teachers and superintendents. It was these external agents who talked of the 'Quincy Plan', something Parker himself was quick to deny arguing that he was merely 'trying to apply well established principles derived directly from the laws of the mind' (Parker 1879 cited in Cremin 1953: 245). While some in professional circles accused him of subverting the traditional business of learning by neglecting the basic exercises of literacy, the success of his system allowed Parker to migrate to the Cook County School in Chicago. If the root of Parker's philosophy was clearly derived from other sources, it was here that he demonstrated his own innovative contribution to the progressive movement as his school became the epitome of his particular conception of the theme running throughout this chapter – that is, the idea of democracy in educational settings. In Parker's words, his school was organized as a 'model home, a complete community and embryonic democracy' (Parker 1894: 450), whose curriculum, as it had been at Quincy, was based around the principle of informality, with subjects being reinforced by methods of communication, notably unique 'Reading Leaflets' which were distributed to the students.

Parker himself was not a natural writer; many of his published works stem instead from lectures he gave to teachers or else from materials developed in preparation for his own teaching classes. Perhaps for that reason it has been suggested by some historians that his own educational philosophy was not greatly endowed with novelty, borrowing liberally as it did from the aforementioned traditions and ideas of Pestalozzi and Froebel. This is most certainly true as his understanding of the child was generically Romantic – an innately good being designed to be encouraged and nurtured through phases of growth. His view of the teacher too was appropriated from elsewhere; he viewed their role as merely releasing the latent impulses towards learning inherent within every child – a view, as we have seen, which had a long historical precedent.

This seeming lack of anything 'new' may explain why he is rarely afforded the same level of scholarly attention as his more well-known contemporaries and why what little literature has been produced has tended to be American in origin. Nevertheless, such judgements are to do Parker a grave disservice. He was himself a modest man, happy to admit his influences and what counted for Parker ultimately, as Jack Campbell (1967) points out in one of the few extended treatments of the man, were the intricacies of practice and not theory. This onus upon practicality and his introduction of the American formulation of democracy into progressive schools mean, therefore, his is a reputation surely worthy of restoration. Nevertheless, while posterity may have been less kind, to his contemporaries Parker's example provided a beacon and source of continuing inspiration.

John Dewey – The American Colossus

John Dewey can, in many ways, be seen as the heir presumptive of Parker and the man who was to most fully carry on his legacy. Fittingly enough, it was to be a torch passed on by children. Upon his arrival in Chicago in 1894, Dewey placed his two sons in Parker's Cook County School and was to forever speak warmly of the practices he observed there. Mutual admiration notwithstanding, however, Parker and Dewey were cut from two different educational and academic cloths. Whereas the former took a view of education that was based on practice and 'doing', only towards the end of his life bothering to flesh out his theoretical work and codify his ideas, Dewey approached the field from the opposite end – he already had a nascent theory and he sought to use educational settings to prove its validity. This theory, as has been alluded to, stemmed from his observance and distaste at what he saw as the evils of industrialization which were detrimental not merely in their directly noxious effects, but because of the confused, fractious and essentially disharmonious communities which the industrial process had served to create. In his early tract *The School and Society* (1899), Dewey recounted those recent changes and lamented the death of the old rural and subsistence way of life which celebrated close familial ties and bonds and a sense of community:

> We cannot overlook the importance for educational purposes of the close and intimate acquaintance got with nature at first hand, with real things and materials, with the actual process of their manipulation, and the knowledge of their social necessities and uses. (Dewey 1899: 23–4)

This passage serves to illustrate what was seminal and indeed progressive about Dewey's philosophy – notably how, for him, the school was not merely seen as preparation for life but that it *was* a representation of life itself. This was reflected in his belief that the school should be a manifestation of democratic ideals and that it should have a purpose of improving and ameliorating the existing external world. In Dewey's words, society had to evolve to become more 'worthy, lovely and harmonious' (Dewey 1899: 28) and the school was irrefutably bound up in that process. Educational change was therefore, by implication, fully enmeshed within the development of societal change. In that, he was going beyond the work of Parker who, while understanding that schools had to be fair, reasonable and of interest to the child, did not see them as having such a critical latent function.

As a consequence of this premise, the term 'democracy' in American progressive educational discourse became loaded with potential connotations which involved aspects of the political, social and the individual. This was, and is, distinctly novel. Many of Dewey's contemporaries such as the influential English legal sociologist Sir Henry Maine retained a particularly narrow lexical view. They saw the word either in purely political terms, as a mere tool of government, or else as a form of 'social contract' which, stemming from Thomas Hobbes, involved an element of servitude to a ruling body in exchange for limited freedom and full protection in law. Dewey's view of democracy though was that it was more multifaceted and fluid and, as he made clear in several of his key works, represented a way of living as much as belonging. He saw the changes which had affected education in recent times, notably those wrought by the doctrines of Fordism, as entwined with the concurrent changes in democratic structure. The school was therefore to be dragged, kicking and screaming if necessary, away from being a mere function of the state to being at the very catalytic heart of its activity through leading by example and constantly innovating in its practices. This carefully refined articulation went far beyond what anyone else had said, and so, acts as the real starting point to any discussion of the American democratic progressive tradition.

Defining this tradition, and the ways in which it can be considered 'progressive' is not particularly straightforward as it is hardly appropriate to refer to Dewey's philosophy as 'child-centred', not least in the way that that phrase has so often come to be used in the contemporary common vernacular. The role and centrality of the teacher, for example, was equally, if not more, important for Dewey and some commentaries have convincingly argued that preparing children for roles in future societies has the potential to negate individual development at the expense of the collective. As Winch and Gingell (1999) point out, Dewey 'has been accused of ambiguity as to whether [his] education is to promote new values in society or to encourage students to improve on the old' (Winch and Gingell 1999: 167). This note of caution is well sounded for Dewey was most certainly *not* calling for a radical educational overhaul. In many ways, he feared change for its own sake, the raison d'être of which was merely to replace the traditional – 'There is always the danger in a new movement that in rejecting the aims and methods of that which it would supplant, it may develop its principles negatively rather than positively and constructively' (Dewey 1938: 6).

A similarly powerful argument stems from the pen of the philosopher of education Amy Gutmann (1999) who, in challenging Dewey's oft referenced quotation – 'what the best and wisest parent wants for his own child, that must the community want for all of its children' (Dewey 1899: 3) – warns that the principles which many 'wise' community members would value most highly, for example, literacy and numeracy, may not be those desired by other communities with differing needs and priorities. Gutmann pithily poses the question:

> If democracy includes the right of citizens to deliberate collectively about how to educate future citizens, then we might arrive at a very different conclusion: that the enforcement of any moral ideal of education, whether it be liberal or conservative, without the consent of citizens subverts democracy. (Gutmann 1999: 14)

Although Gutmann herself is broadly supportive of democratic education, sympathetic to Dewey and has developed a sophisticated way of thinking which has much to commend itself to the American habit, a substantial body of the more hostile criticism of Dewey has indeed frequently emanated from those seeking to view 'progressivism' as a movement on the opposite side of the Atlantic and 'child centredness' as a dangerous and misguided concept relating exclusively to that tradition of writing deriving from Rousseau's *Emile*.

A recent significant contribution to this debate, *Getting it Wrong from the Beginning* (2002) by the brilliant Kieran Egan, is noteworthy as it, although once more demonstrating a sympathy to progressive ideals, argues convincingly that through misappropriation and misunderstanding of ideas, the continued presence in American schools of what are considered to be 'progressive' notions strive, even now, to undermine institutional effectiveness. The chief culprit for Egan is seen as Herbert Spencer, the heavily bewhiskered nineteenth-century English polymath whose writings on education, collected in 1860 under the title *Education: Intellectual, Moral and Physical*, exerted an undue and disproportionate amount of influence on American educators, including Dewey. Spencer's typically Victorian concern with the notion of progress, so Egan believes, conspired to load down and yoke subsequent pedagogues to an unrealistic form of teaching. The author's case is typically convincing, yet, by his own admission, his book 'is not a work of history . . . My topic is current education' (2002: 8) and therefore such attacks surely do not preclude the modern-day historian from offering a narrative based around underlying concerns of influence and value. Judgements on effectiveness can perhaps be better left to others. Where Egan's work *is* significant, though, is that it highlights appreciably not only the often forgotten contribution of Herbert Spencer but also the continuing influence, malevolent or otherwise, Dewey's ideas continue to hold today.

Indeed, it is hard still to overstate the importance of Dewey to American life. While it would be convenient to label him a 'public intellectual' or a 'polymath' in the vein of T. S. Eliot, Bertrand Russell or maybe J. B. Priestley, his voluminous corpus of writings cover such a vast range of topics (politics, education, science, philosophy) in such a serious style that he, as much as anyone else, came to be the touchstone and point of reference for practitioners in a range of fields.[3] As the historian Henry Steel Commager succinctly put it, for an entire generation 'no issue was clarified until Dewey had spoken' (Commager 1950: 100). In that spirit, Dewey involved himself with a range of public causes, including civil liberties, the rights of teaching unions and even the foundation of a new political party, demonstrating his commitment to, and belief in, a practical activism rather than mere ivory tower intellectualism. In discussing his commitment to social reform Spencer Maxcy is right to mention how Dewey both 'spotted trends and tendencies in the culture at large and seized upon them to inform his philosophy' (Maxcy, 2002: xiii) and that he developed 'a new logic and methodology of inquiry for treating philosophical issues which drew upon scientific method and Darwinian evolutionary biology' (Ibid: xiv).

In educational terms, while the American system's principles have waxed and waned over the twentieth century, responding ideologically to political events such as the Cold War, it tended to always do so conscious of its rejection or otherwise of Deweyian ideas and values. At the height of the international tension in the 1950s, Dewey and his supporters even served, somewhat *reductio ad absurdum*, as sacrificial lambs for the United States' failure to overhaul the Russians in sending out manned space-craft:

> the already swelling outcry against the educational system became a deafening roar. Everyone joined in—the President, the Vice-President, admirals, generals, morticians, grocers, bootblacks, bootleggers, realtors,

racketeers—all lamenting the fact that *we* didn't have a hunk of metal orbiting the earth and blaming this tragedy on the sinister Deweyites who had plotted to keep little Johnny from learning to read. (Miller and Nowak 1977: 254)

Overegged as such rhetoric is, it illustrates the polarized caricatures of Dewey as both saint and sinner and his continued presence within ideological and educational debates. Even contemporary teachers still cite Dewey and his practices as vital, not least in relation to confronting the abiding issues facing inner-city American schools still divided over the problematic issues of race and ethnic underachievement. Such therefore is Dewey's stature and the range of his intellectual interests, any discussion here will be, by default, only scratching the surface of his vast output. Nevertheless, the reader should begin to understand that all of his major writings betray a unique interconnectedness which, it is hoped, will become clear through a more detailed exploration of his educational works. In particular, it is imperative in any narrative of progressive ideas to consider Dewey's understanding of the term democracy, how in educational practice, that perhaps differed from the previously discussed New Education Fellowship and its quirkily British circumstance, and finally, how his definition serves to underpin theories of human development and experience.

John Dewey – Life, theory and context

As is to be expected, the corpus of literature by and about Dewey is at once voluminous, daunting and a lifetime of study in itself. However, of all of his works, the most celebrated and well known is undoubtedly *Democracy and Education* from 1916, which ranks alongside Rousseau's *Emile* and Froebel's *The Education of Man* as being among the most important texts in the progressive *oeuvre* and whose reputation and readership extends far beyond mere students of the history of education. For anyone seeking an embodiment of the American liberal educational tradition with its emphasis upon education as a form of democracy including a brilliant reconceptualization of vocational learning, this is the place to start. Jay Martin (2002) has even gone as far as to call it 'the most mature consideration of the many roles of education in America's progressive society' (Martin 2002: 255).

Despite its many seminal qualities, and controversial as it may be to say, it is possible from a stylistic standpoint to argue that Dewey wrote *better* books. *Democracy and Education* certainly suffers from occasional repetition and there are the first signs, perennial in Dewey's work, of the difficulties in understanding and interpretation exacerbated by his love of imbuing simple terms such as 'democracy' with multiple layers of complex meaning. A recommended supplement to this text would therefore be the earlier *The School and Society* (1899) which introduced not only Dewey's own novel orientation of society but the relationship and role that education had to play within it. In particular, this work allows the reader an imagining into the practices of Dewey's early schooling experiments which, as will be made clear, were critical in allowing him to formulate his unique vision of education from the standpoint of practical experience. Furthermore, it is in his two seminal later works, *How we Think* (1933 revised edition) and *Education and Experience* (1938), that Dewey had begun to weave together and connect some of the more disparate aspects of his thought. Drawing on his vast understanding of psychology and philosophy, these books present detailed explorations as to how thinking affects learning and how education can escape and transcend the traditional academic/vocational educational divide. Difficult as these two works may be, they are worth the effort and much of the following discussion will unashamedly utilize ideas first promulgated in these texts.

The explanation as to why Dewey's ideas have had such a long-lasting appeal, and are still required reading for native educational practitioners in training, can be ascribed to their inherently national character which is delineated by three major factors. First, their overall tone is that of a 'middle path' characteristic of American liberalism which tilts towards neither the disproportionate individualism of a Rousseau nor the excessive reliance on the state à la Plato. This path was, and continues to be, cultivated in America's political landscape with complex overlapping systems of government (state, federal and district) designed to promote neo-liberal and free market ideologies. Second, is the influence upon Dewey of pragmatism, a school of philosophy popularized by William James and Charles Peirce and the Harvard School who, as Louis Menand (2001) has made it clear, were 'more responsible than any other group for moving American thought into the modern world' (Menand 2001: x–xi). This they achieved by offering a challenge to the accepted Rationalist and Empiricist European and Continental philosophical traditions. Finally, and most significant of all for those interested in the life of Dewey, the very precise historical contexts out of which his works were to emerge contributed to its very localized character. Specifically, the late nineteenth century provided a backdrop of mass industrialization with the erection of skyscraper high rises so characteristic of American cities and the supplanting of old agricultural forms of subsistence with more mechanized forms of labour.[4] Ken Jones (1983) has identified this latter factor, in particular, as a key feature when distinguishing between these different American and European traditions – 'Whereas Dewey defined educational purpose in terms of the individual's integration into a modern society, the Europeans laid greater stress on 'self realization' and the inner growth of the individual' (Jones 1983: 28).

This industrialization was underscored by the doctrines of Henry Ford whose business models of mass consumption and consumerism and the most efficient ways through which that could be achieved had, furthermore, started to be adopted in American high schools. Education was increasingly perceived through the lenses of efficiency, batch production and there prevailed a clear differentiation between academic and vocational education, with the former intended only for the very few, elite students. The widespread social tensions caused by these processes were to have a direct and ultimately long-lasting impact upon the life of Dewey, as two recent biographies by Jay Martin (2002) and Alan Ryan (1995) have made clear. In particular, these authors have been keen to stress the importance of the effect his early formative years in the turbulent city of Chicago had in shaping his thought and social conscience. His observation of the infamous Pullman strike[5] and its equally notorious quelling by the forces of law and order was indicative of the growing social urban unrest, and his friendships with various social reformers who were responding in a variety of ways to these recognizable problems was to play an important role in instilling him a need to 'put thought and action together and thus create something solid from the chaos [he] encountered' (Martin 2002: 154).

While such biographical detail is, of course, necessary for the reader to appreciate in order to grasp the human motivations behind Dewey's work, it does not explain the paradigmatic intellectual frameworks which buttressed his writing. In that respect, the second of the factors alluded to above becomes of considerable importance as an understanding of the philosophy of pragmatism aids the historian of education when seeking to come to terms with the core of Dewey's thinking in the specific American context. As its name might suggest, pragmatism held that all ideas, values and social institutions found their origins in the practical circumstances and situations of everyday life. The worth of an idea was therefore to be measured in whether or not it contributed to the public good – that is, in a social and not a utilitarian sense. The criterion for making such a judgement, crudely speaking, derived from a scientific habit of mind, the cultivation of which Dewey saw as a vital part of his educational process. Indeed, underlying much of his writing was his particular conception of an 'articulate public' which had received the benefits of a broad arts and science-based curriculum. Given pragmatism's insistence on the synergy between theory and practice, education thereby became important in cultivating individuals to successfully reconcile both.

For Dewey, it was therefore imperative that society and the democratic communities constitutive of such societies were continually evolving, both intellectually and morally. Such a belief rejected, by default, 'absolute' belief systems, principles and dogmas as points of view should be continually open to debate, contestation and not innately rigid. In that regard, Dewey's ideas are close to those of the philosopher Karl Popper whose seminal work *The Open*

Society (1945) argued that societies, like science, should not remain bound by set ideological frameworks but that their component beliefs should remain open to challenge and falsification, ultimately moving continually towards a version of empirical truth. Where therefore would this leave adherence to Marxist ideology or dogmatic devotion to an inflexible progressive philosophy such as that of Rousseau? It was for these reasons that much of Dewey's thinking can be seen as a direct rejection of meta-narrative approaches and as representing change in a more gradual and evolutionary sense through the dissemination of progress and social justice.

Where, though, can Dewey's ideas be said to fit, ideologically, within the context of the American narrative? In educational terms, we have already explored, in relation to gender, how the kindergarten movement became widespread and established within American educational districts thanks, in the main, to its tireless female champions. Although there were differences in the way that the 'kindergarten philosophy' was interpreted, broadly speaking, their establishments represented a particular type of 'democracy' which allowed individual children to express themselves freely without serious fear of reprisal or correction. It would therefore be a fallacy to conceive of the Deweyian tradition as superseding or replacing the kindergarten model. The power exerted by Hegel, for example, on William Torrey Harris has been well documented, but only very recently in work carried out by John Shook and James Good (2010) has it been shown to be equally enduring and pervading on Dewey. Michael Shapiro (1983) also points to the significant influence Froebel's ideas had on the young Dewey and his frequent need for the kindergarten teachers to provide him with evidence for his increasingly scientific, laboratory-school-based theories of child-rearing. Dewey should not therefore be totally divorced from the impact and influence of the earlier Romantic figures or, indeed, the kindergarten movement which they so inspired. As has been stressed in other chapters, progressive educational movements are rarely so easily characterized and this is particularly the case in America, part of whose narrative involved the search for its own recognizable intellectual voice which, inevitably, involved distilling various competing trends and traditions..

Such overlapping tendencies find expression in this relationship between Dewey and the kindergarten movement whose association was bilateral in nature. Not only did he seek to use the data generated in the schools in the development of his own educational theories but, by the same token, they, in turn, acknowledged him as being a catalyst for achieving recognition for their particular teaching methods within the wider academic community and university training departments. In particular, at the level of practice, one key notable determining influence upon Dewey was the work of Jane Addams and Helen Starr, the two founders of Hull House in Chicago. Through their advocacy of meeting children's immediate needs through a range of activity-based programmes they 'enriched Dewey's views of justice and social action, prompting him to rethink aspects of his evolving philosophy and theory of education' (Simpson and Stack Jr 2010: 4). In particular, it was Hull House's pioneering mission statement which convinced Dewey of the need to view education as a means of achieving social justice and reform directly through the sorts of practices and activities which were to be at the forefront of his later writing.

Dewey therefore was clearly drawing upon many of the social reforming instincts and attitudes of his forebears and it would be ahistorical, mistaken and overly simplistic to posit the existence of two divergent and disconnected traditions. Nevertheless, in order to fully recognize the unique impact of 'Deweyism' and, for our purposes, to explore how it came to represent an innovative strand of American educational culture, it is worth focusing upon the differences. Such differences, typically, became more apparent following Dewey's forays in educational practice. How often does practice and the inevitable interpretation of practice serve to clarify and elucidate meaning which is impossible to explicate in the written form! In particular, Dewey had concerns over the psychological approaches adopted within the kindergarten institutions – 'The root problem was that educational practice in the Froebelian kindergarten determined child psychology – just the reverse of the relationship which Dewey proposed' (Shapiro, op. cit. 162). At a wider level, Dewey considered many of Froebel's principles, or at least the ways in which they had been adapted in the kindergartens, as being obsolete and constrictive. The child's day was seen as too regimented, and so, Dewey proposed radically extending the free time available to the child and taking them away from set activities. Likewise, while Dewey appropriated the 'Gifts', he was quick to ensure that they were used to support the work being undertaken in the classroom and not seen as central aspects in themselves around which a curriculum was supposed to fit. In many cases, additional materials of Dewey's own conception such as larger blocks were permitted in the junior schools and teachers found it more appropriate to import popular children's games and songs in place of the more traditional Froebelian entertainments. The justification for this, as was alluded to in an earlier chapter, emanated from a general academic and pedagogic consensus that Froebel's educational devices were increasingly outdated and irrelevant to the interests and needs of the modern school child, a view still held by many practitioners today, but one that carried weight in the emerging culture of America.

Similarly, Dewey himself used the words 'sentimentality' and 'sensationalism' (Dewey 1899: 120) in relation to the Froebelian belief that children could learn to apprehend the external world through the merely symbolic. A cornerstone of the justification for the use of the 'Gifts' was that they allowed for the stimulation of the child's imagination through the internal mental translation of plane shape to three-dimensional space, thus enabling the child to begin to act upon the real world. In a typically practical vein, Dewey argued that this was akin to sweeping, 'make believe rooms with make believe brooms' (Ibid., 118) and that it was assuming too much to pre-suppose that children would be capable of making such an empathetic jump and be able to subconsciously imbibe the spiritual significance of Froebel's ideas. This dismissal points to the very practical understanding Dewey held in relation to his education system which had to be capable of being enacted in real arenas and settings.

This scepticism was a result of his changing conception of the role of play which developed as the ideas of Froebel became superseded in his mind by those of the American philosopher George Herbert Mead. A near contemporary of Dewey (he was born in 1863) and a key pragmatist thinker in his own right, Mead posited that the importance and origins of play arose not from anything metaphysically intangible but from the immediate context of the social environment – a clear example of the ways in which fundamental educational precepts had to be rooted in the 'real' world. Education therefore did not, by default, necessarily have to take place in a specially constructed school such as that proposed by the advocates of Montessori or the kindergarten system. To achieve a 'good' standard of education, it was sufficient to replicate the normal social conditions of man which were not pre-loaded for assigned outcomes. The social environment thus became central to Dewey's educational view as it was in this specific setting that the validity of ideas could be tested and truths emerge by a process of experimental induction.

Dewey and his followers ultimately therefore called for an end to any form of 'play' in the kindergarten sense by encouraging, instead, activities such as farming and mining. This change had about it, perhaps coincidentally, a distinctly American aspect as such pursuits reflected an emerging propinquity and attachment to the newly industrializing power that America was in the process of becoming. The emphasis upon the outdoors served as well to render visible Dewey's ambivalence about a merely urban context to learning. His entire adult life was spent in support of farmers and their interests – they had been hit particularly hard by the Great Depression – and this was certainly reflected in his concerns to move away from, where possible, an education rooted entirely in metropolitan landscapes.

Dewey's ideology therefore can be argued as the product of his total assimilation and then partial rejection of the burgeoning kindergarten movement, a rejection caused by his antipathy towards the symbolic and the potential alienation suffered by pupils solely pursuing their own ends. He was particularly critical of Rousseau in that regard who, he believed, failed to emphasize sufficiently the creation of citizens at the expense of merely pursuing individual development. In discussing Rousseau's scheme of education and his understanding of the ways that humans develop innately, Dewey contended that 'the moral is not to leave them [children] alone to follow their own 'spontaneous development', but to provide an environment which shall organize them' (Dewey 1916: 134). It is thus clear to see how and why the ideas of democracy and society fit into his scheme and, more importantly, how they, in themselves, were a manifestation of a particularly American collage of thinking. All the same, the explicit connection between the idea of 'democracy' and progressive schools is not exclusive to the Deweyian world view. Indeed, we have explored a latent manifestation of it in relation to the British progressive school movement where establishments such as Summerhill and Bedales sought to establish their own miniature communities with the student voice prominent in shaping the school's rules and curriculum. However, in this American context, more emphasis was ultimately placed upon configuration, integration and orientation within a future, distinctively American society rather than a deliberate self-positioning outside of the remit of the strictures of the state.

John Dewey – School practice

Thus far, the discussion has been concerned with detailing not merely Dewey's theoretical ideas but also their direct cultural impact and the way in which they embodied something peculiarly American in their various manifestations. It is now necessary to explore the ways in which these ideas were embodied in practical educational settings and this is particularly pertinent, given the emphasis placed by Dewey, and by others discussing his work, upon the notion of *praxis* – that is, the reconciliation of theory and practice. This is evidenced not merely by his own educational efforts but also by the thousands of teachers raised on a healthy diet of Dewey's teachings. This practical experience was demonstrated through his University Elementary School (commonly known as the Laboratory School) which he set up in Chicago in 1896 as part of his recently acquired university post and which he designed, after that fashion, to ensure the maintenance of 'demonstration, observation and experiment with [the] theoretical instruction' (Dewey 1896 cited in Dewey 1972: 434). Even its very name hinted that it was to be not merely an institution designed to provide its founder with raw data through which to substantiate and develop his theories but also to 'exhibit, test, verify, and criticize theoretical statements and principles' (Dewey, Ibid., 437).

Furthermore, 'Only the scientific aim, the conduct of a laboratory, comparable to other scientific laboratories, can furnish the reason for the maintenance by a university of an elementary school' (Dewey 1899: 88). The triumph of

Dewey's Laboratory School and this strong conviction is indicated by its continued acknowledgement today and it is held up as a cause célèbre in much the same way as, from different traditions and eras, Yverdon and Summerhill often are by those who continually agitate for the eminent practicability of progressive ideas. More prosaically, its fame helped to ensure that Dewey 'became the most famous educator in America' (Martin 2002: 201).

Such a scheme was also important in maintaining a link with the work of his former Johns Hopkins University tutor Granville Stanley Hall who, as we have seen, had very deliberately coined the term 'laboratory' when referring to his own setting which he used as the basis for scientific investigations into adolescence. Dewey too was striving to develop a 'science of teaching' based upon empirical observation and evidence and his school was seen as a test-bed where this could take place effectively. Even today, Dewey is still widely associated among practitioners with the term 'scientific method' and his attempts to devise a workable, practical method in the classroom. The format of the school curriculum was therefore to be based upon a scientific appraisal of the communities needs and there were frequent discussions among the school staff in order to ascertain what these should be.

Despite the enormously experimental nature of the school, however, its structures of governance and discipline were not demonstrably exact nor did it serve merely as an intellectual plaything for its founder. This is evidenced not only by Dewey's own work *The School and Society* (1899), which served to illustrate the theoretical base upon which the school was founded, but also through the memoirs of two former teachers, Katherine Camp Mayhew and Anna Camp Edwards. Although essentially hagiographic, and so right to be afforded a level of scepticism, their jointly written *The Dewey School* (1936) is still one of the most powerfully conceived descriptions of life in a progressive school and is rich in its detailed descriptions of everyday activity. In digesting it, the reader is able to garner an appreciation of the success Dewey had in bridging the perpetual divide between theory and practice and to begin to assess how closely the activities of the school fulfilled the aims of its creator.

One predominant emergent theme is the way in which the local activities were continually linked to aspects of the external world outside the perimeters of the school. In justifying the curriculum's deploying of a range of practical activities such as carpentry, cooking, sewing and weaving, the authors cite the

important industries of the everyday outside world . . . The questions of living under shelter, of living in a home, of daily food and clothing, of protection through the home, and the support of life through food are basic things for all higher civilization. (Mayhew and Edwards 1936: 28)

Likewise, within the context of the laboratory and the kitchen, children were encouraged to perform tasks such as growing corn in a variety of different climates and cooking domestic foods which would relate to tasks carried out in everyday life in everyday homes. Frequently within those activities there is evidence of deliberate attempts to develop children's skills in a range of disciplines simultaneously, thereby encouraging the breakdown of strictly demarcated subject areas. In one noted example – the building of a model farm – completion of the structure involved the inadvertent learning of mathematics:

> the children used a one-foot ruler as a unit of measurement and came to understand what was meant by 'fourths and halves'— the divisions made, though not accurate, were near enough to allow them to mark off their farm. As they became more familiar with the ruler and learned the half-foot, and the quarter-foot and inch, finer work was naturally expected of them and obtained. (Ibid., 83–4)

Examples such as this abound frequently in the text and exemplify the major characteristics of Dewey's education system in action. Broadly speaking, what emerges is a relatively traditional curriculum (mathematics, history and the liberal arts) but overlaid with innovative ways of transmission and communication. Pupils learnt by experiment, enquiry and investigation while, even among the staff, much attention was paid to the ways in which these could be carried out. Teachers met regularly to discuss and coordinate their curriculum strategies. While the Laboratory School had various inherent advantages – it was small in number and pupils were the willing sons and daughters of the professional, liberal middle classes – it served, as we shall later see, to act as an inspiration for many subsequent American progressives drawing on Dewey's ideas. As Robert Westbrook (1993) points out, 'If Dewey did not have a plan for establishing the schools as powerful adversarial institutions in the heart of American culture, he did have a clear vision of what he thought the schools in a thoroughly democratic society should look like' (Westbrook 1993: 8). Such a vision was steeped in the principles of pragmatism, practicality and democracy.

Dewey's yearning to democratize learning was not merely confined to school structures and practices. As his theory became modified, expanded and all-embracing over time, he sought to assess not merely the potential implications that his concepts could have upon the educational curriculum but also how those could relate directly to aspects of mankind's psychology. These concerns were represented most clearly in his belief in the inhering false dichotomy between the academic and the vocational realms of education. Despite being then, as now, an essentially capitalist society, American education was beset with rigid differences between those labelled as 'achieving' students who were of a more academic mind-set and those whose skills lay more in the practical sphere. Although perversely being more indebted to the latter group, there nevertheless existed an unequal weighting in the relative values that society had placed upon them.

Dewey, however, believed differently. In his major contribution to the public debate about vocational education during the years of the First World War (1913–17), he sought to emphasize that the academic and vocational strands of education should not be thought of either as two competing discourses or as being on their own individually sufficient. This cleavage he referred to, cryptically, as an 'Either-Or' (Dewey 1938: 1) which was his term for the way in which mankind 'recognizes no intermediate possibilities' (Ibid). The ideal education therefore was one which combined elements of both in order to give students the widest range of personal capacities. On no account was 'vocational guidance [to] be conceived as leading up to a fixed and irretrievable choice' (Scheffler 1995: 34).

In many ways, Dewey's desire to provide students with a cognitive breadth as well as depth foreshadows the later work of the hugely influential English philosophers of education, R. S. Peters and Paul Hirst, whose intellectual concerns were very much with debating the sorts of subjects a student should study as part of a broad curriculum. Hirst, in particular, was keen to stress that subjects should consist of the acquisition of practical abilities as much as substantive knowledge and information. More pertinently, it was Peters who shared Dewey's concerns that learning should not be seen as a process that ceased when one left school. Instead, for Peters, the purpose of formal education was to prepare young people to prepare themselves as situated lifelong learners through a widening of their 'cognitive perspective' (Peters 1973). In Dewey, these ideas manifested themselves in the processes of constant evolution, both within an individual and their society, which originated from the exigent social questions arising from everyday life. In the process of answering these questions, through both words and deeds, an individual would evolve, and by evolving, aspire towards a 'better' state of being.

In order for that to happen, it was important that such an individual was equipped with a scientific, critically aware habit of mind which had been formed via the various strands of learning Dewey proposed. In the penultimate chapter of *Education and Experience* (titled 'Progressive Organization of Subject Matter'), he was keen to stress the vitality of a learning rooted in conditions of experience and which aroused impulses of curiosity for knowledge – 'It is a sound educational principle that students should be introduced to scientific subject-matter and be initiated into its facts and laws through acquaintance with everyday social applications' (Dewey 1938: 98). Although one of the last published statements Dewey was to make explicitly about education, it was nevertheless still a theme that was to continue to excite debate in a range of fields in the years ahead. The philosopher R. F. Dearden (1968), for example, drawing on Dewey, published seminal accounts contending that education was as much about the development of patterns of reasoning and truth testing while the term 'critical thinker' has entered the lexicon of modern day educational speak.

It should by now be inductively apparent that the sort of progressivism being espoused here by Dewey is ostensibly of a different flavour to many of those outlined in previous chapters. Much of this stems from its flailing poly-mathematic quality and its organic evolution. As a theory of learning, it first involved studying childhood and the characteristic qualities of what it meant to be a child. However, as individual children had to relate to society, Dewey then had to think politically what that society should look like. The good maintenance of that society was dependent on a cultivated scientific mind (psychology) which meant it became conceptualized as a philosophical theory of experience, of which the school was one of the key settings. In much the same way that science relied on experiential testing, verification and, finally, synthesis to find 'truth', so too could educational principles be conceived of in much the same fashion, relying on what Dewey referred to as 'empirical and experimental philosophy' (Ibid., 13). This was only made possible, of course, when the kinds of democratic conditions outlined above had been formed and created to provide the circumstances necessary for such experimental enquiry.

This was not, though, the theory of experience as outlined by other democratic progressives who might have legitimated the validation of any and all experiences of the child. For Dewey, not all experiences were to be thought of as equally educative; indeed, those experiences which served to arrest or distort the growth of further experience were to be seen as 'mis-educative'. In that sense, Dewey was perhaps closer to Rousseau's tutor figure than he may have cared to admit as his educational philosophy carried with it a teleology which was linked to the development of desirable individual characteristics so that children could become 'useful' members of a future society.

Dewey's legacy and social reconstructionism

When considering the legacy of Dewey and those who followed in his not inconsiderable footsteps, it is important to remember that his 'middle' path was not one which garnered universal approval from all educational thinkers. Those wedded to beliefs in scientific effectiveness, including the followers of Granville Stanley Hall, considered his theories too radical while those who sought an educational system based around social reconstructionist principles undoubtedly found Dewey's ideas anaemic and lacking in sufficient social bite.

This latter group is particularly significant for they provided, after the kindergarten movement and Dewey's pragmatic-democracy approach, the 'next wave' of innovating progressivism in America. Although, once more, it is fallacious to view such intellectual movements as superseding each other in a linear way and hardline advocates of Dewey persisted well into the century, in the years leading up to the Second World War and just after, Dewey's ideas were unquestionably subject to critical reflection, supersession and advancement. As had been the case with a number of other thinkers such as Froebel and Owen, it was often familiarity breeding contempt with many of the loudest challenges to Dewey springing from those who had learnt at the feet of the master.

The concern of the social reconstructionists lay not merely with the failings of the Deweyian system itself but more because it seemed to them insufficient in combating a rising counter-reaction against many of Dewey's precepts from those, under the influence of William Bagley, who came to be known as the essentialists. So called because of their adherence to belief in a core of 'essential' knowledge which it was the school's duty to transmit through appropriate didactic methods, the essentialists were broadly aligned against curricula innovation, structural change and attempts to draw upon the experience of the pupil. Much like that earlier hate-figure of progressives, William Torrey Harris, Bagley and his supporters also conspired to maintain an enormous level of influence over educational policy and its implementation within the classroom context. As Wesley Null (2003) makes it clear in his superlative biography, Bagley – professor of education at the Teachers' College of Columbia University between 1917 and 1940 – was among the most prolific, charismatic and prominent of teacher educators in American history who served to act in the public mindset as a viable alternative and outright antithesis to Dewey.

Bagley himself though was no cultural relic; he was as concerned as anyone else with the inhering problems within America and in intentionally polarizing him with the progressives and casting him in the role of the 'bad guy', many commentators have overlooked the subtleties inherent within his thought. This is unfortunate as the differences between Bagley and the progressives stemmed less from their shared political desires to affect social regeneration (in which Bagley believed) and more to do with the way in which they believed that should be carried out within the schools themselves. Far from liberating the child, an activity-based curriculum was considered by the essentialists to have 'robbed American children of their common cultural heritage' (Kliebard 1986: 229). A year before the outbreak of World War Two, for example, Bagley launched a scathing attack on education referring to the 'appallingly weak and ineffective' (Bagley 1938, quoted in Ibid., 192) curriculum which had served to 'enfeeble' a nation. It is little wonder, buoyed by this emotive rhetoric, why the educational curriculum became a keenly contested battleground in the middle decades of the last century.

Further to attempting to ward off Bagley, it was also becoming evident to the social reconstructionists that Dewey's educational 'project' was itself beset with a number of limitations. Most pertinently, it had failed to fully grasp and deal with the widespread social malaise impacting across America. It seemed that while the ideas of democratic schooling were perfectly workable at the micro-level of individual children and schools, they had been less than successful in going beyond the confines of the classroom to address the inequalities residing within the world of adults. Far from being agents for social change, as Dewey had envisaged, progressive schools had tended to exist in a vacuum, isolated from the wider concerns of society. In his seminal work, *Education at the Crossroads* (1938), Boyd Bode summed up the prevailing concern – 'Progressive education must either become a challenge to all the basic beliefs and attitudes which have been dominant for so long in every important domain of human interest, or else retreat to the nursery' (Bode 1938: 5). Typically in such narratives, it was frequently the educational conservatives and formalists who were portrayed as backward-looking in seeking to thwart attempts at progress and advance. Unsparingly, Dewey's clan were thereby cast in the role of limp and unwitting collaborators whose failure to be sufficiently radical and proffer educational solutions based upon a more rigorous democratic mindset had left the progressive movement bereft of direction at a time when radical alternatives were much needed.

As is perhaps easy to construe, the social reconstructionists themselves were frequently political radicals who continually agitated for increased spending on health, welfare and, of course, education. In many ways, their notions of subversion, challenge and a desire to reconstitute society in a mould shaped more equitably are not to be divorced entirely from the critical pedagogy theories developed later by, among others, Henry Giroux and Michael Apple. Given that those authors too are American and are very much concerned with issues of curriculum, it is plausible to once more draw ideological links in relation to their shared concerns over democracy and democratic schooling. For those self-defining as social reconstructionists, unlike Dewey, democracy was associated with not merely initiation into a moral membership which was to put itself to some vague form of 'public good' but, rather more, to be active participants in direct forms of action advancing radical educational, social and political agendas.

George S. Counts, the American firebrand

Perhaps the most daring, forthright and brilliant of the reconstructionists was George S. Counts (1889–1974) whose bullish and thought-provoking writing belie (outside of America at least) his relative obscurity today. Sadly, the scholarship centring upon Counts has tended to be exclusively American in origin and this has proven a contributory factor in his relative under-representation within wider historical narratives. However, as Ellen Lagemann (1992) has made clear in a comparatively recent and very powerful article, current debates over the extent and purpose of testing in schools and the groundswell of interest generated by movements opposed to the social injustices propagated by a loosely defined 'capitalist' system mean that now, more than ever, his reputation and writings are worthy of reinvention and rediscovery. When Counts spoke in characteristically bombastic tones of living in 'troublous times, an age of profound change and an age of revolution' (Counts 1932: 31), he could very easily have been addressing ears attuned to the problems of today. In an age where social and racial divisions continue to be of perennial concern for those in education, 'Counts's vision of teaching in and for a democracy epitomizes the challenges that continue to face educators struggling to reconcile the demands of social justice and individual freedom' (Perlstein, quoted in Cuban and Shipps 2000: 53).

Counts' most famous work, the Depression-era pamphlet *Dare the School Build a New Social Order?*, took few pedagogic or ideological prisoners in challenging the nations' teachers to, quite literally, erect a new society in which students could be better prepared to live harmoniously within a world that, as Dewey had also observed, had been fundamentally transformed by the processes of industrialization. The basis of this short book was a series of lectures Counts had given to the Progressive Education Association, based upon his first sole authored works which had been studies into the Russian education system. Could he have chosen a topic more designed to raise the ire of the conservative sections of the American establishment? And yet, Counts was not seeking to play the role of *agent provocateur*, if anything, his budding analyses were some of the first attempts to successfully weld together studies and experiences of educational practice with meta-narratives emanating from sociology, with prominent concerns over the relationships between class, education and power. Counts was keen to explore how schools operated as social institutions, how they related to other such institutions and the ways in which they could facilitate change.

Counts' essential point was that the Progressive Association which served as the organized mouthpiece for those even loosely affiliated to the democratic child-centred flag had failed in its mission to promote 'social welfare' (Counts 1932: 5). Instead, it had become hijacked by a particular section of American society – the upper middle class – who had ceased to be progressive (under Counts' understanding of the term), thereby undermining the drive towards basic social progress:

If Progressive Education is to be genuinely progressive, it must emancipate itself from the influence of this class, face squarely and courageously every social issue, come to grips with life in all its stark reality, establish an organic relation with the community, develop a realistic and comprehensive theory of welfare [and] fashion a compelling and challenging vision of human destiny. (Ibid., 9)

This sweeping 'vision of human destiny' was one in which cooperation, national planning and economic controls replaced what Counts saw as the worst excesses of rampant capitalism's cruel inhumanity which had stunted morality and left a nations' religious principles in the dust. Schools, he argued, must not be seen in isolation from the rest of society. This, as the failures of Dewey's model attested, was to imperil the urgency of social reform. Although denying it, Counts said much that would have appealed to those of a Marxist hue. Like them, he saw education as a vehicle for transforming individuals and freeing them from the ideological shackles of a false consciousness imposed by wholesale industrial changes. Unlike them, however, he pictured teachers as being at the vanguard of this revolution; it was they who had a collective duty to indoctrinate pupils into the new vision. Failure to do so was an avoidance of their singular responsibility. Many of his statements thereby carried with them associations of duty and obligation which served to swathe his projected revolution in the colours of the American flag. Unlike other socialists for whom the nation state had little meaning and was a barrier to global cooperation, for Counts, it was vital for America as a country to return back to the subsistence values of the past. He, like Dewey, was therefore quite happy to combine the rhetoric both of social progress and advancement and of a return to something approximating frontier values.

For Counts, the cure to the American condition may have been sweeping wholesale change but the symptom was clearly rabid individualism. Intriguingly, as Wesley Nulls (2004) has subtly made clear, in that regard, there was little to choose between both him and Bagley. Bagley believed that the lack of any core curriculum driven by an overarching sense of the common good had left the nation intellectually and vocationally barren and underprepared for being able to tackle the problems of the Depression. Counts too was concerned, albeit from a very different ideological vantage point, that the existing curricula was insufficient in having the potential to combat the social ills being propagated by acute financial collapse. Although perhaps not so wedded to the notion of an 'essential' body of knowledge, many of the points Counts was to make in his 1932 pamphlet were therefore reiterations of those previously made by Badley. Similarly, Bagley was drawing upon an understanding of democracy which was, in the Jeffersonian sense, concerned with the diffusion of knowledge to the majority and which was not to be the preserve of an elite group of individuals. This, for Bagley, was a 'moral' imperative as much as a social one, hence his unqualified demands for highly trained and knowledgeable teachers.

It seems that it was not merely the reconstructionists who had a monopoly on matters of fairness and equality!

It was, however, the latent characterization of Badley as a reactionary from, among others, Dewey, which meant that it was only from the pen of Counts that statements regarding change and the curriculum became acceptable and slotted into an evolving progressive discourse. In that regard, posterity has not been kind to Bagley. Viewed now as a cultural dinosaur, it would be inaccurate to characterize him as a progressive in terms of method and practice but, in regard to the concern he showed with the democratic dissemination of knowledge, one can identify him as tapping circuitously into that distinct strand of American thinking which has characterized much of their educational narrative across the century.

However, for all of Bagley's claims to be misunderstood, he lacked something of Counts' electrifying presence and provocative speechmaking. Many listening to Counts throwing down the gauntlet to the nation's teachers were struck dumb by the power of his oratory which had the effect of creating a seismic shift in educational circles; after 1932, as Herbert Kliebard reminds us, 'the Progressive Educational Association was never the same' (Kliebard 1986: 195). Counts' ideas now held sway and he was able to recruit to his cause many young, idealistic teachers, ostensibly from the teaching college at Columbia University. The journal *Social Frontier* succeeded in promulgating Counts' views and received a very vocal backing from such key figures as William Heard Kilpatrick, John L. Childs and Harold Rugg. Those at the vanguard of the movement were described appropriately as 'anti gradualists' – change, for them, was something that had to be immediate, instantaneous and enacted by a national army of vocal and militant teachers. Their vision was at once both utopian and practical, seeking as it did to overturn the social injustices propagated by capitalism through the direct action of the state's most trusted employees. Even the accusation of indoctrination was turned on its head; indoctrination (a term openly used by Counts and his supporters) was a *good* thing, necessary if the teacher-planned future society was to be democratic and reconstructed from the ashes of the old.

It was thus George Counts, and those whom he inspired, who added an additional layer to the 'democratic' education of Dewey and who began to talk of an 'ideal' society not merely in the abstract but as something concrete, desirable and, above all, obtainable through direct action. Such a vision was driven by the need to remove rabid inequalities, level the educational playing field and, in the process, facilitate individual expression. By so doing, much of their rhetoric drew on a particular vision of the American past which enshrined virtues of neighbourly cooperation, equal rights and direct participation as members of communities – be they schools, towns, professional bodies or the nation more generally. In this way, it can be seen that although advancing the course of progressivism, the reconstructionists too were drawing upon that unique formulation of democracy which was so dear to the American nation and which had underpinned the previous century of their educational theorizing.

The legacy of Counts and Dewey

Towards the end of their lives, both Dewey and Counts migrated away from education. Dewey's later writings became more explicitly philosophical (his last published book was titled *Knowing and the Known*) while Counts became entangled in the murky world of politics, working with the nascent American Labor Party and by establishing the Liberal Party as a left-leaning alternative organization to those in the centre. In many ways, though, the history of American progressive education over the course of the last 60 years, since Dewey's death, has been shaped by reactions to their earlier tenets and writings. Understandably, the reception afforded to Counts has been significantly more hostile than that given to Dewey. Through his leftish posturing and occasional demagoguery, his has been a system of education which has frightened and upset the safe American middle with its traditional aversion to extremist radical politics. Even, as we have outlined, during the Cold War period, cultural conservatism meant it was hard for even more 'soft' progressive ideologies to make any headway and impact in schools. Dewey's liberal ideology, for example, was given Communist connotations and seen as not only being potentially corrupting of the nation's young but also as failing students for not giving them sufficient skills with which to compete in the global marketplace – a key consideration at the time of the Cold War.

Utilizing the dialogue and rhetoric of standards and comparison, the seminal document *A Nation at Risk* (1983) provided a particularly powerful example of how far Dewey's stock had fallen as it seemed to associate failing standards and a general educational mediocrity and malaise with the dominant discourses which Dewey sought to put forward – once more, child-centredness was characterized as all play and no work. This has remained a constant threat to progressivism in an age of markets and choice, as has been illustrated by anxieties raised over former President Bush's *No Child Left Behind* Policy (2002). Even Dewey's status as an American 'sacred cow' and seemingly canonical figure has come under attack in recent times. Works such as those by Allan Bloom (1987) and E. D. Hirsch (1987) have sought to question the enduring desire to pay lip service to Deweyian notions of schooling and school practice. While these works were not educational in their focus, concerns have also been voiced in relation to many of the practicalities of Dewey's system. Much of the anxiety over standards, for example, can be found in Diane Ravitch's *Left Back: A Century of Battles over School Reform* (2001) which 'notes John

Dewey's influence in generating at least two of the misconceptions that now cripple American education: the use of schools to solve social and political problems and the depreciation of academics in favour of assorted "activities"' (Edmondson III 2006: 4). In a similar vein, Charles J. Sykes's *Dumbing Down Our Kids* (1995) exposes similar troubles in the education system and seems to heap much of the blame for this with the progressive school movement. Nor should it be thought that these are right-wing polemics; instead, they are serious academic contributions which indicate that there is not yet a consensus on Dewey's legacy and that his educational project is still up for contestation.

However, for all the pessimism, what progressivism has existed in the United States context has really been driven by two key thrusts. The first has been that of critical pedagogy which will be considered in a later chapter and which has tended to draw, somewhat ironically, given that many of its theorists have been North American, upon a European body of literature, notably that of the Frankfurt School. The second has been a more 'mild' form of progressivism which has continued to draw from the wellspring of Dewey and his notions of school democracy, albeit not always openly or explicitly. On the one hand, this audience has been academic, and for every work prepared to lambast Dewey, there have been an equal number, of which Alfie Kohn's (1996 and 2000) are the best examples, which have sought to invoke his ideas as a corrective against the increasing adherence to testing, standardization and tables. More importantly, his ideas are still widely taught at education colleges and in university departments and while they may not always be fully understood – a perpetual difficulty when one separates education from the rest of his philosophy – they are at least subject to critical review and appraisal from those going into the field of teaching as practitioners. Today, a long list of schools and colleges from Los Angeles to Maine define themselves as 'progressive' and their mission statements frequently invoke Deweyian notions of democracy and cooperation. Admittedly, such terms are somewhat open to disputation and the range of practices in these schools is undoubtedly greatly various; however, it provides at least numerical evidence of the perennial regard with which child-centred ideas are held in the educational establishment and attempts to kick against the pricks of governmentally imposed doctrines of examinations and measurement.

Much of the reason why such ideas have become ingrained in this way stems from the work done by William Heard Kilpatrick (1871–1965) – a colleague and self-confessed disciple of Dewey – and the example he set in acting both as a university academic and educator. Significantly, as a self-respecting Deweyian, he did not believe in the separation of academic theory and vocational practice and the promulgation of such an agenda has been at the heart of much of the subsequent training of teachers in America. In an important article, Kilpatrick adumbrated what he called the 'Project Method' which was a system of education devoted to 'wholehearted purposeful activity in a social situation as the typical unit of school procedure' (Kilpatrick 1918: 334). Such a system, which sought to integrate learning around a theme rather than discrete subject areas with the teacher as a guide and facilitator, clearly owed a considerable debt to the classrooms of Dewey's Laboratory School which Kilpatrick observed first-hand. Like Dewey, his was not a system built upon airy contention but a practical, reasonable and workable method and its development exemplifies one way in which such progressive ideas have maintained their currency in America's schools.

Aiding this process has been the decentralization of the American curriculum. As Robin Alexander (2000) observed, the clear historical demarcations between state, federal and district level meant that their teachers have been free to pursue more innovative and inclusive educational strategies within the classroom, unencumbered (at least relative to other countries) by centrally imposed direction. While this has decreased in the 13 years since Alexander's pioneering study, examples from American history show how such structures have allowed for developments to occur. The work of Herbert Kohl, for example, in pioneering open plan classrooms is a case in point. Drawing from his own teaching experiences in New York, his short text *The Open Classroom* (1969) advocated a system of 'open and creative' teaching in order to be less authoritarian within the context of the classroom and allow for student differences to be articulated more peaceably and their opinions and values respected. Much of this derived from adjusting and making 'open' the layout and spatial configuration of the classroom – specifically by removing internal walls and barriers so as to facilitate ease of access and group and project work in the classroom. In every sense, this was 'community' schooling.

By contrast, in language reminiscent more of Counts, Kohl talked of 'authoritarian' learning, which he equated with 'closed' schools which 'teach people to be silent about what they think and feel, and worst of all [they] teach people to pretend that they are saying what they think and feel' (Kohl 1969: 116). It could be argued that Kohl here overemphasizes the importance that architectural design can have in shaping ideology and reduces a school's ethos to its physical manifestation and configuration, yet there is much to take from his commitment to open and free schooling and the democratic ideology it espoused. In particular, in seeking to adjust the school's layout in this way, Kohl was invoking the idea that democracy, such as it was, could be reflected in a school's design and architecture and was not merely confined to a curriculum or philosophical approach to education. Coincidentally (or perhaps not given the liberalizing ethos of the time), in Britain, the Building Bulletins issued by David and Mary Medd (nee Crowley) were also positing the development of open plan classrooms and these were influential upon the Plowden Report's views of architecture. Kohl's definition, like that of Plowden, sought to therefore expand school 'democracy' to incorporate explicitly those aspects of school which had hithertofore received only tacit recognition.

It was perhaps the most significant part of Kohl's argument that he very deliberately cites his experiences in the '*black* ghetto' (Ibid., 11, italics added), signifying an important reason for the continuing attraction Dewey's ideas seem to have for practitioners and why such beliefs refuse to go away. Democracy is as much about global representation as it is about child-centredness and in coming to terms with, and looking to overcome, ethnic division and underachievement, many have seen the democratic school as a way of bridging those difficult divides. The term 'democratic' is in itself perhaps slightly outmoded; the academic-turned-head-teacher George Wood (2005) has talked instead of the 'restructured' school and has convincingly shown, illustrating his case with practices drawn from his own pioneering Federal Hocking High School in Ohio, how the desire to create a 'finishing school for democracy' by creating good citizens with desirable virtues is still pertinent in the American educational mindset. Indeed, the influence of Dewey (and, for that matter, Thomas Jefferson) is tangible in the descriptions of his school, which relies upon periods of unstructured time for free activities, a thorough understanding of content at the expense of examination preparation and student involvement in the running of the school through participatory councils, fund-raisers and interviewing for teaching positions.

The term 'restructured' is apt in this context for the recent 'small schools' movement in America overseen by Deborah Meier (a friend and collaborator of Wood's) sought to fragment American schools from large, thousand-strong centres into institutions with no more than 200 pupils. While this could be seen as no more than an exercise in bureaucratic streamlining – and questions have been raised as to the possibility of ever equalizing such numbers – in a way, it perfectly represented the recent trend in American education to maintain and manifest the idea of democracy in schools by providing the conditions and environment in which children can be more active participants in their own learning. Smaller schools, of the type proposed by Meier, would thus be able to facilitate this by affording children more opportunities for teacher–pupil contact time and individual programmes of study. Woods' work therefore serves as a call to arms to the teaching profession to retain a link with the past and ensure that American education maintains its commitment to democracy and democratic forms of culture. This is clearly not progressivism of the European and Romantic variety; perhaps, it was only the still broadly unloved Counts who came close in recent times to adumbrating a singularly child-centred curriculum, and so, it may be somewhat fatuous to compare the two traditions. Analogously, the same point could be applied in relation to broader political concerns where 'left' and 'right' aspects of the political spectrum have different connotations. Nevertheless, as American society and culture has found its voice across the century, so it has established its own progressive tradition – one dependent on democracy, society and the child's place within it. Its continuing and burgeoning evolution today – in the forms of architecture, school size and configuration – perhaps provide the greatest monument to the work of the forefathers.

Notes

1 The Alcott family life was immortalized in Louisa May Alcott's classic semi-autobiographical account, *Little Women*.
2 Transcendentalism refers to the large philosophical grouping of writers and intellectuals, the most famous of whom – Longfellow, Whitman and Thoreau – believed in the 'transcendence' of life beyond that experienced by the senses. Taking progressive stands on women's rights, the abolition of slavery and education, their views on the natural world encouraged Americans to adopt the virtues of self-reliance and individualism.
3 As one example, the University Library of Cambridge credits 71 books under the search term 'John Dewey'.
4 It was these changes in Europe which had so impressed the young Emile Durkheim that he set about explaining them relative to the changing nature and shape of society, which he referred to as mechanical and organic solidarity. In America, it took until the twentieth century with the work of Robert Park to fully explore the sociological dimension to urban living.
5 The Pullman Strike of 1894 was a conflict between the labour unions and the railroad companies with its origins in the town of Pullman, Illinois. Throughout the course of the strike, 13 workers lost their lives.

Key reading

John Dewey, *Democracy and Education: An Introduction to the Philosophy of Education* (New York: The Macmillan Company, 1916).
Lawrence Cremin, *The Transformation of the School; Progressivism in American Education, 1876–1957* (New York: Knopf, 1961).

Further reading

Jay Martin, *The Education of John Dewey: A Biography* (New York: Columbia University Press, 2002).
Louis Menand, *The Metaphysical Club: The Story of Ideas in America* (London: Flamingo, 2001).
John Dewey, *Education and Experience* (New York: Kappa Delta Pi, 1938).

7

Social Reform

Introduction

Writing in 2009, the historian Edward Vallance in his marvellous survey of the kaleidoscope of radicalism referred presciently to 'the enduring power of the idea of a "radical tradition"' (Vallance 2009: 15). It is therefore clear that one of the common factors across time which drove and gave impetus to 'radical' groups as ideologically disparate as the Levellers, the Diggers, the Chartists and the Suffragettes can, crudely, be said to have been a desire to improve and better the lot of the disenfranchised and marginalized groups within society – women, the working class, religious dissenters and so on. Consequently, it is perhaps unsurprising that, in the context of radical social movements and amid deep-seated and often revolutionary calls for 'root-and-branch' change and reform, education has often had a central role to play. It is a common opinion, for example, of the 'left' in England that self-improvement stems from self-enlightenment, which itself, in turn, emanates from education. Even today, left-wing fringe groups frequently run didactic courses for their incumbent members. Brian Simon, in discussing the radical tradition in education, referred to 'that [tradition] which sees educational change as a key aspect (or component) of radical social change' (Simon 1972: 9). The term education, in this particular context, has, therefore, an ambiguity of meaning, referring to the very fact of enlightening individuals as well as the pedagogic processes through which this may occur.

However, as shall be demonstrated in this chapter, radical ideologies and progressive practice have, in the past, often been reconciled and the two are far from mutually exclusive. It is perhaps self-evident that progressive education should (or *could*) go hand in hand with wider concerns of social reform; progressive educationalists, after all, ascribe great importance and centrality to the notion of the child and, as has been seen, this almost always involves their physical as well as mental well-being. Nevertheless, few progressives have sought to incorporate their theories of child development into any larger scale analysis of society or, even further, to agitate directly for social change while dreaming of a distant utopia. This has been implicitly made clear in previous chapters. Some educators such as Mary Wollstonecraft were clearly a product of their literate, middle-class upbringing with no great desire to educate the mass numbers of the working class; others such as John Dewey had a distinctly ambiguous relationship with those agitating for radical social change while those such as A. S. Neill were disdainful of all political creeds (even to the extent of supporting the continuance of private schools), so it is a falsehood – albeit a persistently convenient one – to associate 'progressivism' with 'radicalism'.

Conversely, the writings of historians like Harold Silver (1975) and, especially, Brian Simon (1972), which elaborate this unique relationship between education and radicalism incorporate the writings of men such as William Godwin, Thomas Paine and William Morris who, while to a man recognizing the major role education had to play in alleviating the worst excesses of the state, were neither practicing educators nor, perhaps for this reason, were they concerned with adumbrating philosophies which could be deemed to be contributing to the 'progressive' tradition. Indeed, much of their received radicalism stemmed from their diametric opposition to the teaching and practices of the existing voluntary and religious schools who relied upon a curriculum heavily, and unsurprisingly, devoted to religious teaching and the acquisition of 'dead' languages – Greek and Latin. In that respect, as Simon makes clear, one of the continuities that can be seen in this tradition is 'the emphasis on science and scientific education as the means to truth' (Ibid., 10). While therefore the reader is encouraged to seek out these primary works as, beyond their huge historical importance, they do contextualize more broadly the intellectual and social background which framed much educational thought, such writings will intentionally not be discussed or considered within the context of this chapter as the focus here remains upon practices and ideas that can broadly be considered 'progressive'.

In addition, as Silver has pointed out, the term 'radicalism' has also been used to refer to a tradition among members of the middle class whose commitment to the expansion of education 'contained a degree of condescension [and] a notion that education was a cheaper and more effective form of social protection than prisons and punishment' (Silver 1975: 97). This was particularly noticeable within the later Christian Socialist movement who, somewhat paternalistically, sought to use their education to steer the working classes away from violent revolution, rhetoric and insurrection. Few of these groups could, in any sense, be considered educationally progressive!

Equally, some of those with grave and direct concerns as to the health and well-being of children – for example, the McMillan sisters (Rachel and

Margaret) – are rarely thought of as educational progressives and have been often shamefully overlooked in that regard by previous historical narratives. As has been made clear, however, in view of the theme of 'social reform' and its relationship to such educationally progressive philosophies, equal consideration must be given to those ideas whose values are as much about the fitness of the body as of the mind. It is perhaps little wonder that those writing on this issue, particularly the McMillans, frequently sought to link progressive educational theory and rhetoric with issues of a more general concern and the future of the well-being of the nation.

Robert Owen and New Lanark

Perhaps the most pertinent historical example of this peculiar combination of education and social reform stems from the work of the Welshman Robert Owen (1771–1858), particularly during his time in charge of the celebrated 'model village' of New Lanark, situated in the picturesque county of Lanarkshire in the Scottish Lowlands. The Lanark village was to serve as the location for an historic attempt at founding a miniature community based around the communitarian philosophy and proto-socialist beliefs of one man. Although initially founded by the entrepreneur David Dale who constructed cotton mills and rudimentary houses for its workers, it was after its appropriation by Owen in 1800 that Lanark was moulded into the communal form with which it is best associated today. While still a thriving cotton mill, it became celebrated for its pioneering attempts at collective living, including the sharing of facilities and houses, primitive forms of social security and insurance and, most importantly for our purposes, radical forms of schooling.

This was not the first time, of course, that an individual had endeavoured to construct an autonomous self-sufficient community in this way. Famously, the Alsatian pastor Johann Friedrich Oberlin (1740–1826) had earlier set a unique precedent by seeking to actively better the lives of peasants in the village of Walderbach, situated in the Alsace-Lorraine valley. This he had achieved through the construction of bridges and civic works, by increasing agricultural production and, crucially, through the building of schools. His incentives and motivations were, however, quite different from Owens for Oberlin was seeking to combine, theologically, both the spiritual and the earthly realms and saw one way of doing this as through harnessing the nobility of labour which was, he believed, the craving of the soul. The schools and chapels he built were therefore ostensibly directed towards affecting a unity with God and not, as was to be the case with Owen, for creating a specific tailored environment suitable for harmonious living and growing children. In addition, we have no first-hand accounts detailing evidence of progressive educational practices within Oberlin's particular community. Although Oberlin is therefore worthy of tacit acknowledgement for his bold attempts at group living, he was not in any sense seeking to conjoin these beliefs with any form of radical educational or social practice.

Oberlin's background was that of a humble (albeit fiercely intellectual) pastor. Owen, by supreme contrast, was recognized and respected in his time as 'the prince of the cotton spinners' with the ear of many influential Establishment figures and an enormous personal fortune to boot. All the same, despite these obvious advantages, Owen's posthumous reputation has been characterized by a degree of fluctuation unusual for a man so famed and revered by his own contemporaries. His unique brand of communitarianism, for example, seemed latterly out of step with the mid-nineteenth-century economic boom which was glossily represented by the pomp and splendour of the Great Exhibition. Similarly, the later rise of more radical ideas in the forms of Marxism and socialism offered new and far more direct and practical solutions to the encroaching problems of mass industrialization and working class unrest. As such, while lip-service was frequently paid to Owen, and he was identified by such luminaries as Karl Marx, Henry Hyndman and John Stuart Mill as being the 'father' of both the British socialist tradition and of the cooperative movement, it took until 1969 and the pioneering work of J. F. C. Harrison in his seminal book *Robert Owen and the Owenites* for historians to fully come to terms with and appreciate the importance and significance of the Owenite movement and of Owen's own writings. Prior to Harrison's endeavours, academic assessments of Owen had tended to be dismissively hostile; E. P. Thompson, for example, denigrated Owen as 'a preposterous thinker' and 'a mischievous political leader' (Thompson 2001: 136).

Nevertheless, while Owen's central precept – that an individual's character was formed exclusively by their environment – has long been debated and clamoured over by philosophers and psychologists seeking to reconcile the pulls of nature and nurture, it seems that his actual educational practices, and specifically, their contribution to a continuing progressive discourse, have been relatively disregarded. Only a small work by John Siraj Blatchford (1998), himself better known as an expert in technological learning than as an historian of education, and part of Ian Donnachie's marvellous (2000) biography (surprisingly the first in over 50 years) have attempted recently to explicitly explore Owen's educational philosophy.[1] This philosophy can best be comprehended today from observation of the site of New Lanark (rightly accorded UNESCO World Heritage Site status), personal memoirs and accounts of workers and managers but, most vitally, by examining education within the context of two of Owen's most significant published writings. These are *A New View of Society*, his 1813 treatise comprising four singular essays addressing aspects of human character, communitarian principles and their application to wider aspects of society[2] and the 1816 *Address to the Inhabitants of New Lanark* delivered by Owen on the opening of the Institute for the Formation of Character on 1 January 1816.

These works are especially appealing as they represent rich historical exemplars of the Enlightenment view – explored earlier in relation to Rousseau's *Emile* – that through the application of reason, general laws and principles governing human nature can be deduced and used to combat ignorance manifesting as (often religious) superstition. This observation serves to illustrate the important point, hopefully implicit throughout the narrative, that intellectual trends and epochs are not conveniently defined and demarcated in time but by, in Michel Foucault's (1972) terms, epistemic breaks and ruptures. Ideas and movements overlap; Owen was writing and conceiving of these works from 1811, and yet, they betray evidence of rationalist notions emanating from an earlier period. *A New View of Society*'s radicalism and unconventionality stems, therefore, not merely by its reference to, and promulgation of, innovative educational practices but also the way in which it deploys a particular philosophy to critique social issues. Owen's stress, in particular, upon the happiness of the 'lower' orders marks it out as particularly distinctive.

These were not, though, the rantings of a countercultural cult leader of a fringe movement. While it is true that they were perceived as highly radical and Owen himself later became pseudo-messianic in his millenarian posturing, during his writing of these works, he remained a model liberal capitalist in the mould of the elder Robert Peel or Richard Arkwright, known and valued in intellectual and political circles (he contributed, for example, to various Royal Commissions relating to the Poor Law) and a follower of the widely respected liberal and utilitarian principles of Jeremy Bentham. Such was his afforded status, he felt able to dedicate *A New View*, somewhat incongruously, to the Prince Regent – himself no great advocate of social reform! The overarching 'do as I say' paternalism of the factory oligarch remained therefore a pervasive influence throughout his early life and these works need to be contextualized as such.

Robert Owen – Beliefs

In the course of the writing of *A New View*, and culminating ideologically in his later 1821 *Report to the County of Lanark*, Owen came to adopt the position with which he is associated in the popular imagination today and which inflected all of his later writings and practices. This was that both character and habit were formed solely by environment and aspects of community:

> Any general character, from the best to the worst, from the most ignorant to the most enlightened, may be given to any community, even to the world at large, by the application of proper means; which means are to a great extent at the command and under the control of those who have influence in the affairs of men. (Owen 1949: 14)

This association of character defects with lack of 'proper guidance and direction' stood at odds with the overwhelming contemporary view, later put forward by many Victorian moralists, that the social ills of poverty, ignorance and vice were due to flaws and weaknesses within a person's character and, as such, responsibility for their alleviation lay not with the state, taxpayer or private charity but with those individuals themselves. The classic Victorian text by Samuel Smiles, *Self Help*, published in 1859, which propagated and celebrated the virtues of individual fulfilment, desire and learning with its rags-to-riches tales is a notable example of that particularly stringent viewpoint. This was, after all, the age of the autodidacts who were held up as celebrated examples of the rewards of hard graft.

Such ideology was more tangibly manifested in the setting up of the workhouses through the Poor Law Amendment Act of 1834. This was at the expense of the old Speenhamland system of outdoor relief which supported the destitute through imposition of a tax, paid for by local rate payers. The new Act, which Owen himself tirelessly opposed, was designed, through a grizzly logic, to be both efficient for the government and induce people to find work, thereby avoiding poverty and not having to end up in a workhouse. Conditions inside were made so bad so as to be intolerable – poor food, familial separation and meaningless tasks to fulfil. Such institutionalized brutality was designed to provide this perverse stimulus for people to get out and find gainful employment rather than suffer inside. Crudely speaking, it was the common belief that an individual's straitened circumstances could be attributed solely to themselves and their defects of character which would be remedied through a harsh and spartan regimen.

At the heart of Owen's reasoning, however, and what made him so revolutionary, lay the conviction that it was impossible to divorce people's lives from more global factors such as opportunities for employment, their financial positions and the character of their home life. Even though the centrality of aspects of the environment had been articulated by previous theorists, Owen was unique in his application of the idea to the context of a proto-industrial society, a paternalistic environment in which workers could have their characters moulded and their working and living conditions shaped and improved. In that respect, as both Harrison and Harold Silver point out, it is a mistake perhaps for us to casually and loosely characterize Owen alongside others such as Pestalozzi and Froebel as his educational techniques were indicative of a much wider societal viewpoint than the mere instruction of the children within institutions. Even Pestalozzi's vision was one based on a spiritual naivety rather than the evidence of an advanced industrial state.

In his discussion of crime, for example, Owen was quick to attribute it – in a remarkably prescient statement, given the later work that was to follow in relation to social ills by various philanthropic investigators – to the trappings of poverty with its attendant cycle of low wages, starvation, misdemeanour, and punishment. There is something cutting and almost satirical in the way in which he forcefully argued that it was only through an accident of birth that those in positions of authority (in this case a judge) were not themselves in the dock:

> Had the present judges of these realms been born and educated among the poor and profligate of St Giles's or some similar situation, is it not certain, inasmuch as they possess native energies and abilities, that ere this they would have been at the head of their *then* and, in consequence of that superiority and proficiency, would have suffered imprisonment, transportation or death? (Ibid., 25)

Despite the frequent evidence of his empathetic conscience, there was however certainly a Puritanical streak to Owen and he vigorously opposed gambling, drunkenness, promiscuity and vice. Yet, such views on society were marked by his desire to apply rational principles to work towards the alleviation of such destitution. Education was the catalyst for these principles, and in the first essay of *A New View*, he talks in grandiose, international language about the need to educate children according to those precepts:

> These [educational] plans must be devised to train children from their earliest infancy in good habits of every description . . . They must afterwards be rationally educated, and their labour be usefully directed. Such habits and education will impress them with and active ands ardent desire to promote the happiness of every individual . . . .(Ibid., 20)

Owen drew links later on in his book with the earlier initiatives undertaken by Andrew Bell and Joseph Lancaster to give credence to his ideas and to defer potential accusations that his proposals were those of an idealist, visionary or mad man. One must remember how radical such ideas were in the context of evolving, industrial England. By a similar token, Owen referred in his texts to examples drawn from the Continent which had already been visited and legitimated by reformers, for example, schools in Bavaria and the Netherlands.

The emphasis upon environment as the central determinant of an individual's character led him to take steps to ensure that children's upbringing was not made toxic by the potentially corrupting effects of families. As Harrison makes clear, 'Owen regarded the family as a fundamentally divisive force' which 'served to isolate men from each other, and to breed loneliness and self-centeredness' (Harrison 1969: 60). These concerns were shared by other communitarians and thinkers such as William Cobbet. Owen therefore made conscious efforts to ensure filial separation as early as was physically possible – 'the child will be removed, so far as is present practicable, from the erroneous treatment of the yet untrained and untaught parents' (Owen, op. cit., 41).

In practical terms, this involved the setting up of innovative play areas and schools designed to be attended and utilized by the children of the local artisans while their parents worked in the factory. Although attendance was not compulsory, it was certainly Owen's belief that the character of the child was 'correctly or incorrectly formed before he attains his second year' (Ibid., 40), and so, early years education was seen as crucial to formative character development. Here again is an example of Owen breaking with previous precedents in rejecting the lessons of Pestalozzi and his reliance on the mother as the lightening rod for moral example. Certainly, Owen and his later advocates and followers – for example, William Maclure and James Greaves[3] – were well versed in the progressive canon; yet, as Harold Silver (1969) points out, Owen was quite prepared to strike out in innovative directions, cherry picking ideas in relation to the curriculum but not necessarily to matters of pedagogy which were very much his concern and where he sought to provide the most direct forms of advancement.

At the heart, therefore, of Owen's educational project – and where the child's environment was to be fashioned – lay the slightly sinisterly and Orwellian-titled Institute for the Formation of Character which, from 1814, with his business partners at a distance away in London and with himself now reinstated as director of New Lanark with a ready supply of capital, Owen could fully develop and turn into a propaganda vehicle to demonstrate how his formative educational ideas could be applied in practice. Perhaps the best description of the institute comes from Robert Dale Owen (Owen's son) in his panegyric *Outline of the System of Education in New Lanark* (first published in 1824) and, given its centrality in any understanding of the Lanark classrooms, it is worth quoting at length:

> The principal school-room, [is] fitted up with desks and forms on the Lancastrian plan, having a free passage down the centre of the room . . . It is surrounded, except at one end where a pulpit stands, with galleries, which are convenient, when this room is used, as it frequently is, either as a lecture-room or place of worship.
>
> The other apartment, on the second floor . . . has the walls hung round with representations of the most striking zoological and mineralogical

specimens, including quadrupeds, birds, fishes, reptiles, insects, shells, minerals etc. At one end there is a gallery, adapted for the purpose of an orchestra, and at the other end are hung very large representations of the two hemispheres; each separate country, as well as the various seas, islands etc. being differently coloured, but without any names attached to them. This room is used as a lecture and ball-room, and it is here, that the dancing and singing lessons are daily given. It is likewise occasionally used as a reading-room for some of the classes.

The lower storey is divided into three apartments, of nearly equal dimensions, 12 feet high, and supported by hollow iron pillars, serving, at the same time, as conductors, in winter, for heated air, which issues through the floor of the upper storey, and by which means the whole building may, with ease, be kept at any required temperature. It is in these three apartments that the younger classes are taught reading, natural history, and geography. (Dale Owen, quoted in Simon 1969: 149–50)

What is perhaps most striking about these rich descriptions, and indeed those of Owen himself in his autobiography, are how modern the classrooms sound certainly in comparison to many contemporary schoolrooms which were often sparsely decorated and basically designed. As a case in point, they differed markedly from the aforementioned 'instruction factories' (Harrison 1969: 160) of Bell and Lancaster who had insisted on enacting the monitorial system with its tedious rows of desks and tables. Modern historians of education have been quick to seize upon the underlying importance of such ideas. Catherine Burke and Ian Grosvenor (2005), for example, have pointed out the common misconception in the traditional view of seeing the classroom space as a 'static other' devoid of historical meaning. Frequently, they argue, the design of classrooms and school buildings echoes, intentionally or otherwise, particular educational and didactic philosophies and this is especially significant in relation to New Lanark. In this case, underpinning the classroom was a programme of learning designed to be both relevant and engaging for the young child. Traditional learning devices such as copy books were abandoned early on, the Bible was placed on an equal footing with adventure stories and children were encouraged to express themselves in words and images.

Indeed, what are not mentioned in the above descriptions of Dale Owen are books and it is known that Owen himself had, if not enmity, then at least a vague distrust for the educative value of the written word. This philosophy was reflected in the choice of teachers for the school. The first was James Buchanan, a former handloom weaver and a 'simply-minded, kind-hearted individual who could hardly read or write himself' (Owen 1857: 139) and his assistant, Molly Young, a 17-year-old village girl. While it would be tempting to justify their unlikely appointments by fanaticizing about Owen immersed in the ideas of Rousseau and the noble lives of Godly peasants, in truth, their selection owed, as Ian Donnachie (2000) has pointed out, more to the simplicity and gentle nature of their characters. After that fashion, Owen's instructions to his staff were simple – '. . . on no account [are you] ever [to] beat any one of the children or to threaten them in any word or action or to use abusive terms; but [you are] always to speak to them with a pleasant voice and in a kind manner' (Ibid). In many ways, Owen's directives in this particular instance do bear witness to the influence that Pestalozzi had on his thinking, with the latter's specific highlighting of kindness towards children. It is also worth pointing out that such emphasis bears similarity to Jeremy Bentham's diktat of the 'greatest happiness principle'[4] which was equally important in the shaping of Owen's political and social viewpoint.

Under this aspect, much of the day-to-day life of the school involved emphasizing the importance of happiness. While this virtue had been repeated *ad nauseum* by other progressives, what makes it pertinent in the case of New Lanark was that it was being deployed at a particular time and a place where punishment and beating of children was commonplace. Hardened Scottish Calvinists around Lanark were 'convinced that such punishment and pain [was] necessary to prevent the ultimate destruction and damnation of their children's souls' (Greven 1991: 62). For Owen, this was tantamount to a form of child abuse and served to reinforce his deeply entrenched and controversial views regarding organized religion. Punishment of the young, he argued, could never achieve its stated aim of changing and reforming character, merely, instead, humiliating and making fearful and intellectually impotent otherwise intelligent children. Owen's precepts concerning happiness, with the teachers setting the appropriate example, were therefore expected to filter down through the school and workplace. The fundamental principle instilled into a child entering the institute was that 'he is never to injure his play-fellows; but that, on the contrary, he is to contribute all in his power to make them happy' (Owen 1949: 40). Older pupils were therefore expected to take upon a responsible, fraternal role with the younger ones and this was particularly encouraged during games playing and activities.

Owen's conception of happiness was therefore novel, not merely for its operation in a specific environment but also because it seemed to repudiate the contemporary idea that 'the greatest good for society could be achieved through individual hedonism' (Siraj-Blatchford 1998: 50). Instead, New Lanark promulgated the view that happiness was to be thought of not in terms of the seeking or achieving of an ephemeral, pleasurable individual state, but as the outcome of a 'rational' form of living. Happiness of the individual was intimately connected with the happiness of the wider community and in giving priority to the latter ideal, individuals would implicitly elevate, refine and heighten themselves and their emotions. This had an important knock-on educational effect too for it required a very specific conception of the child-citizen, one imbued with not merely a moral awareness to give aid to individuals but also a more practical responsibility as regards their basic welfare. Citizenship education (otherwise known as civics) therefore formed an important cornerstone of the New Lanark curriculum as it sought to promote messages of social cohesion, stability and togetherness. Owen's desire to link school and community under an aspect of universal 'morality' and happiness predates, albeit in a more microcosmic way, the later ideas of John Dewey and demonstrates, once more, the enduring importance of Owen as an educational progressive of longitudinal importance.

Elsewhere, the influence which Pestalozzi affected, directly and otherwise, upon Owen has been mentioned, and nowhere more was this apparent than in the curriculum which he delivered, which consisted of natural sciences, geography, ancient and modern philosophy and, as we have mentioned, civics. While these classes tended to take the form of a 'lecture', they were frequently illustrated with maps and pictures and children were encouraged to be tactile with the various exhibits scattered around the classroom. Geography also allowed for the use of that tried and trusted progressive stratagem of learning externally through field studies in the Scottish countryside. For those children of an older age, dancing, choral harmony singing and, somewhat oddly, given his avowed hatred of warfare, military drill became added to the curriculum and it was these huge demonstrations of coordinated movement that so impressed many of the 20,000 visitors the institute received in the decade following its opening. It is clear, beyond the undoubted physical and intellectual benefits such things conferred, why such activities were important to Owenite thinking, with their emphasis upon cooperation, synchronized movement and sense of individual fulfilment within the confines of a larger group.

While it is certainly true that Owen's philosophy was based upon Enlightenment principles, it clearly carried with it much of the former Romantic sentiment regarding the unique and sacred nature of the child and the 'special' period of childhood. For many other capitalists and industrial employers, it was inconceivable that young children should not work in factories. Children were viewed, under that aspect, as 'apprentices', a perverse term which obscured the grim and horrific realities of their working conditions. They were treated little better than slaves – grist, quite literally, to the mill. For Owen, though, the creation of a new society demanded a fresh conception of the role and status of the child. One of the first actions Owen took on arrival at New Lanark was therefore to refuse to employ any child under 10 and he ceased to use pauper labour. Quite simply, a 9-year-old child was not a 'little adult' and it was neither morally acceptable nor justifiable to compel them to go and work a 12-hour day in a factory alongside their parents and older siblings. Such a child was a human being undergoing a phase of growth that had its own distinctive traits and attributes. Although this view was in no sense unique to Owen, and had been put forward by others beforehand, this was the first time it had been advocated so vehemently from someone operating within a sphere of power and control – a factory owning capitalist.

Alongside the re-education of young children went a programme of adult education based around a series of evening classes and lectures given by Owen himself. Prior to his reduction of the standard working hours, attendance at these classes was low, at less than 100 scholars a night. Once this lessening was implemented, however, there is evidence of numbers quadrupling to an average of 400 scholars a night throughout the latter half of 1816. Owen contended vehemently that if people were educated and well informed, then they would be more successful and happier in the context of communitarian living, thus contributing more to the aggregate harmony of the community – a principle which he undoubtedly derived from his knowledge of Pestalozzi's Yverdon School. In addition, 'enlightenment' through education would demonstrate to men the true nature of the left-behind external society where their fears and prejudices were formed, irrationally, by virtue of their injurious environments. While these ideas may not seem progressive in a pure sense (that is, not associated with children), it must be remembered that one strand of progressive philosophy, as espoused by Froebel and discussed in an earlier chapter, was the notion that development, at both the emotional and cognitive level, is a continuing process of 'eternal' progress that does not end upon reaching adulthood. While Owen's concerns were grounded far more in earthly social realities than ethereal German metaphysics, it is another example of Owen's practices chiming with the beliefs if not the practices of other progressives. As one Owenite, James Hole, was to pithily surmise, 'Education is not an affair of childhood or youth, it is the business of the whole life' (Hole 1853: 44).

New Lanark – Legacy

There is little doubt as to the historical success and persistent longevity of New Lanark; however, any assessment of Owenism as a social movement would have to consider it a 'failure', albeit a very glorious one. Owen's three largest subsequent communities, New Harmony, Orbiston and Queenwood, which were intended to export the legacy of their Scottish predecessor to a global level, all ultimately collapsed due to a combination of economic and social difficulties and we have few extant records detailing the histories and goings on at many of the smaller communities which derived their inspiration, impetus and ideology from Owen. Generally, the larger communities struggled to accumulate capital and funds, had difficulty managing the enormous land areas they had unwittingly purchased, suffered due to their heterogeneous and diverse membership and split apart due to resentment over Owen's appointees, many of whom struggled to properly implement his system.

Those who stuck rigidly to the old Owenite communities and ideals patently failed to adapt to the changing nature of the modern world, particularly after the tumultuous events of 1848. A marked failure to admit the dominance and triumph of advanced capitalism meant that they were sluggish, if not in performing a *volte face*, then at least in failing to adapt their ideas for the new incumbent age. Even when such time came, change seemed grudging. As Harrison points out, 'they groped towards a new psychology and a new sociology within the terminology, common also to their non-Owenite contemporaries, of moral, mental and social science' (Harrison 1969: 237). The remains of Owen's theories thus became supplanted, supplemented and ultimately overtaken by a boom in the economy and a radicalization of the left, until eventually, the communitarian spirit, such as it had been, no longer existed and Owenism was reduced to the status of historical artifact.

Nevertheless, if anything can be said to have been successful and highly regarded about these nascent communities, it was their systems of education, where evidence abounds of the continuation of many of the progressive practices which had been carried out so triumphantly at New Lanark. Crucially, the Pestalozzian ideas which had begun to be increasingly utilized there now found their full fruition in these new centres of intellectual learning and pedagogy. Every child was to learn to be literate and numerate supplemented by science, geography, natural history and, like Rousseau's Emile, a trade. Such classes were to provide the child not only with mental and manual skills but also, in the words of a contemporary commentator, 'knowledge of himself and of human nature to form him into a *rational* being' (Simons 1941: 101 italics added). Even in the most basic of communities, the provision of education was written into their constitution.[5]

Nowhere was this more evident than in the New Harmony colony situated in Indiana under the guidance of Robert Dale Owen, Owen's aforementioned son. While several Pestalozzian progressives, including Marie Fratageot and Phiquepal d'Arusmont,[6] were also persuaded to make the Atlantic crossing, it was primarily the Scotsman William Maclure who, alongside Dale Owen, was the driving force in seeking to combine progressive educational methods with application to manual work which was ideally suited to the frontier existence the community enjoyed. In keeping with his joint discipleships of Pestalozzi and Owen, Maclure oversaw the education of children from the age of two onwards away from the influence of adults and their patterns of learning were thus commensurate with their individual levels of ability. The material goods produced by the children were then sold to further subsidize the activities of the school itself which was similarly in keeping with the communitarian, self-sufficient ethos. Given Maclure's later role in publishing various educational treatises, he can rightly be credited with inculcating a progressive mode of thinking and practice into the budding American education systems. In addition to these New Harmony successes, the Orbiston community suffered from ill discipline until it was taken over by staff previously employed and trained at New Lanark; while such was the strength of the educational centre at Queenwood in Hampshire that it was maintained, subsequent even to the demise of the original population. Furthermore, large-scale group activities such as dancing and theatrical productions continued unabated. Perhaps the continuing successes of the educational aspects of Owen's philosophy attest to their radical, progressive and, ultimately successful, nature.

While these communities were founded directly by Owen and run by those individuals handpicked by the master, there were those who, taking inspiration from his example, attempted to take charge of their own miniature societies in much the same way Owen had in Scotland. Owen's uniquely altruistic business model thus proved influential on various members of the philanthropic middle class, themselves determined to found new world orders or else to enjoy the trappings of demagoguery while it lasted. The two most prominent of these were John Minter Morgan and Robert Pemberton, who sought to design communities very much along the lines of New Lanark. In many ways, paternalistic beneficence of this kind was to prove a precursor to many of the later initiatives designed to improve the conditions for children within schools, for example, the pioneering work of the McMillan sisters and the measures and provisions involved in formulating the Liberal Government's Children's Charter. These second wave of institutions thereby provide an important historical and ideological link within the chapter's overarching theme of social reform as they advanced Owen's primitive ideas on welfare into the Victorian Age when concerns over health became more paramount.

In keeping with the socially reforming precedents established by Owen, the initial driving force for men like Pemberton and Morgan were attempts to perpetrate their own visions of utopia. Such grand designs were additionally given impetus by their increasingly frequent public disagreements and criticism of Owen. Morgan, for example, lamented Owen's attack upon organized religion and ended his days attempting to found communities based upon a form of Christian socialism. Robert Pemberton was more concerned to distance his acolytes entirely from any whiff of industrialized society, and in his work *Happy Colony* (1854), outlined plans to establish a colony in New Zealand. Pemberton's planned (though, sadly, never realized) 'philosophical model infant school' was based on a more mystical interpretation of Owenism. Another follower, James Hole, worked closely with the burgeoning Mechanics' Institutes – an extension of Owens' adult education classes – which he saw as best embodying the communitarian and association spirit inherent within his master's writings.

Nor was it solely through physical educational experiments that the gospel of Owen was spread. In addition to being a benefactor, John Minter Morgan was a widely published pamphleteer and author who attempted to synthesize his ideas through his Church of England Self-Supporting Village Society, which consisted, in essence, of building self-sufficient communities with the addition of a vicar and a place of Christian worship. Religious disagreements aside, he shared with Owen a belief in the transformative power of gentlemanly philanthropy, a profound contempt for the existing systems of looking after the poor and pessimism at the consequences of mass industrialization, all of which he voiced in his copious writings. While many of these experiments were ultimately short-lived and more in the heads of idealist visionaries than on the ground, in bricks and mortar, they nonetheless served to exemplify the continued legacy not just of Owenism but of the desire to seek rapprochement between social reform and progressive educational practices.

The Chartist contribution

The experiments in living and schooling detailed above were of a very particular flavour – usually middle class in origin with a healthy dose of philanthropic beneficence thrown in for good measure. While they nonetheless aspired to relative levels of equality, in general, such ideas did not extend to overturning and disrupting at a national level the rigid and top-heavy power structures that prevailed throughout the early decades of the nineteenth century.

There were though certain more radical groups, of whom the Chartists are the most important, who did pursue such aims campaigning not merely for a universal (male) franchise but also for an end to the squalor and lack of regulation concerning living and working conditions. As the Chartist historian Dorothy Thompson explained, the middle decades of the nineteenth century were a time when 'thousands of working people considered that their problems could be solved by the political organization of the country' (Thompson 1984: 1). Unsurprisingly, therefore, Owenism has been commonly recognized and identified by social historians as providing a precursor to many of these later ideas, especially given its emphasis upon the amelioration of the worst excesses of the artisan existence through the reduction of working hours and by ensuring workers were looked after in the event of accident.

Nevertheless, ideological continuities aside, for the historian of education, within the context of a movement as altogether radical as Chartism, one can identify distinct formulations of progressivism which relate not merely to Owen's communitarian principles but also to the idea of mass social reform.

It is perhaps convenient to bracket Robert Owen with Chartism. After all, as Malcolm Chase (2007) has pointed out in his authoritative study, many members of his failed Grand National Consolidated Trades Union later went on to become committed Chartists, founding more politically radical groups such as the National Association of United Trades for the Protection of Labour (NAUT). Similarly, Owen himself maintained at least a passing interest in later Chartist activities, although he could never bring himself to fully support their more violent and insurrectionary methods and tactics. The situation is made more confusing as any attempt to define when and where Chartism began is fraught with difficulty. Much has been written on this – perhaps the best guides are those of Malcolm Chase (2007) and Edward Royle (1986) – and it is neither possible nor necessary to detail the historiographical debate here except to say that it is not overtly simplistic to discuss its foundation in the context of dissatisfaction with the 1832 Reform Bill and anger at the lack of improvements being made in relation to social and industrial conditions.

What is important to stress though is that, as was the case for Owen, education was an important part of Chartist thinking and, in that regard, two of its key members stand out for their development of theory and practice and for the huge significance they ascribed to the business of learning – William Lovett (1800–77) and Thomas Cooper (1805–92). The former is well-known to historians as one of the founders of the London Working Men's Association and as being a leading Chartist agitator and formulator of the movement's ideology and discourse. Cooper, by contrast, has tended to be relegated to the 'also ran' category of Chartist notables subject, only very recently, to critical attention through an excellent joint biography by Stephen Roberts (2008) encompassing Cooper and his fellow Chartist prisoner, Arthur O' Neill. Aside from his educational pronouncements, Cooper's main claim to fame resides through his autobiography, which is unexpectedly lively and overshadows Lovett's own contribution to that genre and an overlong, Milton pastiche poem *The Purgatory of Suicides* (1845) which, while matching Milton's *Paradise Lost* for length, lacks in the course of its 944 stanzas any of that other poem's notable genius. Nevertheless, both works, in their own ways, exemplify the strong continuing link in a tradition which recognized education as a site of hegemonic struggle where the mutual processes involved in education at the level of the classroom tie in with what Henry Pelling (1971) identified in Chartism as the common interests of the whole of the working class.

The contribution of William Lovett

Traditionally, writings on Chartism had, understandably, been keener to focus upon the broader political and social origins and implications of the movement rather than explore its distinctive educational contribution. It was therefore not until the pioneering historian of education, Brian Simon, writing in 1972, first recognized the transcendent importance of William Lovett as an educator in the progressive tradition concerned as much with theory and detail as purpose that this omission became righted:

> [Lovett] made a deeper study of the techniques and methods of education than most of his contemporaries, so that his tract stands out as a comprehensive treatise on education from the Radical point of view, covering not only organisation, but also its content, methodology and ethos. (Simon 1972: 17)

The tract in question was Lovett's *A New Organization of the People* (1840), written while its author was imprisoned in Warwick Gaol following the breakup of the General Convention of the Industrious Classes – an aborted attempt to bring together the myriad of radical groups scattered across Britain. The resulting book is divided into three main sections – the first, a general introduction outlining the Chartist case, the second outlining the rules and regulations for a National Association of the United Kingdom for Promoting the Political and Social Improvement of the People and, finally, an essay on education. While all of it is written in a readable, pithy and direct style, it is the latter two sections that, for the historian of progressivism, are the most important. Broadly speaking, with its international emphasis, its argument that the root causes of social evils were in the present organization of the people and, in noting and raging at the gross inequalities between rich and poor, the work bears a remarkable similarity, and betrays an ideological debt, to the earlier works of Owen. This is especially noticeable in the ways in which Lovett tries to ultimately justify the task of education as having a role to play in bringing about the concept of a general 'social happiness'.

Lovett's justification for the provision of education – as well as other forms of social reform – stemmed from the types of definition relating to human rights which resided in Thomas Paine's hugely influential *The Rights of Man* (1791) which saw rights defined, broadly, as 'reciprocal justice' which were to be protected by government unreservedly without recourse to legal charters and devices which could revoke such privileges.[7] The right therefore to an education became implicitly embedded in the discourses concerning social rights and derived from the concept of society itself, the term society being taken to mean a union for mutual benefit. Education thus enabled an individual to 'understand and share in all the benefits of society' (Lovett 1840: 123)

Many of Lovett's plans for education seem indeed to have reflected the more progressive features and aspects of New Lanark. For a non-educator (he was a cabinet maker by trade), Lovett's text is remarkably prescient and detailed in describing not merely the logistics of his ideal school but also the sorts of behaviours and characteristics to be expected of those responsible for the teaching of the children inside and it is remarkably wide-ranging in the ground which it covers. At the level of the classroom, *A New Organization* proposed detailed plans and rules for the day-to-day running and design of the school and its operations. A curriculum was suggested that took account, as had Owen, of the need to educate children for the role of being a 'good citizen.' Furthermore, Lovett outlined different approaches and methods to teaching his desired curriculum and the final part of the book consisted of exemplar lesson cards for prospective teachers concerning topics as diverse as mineralogy, truth, morality and the internal workings of the human stomach.

More than that though, Lovett's writing sought to democratize and make more progressive the wider institution of education in developments and suggestions which were wedded to his desire to create a 'new organization of the people'. Moving away from the minutiae of the classroom, the book broadens out to discuss the control of schools through local boards (providing yet more emphasis upon community at the expense of a centrally controlled system), the election of 'superintendents' and the selection and training of teachers. On this latter point, there is more than a hint of Froebel in relation to the importance Lovett placed upon the correct modes and methods of training, describing the foundation of the teacher training schools as 'one of the first objects of the association' (Lovett 1840: 76). For Lovett, teachers, as was to be the case for their future students, were to be educated holistically in a range of cognate disciplines and this was to be reflected in the training facilities. Lovett describes a typical training school as having a 'library, museum, laboratory, sitting rooms and sleeping-rooms for the teachers' (Ibid) while 'great care and discrimination would be necessary in guarding against the admission of persons who possess neither the disposition, aptitude, nor capabilities for efficient teachers' (Ibid., 77). The role of the teacher was therefore one to be considered as a specialist with relevant and articulated training in what today we would consider educational psychology and child management. Even the teaching assistants were expected to be literate and skilled in a range of aptitudes. As Brian Simon in an earlier work pointed out, according to Lovett, the task of those involved in pedagogy was,

> not as that of imposing knowledge and habits on the children, but of assisting them to acquire knowledge and habits through their own activity, so exercising their reason and moral judgement that they come to understand for themselves and know aright. (Simon 1960: 265)

When one considers how the concern of many contemporary school teachers was the preservation of social order through moral abeyance often administered through physical punishment or else the rote learning of facts in a Gradgrindian style, such passages are breath taking in their progressiveness and novelty. Lovett himself was, in fact, directly critical of aspects of the contemporary curriculum which focused exclusively upon the learning of the '3Rs' and, at a higher level, Greek and Latin.

In addition, Lovett was keen to stress the role that women could play in the teaching profession (predating the British interest in the Froebelian society) and, like the earlier Romantics, he saw female pedagogues as 'supply[ing] the place of an attentive, kind, and intellectual parent' (Lovett, op. cit., 77). While limiting the role of women merely to the teaching of the very young in his schools, Lovett outlined in some detail desirable personal characteristics, including knowledge, empathy, good health and compassion which, once again, strongly indicated the seriousness which he considered the role of education had in reformulating society.

The school itself was envisaged as being divided into three different levels – the ground level for infant teaching (3–6 years taught by women), the next level for those in the prep school (6–9 years), and finally, the high school on the top level for those 9 years and over. Pervading throughout these various levels of schooling were certain key themes which make distinct Lovett's contribution to progressivism, particularly as it applied in the British context, which had been, to that point, slow in adapting to the more forward-thinking Continental ideas. Foremost among these was the need to recognize that the educational process was one which had to encompass 'all the faculties of mind *and body*' (Ibid., 64, italics added). In passages remarkable to the contemporary reader for their foresight in light of later developments, Lovett stressed – through the quotation of statistical data – the importance of healthy diet, fresh air, warm clothing and exercise within the context of the school, not merely for their restorative benefits but because they provided the necessary nourishment which allowed the mind to thrive.

Key as well to Lovett's progressive philosophy was an education which placed equal emphasis on moral as well as intellectual learning. In strongly worded phraseology, Lovett took sideswipes at those whose moral intentions were good but who lacked the intellect to avoid being deceived and, conversely, those individuals of 'great intellectual attainments without morality' (Ibid., 66) who Lovett seemed, perhaps unsurprisingly, to associate with the more well-to-do classes, who were guilty of manipulative and amoral exploitation of the 'people'. While recognizing that innate differences inevitably existed between individuals in relation to their physical and intellectual prowess, Lovett's form of moral education was designed to raise and enlighten individuals beyond their current, base preoccupations with 'gluttony, drunkenness, profligacy, debauchery, and extreme vice' (Ibid., 67). Such statements clearly carried debts to Owen who equally saw immorality and vice as a contributory factor in restricting the working classes from achieving a more enlightened state. Additionally, the stress Lovett placed on 'education as community' has been seen elsewhere in kindergartens, Deweyian institutions and Fellowship schools.

Perhaps the only difference between those institutions and Lovett's proposals were that his was a message writ large with the purpose of education being not merely to unite people together in a shared consciousness so as to campaign for wider social and political rights but ultimately to push directly for greater representation through the implementation of the People's Charter.[8] One of the common justifications of the time for denying the working classes political rights and the franchise was that they were too ill-educated to use it responsibly. It is clear that Lovett (and Chartism, more generally) sought to therefore address this prejudice by proposing a system of universal education that would emancipate and provide independence and awareness as much as it would enlighten.

Further to his overarching political aims, the intangible notion of the school environment became a pervading concern for Lovett; in his wonderful phrase, the school was to be 'a little world of love, of lively and interesting enjoyments' (Ibid., 77) and this was facilitated not merely by the predisposed attitudes of the trained staff but through unique and innovative configurations of design and a novel approach to architecture. He advocated the use of playgrounds in his school for children's exercise and games with additional planted areas and gardens for horticultural instruction. Furniture and fittings in the school were designed to relate directly to the instruction envisaged. As in New Lanark, corporal punishment was banned as 'blows and injudicious privations only strengthen a harsh disposition' (Ibid., 41) and desirable personal characteristics – compassion, kindliness and consideration – which Lovett demanded of his incumbent staff have already been noted elsewhere.

More so even than for Owen, Lovett saw the school environment as being not exclusively a finite one, constructed solely for the education of children through the basic teacher/pupil relationship. Instead, the school building was envisaged as the central part of a wider, more radical and progressive project, with a set of facilities working towards the education of children and, crucially, adults in a context outside of the traditional classroom. For example, the school hall was conceived of as a place where public lectures could take place 'to interest the young, and stimulate the mental energies of the adult' (Ibid., 50) although quite how lectures relating to 'physical, moral and political science' were to act as 'fruitful and never-ending sources of delight', Lovett does not say. Readings and discussions were encouraged which were designed to not merely stimulate political and social debate but also to arrive at some form of reality-approximating truth which Lovett saw as emanating in the cauldron of debate and social exchange. This desire to increase literacy through the publication and dissemination of information in various forms of media was undoubtedly one of the defining and most successful characteristics of the Chartist movement. At its height in 1839, for example, the *Northern Star* newspaper edited by Feargus O' Connor achieved a circulation of 50,000 and its pages were full of contributions from its largely working-class readership. New methods of communication allowed the Chartist movement to be far more nationally coordinated than any previous Radical group, in particular, via its two major hotbeds of London and Birmingham. Lovett, it seems, was keen to draw upon this well spring of social spirit.

Nor did Lovett limit himself merely to the discussion of higher, more intellectual pursuits; various elements in his design are indicative of the pioneering notions he held with regard to the physical happiness of the population as a whole. Dancing and music making were to take place in the school hall and were to act as a tonic and light relief to the other, more cerebral pursuits. Lovett believed that the opportunity to quick-step and waltz would alleviate the working man's unhealthy desires towards drink and general hedonism. Hot and cold baths are also cited in the text as being a preserver of health and recommended to all adults. Again, this recognition that physical well-being and vigour were intrinsically bound up with educational performance is far-sighted and progressive in the extreme.

Nonetheless, Lovett, and perhaps Chartism more generally, differed fundamentally from earlier social movements and experiments in living in placing an emphasis upon self-enlightenment. One of the underlying themes of Lovett's tract was a clear desire for the working classes to take an active participation in the determination of their own fates, striving continually for change rather than mere acquiescence in the face of the perceived injustices of society. This was indicative of Lovett's view which held that class progression was not merely awareness of one's social position relative to other, more privileged strata but that it should also be representative of a consciousness relating to an active engagement within the membership of the working class movement. This was in contrast to Owen who, although seeking comparable social amelioration and improvements, only saw it as possible, ultimately, by the subsuming of the individual into a microcosmic community under the aegis of his own ideology. We know that there were occasional disputes among the Lanark workers and their management and it is hard to imagine Owen's particular system operating outside of that Scottish community which came ready equipped with a distinct Calvinist deference to authority and hierarchy. Similarly, his large ego, gift for demagoguery and self-publicity, combined with his descent into an almost radical millenarianism, is indicative of a certainty of purpose and strident self-belief that stands in contrast to the more bookish

Lovett. Indeed, it was these personal characteristics that Lovett so despised in several of his rival Chartists, particularly the bullish O' Connor.

Thomas Cooper – The self-taught Chartist

A man such as Thomas Cooper (1805–92) was, in many ways, the self-enlightened autodidact par excellence and his life, career and achievement represented all that was good (and bad) about Chartist educational ideology. As Stephen Roberts (2008) has made clear, Cooper's early life constituted a period when he read voraciously, absorbing himself in dense philosophical and theological works as well as the poetry of Shakespeare and Milton which was to remain continually dear to him throughout his life. In many ways, Cooper's early conversion to Methodism and, despite minor theological fluctuations, continuing adherence to a muscular form of Christianity exemplify his educational work which was at once designed to liberate and enlighten, yet often comes across as preachy and dogmatic. This is not to say though that Cooper was insignificant within the Chartist movement; indeed, he more than any other perhaps embodied best, both ideologically and physically, the twin concepts of dedication to lifelong learning and intellectual self-respect so dear to the Chartist heart.

His noble ideals floundered, however, in his two biggest educational posts as they came up against the earthy realities and expectations of the working man. In his first teaching post in Gainsborough in the county of Lincolnshire, while preferring to teach Latin, he found, 'the parents of pupils . . . wanted their children to study arithmetic and reading and writing' (Roberts 2008: 44). Additionally, when later setting up his adult education classes in Leicester, despite early successes with numbers growing to nearly 300 within five weeks, he soon found that people resented giving up what spare time was available to them to discuss the finer points of the political ideologies of Tom Paine and William Cobbet. Cooper rather forlornly records in his autobiography being told by one of the workers, 'What the hell do we care about reading if we can get nought to eat?' (Cooper 1872: 172) If his formal attempts at trying to run a school seemed therefore to reach an impasse, such failures did not bring to a halt Cooper devoting the remainder of his life to travelling the length and breadth of the country in a Herculean toil to address audiences as a Baptist lay-preacher spreading a message of forthright worship and self-improvement. His biographer calculates that, by 1866, he had addressed 3373 such crowds including, by 1885, eight visits to the town and people of Halifax alone. One is not perhaps sure who to feel sorry for more.

Cooper was though, in many ways, a remarkable man driven by an ethic that today seems indelibly associated with 'the Victorians'. There is, admittedly, little perhaps in his work that could be called 'progressive' in terms of educational philosophy. He named his classes after his heroes who, characteristically, were Shakespeare, Milton and Philip Sidney and his style of teaching, from what records we have, indicate a heavily didactic approach based around group reading and public lectures. Nevertheless, while Cooper was not progressive in thought per se, his writings, particularly his autobiography, are perhaps the clearest explanation and justification for the particular connection between education and social reform and the way in which knowledge was seen as a device for liberation and emancipation of the soul and body. Cooper, more so than perhaps any other major Chartist, reached a large audience both through his lecture tours and his extensive publication output which amounted to 18 books, 10 pamphlets and an editorship of 7 periodicals. He sought to continually instil into those readers and interlocutors the basic desire to self-improvement through education, which accords with what today would be labelled 'life-long learning'. While some of his writings, for example, the *Triumphs of Perseverance* and the *Triumphs of Enterprise*, stray dangerously close to the territory inhabited by Samuel Smiles and the 'self-helpers', Cooper's corpus of work was enshrined in a more grandiose vision which encapsulated and envisaged mass liberation of the downtrodden through the power of understanding and learning. The climactic passages of the *Purgatory of Suicides*, for example, betray this largesse by declaiming, 'Earth's children raise their universal song/Of love and joy' (Cooper 1845, Book X, Stanza 125, lines 1–2) and the poem's end anticipates the day when 'Truth's young light disperse old Error's gloom' (Ibid., Stanza 126, line 8).

For Cooper, truth in this context was represented by the system of learning he advocated which would allow for the individual to apprehend the 'truth' of their condition and their position in the world. In contrast to Shelley's *Mask of Anarchy* with which *Purgatory* shares some ideological similarities, this was not limited to political and social freedom but also intellectual and Cooper was explicit upon this point. In many ways, his whole life was spent in pursuit of the furtherance of this one belief as he slaved remorselessly to enlighten through both his writing and teaching. It should, of course, be remembered that he envisaged salvation as residing more within the pages of Classic and canonical literature rather than through Lovett's and Owen's progressive methods which aimed at liberating the inner child. Given this, it may appear erroneous to include him in a narrative concerned with progressive educational methods, yet Cooper's desire for, and genuine belief in, the potential bettering, both physical and intellectual, of large swathes of the population was indisputable, and so, any exploration of education and social reform must include reference to him. If we consider an aspect of progressive education to be the liberating and emancipatory effects which knowledge can bestow – and we see this manifest in the later critical pedagogy movement – then Cooper can certainly be considered an important part of that tradition albeit one rooted firmly in the autodidactic and Christian virtue principles of the nineteenth century.

Changing attitudes to social reform

In many ways, Lovett's *Chartism* signalled the end of a particular Radical tradition in education. As social historians like Harold Perkin (1985) have made it clear, the vestiges of radical Chartist and Owenite beliefs spilled over into new fights as the century progressed towards its end. Many old campaigners were now shifting their focus instead towards the battle for free and secular education which became prevalent around the time of the 1870 Education Act. There were, in addition, constant conflicts, both ecclesiastical and political for control over the newly created School Boards while the budding trade's union movement concerned itself with opening up educational opportunities for its members. In addition, as Harry Hendrick (1997) has convincingly demonstrated, there occurred a general transformation in the paradigmatic conception of childhood at the end of the nineteenth century, with the view that the child was seen less in individualistic laissez faire Victorian terms and increasingly as 'the child of the nation'. This was a precursor to the post-war views regarding the child as an emergent property of the fully fledged Welfare State and signalled a move towards the British state assuming a form of responsibility for the condition of its citizens. Indeed, whatever the motivations for example behind the 1870 Education Act which provided for a system of national elementary schooling, it must be at least credited as the first time that the State had taken any form of significant overall accountability for educational provision. Perhaps most appreciably of all, the results of this shift were to be found in the broad raft of Liberal social reforms of 1906–14 which came to be known, as far as education was concerned, as the 'Children's Charter'.

While, as has been well documented, much of the motivation behind these reforms stemmed from the need for imperial preservation, and thus, the long-term sustainability of a global military hegemony, there was clear evidence of the substantial impact that philanthropic social reformers were having upon embryonic policy. The famous studies of William Booth and Seebohm Rowntree in the cities of London and York, respectively, emerged out of a belief (in the latter's case, a Quaker belief) that social reform was a necessity for moral as much as for economic imperatives. Their statistical evidence gave a scientific, quantitative legitimacy to very real concerns over the 'state of the nation' question which was then preoccupying thinkers and policy makers.

These concerns were aggravated by fears relating to juvenile delinquency, the formation of 'blind alley characters' through the haphazard system of entry into the labour market and the concern over Granville Stanley Hall's newly emergent concept of adolescence with its universal connotations of *sturm und drang*.

Many of these anxieties, perhaps indirectly, provide the observer with a thread of continuity from the past as they emphasized strongly that not only was the plight and fortune of society at large linked to the plight and fortune of the child but also that it was urban environments where this plight was felt most strongly. In many ways, the introduction of compulsory elementary schooling had made it possible for children to be observed en masse and comparative data relating to their physical condition to be more readily available. Most famously, this had resulted in the Egerton Commission (1889) which attempted a reclassification of special educational needs on the basis of a spectrum along which children could oscillate, rather than a mere presence or absence of mental illness.

Much the same was true of health and this became only too evident in the contents of a series of reports and enquiries into various aspects of children's well-being facilitated, as has been made clear, by the opportunities for observation afforded by the panoramic classroom setting. By far, the most significant of these investigations was the Report of the Committee on Physical Deterioration, set up in the aftermath of the Boer War in 1902 and which reported back two years after the successful prosecution of the conflict. The Report had been initially commissioned to explain why four out of every ten recruits had been turned away on the grounds of ill health – frequently through conditions such as rickets, stunted growth and general malnourishment. While not considering that such problems were part of a long-term trend in the decline in health of the British population, the Report did recommend meals and health checks for the poor as a compulsory element in the nation's schools in an attempt to provide a basic level of nutrition and care to the population.

These recommendations did not arise though merely as a result of a tortuous campaign on the South African *veldt*. While there were always those, on both sides of the political divide, who feared that the State taking up the basic functions of parental responsibility was an unnecessary and costly burden and imposition into the lives of its subjects, there were also those for whom such reforms were long overdue. The most noteworthy of these campaigners were two remarkable sisters, Rachel (1859–1917) and Margaret McMillan (1860–1931), whose achievements in relation to national policy and practice were, by any estimation, monumental. Oddly, it would not perhaps be unfair to say that much of the attention focused upon them has emerged more from writers concerned with early childhood and nursery education than from historians of progressivism. Works as traditionally authoritative as those of W. A. C. Stewart (1972), for example, fail to mention them, even though they do make reference to the reforming efforts of Owen and Lovett.

The McMillan sisters and a nation's health

Born in New York to emigrant Scots, the sisters returned home, following the premature death of their father, to be schooled in Inverness and it was in nearby Edinburgh where Rachel's social conscience was first awakened which, through their seeming inseparability, inevitably percolated to her sister, setting a symbiotic pattern which was to continue for the rest of their lives. For all their cosmopolitan background, however, it is for their efforts in stolidly English districts – specifically their work in schools in Bradford and more significantly around the areas of Bow, Deptford and Peckham – that was to account for their lasting fame as contributors to this unique aspect of progressive thought. Much like Pestalozzi at Yverdon or Neill at Summerhill, the McMillan's and 'health' are forever indelibly associated with those parts of impoverished East London.

Both sisters emerged out of the Socialist movement; we know from Margaret's three foremost biographers – D'Arcy Cresswell (1948), Elizabeth Bradburn (1989) and Carolyn Steedman (1990) – of the key political contacts that she made in moving to London which provided her with a formative political education. One could not then throw a stone in Bloomsbury without hitting a social thinker and through encounters with George Bernard Shaw, the Webbs, Annie Besant, future ILP leader and MP Keir Hardie and even Kropotkin, the McMillans became convinced of the necessity of socialism, attending meetings, rallies, marches and strikes. Margaret's social work in feeding and alleviating the distress of the poor in the stricken Whitechapel district prefigures that done later on by another notable middle-class convert with a social conscience – future Prime Minister Clement Atlee. It would not be an overt generalization to say that all of their educational thoughts and ideas were couched and enveloped in a basic Marxian class analysis of society – that is that the root cause of suffering stemmed from economic poverty, a variation on the theme established by Owen.

Political creed aside, much of the driving sentiment behind their work lay, as Viv Moriaty (1999) has made clear, with the need to, in some way, compensate urban children for their loss of the, 'secret idyll of childhood' (Moriaty 1999: 17). Turn of the century literature, for example, Frances Hodgson Burnett's *The Secret Garden* (1910), J. M. Barrie's *Peter Pan* (1911) and, from a later period, Arthur Ransome's *Swallows and Amazons* (1930) contributed to a general belief that nature and the outdoors could provide an antidote for urban living and its associated poverties. Nowhere were these urban problems better illustrated than in the town of Bradford where in 1893, the year of the McMillan's arrival, infant mortality stood at almost one-fifth and an equally high percentage of children suffered regularly from curvature of the spine, hollow chests and rickets, which were telltale symptoms of poor diet. While the city was one of the early progenitors of the Labour movement and local authorities encouraged the use of public facilities such as libraries, many adults simply were physically too weak and starved to use them regularly. Margaret McMillan not only realized the value of the outside world but, by using her platform as a prominent member of the Bradford School Board, begun a lifelong fight to ensure that such hideous injustices would not affect those of the later generations. The seven formative years spent in Bradford, while not yet making her name nationally famous, allowed Margaret McMillan to develop, through empirical observation and work done at the microcosmic level, fundamental aspects of her philosophy which were to be reflected in all of her subsequent writings and practice.

We know from her various biographers that she was well versed in the works of Rousseau, Pestalozzi, Froebel and Seguin and the general permissive and progressive aspects of their philosophy were incorporated not merely into her own practice in Bradford's Belle Vue School but also across the district through her skilled administration. Her visits to the Froebelian Kindergarten in Kensington with its free learning programmes, welcoming environments and emphasis upon play further convinced her of the need for more widespread progressive methods in the classroom, to allow children to express themselves and for their views to be taken more seriously. Typically, her ideas found opposition among other teachers who preferred to adhere to the conventional '3R's' approach, believing that this more concrete knowledge ultimately provided the best opportunities for children of the working classes.[9] It was perhaps this intransigence that was the catalyst for Margaret McMillan's finest and most readable early work, *Education through the Imagination* (1904), published following her Bradford experience, and which clearly demonstrated her progressive credentials were as much practical as biological and theoretical.

The rationale for the book, as stated in the preface, was to take issue with the received popular wisdom at the time which 'does not incline to regard imagination as a very important faculty at all' (McMillan 1904: ix). McMillan's justification for the imagination was not however merely that of the Romantics on the grounds of self-contemplation and communion with a higher power. Instead, imagination, even as expressed among the artisan class, was something that was of benefit more broadly to society as a whole. This was not through the continual collective and communal enjoyment society could gather from an appreciation of art and the aesthetics but because imaginative workers would be better workers who could compete more productively in the global marketplace. In a key utterance, McMillan sought to equate prevalent didactic teaching methods with the enduring decline in British economic performance:

> The learning of facts and of formal arts, the training of the verbal memory, the discipline of the class-room and school may be good things in their way. But when the youth of the country have left the school-room, when they are out in the open of industrial life, competing with educated workmen of other lands, mechanical training and formal attainments will not carry them far. (Ibid., xi)

McMillan's writing thus invoked pertinent, topical debates and concerns over the 'state of the nation' question to begin to provide sympathy for, and justification of, her main progressive philosophy. In this particular work, McMillan was concerned to demonstrate that it was precisely the lack of attention paid to children's imaginative development in schools that had led to a decline in standards within many areas of public life. Whereas once, 'the people [were] very far beyond the average of the most favored nations' (Ibid., 8), British children now, with their imaginative growth stunted, could no longer fulfil their potential and such latent possibilities, as McMillan explained through reference to a range of complex literature, applied to concepts as broad as movement, emotion, aesthetics, science, art and construction. Progressive educational methods were therefore seen as existing not merely for providing knowledge for its own sake but also as giving children an opportunity to develop attributes that could contribute more broadly to social welfare.

It was more than this, though; Margaret McMillan was, in her own quiet way, attempting to redefine the role of the teacher who she felt had been constrained by recent legislation and theories of practice. She opposed, for example, the received wisdom that classrooms should be silent and considered it important for teachers to have elocution lessons to allow for 'voices full of subtle intonations which would make conversation quite a delightful thing' (McMillan 1896). Music, which she argued was 'beyond the pale of the elementary teacher' (McMillan 1904: 42), played a considerable part in her thinking due to children's innate and natural responses to its sounds. Furthermore, her explicit concern for the health and well-being of the child meant that the teacher's position was now being re-conceptualized to include being as much a pastoral carer rather than a mere supervisor and deliverer of information, as had been the tendency under the previous system of payment by results. In light of the close links which now exist between schools and social and child welfare services, it is possible with hindsight to see how pioneering McMillan's notions were. Indeed, Albert Mansbridge, her first biographer and founder of the Workers' Educational Association was to formally write that 'The importance of [her] work in Bradford lies in that fact that it has influenced profoundly education in England . . . The flame of her spirit lit fires in Bradford which were never put out' (Mansbridge 1932: 51).

McMillan's triumph in that regard was to ultimately fight, and win, two crucial battles at a national political level to achieve tangible classroom reforms – those concerning school meals and health checks. She had realized in Bradford that it was as much poor diet and health rather than facilities or opportunities which were the limiting factor on a child's life chances. Money thrown at educating starving children was money wasted as they were ultimately incapable of learning effectively. These factors became more apparent upon the sisters' arrival in Deptford in 1904, Margaret at the invitation of the London County Council, to oversee the management of three schools in the Deptford region. London was Bradford writ large, yet the capital also provided her, as it had with the suffragette Pankhurst family, direct access to political figures who could drive through legislation in Parliament, for example, Arthur Henderson and the future Labour prime minister Ramsay MacDonald. While the McMillan's direct contribution to the development and formulation of the resulting legislation is not known and was, ultimately, intangible (neither, after all, were MPs), there is no question that their authority and skills of persuasion, reason and conciliation were vital to its passing. While the legislation was adopted by the emerging Labour Party as its own, and was appropriated as part of the parties reforming tradition, it must be remembered that the various pieces of Acts of Parliament were passed by a Liberal government, thus testifying to the appeasing skills of the McMillans who, pragmatically, did not lose sight of their overall objectives at the expense of partisan politics. While it has traditionally been Margaret who has been seen as the progenitor of the development and detail, she herself was quick to emphasize the role Rachel had played in her crusade – 'It was she who, when all was falling to pieces like a broken chain, forged and reforged the links, recollected us all and still held to our purpose' (McMillan, 1927: 116). Given their closeness to one another, it is difficult and disingenuous to attribute and apportion success; like any intellectual friendship ideas, inspiration and support were both mutual and inestimable.

The resulting legislation – the Provision of Meals Act 1906 and the Administrative Provisions Act a year later – were the first major attempts by the State to seriously consider the welfare of its children. Now, the newly formed Local Education Authorities were encouraged to feed children in their schools, although not at a universally designated time, and they were legally required to perform medical inspections. The rest of the McMillan's achievements can therefore be seen in light of trying to not only enact the existing legislation concerning children but to demonstrate to parents more generally the inherent value that health care and treatment could have on preventing disease and illness.

The concretization of this philosophy came in a series of pioneering institutions established by the sisters in a brief and fertile period prior to, and just after, the beginning of the First World War. The health clinic in Bow (opened in 1908) and the Deptford treatment centre (1910) served to embody Margaret McMillan's 'new crusade' (Bradburn 1989: 111) which was to ensure that education and society, particularly during the vulnerable primary years, was concerned as much, if not more, with the physical well-being of children than with their mental stimulation. The child was now emerging as an object of enquiry in their own right, independent of existing frameworks and preconceptions. As in her earlier writing, McMillan's justification for the necessity and potential expense of such centres of health was at the macro level – 'The whole purpose or aim of Public Health is . . . not the health of individuals but the security and progress of the whole nation which is here involved in the elimination or tolerance of preventable disease' (McMillan, quoted in Bradburn, 122). In that sense, as Carolyn Steedman (1990) has pointed out, the body of the working-class child was becoming politicized, reconstituted and held up as a form of democratic socialism.

As an adjunct to her health centres, the McMillans founded a series of open-air night camps and even a night school where children would spend time in the outdoors which was seen as a way of preventing disease in its initial stages rather than merely attempting to cure it once it had spread into the school population. Once more, in this regard, their ideas were ground-breaking as they fell in with much of the radical contemporary thought which had begun to emphasize prevention, rather than merely cure, of sickness through better health care (there was a National Insurance Act in 1911) but also through the necessity of improved housing and sanitation. The tragedy for McMillan was that it was only well past her lifetime that such ideas – for a combination of reasons, not least of all, the debilitating economic effect of the War – began to be accepted in the context of mainstream politics.

What was perhaps most unique about these nocturnal establishments was that they placed enormous emphasis upon those children of pre-school age of five years and under. As previous chapters have manifestly demonstrated, progressive educational theorists dating back to Comenius had all emphasized the importance of the first five years of the child's life in their future development and the McMillans, through their open-air nursery school in Deptford, attempted to give very young urban children opportunities not merely to relieve themselves of the grime, smog and squalor of the large cities but to articulate themselves more freely through play and self-expression. Crucial to this was the continuing influence that the French psychologist Edouard Seguin (1812–80) was having upon the sisters' thought and practice. Having pioneered hygiene treatment in a children's mental asylum in New York, Seguin had written of the need for developing self-reliance and independence in young children through the development of tasks which served to stimulate their senses in conjunction with their intellect. While Seguin's work – as we have seen in the discussion pertaining to Montessori – had concerned those suffering from mental retardation, McMillan realized that such principles could be equally successfully applied to her children. While they were not mentally abnormal or handicapped, they were suffering a form of deprivation – notably that of the soul. This deficit manifested multifariously in sensual, physical and imaginative aspects and was a result of an urban upbringing which had deprived them of the innocence of their childhood and contributed to a general dulling of the senses.

To alleviate this distress, the camp schools pioneered a range of progressive activities designed to 'let the young live and move in close intimacy with the forces, and changes that develop not only the muscular brute force organs, but the higher and finer nerve processes and brain centres as well' (McMillan, quoted in Bradburn, 142). Young children were encouraged to wander in the specially prepared garden, becoming involved with the herbs and plants while learning how to wash and dress themselves. Older children were left to draw and write, sing and dance and play a more responsible role within the school community through the setting of tables and cutlery. In the notoriously grimy East End of London, the McMillans had pioneered their own version of utopia.

The significance of these schools was two-fold. First, they were innovative in the practices they pioneered and the activities they facilitated which allowed the child to experience the joy and gaiety of being young. They did so not merely out of a slavish sense of ideological duty to the tenets of Romanticism but because the McMillan's well understood that such activity was bound up with the health of the child. With increasing scientific understanding as to the direct correlation between physical well-being and the expression of intellectual potential, they realized that the sole way of releasing the 'child within the child' was through placing them into an environment that was both clean and away from the debilitating effects of urban living. In that sense, they second reflected much of the *fin de siècle* concern over the rise of the city which came to be symbolic of spiritual and sensual deprivation. Romantic educational tenets were thus ramified with questions pertaining to the 'state of the nation' and the incipient squalors which investigations had revealed.

After Rachel's death in 1917, Margaret's work became more explicitly focused upon the development of nursery education and she produced two key works, *The Nursery School* (1919) and *Nursery Schools: a Practical Handbook* (1920), both of which were designed as companion pieces for those practitioners involved in the education of the very young. In acknowledging the 'wonderful success' (McMillan 1919: 1) of the infant welfare movement and consciously not mentioning the term in her book, Margaret McMillan was tacitly indicating the achievement of her various campaigns and it was clear that her focus had now shifted to ensure that nursery education was enhanced through more holistic considerations and chapters of her book pertain to the school garden, its size and configuration of the buildings. While best remembered for their achievements in children's health, it must be noted that fitness was not only of the body; the mind also had to be cultivated and the mind/body duopoly was manifested clearly in their progressive practices which sought to liberate and encourage good habits. The orientation of the school, as outlined in these late works, thereby became an important way in which this was facilitated with classrooms, gardens and grounds being designed to enable self-expression through freedom of movement.

In that sense, one can identify the McMillans as being an important link with other thinkers, particularly those psychologists who had made it their business, as we saw earlier, to probe the developing minds of young children. The Malting House School of Susan Isaacs, for example, was very similar in character, if not purpose, to the open-air schools with interactive activity areas and animals and plants to be cultivated and studied. By then though, with the resultant advances in medicine, concern over physical defects were seen as passé and attention was switching more explicitly to the development of the mind. Reform was not about meals and nurses but curricula and school structures. In particular, much ink was spilt over the value of nursery education and, in seeking to justify its importance, many writers, including certain members of the New Education Fellowship, had recourse to cite the earlier examples of the McMillan sisters. Perhaps no greater testament can therefore stand to the history of progressive social reform than the protected status we today afford children, both in law and the popular imagination and our understanding that deprivation of both the soul and the spirit is to rob a child of its essential qualities.

Notes

1 Perhaps part of the enmity towards Owen and other social reformers has been the slightly sniffy and suspicious attitude we hold today regarding their motivations, intentions and forthright Christian overbearance. The title of a recent BBC 2 series presented by Ian Hislop ('the Do Gooders') is an accurate summation of the modern position.

2 There were several re-issuings of the work overseen by Owen himself, notably in 1816, with very minor amendments made to the text. The most significant of these was the dropping of the dedication to William Wilberforce perhaps because of the latter's opposition to Owen's anti-religious sentiments or possibly because Owen felt some kind of (guilty?) association with his own cotton profits and the slave trade.

3 William Maclure was a Scottish merchant who moved to America and, having there made his fortune, retired to pursue his interest in education. Having

visited Yverdon, he came to the attention of Owen and was instrumental in the founding of the later New Harmony colony. Likewise, James Greaves spent four years studying as a pupil teacher under Pestalozzi and in later life, while publicly disagreeing with Owen, continued his legacy through a series of schools and organizations.

4 Bentham's much cited aphorism, 'It is the greatest good to the greatest number of people which is the measure of right and wrong' is certainly an accurate reflection of his hedonist position (he went as far as to develop a mathematical measure of pleasure – the felicific calculus) but it, of course, raises issues as to the preservation of individual rights, what counts as 'valid' pleasure etc. In educational terms, as we have seen, these issues have been raised, albeit tangentially, to attack progressive methods – is education solely about making children happy regardless of the activity? Should schools cater for *all* children's desires?

5 This seems to be a peculiarly American attribute; even in the early colonies founded by the English Puritans such as John Winthrop's 'City on a Hill', literacy and education were seen as vital to the well-being of the community.

6 Maclure had met both Frategot and d'Arusmont from his earlier travels in Paris, the latter opening up his school in Maclure's apartment.

7 There is an obvious indebtedness here to the work of John Locke and his *Second Treatise of Government,* which argued that the main role of government was protection of private property and the individual's personal transactions.

8 The People's Charter (part authored by Lovett) was first published in 1838 and contained the six stipulated aims of the Chartist movement – universal male suffrage, a secret ballot, payment for MPs, equal constituencies, an end to the property qualification and annual parliaments.

9 This may seem surprising, given Bradford's reputation as a Labour-supporting town; however, there was always strong support in the Labour Party for not only traditional forms of curriculum but also selective institutions, such as grammar schools, which provided a 'way out' for working class children. This explains the Attlee Government's general acceptance of the 1944 Education Act.

Key reading

Robert Owen, *A New View of Society: Essays on the Formation of Character,* With an introduction by G. D. H. Cole (London: J. M. Dent & Sons, 1949).

William Lovett, *Chartism: A New Organization of the People* (London: J. Watson, 1840).

Margaret McMillan, *Education through the Imagination* (London: Swan Sonnenschein, 1904).

(continued)

Further reading

Malcolm Chase, *Chartism: A New History* (United Kingdom: Manchester University Press, 2007).

Brian Simon, *The Radical Tradition in Education in Britain* (London: Lawrence and Wishart, 1972).

8

Critical Pedagogy

Introduction

The late twentieth century can be characterized intellectually by the rise and encroachment of 'postmodernism' and the resultant onset of the climate of 'postmodernity'. Although in themselves indolent terms which preclude easy definition, they have nevertheless become associated with certain specific epistemological and ontological features which relate to, and have become intertwined with, the continuing changes and transformations of modern societies and modes of thinking. Most pertinently the questioning of the existence of 'Truth' has arisen as does the onus placed upon interpretation, subjectivity and unique and distinct *truths*. Postmodernism has therefore conjoined itself with approaches to social theory that emphasize the individual at the expense of the collective, or in sociological terms, prejudicing subjectivism over structuralism. For writers working in these fields, how individuals understand, perceive and act upon the world around them is more significant than attempting to locate such action within the framework of larger social structure.

Famously (or perhaps infamously), these considerations over knowable truth arose in the French sociologist Jean Baudrillard's 1991 declamation that the First Gulf War did not actually take place as we had been led to believe. Although somewhat misunderstood and therefore ridiculed as nonsensical ethereal babble, Baudrillard's point, which was that had the mass of invading American soldiers stayed at home, more would have been killed in car accidents than were actually lost in the fighting, threw into question not if the event took place, but whether it should, in fact, be labelled as a 'war' merely because it had all the features of one – hostile rhetoric, invading armies and so on. For all of Baudrilliard's supposed flippancy, his point was therefore a serious one as he invited audiences to be critical in questioning the accepted versions of events (the 'truth') as presented through official sources. In drawing upon the concepts and problematic nature of terminology and nomenclature, Baudrillard was thus adumbrating, albeit in a characteristically mischievous and provocative way, considerations of language which have represented one of the key concerns of postmodernists.[1]

This trend has been particularly conspicuous in writing connected to historiography and the theory of history. Noteworthy authors such as Alun Munslow and Keith Jenkins, drawing upon the burgeoning canon of difficult and complex postmodern literature such as that of Baudrillard, Jacques Derrida and Hans-Georg Gadamer, have sought to throw into question and doubt the whole historical enterprise by asking searching questions concerning the historian's practices and the inhering difficulties in reconciling truth and interpretation. Can we ever, as historians commonly claim, know the 'truth' about the past? By extension, should therefore historians blindly follow the diktats of Leopold von Ranke and his latter-day disciples Arthur Marwick and Geoffrey Elton in claiming for themselves the right to tell historical truth through recourse to allegedly simplistic positivist causality? Whose truths are therefore being represented in historical archives and the histories which are produced through their utilization?

Significantly, such speculations have not merely been the intellectual machinations of other worldly philosophers for whom such ephemera are academic parlour games and thus divorced from scholarly practice. Were that the case, they would be easy to ignore and dismiss. However, both Munslow and Jenkins identify themselves first and foremost as historians and are therefore seen as members – albeit often unwelcome and noisy ones – of a community of practice which has prided itself on 'doing history' in a very particular way. In its own way, though, this proximity has served as a much-needed prod for mainstream historians to elaborate both substantive and methodological transparency in their practices and assumptions. As was discussed in the introductory chapter of this book, historians of education working in interdisciplinary departments and faculties have been particularly strong in that regard. Despite their best efforts, however, the trend among social scientists in recent years has been to favour a kind of methodological individualism which reflects the importance ascribed to understanding the past and its causes by recourse to individual action. In that sense, the legacy of Max Weber has been greater than that of either of the other sociological 'founding fathers' (Emile Durkheim and Karl Marx), both of whom relied heavily on structural forces in developing their theories of social action.

To prejudice the 'verstehn' theory of individual action and agency over that of large-scale structure in this way has thereby served to act as the gravedigger for the meta-narrative. In famously declaring the 'death of history', Francis Fukuyama (1992) was indicating the redundancy of the old Whig, Marxist and (to some degree) feminist narratives with their nods to pre-destination and determinist frameworks. Although the end referred to by Fukuyama was the triumph of American style neo-liberal capitalism, and in that sense, he was anything but a postmodernist, his powerful pronouncements served to call once more into question adherence to accepted versions of history relying on overarching patterns into which events could be placed according to a particular author's teleology.

These issues and debates may seem far removed from the field of progressive education and its practices and, in a philosophical sense, they are. Nevertheless, to draw such a link is not so tenuous an exercise as may first appear for every age can, to some degree, be recognized as having certain intellectual features which underpin, define and give weight to its assumptions about society and its constituent parts including, inevitably, education. We have seen already the Early Modern view of childhood (or lack of it), the Romantic view and that of the Victorian Age, to name but three. All of these were partially determined by corresponding views about the nature of humanity, society and the social order which themselves had been shaped by advances in science, technology, knowledge of the human mind and politics. If one could therefore appropriate a term from the postmodernist discourse to sum up its prevailing ethos, it would be 'opposition' – in this case, opposition to accepted dogmas and a desire to challenge established claims on 'Truth'. In that sense, then, postmodernity provides both the intellectual surround and the ideological explanation for the last strand of progressive education to be considered in this narrative which is that of critical pedagogy. As will therefore be implicitly clear throughout the following discussion, these ideas of postmodernism and postmodernity have served to inform many of the works of the writers labouring under that particular ideological umbrella, in particular, their stand against blind acceptance of supposed educational and pedagogic reality and dogma.

Critical pedagogy

Like the New Education Fellowship from an earlier part of the twentieth century whose 'membership' could be more accurately described as an informal gathering renowned for ad hoc intellectual discourse, critical pedagogy as a term encompasses a broad range of educational thinkers, perspectives and some very distinct practices. This latter point is especially important here, given the very specific geographical contexts – Latin America and South Africa – in which it emerged. This has given rise to important considerations as to whether aspects of the movement, particularly the de-schooling ideas of Ivan Illich and Paulo Freire, can ever be successfully exported to locations which are not at the same stage of political development – that is, labouring under the banner of severe inequality and under-privilege.

Moreover, critical pedagogy draws upon a wide and disparate range of intellectual theories such as feminism, postcolonialism, Marxism and discourse analysis and buttresses itself by citing key theorists, many of whom, such as Edward Said, Franz Fanon and Michel Foucault have, at best, only a tangential relationship to education and its practices. This can be physically evidenced from a reading of the academic journals devoted to the substantive field where educational concepts are often intertwined with aspects of grand theory. Critical pedagogy should therefore be seen in light of the recent fracturing in ideology and of the self that postmodernism has facilitated and which has featured strongly in the work of the important Spanish sociologist Manuel Castells, himself a key advocate of these ideas. This contested nature of theory and its relationship to practice therefore makes it all the more difficult to define and elaborate critical pedagogy in any succinct way.

Further to that, the historical origins of critical pedagogy, often in less economically developed countries, betray its power as a device for emancipation and the ways in which it has sought to act as a demonstrative corrective to seemingly accepted truths and belief systems, be they racial in apartheid-ridden South Africa or economic in the slums and shanty towns of Latin America and, more specifically, those of Brazil. Progressive education through this lens has thus taken upon a political dimension and the fight for equality has often been associated, understandably, with demands for basic democratic rights and freedoms. As Douglas Kellner puts it,

> Critical pedagogy considers how education can provide individuals with the tools to better themselves and strengthen democracy, to create a more egalitarian and just society, and thus to deploy education in a process of progressive social change . . . .[it] involves teaching the skills that will empower citizens and students to become sensitive to the politics of representations of race, ethnicity, gender, sexuality, class, and other cultural differences in order to foster critical thinking and enhance democratization. (Kellner in Trifonas 2000: 197)

The need to 'strengthen democracy' is important in this context for the term democracy is not simply associated with the right to vote and basic political representation; much of the writing of critical pedagogues has, in fact, been more subtle and has attempted to explore how even so called 'democratic' countries such as Britain and the United States with 'developed' educational systems have inbuilt fundamental inequalities which serve to innately favour one (dominant) class over another with knowledge, like monetary currency, having an exchange value which can be traded in the economic global marketplace. This definition of democracy can therefore be seen as an extension of that propounded by John Dewey and goes some way to explaining why, through his belief in the transformative power of education through social reconstructionism and his criticism of mechanical models of learning, many critical pedagogues have taken him as an inspirational and ideological 'jumping off' point. One of the aims therefore of critical pedagogues has been to make real the inequalities hidden within a range of education systems and this has often been achieved, logically enough, by seeking to initially emancipate children in the classroom. Frequently, as in the work of the American scholars Henry Giroux and Michael Apple, this has entailed overlap with strands of neo-Marxism, particularly through their distinct understandings of power and power relations within schools. This thereby reinforces the difficulties involved in attempting to neatly categorize and bracket educational thinkers together under a common umbrella.

While critical pedagogy can thereby be seen as forward-looking through the philosophy it appropriates and the vision it promotes, politically, it finds its roots in the past and, specifically, through drawing upon the writing of the 'Frankfurt School'. The School's social critiques, which emerged during the interwar years, and their anti-establishment tone ensured their continuing popularity during the radical decade of the 1960s. Principally, they saw consumer culture (particularly as deployed through the new 'mass' media) as promoting ideological indoctrination of the worst kind which served to create, in Herbert Marcuse's famous words, 'one dimensional men' devoid of the desire and ability to challenge accepted truths and wisdom. Basing their approaches, characteristically, upon aspects of both Marx and Freud, those affiliated to the Frankfurt School offered sophisticated and withering analyses of capitalist societies, with a particular emphasis upon the concepts of 'false realities' generated by all-pervading forms of media which acted as an updated version of Marx's 'opium of the masses'.

It is, perhaps, therefore unsurprising that many critical pedagogues have drawn inspiration from such writers as Marcuse, Adorno and Horkheimer and their stringent opposition to prevailing power structures within society. As Joe Marshall Hardin (2001) points out, 'Critique and resistance are admirable goals . . . but they remain too vague unless teachers also encourage [students] to see the very real relationship between rhetorical production and the material conditions of their own lives' (Hardin 2001: 55). Although writing here about classroom musical composition, Hardin's point is an important one as it serves to clarify how some critical pedagogues have not seen inculcating resistance as necessarily the sole purpose of classroom education. Indeed, Hardin's work articulates the view that while children should be free to espouse their own values and opinions, their rhetorical engagement and analysis should be more detached. In other words, he refuses to promote and countenance one set of political values and beliefs over another which is in itself in opposition to other critical pedagogues who have been stringent in their adherence to education as developing a social awareness, often itself of a leftish nature.

Regardless of Hardin's political beliefs, however, this point is further significant as it serves to emphasize the ways in which certain critical pedagogues consider that cultural experiences structure and form identity, experience and modes of communication. This formulation represented an extension of the writings of Marx who had previously given sole primacy to economic conditions in shaping identity. This 'humanist Marxist' approach served therefore to explore the ways in which aspects of the state 'superstructure' (culture, family etc.) acted themselves as agents of control and indoctrination, rather than as merely being adjuncts of the economic 'base'. After this fashion, education was thus seen as a key battleground in which discourses and value-systems competed for dominance and hegemony while schools were conceptualized as sites of cultural transmission and reproduction. Teaching too became seen as a political act and never something that was ideologically neutral and straightforward, hence the reason why it has played such a huge part in the writings of so many of these thinkers.

In encouraging its adherents to use education as a device to challenge certain received wisdoms and to question our fundamental taken-for-granted assumptions as to what the purposes of education are and should be, critical pedagogy once again reflects the dominant postmodern intellectual *zeitgeist*, which has been more prepared to legitimate all forms of art, creativity and culture. In that way, postmodernism has sought to 'democratize' and make more readily accessible media which have traditionally been seen as the preserve of those few with the ability to 'read' and understand it in the appropriate way. One of the side effects of this in, for example, art has been a challenge to Western assumptions as to the constitution of skill and beauty – can not cartoon images, consumer products and 'found' object also have aesthetic value? This parallels perhaps the unorthodox classroom methods which, as we shall see, have come to form part of the modus operandi of critical pedagogic discourse.

As should perhaps be clear, there is significant overlap between critical pedagogues and Marxist educationalists – a relationship recently explored by Peter McLaren (2013) who argues that the tools of critical pedagogy are naturally conducive to being used in a particularly revolutionary way. Many of the former group would confidently declare allegiance to the ideas and ideals of the latter while many Marxists have articulated public sympathy for the continuing efforts in championing those in less privileged pedagogic settings. The work of Paulo Freire, for example, is permanently underscored by a form of dialectical materialism which sees human destiny as residing in the innate conflict between workers/labourers and those who control the means of production – landlords, factory owners, business leaders, head teachers and so on. Where Freire, and the de-schoolers, are to be differentiated from other Marxists, however, is that they see education and the school as an additional battleground where the inequality of those relationships also manages to manifest itself, with the teacher playing the role of the oppressor and the pupil the exploited party.

Nevertheless, the focus of this narrative has throughout been progressivism and the ways in which certain of its activities have been developed and enacted in (frequently) school-based contexts. As Madan Sarup (1978) points out, one of the key criticisms of many of the Marxist educationalist texts, even Samuel Bowles and Herbert Gintis' (1976) pioneering *Schooling in Capitalist America*, is that while identifying the sickness, they fail to prescribe a cure and there is little in their works which relates to any form of tangible teaching theory and practice. Although acknowledging that the hierarchies of capitalist societies are reflected in schools through streaming, testing, stratification and selection, they rarely seek to offer solutions as to how the content and subject matter of the curriculum can serve to break down these class-based divisions. As such, theirs, as Henry Giroux (1981) has acknowledged, is a rigid structuralism which fails to account for the subversive possibility of human agency and is thus quite pessimistic in outlook. Questions such as how schools should, at the level of classroom practice, go about the task of 'levelling the playing field' and creating equal opportunities for all are thus not satisfactorily answered. It is perhaps understandable why this is the case; Marx himself devoted an insignificant amount of space to educational considerations while many of the aforementioned writers are, by trade, sociologists whose concern has been in locating the school and its role within the wider context of social structure and who may thereby lack the necessary discipline-specific knowledge of education and the subtleties of classroom practice to delineate an appropriate curricula framework.

The reader should therefore be aware that the focus of this chapter shall be upon those aspects and adherents of critical pedagogy who have attempted to elaborate radical educational perspectives through explicit considerations of practice rather than those who have sought to merely locate the school within a theoretical framework. Such is the heterogeneous nature of critical pedagogy that it would anyway be a mistake to equate it with radical political posturing. The far-left after all do not have a monopoly on the fight for basic political rights and representation!

The following discussion will, in addition, attempt to explore the ways in which critical pedagogy has emerged in two distinct settings – the developed world of the United States and in the developing nations of Latin America and South Africa. As will be made clear, there has been significant reciprocity involved in the exchange and transmission of ideas but it is a matter of debate, raised by Ecclestone and Hayes (2008), as to the extent to which certain of these ideas can indeed be applied in Westernized settings. In their provocative discussion of the therapeutic nature of modern education, they steadfastly refuse to 'adopt the safe form of verbal radicalism of liberals who cite the emancipatory rhetoric and beliefs of educators such as Paulo Freire without any recognition that the structural and material conditions that shaped it are starkly different from current conditions' (Ecclestone and Hayes 2008: 161). Current conditions, in this context, refer to those settings whose economies are not predominantly agrarian and industrialized – in other words, what could broadly be considered 'the West'. There are therefore long-standing complexities involved in attempting to appraise and outline the broad movement known as critical pedagogy and the way in which it can be considered as something uniformly 'global'. These inconsistencies will become apparent throughout the course of the chapter.

The de-schooling Movement

One particular arm of critical pedagogy is the movement commonly known as de-schooling, which in many ways is its most famous manifestation. Indeed, such is its prominence that de-schooling is popularly and sometimes incorrectly conflated with critical pedagogy and, while sharing common residual features, is also distinguishable through various subtle ideological distinctions. A recent (2008) de-schooling reader edited by Matt Hern, for example, included not just pieces from the usual suspects (Ivan Illich and John Holt) but also figures as diverse as Leo Tolstoy, Rabindranath Tagore and A. S. Neill's daughter, Zoe Readhead, indicating not merely that de-schooling's principles have a long (very long!) historical genesis but also that it is possible to suggest that a school as 'anti-authoritarian' as Summerhill can be considered part of the movement. Is it the case in the modern climate that any school offering an education which 'builds critical thinking for active engagement and democratic self-governance' can be said to be actively demonstrating de-schooling principles?

This would certainly stand in opposition to certain pronouncements from Ivan Illich who argued that any attempt at schooling, even ones as radical as Summerhill, were still legitimating the idea that the school as an institution was the sole way of introducing and indoctrinating children into society. As Illich puts it, 'Even the seemingly radical critics of the school system are not willing to abandon the idea that they have an obligation to the young . . . an obligation to process them into a society which needs disciplined specialization' (Illich 1971: 67). Can therefore 'schools', as we understand them, be institutions for de-schooling or does that, in itself, represent an implicit ideological tautology?

Further confusion arises from a pertinent essay included in Hern's *festschrift* to Freire, referenced above. In this piece, Esteva, Prakash and Stuchul offer a potent condemnation of the work of Freire, whose ideas, they argue, 'served the system he wanted to change' (Hern 2008: 92). This further suggests that the de-schooling movement is not by any means united and even those broadly sympathetic to its ideals can find much to criticize in one of its sacred cows. Nor was this an isolated incident of mutiny; a 2004 anthology of essays published in 'Rethinking Freire: Globalization and the Environmental Crisis' and edited by Chet Bowers and Frederique Apffel-Marglin served to offer a potent analysis and critique of Freire's model as applied in a range of Third World Countries. In this book, Freire and his supporters stood accused of failing to take sufficient account of two recent trends – 'Third World grassroots resistance to economic globalization and the ecological crisis' (Bowers and Apffel-Marglin 2004: viii) – an oversight caused by underpinning their assumptions with a broadly Western system of values. Although the 'Westernness' of Freire's beliefs are clearly a matter for scholarly debate, the authors here argue powerfully that the ability of his ideas to act as the vehicles for global emancipation has been both repressed and stunted.

However, such academic disagreements seem to (respectfully) represent little more than ideological nitpicking. There is clearly a world of difference between such works which emanate from those innately sensitive to the ideals of de-schooling and attacks from scholars such as Robin Barrow (1978) whose mission has explicitly been to deconstruct and deride the movement *in toto*. Barrow's corpus of work is both significant and profound and there is clearly much to ponder in his argument as to how emancipatory de-schooling can legitimately claim to be. Nonetheless, his is a work of philosophy and, in the context of an historical narrative such as this, it is possible to side-step its implications and focus instead upon the protagonists of this particular group without recourse to, perhaps, consider the extent of their radicalism as is Barrow's avowed intention.

Such works do, however, provide a rejoinder which is a particularly timely tonic when taking into account the ideological slant of de-schooling. It must be made clear that many of its intellectual suppositions have emanated from a particular left-wing viewpoint and are, as such, not to be shared by all. It is sometimes difficult, especially when confronted with such powerful prose and emotive discussions of 'oppression' and 'inequality', to be anything other than converted to this particular way of thinking. Any right thinking person would, after all, surely seek to oppose coercion in any of its manifestations. When the cause was as transparently unjust as in South Africa, this tendency becomes exacerbated. However, the symptoms and cures prescribed by the de-schoolers are not the sole solution and so the reader would be well advised to adopt a questioning approach when reading any related literature and to be conversant with alternative approaches such as those which advocate the dominance of the market and are oriented towards neo-liberalism and a target driven culture. While this would be advisable for any writer or movement within the progressive canon, it is of particular importance in this case, given the proximity of these events to our own time and the contested ground that education still occupies among theorists of all political hues.

This mystification of de-schooling has though arisen in part as the central figures involved – Ivan Illich (1926–2002) and Paulo Freire (1921–97) – provided a corpus of writing and theory which has continued to prove significant and influential today, evidenced by its continuing popularity among idealistic trainee teachers and restless undergraduates. Their place together at the forefront of this chapter should therefore need little justification. The relationship, at least personally, between the two men was close and, despite recent ideological disputes perpetrated by the followers of Illich, it would not be wrong in the first instance to conjoin them together, particularly given the comparable Latin and Southern American locations and contexts in which they operated and wrote.

Famously, Freire came to hold positions within the Brazilian Department of Education and was to prove influential in promoting curricula innovation. Likewise, Illich founded his CIDOC (Intercultural Documentation Centre) in Mexico originally as a Catholic missionary training centre but which rapidly expanded to serve as a Mecca for the intellectually curious, including drop-out hippies and pacifists to earnest Catholic priests intent on spreading the gospel of the Church. Such was Illich's success at CIDOC in providing a sophisticated analysis of poverty and the Third World that he invoked the ire of both the Catholic Church and the CIA.[2] This was not altogether unsurprising, given that much of his criticism was directed at American and Catholic philanthropic efforts to assist and aid in combating the widespread poverty within the Third World. For Illich, such attempts reeked of cultural and ideological imperialism and were designed, ultimately, to impose particular Westernized structures and viewpoints upon developing nations. Taking therefore its cue from Illich, much of de-schooling was to be latterly concerned with promulgating a 'national' as much as an 'educational' awareness and in seeking to develop politically aware and active citizens. Indeed, the extent to which de-schooling has been characterized by the formation of these political identities has proven the foundation of some critiques such as that put forward by the journal *Social Policy* in the early 1970s which have sought to suggest geographical limitations to the spread of de-schooling. How can a movement which seeks to promulgate such strong nationalist sentiments among the working classes and which arises out of a very specific agrarian, class-based relationship be exported outside of that environment where the social and political contexts may be radically different and, in some cases, non-existent?

The Challenge of Freire and Illich

Of the two writers, it is perhaps Freire whose work has had the most global impact, evidenced by the range of centres and organizations founded to preserve his legacy.[3] His seminal text, *Pedagogy of the Oppressed* (1970), in particular, has served as required reading for anyone with designs on changing the educational structure in which they operate and continues to be a set text on many teaching degree courses, given the way in which it seeks to emancipate and offer a voice to disadvantaged groups within society. Furthermore, although espousing an 'extreme' philosophy, it does so in a fair and reasoned way, which has led to its intellectual advocacy among even those with contrasting ideological viewpoints. This was characteristic of the man himself; all testimony reveals him to be a gentle man of great humility and able to temper his profound convictions with a pragmatic streak, evidenced by his willingness to assume certain 'establishment' positions which he used to highlight the inequalities he saw as bedevilling the education system of Brazil.

While Freire's canon is relatively substantial (and, confusingly, includes several revisions of earlier works), at its heart is a key relationship between oppressors and the oppressed which acts as the central driver for much of his philosophy. One term above all – *praxis* – came to be fundamental to his project and represented Freire's way of articulating the need to act on reality rather than merely apprehending it which, in his terms, amounted to a passive legitimating of social inequality. This reflects the way in which much of Freire's rhetoric is action-based and sees human relationships as existing through the contexts of oppression, rebellion and challenge. In a powerful call to arms Freire declares:

> It is only when the oppressed find the oppressor out and become involved in the organized struggle for liberation that they begin to believe in themselves. This discovery cannot be purely intellectual but must involve action; nor can it be limited to mere activism, but must include serious reflection: only then will it be a praxis. (Friere 2000: 65)

This is very much Marxian language and terminology and hints at Freire's political sympathies; however, it is by no means straightforward to a label him a 'Marxist' after this fashion. While his work was embedded in the discourse of class struggle and his educational philosophy was similarly rooted in the belief that human beings could ultimately change the world for the better, Freire was reticent to advocate violence and armed struggle. Likewise, his Catholic upbringing meant his relationship with religion (anathema to true Marxists) was decidedly ambiguous. Freire thus used established Marxist categories to explain aspects of the world to his reader but only insofar as they acted as the framework for his educational viewpoints. In the sense that this was Marxism, it was a very particular South American formulation of it.

In his equally famous *De-Schooling Society* (1971), Ivan Illich promulgated a very similar diagnosis to Freire. For him, schools condition pupils to become customers in a technological world with its 'futile promises of salvation to the poor' (Illich 1971: 15). This repudiation of technology nests comfortably with many of the previously mentioned ideas of the Frankfurt School who saw consumerist culture as being at the heart of the contemporary problems of society. Illich calls the controllers of these cultures the 'technocrats' and argues that technologies, while in themselves conferring positive benefits, need to be developed, which fall outside the control of these keepers of power and their big corporations and are thus genuinely democratizing in their attributes. Like Freire, he saw centralized education as a device for maintaining inequality and using smoke and mirrors to construct an illusion of hope and progress which schools serve to legitimate.

In the second chapter of his book, Illich deconstructs this anatomy of the school and argues that the pupil subservience is maintained by recourse to modern conceptions of childhood, with young people being seen as in need of 'protection' and 'governance'. As has been referred to in previous chapters, much has been written on this (notably by the historian Harry Hendrick) and the notion that constructions of childhood serve to institutionalize young people is a powerful one. For some readers, Illich here may carry the argument too far yet, in the context of 'poorer' South American countries where young people are more active in the circumstance of communities and daily life, it represents an accurate inference. This indoctrination process is achieved, for the most part, by the efforts of the teacher who, according to Illich, propagates three functions – that of custodian, therapist and preacher. All of these terms are very deliberately chosen for they carry overtones of control, power and guardianship and reflect the many functions of a school in transmitting 'official' culture, doctrine and dogma.

There are therefore two key areas into which these classic texts of de-schooling writing probe. First, are their attempts to explain how social inequalities are maintained through the education system and, second, they endeavour to answer the question as to 'how [then] is it possible to carry out the pedagogy of the oppressed' (Freire, op. cit. 54), particularly given that those subjugated individuals have no political power by which to democratically enact change? It is from this second interrogation that de-schooling's inherently progressive educational philosophy derives for equality can, they contend, only be achieved by obliterating the traditional classroom power relationship of pupil and teacher. Indeed, as we shall first examine, it was Freire who believed that pedagogy (he is reluctant to use the term teaching) should consist initially of unveiling the world of oppression and then, as a pedagogy of all peoples, acting as a force for 'permanent liberation' (Ibid).

Central to Freire's thesis of oppression and its maintenance was his notion of 'educational banking' which forms an important chapter within *Pedagogy of the Oppressed* and frames much of his subsequent thesis. In terms which resonate powerfully with the modern age where economic and 'recessionist' jargon is becoming ever more a part of our existence, he posits a powerful analogy between the bank and the school. In much the same way as one would 'deposit' money into a bank, so schools and teachers 'deposit' knowledge into their pupils. Like banks, this share is, ultimately, unequal with some (those with sufficient levels of capital) benefiting at the expense of others (who are lacking). It is only those students who are seen as being able to sufficiently repay the institutional investment (financially and intellectually) who will serve to gain from the system. Clearly, a theory for the modern world!

Inherent within this key notion we once more see Freire drawing upon the language of opposition – the depositor and the receptacle, the knowledgeable and the-need-to-know. As he so bluntly puts it, 'The teacher presents himself to his students as their necessary opposite; by considering their ignorance absolute, he justifies his own existence' (Freire, Ibid., 72). Freire thus sees the inequalities of a 'banking' system of education as holding a mirror to society more globally with access to knowledge, the imposition of discipline and educational choice being in the hands of an oppressor represented, in this particular case, by the teacher. Freire was not offering, however, a critique of the teaching profession per se but instead arguing that much of their practice derived from their experiences as deliverers of officially sanctioned knowledge or 'culture' which it was their duty to transmit. It was hardly the fault of teachers that the only routes into their chosen profession were monitored by the gatekeepers of the State! Such a thought ultimately precluded him from being pessimistic about the opportunity for teachers to be active agents of social change and to reject the notion of official compliance.

Within this 'banking' system of education, the natural spirit of childish enquiry was blunted – 'The teacher's task is to organize a process which already occurs spontaneously, to "fill" the students by making deposits of information which he or she considers to constitute true knowledge' (Ibid., 76). Freire thus contended that the innate responses of children to the world are elbowed aside in favour of the teacher imposing instead a straitjacketed and socially accepted view both of behaviour and learning. Knowledge never therefore emanates from children themselves and opportunities for independent enquiries are lost. This serves to dull any attempts at critical thinking and preserves the social order through stressing the values of obedience, passivity and conformity. As such, supporters of Freire have argued that the notion of 'educational banking' goes far beyond South America and, for that matter, crude Marxian notions of false consciousness. Instead, they argue that it offers a much broader understanding of the way in which educational systems allow for subservience to any and all value systems, including those within the context of the Western world where oppression, although less obvious, is still perpetrated on a daily basis. As we shall see later, this forms the basis for many of the critiques of writers such as Peter McLaren and Henry Giroux.

Freire's pseudo-financial metaphor for knowledge as something to be deposited transferred and re-cooped as if it were market place currency is reflected too in the pages of Ivan Illich. Indeed, Illich's work interrogates to a deeper level the process by which knowledge is compiled and re-assembled for student and pupil digestion. Although he prefers the term 'package', Illich nevertheless reiterates that individual success in schools is judged on how well students can assimilate, consume and replicate these packages. Very often, they reflect nothing more than a set of standards that societies (and its ruling 'technocrats') deem as valuable; educational 'success' then can be seen as a result of successfully enmeshing oneself within concurrent political demands and ideologies. As such, conservative values are inculcated within the moral and social fabric of a country and it becomes the role of the 'custodian' teacher to ensure their transmission and foster an allegiance to their representation. In his last work, published posthumously in 1998, Freire referred to the teacher as a 'cultural worker', thereby emphasizing the key role they had in transmitting long-standing belief systems or, put another way, the culture of a particular country. One of the key side effects of this is that the curriculum becomes limited to a package of quantifiable 'credentials' in which imagination and free-thinking have little place. Indeed, such freedom of thought is central to many of the key writings of de-schooling for it is this attribute that is seen as the most significant catalyst in precipitating change.

These theories have proven particularly influential among theorists such as the American sociologist Michael Apple (1942–), who have similarly argued for the interwoven relationship between schools and their political surrounds, particularly (in the case of Apple) within those societies oriented, like the United States, along free market and neo-liberal lines. Like Freire, Apple's corpus of work has involved interrogating common assumptions about the school system and the way in which certain 'kinds' and 'types' of knowledge are more readily recognized and legitimized in the market place. According to Apple, the unequal distribution of knowledge within schools (he refers to it coming in 'packets') is replicated across society at large, allowing for the reproduction of structures of inequality and the maintenance of power to be contained within the hands of small governing elites.

Such ideas have been further developed by the equally important English sociologist Stephen Ball who, in common with others in his field, articulates the view that knowledge has become a commodity with exchange value to be ultimately redeemed and recouped later in life. This is termed 'credentialization' and is used by Ball to explain how occupational mobility is restricted to those with further education and who have the appropriate life 'credentials' such as extra-curricular achievement, experience of volunteering, travelling and so on. Far from being valuable for its own sake, knowledge has thus become a tool which a privileged few can use to unlock certain doors on their way to success.

This accords with the type of analysis that Ball has explicitly set out in his recent book, *Global Education Inc* (2012), which argues powerfully that twenty-first-century systems of education have been appropriated and corrupted by neo-liberal forces, franchises and big businesses. Educational policies, according to Ball, are now sold as profitable commodities with responsibility for their implementation lying with non-accountable external agencies and quangos (quasi autonomous non-governmental organizations). Even the training of teachers – one of the 'sacred cows' of the state – has now been hijacked by private companies, as in the example of 'Teach for America' in the United States and 'Teach First' within the United Kingdom.[4] This corporatist ethos is also reflected in the way in which the architecture of many new school buildings consciously apes commercial and 'city' structures, many of whom are sponsored anyway by private organizations. Given the be-suited corporate image and strategy style of such groups, there is much in Ball's argument and overall critique which would have appealed to Freire!

However, if such discussions represent a particular diagnosis of the problem, then much of Freire's work was equally concerned with exploring the mechanisms by which education could make societies more equitable. The solutions to this, he argued, lay less in the content of the curriculum but more in the pedagogical approach by which it was deployed. As Apple, Gandin and Hypolito (2001) put it, 'Emancipatory education for Freire is never a simple transmission of knowledge . . . Rather, knowing is constructing oneself as a subject in the world, one who is able both to rewrite what one reads and to act in the world to radically alter it' (Apple, Gandin and Hypolito in Palmer 2001: 130). Freire argued that the impetus to read and write and to do so creatively was heightened when children realized that such activities enabled them to gain privileged insight into the power networks in which they were embedded and to which they were subjected and bound. This draws very much on the Marxian precept of 'false consciousness' and, like Marx, Freire believed that this awareness was critical in enabling a transformation of society through the enlightening of individual consciousnesses.

The processes of de-schooling

Having outlined above the prevailing global framework, it is now important to give some consideration as to the way in which these conditions could be overturned through the mechanisms of education. In particular, how do the de-schoolers propose affecting change in a world so deeply imbued with oppressive values and rituals? This would seem to be a difficult task, given that much of their work is predicated upon the assumption on a deep-seated permanence of the very ideals which they seek to overthrow! If these values and ideologies were not so severely ingrained within the social structure of society then, perversely, would there be as much need for their specific methods of re-education? However, pleasing ironies aside, it is through the consideration of proffered solutions that not only do key progressive educational tenets emerge but that degrees of divergence in relation to the proposed resolutions to common problems become apparent. This gives us the clearest indication to date of the different inflections within de-schooling approaches. In many respects, it is the suggestions of Illich which are the most radical here for it is in his work that we see proposals for wholesale 'root and branch' changes to education systems and not merely the adaptation and transformation of the strictures of existing educational institutions.

In his *De-Schooling Society,* we therefore see Illich going beyond merely attempting to alter pupil awareness and consciousness within the context of a decentralized or less formal centre of learning; while that is required, it cannot, he argues, take place within institutions as ultimately, they will themselves become subsumed by the rules of the technocrats. Illich therefore calls for a breakdown in all forms of schooling and posits instead his theory of 'learning webs'. In common with many other de-schooling theorists, the notion of community was central to his pronouncements as it was in the context of local communities where Illich saw education as being recast and the 'webs' spun. In particular, he elaborated a particular framework for relationships which was comparable to that of a master and an 'apprentice' student. Such an association was destined to be intimate and outside of the normal regulatory educational frameworks but one which also taught practical knowledge and skills, historically often regarded as second-class within schools. These 'skill exchanges' served as an alternative model by which the transfer of knowledge could take place, thereby side-stepping many of the more conventional routes, which were themselves riddled with unequal distributions of power. Likewise, the context of 'community' served as the basis for what Illich referred to as the *de-institutionalization of resources* – that is to say, that potential resources for learning should not be demarcated within specific sectors of the community. A shop, for example, may be thought of as a place where one could learn rudimentary mathematics such as addition and subtraction or a skill such as fixing specific equipment rather than merely a place for economic exchange and barter.

This may seem fanciful whimsy, yet it is an important concept as it serves to highlight the ways in which Illich saw knowledge exchanges (even those based around authoritarian ways of learning) as potentially liberating when they took place outside of the official state-sanctioned institution of the school. In Illich's utopia, the custodians and guardians of knowledge were no longer the teachers (agents of the state) but individuals with skills who have, he argues, far more logical right to be those transmitting instruction and knowledge in a non-hierarchical way. Are not, after all, their skills the ones which have more immediate and long-lasting value in the context of everyday living? In this, there are shades of Rousseau's recommendations to Emile to learn a useful skill which could benefit both himself and the community as a whole. The way in which both parties were to go about this process of learning was designed to be reciprocal between learner and instructor and Illich was keen to stress the cordial nature of these skill exchanges which were designed to be available for all through the skills 'bank' which would act as a catalogued repository of abilities which were capable of being communally shared.

Interestingly, for one whose concerns lay in de-centralizing the mechanisms of education, Illich's recommendations placed an onus upon the central strictures of power – 'governments . . . employers, taxpayers, enlightened pedagogues, and school administrators' (Illich, op. cit., 103) – to enforce change. One way in which this was to happen was through his suggestions for authorized vouchers to be spent as individuals saw fit on the skills of their choice. Clearly, there would have to be some form of organized social policy in place to oversee these exchanges and permit them to take place. Likewise, his central repository of skills could not, presumably, emerge spontaneously and would need to be authorized and coordinated by a centralizing body.

These are points worth noting as they serve as a contrast to the solutions presented by Freire offering, in passing, an indication of the heterogeneity of the de-schooling movement. Although he too was concerned with collective understandings, action and the liberation of the people, Freire's was not emancipation based upon skills exchanges and clearly defined webs of learning. Instead, Freire proposed that the basis of radical action should stem from particular activities undertaken by those in schools to change modes and ways of thinking. Central to this was developing a dialogic relationship between students and teachers which he refers to in his early work as 'problem-posing' education. These problems did not relate to specific substantive queries but more to reaching a general understanding of the world through mutual discovery by both student and teacher – indeed such is the relationship between the two that the terms become interchangeable in Freire's language.

This rhetoric is progressive as it empowers the student to become a critical thinker, values their opinions and puts them on a passage to self-discovery. As we have seen with so many other child-centred thinkers, these approaches are valid across the whole spectrum of the curriculum and do not relate exclusively to those subjects which one would imagine could be more readily politicized, such as politics, history and economics. As Freire himself makes clear, it is only when children partake in this kind of investigation that their educational experience becomes validated – 'Problem-posing education bases itself on creativity and stimulates true reflection and action upon reality, thereby responding to the vocation of persons as beings who are authentic only when engaged in inquiry and creative transformation' (Freire, op. cit., 84). The term used for this activity-based approach is *conscientization*[5] which is the process of developing a critical awareness of reality through reflection and action. In many ways, this serves as the end-goal to the progressive activities described above and is further developed in Freire's second book, *Education for Critical Consciousness* (1973), which explores in more depth how this singular development takes place. The three levels of consciousness to which he refers – naive, magical, and critical – represent the conversion from blind naïve acceptance to fatalistic stoicism to, finally, an understanding of the world as it essentially is.

These developments are important to contemplate here for they served to give intellectual stimulus to global movements who recognized the significance of the relationship between education and social justice. The most radical South African anti-apartheid group, for example, was Steve Biko's Black Consciousness whose very name betrays the importance it ascribed for the need to raise critical and cultural awareness by identifying and celebrating one's status as a minority. Much of Biko's activity took, as its starting point, the need to directly oppose apartheid through not only the promotion of social justice but also by encouraging a more militant attitude among his followers in directly challenging the oppression of the dominant class. In part, this was facilitated by education and the need to raise awareness of what it meant to be a *black* South African. Even before Biko, writers from other parts of Africa, such as W. Senteza Kajubi (1971) in Uganda, were considering the possibility of dispensing with traditional forms of schooling which were seen as having failed to adequately respond to the needs and problems of developing countries. In both cases, a particular model of education – informal, anti-traditional and rooted in a particular African discourse – served as vehicles for addressing very real and prevalent needs and deficits. As was stated earlier, it is easy therefore to apprehend how critical pedagogy became intertwined with theories of race, ethnicity and gender, particularly as it became a vehicle for challenging various manifestations of oppression.

One of the inhering complications, however, with accommodating Freire's work (and indeed, that of Illich) within a 'foreign' context, beyond the contrasting social and political landscapes, is the problems it poses in relation to the re-conceptualization of the role of the teacher. Given both of their attempts to dismantle and break down the traditional dialectic classroom-based practice, it is asking much of teachers to abandon not merely their training but also centuries of patterns of educational practice. This would require a confidence and daring not traditionally associated with the professional mainstream who in recent times have, as Larry Cuban (2009) points out, been crowbarred into adopting approaches to teaching which serve to satisfy government targets of testing and attainment. No matter how innovative a teacher may actually be or how confident they may feel about their day-to-day practice, critical pedagogy ultimately seeks to transform the role of teacher into one of the 'transformative intellectual' (Giroux and Aronowitz 1986). In practice, this means teachers working with their students to interrogate and make meaning of the diverse range of experiences they have and to produce out of these a child who is a critically aware citizen of the world. No easy task!

Such a transformation also poses logistical problems. In considering why so few teacher-researchers have written about conscientization in relation to young people, Antonia Darder (2002) cites the intellectual complications involved in 'the ability to reflect and critique one's thoughts, actions, and motivations . . . ongoing dialogue with peers and mentors . . . awareness of self and environment in a particular place and time, within a historical and cultural context, and a particular political landscape' (Darder 2002: 179–80). If this may be too much for some teachers, for others, it is impossible or undesirable to attempt problem-posing education with young children as the subject matter may be 'too intense for younger sensibilities' (Ibid). In describing her experiences of critical pedagogy, Darder cites the cases of teachers who themselves are sympathetic to the ideas of critical pedagogy, yet lack the faith in either their students or themselves to fully enact the doctrines of Freire. Issues of professional confidence thus become ones to consider in this context and these may be matters which are problematic in countries where mechanisms for teacher development do not seek to engage in the complexities of learning theory or which do not have a long history of public sector empowerment. This may serve to throw into further doubt the potential for critical pedagogy to act as a global vehicle for educational transformation.

Critical pedagogy in the United States

The previously discussed manifestations of critical pedagogy represent a key arm of the movement, notably one concerned with political representation, empowerment and a general enfranchisement of the downtrodden. Nevertheless, as J. Martin Rochester (2003) points out, 'the critical pedagogy school has [also] managed to carve out a respectable niche in *America's* schools of education' (Rochester 2003: 77). Much of this has been through the widely disseminated scholarship of not only Michael Apple (whose work has been alluded to earlier) but also important scholars such as Henry Giroux (1943–), Joe Kincheloe and Peter McLaren, to name but a few, who have between them produced a copious and wide-ranging body of research seeking to not only promote the ideas of Illich and (particularly) Freire but also to apply them in the wider context of North America through filtering certain of the latter's key concepts through the lens of European critical theory.

Such nowadays is critical pedagogy's 'respectable' academic status, even journals as reputable and upright as the *Harvard Educational Review* have carried articles pertaining to support its ethos and justify its significance as a movement for change in educational circles. Likewise, within many American schools and colleges of education, critical pedagogy is increasingly being given more status and representation and not merely as an historical and sociological curiosity merely to be studied tokenistically. In that respect, both Giroux and McLaren represent this trend as both are, like Apple, practising academics and were, briefly, working together at the University of Ohio as well as co-editing volumes and acting as symbiotic valuators of each other's work. These relationships serve to demonstrate not only the highly theorized and nuanced form that critical pedagogy now takes but the way in which a burgeoning community of practice has developed round it through the dissemination of teaching and discipleship. As an example of this, a key text for many aspiring teachers continues to be McLaren's *Life in Schools: an Introduction to Critical Pedagogy in the Foundations of Education* which, as of 2006, was into its sixth edition – testament to its continuing popularity and high reputation. As was the case with the earlier work of William Kilpatrick at the Teachers College of Columbia University, education colleges and their in situ academics have seemingly retained their reputation as purveyors of 'radical' ideas!

Henry Giroux, in particular, is often seen as the standard bearer for this strand of American critical pedagogy and reading his work, it is easy to see why. Even at its most complex, it retains the important characteristics of being readable, powerful and compelling, yet bound together with a particular aphoristic quality. He is also a writer of Stakhanovite proportions,[6] having published over 40 books and 100 articles and book chapters which have evolved from being confined to the field of education to, more recently, moving towards considerations of culture in its broadest sense and the ramifications these theories may have in this wider context. While in a work of history such as this, it may seem somewhat erroneous to be discussing a man still living and contributing to the educational discourse, Giroux's contribution to the critical pedagogical movement is too large to ignore and too seminal to register as an appended footnote.

Furthermore, those shifts in ideological emphasis (most noticeable in the work he has been producing from the mid-1990s) mark out a very distinctive educational philosophy which encompasses the new media – itself a form of pedagogy – and the ways in which that seeks to exert control through the promotion of a form of instrumental reason. Giroux argues that contemporary activities, including but not solely limited to schooling, are measured according to the value that they are seen to possess and not always through the beauty of the things in themselves. In that respect, Giroux is consciously echoing many of the writings of the American philosopher Maxine Greene whose profound discussions of the arts have resisted attempts to impose any criteria of immediate gratification at the expense of longer lasting intellectual curiosity.

These concerns are further unsurprising, given the profound intellectual debt Giroux owes to the writers of the Frankfurt School and their more substantial commentaries upon consumer culture. His, unlike theirs, is not however a pessimistic vision; inherent within his work, as is the case with many critical pedagogues, resides a hope that an articulate and educated citizenry can make a difference in combating many of the social evils in society. His work is therefore underpinned by a morality and humanity which credits individuals and those in education with being able to make some form of tangible difference to the unequal balance of power. As has been made clear by Giroux in interviews and biographical accounts, his own experiences as a high school teacher were seminal in that regard for they demonstrated to him the necessity of overlaying daily practices with a stylized academic discourse in order to legitimate the sorts of teaching methods he saw as urgent in American education.

It is further in this later work that Giroux betrays his significant intellectual debt to postmodernism. Moving away from the Modernist ideas of the Frankfurt School, with its emphasis upon high culture and 'core' sets of values, postmodernism's articulation of the breadth of human voice and experience – both racial and sexual – provides the basis for a curricular philosophy which does not allow for the under-representation of marginalized groups. Likewise, the rationality inherent within Modernity is seen by Giroux as a force for legitimating value-neutrality which, for him, is not (as it claims) fair and equitable but represents instead a form of inaction and inertia. The classrooms envisaged by Giroux would therefore seem to be diverse places of cultural and value pluralism which encourage life narratives and constant pupil self-reflection, all of which accords with particular aspects of postmodernity. If progressivism can be defined in any way as individualizing the learning experience and valuing those contributions, then Giroux is most certainly one of its staunchest advocates.

Although not ultimately posting an 'irrational' approach to teaching in favour of achieving his diverse aims, Giroux brilliantly sidesteps many of the critiques of postmodernism, particularly those which point to its relativistic character and posits a view of education which celebrates multiple classroom truths and emphasizes the vitality of individualism. Education, for Giroux and his colleagues, is therefore a democratizing process which seeks to give a voice and represent all young people. In that sense, it fits with the long established tradition in American progressive educational writing stretching back to Dewey, which saw education as a mechanism by which the composition of society could be continually re-structured and re-constituted. This gives further support to the idea that this strand of critical pedagogy is one which is particularly Western in its composition and application if only through its attachment to a very particular intellectual and ideological tradition.

The limitations of critical pedagogy?

There are several key criticisms of the work of Henry Giroux which can be used to highlight some of the potential limitations of critical pedagogy as a movement and, particularly, the way in which it has been translated into the Western context. These are potent to explore for they serve to throw into dispute critical pedagogy at a time when it is still finding its feet intellectually and thereby remains a contended concept within educational narratives and rhetoric. Its methods, for example, have yet to become fully embraced by any government-sanctioned framework for learning while the idea of directly politicizing education through the role and voice of the teacher remains, understandably, controversial, particularly in Western systems of pedagogy which, rightly or wrongly, are being continually driven by standards, results and league tables.

When discussing critical pedagogy, it is therefore initially important to consider the inhering problem of attempting to translate the passionate rhetoric of Giroux and others into tangible classroom action. Although both Freire and Illich stressed forms of *praxis* with an emphasis upon realistic classroom-based practice, would 'learning webs' and the impassioned process of conscientization of Freire hold much currency in British, American or European cultural settings? It is clear that Giroux and others wish to subordinate the learning of English, mathematics and science (the so-called 'key subjects') to the development of critical faculties and the need to engage in a conscious struggle against the inherently 'unjust' values of society. However, we here come up against the fallacy of postmodernism. Although denying the existence of 'objective' and 'truthful' knowledge – as exemplified through the teaching of English and culture which is frequently representative of canonical and dominant narratives – critical pedagogues have no qualms themselves about putting forward values that teachers should cultivate with their students. In particular, the sort of society which is seen as 'desirable' is one which is defined exclusively by Giroux and his colleagues. To put it simply, the social and political assumptions underpinning critical pedagogy may be flawed. Even if they are not, why should not the views of other educators be considered when defining a set of desirable educational outcomes?

Similarly, are the classrooms of critical pedagogy which are at the hub of challenging the status quo representative and accommodating of a range of viewpoints or do they solely promote counter-cultural values? Are dissenting voices allowed? This is perhaps not a fair critique as there have been too few settings where these ideas have been applied; however, it serves to illustrate the potential difficulties involved in promoting the sorts of ideas elaborated by Giroux and his colleague Peter McLaren. The instruction factories which Giroux identifies, particularly in his key work *Schooling and the Struggle for Public Life*, would seem to disparage many of the attempts at innovation attempted by teachers who, as a profession, have tended to be at least sympathetic to child-centredness in their mindset. Are schools really places where 'students traditionally sit in rows staring at the back of each others' heads and at the teacher who faces them in symbolic, authoritarian fashion'? (Giroux 1988: 37) Are 'events in the classroom governed by a rigid time schedule imposed by a system of bells and reinforced by cues from teachers'? (Ibid) Even if, as Giroux would argue, this is not the fault of teachers but of an ideological state of mind which values conformity over innovation which is subsequently reflected in policy, does Giroux allow for the regular acts of subversion which teachers undertake on a daily basis? Are teacher training colleges and institutions really so mechanical as to produce identikit teachers lacking in ideas and novelty and destined to conform and comply? Various academic studies done in British schools, for example, those of Elizabeth Wood (2008 and 2010) indicate that even where there is a high level of state interference and regulation of the curriculum and its key elements such as play, it has still been possible for teachers to innovate and challenge. In the latter article, Wood also discusses these trends in explicit relation to emerging critical pedagogies, indicating perhaps that the relationship is more complex than may first appear. Indeed, Giroux's contention that the teaching profession has become increasingly de-motivated and de-skilled may not be a result solely of the introduction of having a reduced autonomy within the classroom and could plausibly be linked to any number of other external factors.

For Giroux, the purpose of the school should be to produce students who are politically engaged and active in seeking to challenge and overturn the inequalities inherent inside the education system, and therefore, society at large. This is achieved by developing within them a critical and political consciousness and mindset. Is this, however, just and equitable failing, as it does, to stress and promote marketable and transferable skills which may be needed in the market place later in life? Admittedly, once more, this may be to somewhat miss Giroux's point as he would surely question why these attributes, above others, are the ones given priority in the adult world and it may ultimately be too simple to dichotomize critical thinking and employability skills. Nevertheless, should one be sacrificing children on an ideological altar, merely to validate an educational theory or can mechanisms for change be more closely regulated through considerations of policy and the like?

The above points are not meant as active disparagements of the work of either Giroux or his colleagues. The publications they continue to produce are seminal and resonate strongly in our modern age, itself beset with ideological and educational consensus and conformity. Indeed, it is only contentious *because* it is so original and provocative. It is worth, however, being aware of the debates which surround critical pedagogy which stem, in part, from the highly politicized nature its advocates attribute to the very act of teaching. They have served to problematize education in a wholly innovative way which stems not merely from philosophy, science or theories of learning but from notions of politics and power, particularly in relation to where it resides within the context of the school and where the school sits in the bigger picture of society. Whether one concurs with this political conjoining or not, what is indisputable is that many of the recommendations which have been put forward by the de-schoolers have contributed in innovative ways to the progressive educational tradition and have raised new and direct questions for practitioners working in the field.

Notes

1 Drawing upon the 'linguistic turn' of twentieth-century philosophy, which began with Wittgenstein and Russell, many postmodernists have explored language and text as innately problematic media for conveying meaning and truth.

2 It was while working in Mexico that Illich produced his classic *De-schooling Society*.

3 The Freire Institute in England, as one example, is attached to the University of Central Lancashire and there are comparable organizations to be found in (among others) Spain, South Africa, Finland and North America. Of the latter, the Paulo and Nita Freire Project for Critical Pedagogy founded by Joe Knicheloe is the most important.

4 Teach First, founded in 2002, is an independent charity which offers an alternative route into teaching for aspiring graduates. Its critics have argued that it its corporate image and brief training period are divorced from the more earthly realities of education.

5 This term is sometimes referred to in the relevant literature as 'consciousness raising'.

6 In that he is hardly alone; Peter McLaren has been involved in the publishing of over 40 books while at the time of his death, Joe Kincheloe was in the process of writing and editing his 60th book.

Key reading

Paulo Freire, *Pedagogy of the Oppressed, 30th Anniversary Edition* (New York: Continuum Published Company, 2000).
Ivan Illich, *DeSchooling Society* (New York: Harper & Row, 1971).
Peter McLaren, *Life in Schools: an Introduction to Critical Pedagogy in the Foundations of Education* (Boston, MA: Pearson, 2006).

Further reading

Henry Giroux, *The Giroux Reader (Cultural Politics and the Promise of Democracy)*, Christopher Robbins (ed.).

Conclusion: Methodological Reflections

Wither Progressivism?

As has been alluded throughout the course of the previous pages, many of the more dominant narratives concerning progressive education and the progressives are based upon an implicit teleology, which is linear in both its scope and formation. This is particularly true of older accounts written before the established challenges laid down by the postmodernists whose influence and importance has been acknowledged in the preceding chapter. Here the more 'mild' progressivisms of Locke and, to some extent, Rousseau ultimately give way to the more 'radical' viewpoints of the de-schoolers and those who seek to locate the school as a political entity in relation to more partisan trends and ideologies. Along the way, minor figures and those less frequently discussed are seen as 'props' and 'adjuncts', whose sole purpose is to contribute to, and intravenously feed, an historical discourse dominated by the few who acquire the status of 'major writer'. This has been noted in relation to, for example, those individuals such as Edmund Holmes and Ovide Decroly whose stock today is in negative disproportion to the influence they in their own times exerted.

Although these kinds of teleological approaches were dismissed by Michel Foucault as the 'search for silent beginnings' (Foucault 1972: 4), the idea of a progressive 'view' has been advocated by (among others) the historians Blenkin and Kelly (1981), who wrote that in any discussion of progressive ideas, one 'must begin with the theories of Jean Jacques Rousseau, since it is here that they are first articulated' (Blenkin and Kelly 1981: 16). In the same way, Lawson and Peterson (1972) in their discussion of progressive education also claimed that progressive ideas stemmed directly from Rousseau's *Emile*. John Darling (1994), in fact, justified his reference to a progressive 'philosophy' by assuming a common, '. . . set of ideas about the nature of children, the nature of knowledge and the nature of life itself' (Darling 1994: 5). As Peter Cunningham (2001) has therefore noted, historians such as those referred to above 'had shown for some years [before] that there could be a sense of common purpose between parties motivated by different ideas, the sense of a "new education movement"' (Cunningham 2001: 433).

Nevertheless, this overarching contention means that there has been a shared collective tendency to become locked into observing progressivism as a homogeneous entity with common traits and characteristics which can be easily identifiable and recognizable at any point across time. These characteristics as they have traditionally been conceived include the notion of a child-centred curriculum, activities directly relevant to the needs and desires of the child, the child as an active learner and a high degree of freedom within the context of the school setting for both teachers and pupils. Certainly, within the popular mind-set, the existence of at least one of these has been frequently cited as evidence of child-centredness, with all of the attendant problems and debates which that inevitably brings.

To think in these terms does perhaps more harm than good as it ultimately obscures the truth as to what the various protagonists of progressive education of the past were trying to do in the context of their writings and educational statements. It does this by potentially falsely implicating such individuals in a round-table and temporally free floating teleological conversation with a shared sense of assumptions and beliefs. Such historical writings tend also to be characterized by insufficient reference to the dynamic relationship between an individual writer's thought and the contemporary contextual networks of thought to which they contribute and from which they draw. Under this aspect, can one legitimately compare the ideas of 'progressive' educationalists as diverse as Jean Jacques Rousseau to those of, say, Friedrich Froebel or Maria Montessori, given that, as we have seen, the historical contexts in which they wrote were wholly different? Ultimately, although it may be valid to compare individual progressives at a level of 'similarities and differences', it is surely a fallacy to assume that they either do or, in some cases, do not fit in with a particular historian's teleological conception of how progressivism has evolved.

In pursuing such a fallacy, it therefore becomes almost a matter of inevitability that one will descend into both anachronism and prolepsis. The former often displays itself via a series of caricatures which crudely stereotype individual thinkers, often according to the moral and social frameworks of the present. This theme, as was elaborated in the introductory chapter, has been a prominent concern of the leading historian of ideas, Quentin Skinner, whose work is being increasingly cited by those such as Kevin Brehony (2001) and Philip Gardner (2010), who have been cognizant in recognizing the possibilities of the application of such ideas to the writing and construction of educational history.

And these ideas *are* important. In his own field, Skinner cites examples of writers who refer to Niccolo Machiavelli as an 'evil man' and Rousseau as a 'totalitarian' (Skinner 2002: 65), thereby, in the process, utilizing anachronistic terms and concepts very much alien to the subjects themselves. For Skinner, by ignoring the very particular social and intellectual contexts in which texts are produced, historians have tended to ignore writers' original intentions as they emerge in their published writings and have instead mediated those intentions through the lens of the present. Although unnecessary here to recount the detail, development and inflections of Skinner's very sophisticated methodological model – and there has been much written on this often from scholars in Europe who do not share the British establishment's conservatism – it is sufficient to note that they have impacted (and continue to do so) upon a range of cognate fields. In the same way, therefore, that such sophisticated notions have achieved wider recognition through the endeavours of, among others, Duncan Bell (2007 and 2009), a scholar working in the area of international relations, so historians of education are equally seeking to rectify the 'mistakes' and 'limitations' of their forebears by making their own historical understanding commensurately more sophisticated.

Such analysis also goes some way to addressing the second of the issues concerning historical writing – *prolepsis*. Broadly defined, prolepsis is the capacity of historians to impute to individuals of the past a particular teleology that is at once unrealistic and demands that those individuals had some concept of events that have yet to unfold. A pertinent example might be those educational (and social!) historians who saw Mary Wollstonecraft and Maria Edgeworth as somehow prefiguring or predicting the emergence of the suffragettes and the feminist movement. While this contention may not, in itself, be incorrect, it nevertheless runs the risk of placing writers and thinkers within an unexpected and wholly retrospective continuum and failing perhaps to fully appreciate the specific audiences they sought to target, the responses generated by their work and, at the risk of repetition, the intentions embedded within their texts.

These issues have been at the forefront of recent published work in the history of education, notably from Howlett and McDonald (2011), which has sought to at least question the ways in which historians of education have attempted to interrogate their subjects through more nuanced understandings of language and greater transparency in their methodological practices. Further to those examples a commemorative (fortieth anniversary) edition of the flagship *History of Education* journal published as recently as January 2012 contained a number of pieces by leading figures in the field such as Jane Martin and Joyce Goodman, which actively demonstrated a more critical awareness of issues relating to, for example, biography and its relationship to narrative as well as appraisals of the way in which a variety of educational themes have been re-considered in light of emerging historiographical trends and critical lenses. As Martin herself comments,

> We see [now] history [of education] writing that places figures very carefully and securely into their various milieux, takes intellectual developments seriously and allows us to think about ways of bridging the 'old' and the 'new' histories, offering a mode of explanation that enables the writer to craft a narrative of events interwoven with analysis of structures. (Martin 2012: 101)

Martin herself has further explored the link between biography and identity in her recent (2010) and thoroughly engaging work on the life of the pioneering socialist educator Mary Bridges Adams who herself could easily be seen as fitting into a very particular tradition of social reformers of the sort delineated in Chapter 7. Such enlightened intellectual contributions – both theoretical and biographical – have themselves meant that historians of education are very much in the vanguard of methodological thinking and its continuing application to historical writings. This is in stark contrast to those working in more traditional and 'mainstream' fields of history, for whom such reflections are often seen as unnecessary exercises in naval-gazing and parlour game pontificating, which ultimately obfuscates the true business and purpose of academic scholarship.

A simplified example of where such nuanced thinking could be seen to impact comes when one examines how a term such as 'freedom', which itself is seemingly integral to the progressive discourse, carried with it a range of different connotations for three progressives, all of whom have been central to the context of this narrative – Rousseau, Dewey and Montessori. For Rousseau, as we have explored, childhood 'freedom' was of a very specific type, which does not always sit easily with our present-day conceptions and associations with a looser form of individual liberty and licence. Rousseau's Emile was free only in so far as he was allowed by the grace and benevolence of his tutor. Although the child learnt through the application of his own reason and endeavours, it is unclear if Rousseau intended this system of education as one for those who were to occupy a very specific position within his idealized State. As much as within any other contractarian theorist, the security of civil freedom was ultimately counterbalanced by a corresponding diminution of an individual's natural freedom. To further obfuscate the issue, it is equally uncertain if *Emile* as a text was a pastiche and an attempt at parodying certain prevailing traits and personal characteristics of the bourgeoisie, whose child-rearing practices were seen by more maverick thinkers such as Rousseau as not always in the best interests of the child.

This approach stands in contrast to the 'freedom' as later conceptualized linguistically and ideologically by John Dewey. Although within the opening pages of his *Schools of Tomorrow* (1915) paying fulsome tribute to the work of Rousseau – he refers, for example, to the philosophy of *Emile* as sounding the 'keynote of all modern efforts for educational progress' (Dewey 1915: 1–2) – Dewey's conception of freedom was one which was not predicated upon any prior teleological position. Although this may not, on the surface, appear to conflict with the intentions of Rousseau, when one explores the attitudes both men held towards Plato and his *Republic,* the important divergence of belief becomes clear. While, as we have seen in Chapter 2, Rousseau greatly admired Plato's writing, Dewey was more critical of his *a priori* position – 'Plato's starting point is that the organization of society depends ultimately upon knowledge of the end of existence. If we do not know its end, we shall be at the mercy of accident and caprice' (Dewey 1916: 102–3). Such a statement indicates how the freedom accorded by Dewey was one which was not only natural but also organic and whose spontaneity found an echo in the shape of future societies whose configuration and structure 'emerged' from the freedom accorded to its individuals. Freedom was thus a wholly emergent property. For Plato (and by extension Rousseau), freedom was permissible only in so far as it accorded with the future shape of their imagined and pre-designated utopias. In the case of Rousseau, as we have seen, this involved the necessity of individuals conforming to a 'general will' while, for Plato, it involved acceptance of a heavily stratified tri-partite society, with rigid demarcations between those destined to rule and those intended to follow. This form of questioning also allows for a more sophisticated discussion and attempts to understand the complexities inherent within Rousseau's ground-breaking text.

Montessori also offers us a very particular definition of 'freedom' and one, again, which carries with it a wholly different connotation to those of her forebears. Her 'freedom' was distinctly non-political and emanated from an empirically scientific basis and the workings of the child's cognitive mechanisms. Within the context of her educational philosophy, 'freedom' as she used the term did not though equate with license and the pleasures of freedom extended only as far as children were willing to respect their personal freedom, the safety of others and the sanctity of the shared environment. Although Montessori sought the ultimate liberation of the child's mind, this was through the use of particular didactic 'apparatus', which was criticized by some as being restrictive and contrary to her overall pronouncements about child 'freedom'. Tellingly, John Dewey took to task this apparent contradiction. In discussing generally the Montessori Method, he wrote sternly:

> But there is no freedom allowed the child to create. He is free to choose which apparatus he will use, but never to choose his own ends, never to bend a material to his own plans. For the material is limited to a fixed number of things which must be handled in a certain way. (Dewey 1915, op. cit. 157–8)

While Dewey's had other axes to grind – notably the early reading age and phonics usage within Montessori Schools – it is right to single out this criticism as it indicates a fundamental linguistic and ideological disagreement between two thinkers long conjoined together. While this may appear an obvious point to raise, it is indicative of a deeper and far greater heterogeneity within the progressive movement and raises awareness of the need to be aware of this diversity when considering individual writers of the past and the way they have been conceptualized.

The discussion of 'freedom' is one which has also been taken up by a number of educational theorists keen to disabuse us of the notion that progressivism is automatically to be associated with a particular type of individual autonomy and freedom. William Marsden (1997), for example, has argued strongly that traditional progressive notions of learning, particularly those surrounding the period of the New Education Fellowship and which were built upon the notion of innate qualities, have on occasion embodied a fundamentally conservative ethos as they do not ultimately allow people to have 'no limits' set on their potential. This would perhaps be the case with the Idealism of Froebel which indicated that at birth an individual was comprised of all that they were to become. The notion that progressivism can be a contradictory entity was further tacitly reflected in an utterance made by A. S. Neill, who chastised Maria Montessori for her belief that her very specific apparatus was only considered 'useful' when children had completed its various components in order and, by her definition, successfully. As he put it, 'the Montessori system . . . is an artificial way of making the child learn by doing. It has nothing creative about it' (Neill 1968: 37). Although Neill could be considered exceptional in relation to nearly all other progressives (of the figures discussed here perhaps only Homer Lane comes close to echoing Neill's egalitarian spirit) even a seemingly trite statement of this type indicates the multifarious nature of progressivism and the problems of characterizing individuals long since thought to exist within a particular educational tradition. Indicating his sense of self-ostracization from others, Neill even claimed never to have read any of the works of Rousseau!

Although there are potentially a huge number of examples as to where such conceptual difference could be elaborated, these issues are important to highlight for they serve to show that even within a volume broadly contained under the title of 'progressive education', there is enormous range and difference and it would be a mistake to consider all progressives as fitting into a pre-delineated 'tradition'. If nothing else, methodological considerations of the sort referred to above need not become attempts to rewrite history *ex post facto* but to stand instead as fundamentally democratic expressions which seek to raise the achievement of figures of the past to a higher level (including those not traditionally discussed) and to more fully recognize those achievements by appreciating the particular historical contexts in which they were produced.

Can progressivism progress?

While such methodological contentions would seem to some to 'take the fun out of history' and deny the pleasure of both its literary and aesthetic creation and reception, in a way, it has meant that thinkers of the past have become more individualized and thereby ultimately more highly valued for the distinctive contributions they have made. One of the initial motivations behind Skinner's theory in the late 1960s, for example, was, as Robert Lamb (2009) helpfully reminds us, to oppose both the 'great text' view of history and the rising phenomenon of determinist history as espoused (frequently!) in Marxist histories of the period. In thus giving primacy to the granular level (that of the individual author and their historical contexts), it has thereby meant educational history, and particularly that associated with progressivism, has become increasingly more detailed, nuanced and specialized with increasingly sophisticated attempts made at mapping those ideas of the past onto the strictures and structures of the present. It has also meant that the remit of what counts as 'progressive' has become broader, with the identification of competing progressivisms and their related discourses and the absence of what, in Skinner's terms, are known as 'perennial ideas', which are those that exist in time and are independent of human input and agency. The introductory chapter in this book referred to the work of A. O. Lovejoy and his 'unit ideas' typify this tendency, which would ultimately locate and pinpoint a concept such as progressivism as identifiable at various points across time. It is to be hoped that the previous pages have instead elaborated the multifarious and elaborate manifestations of progressivism in a range of different historical times and places.

An appropriate case in point is the large corpus of recent work produced by Tina Bruce, who has sought to locate and apply the ideas and practices of Friedrich Froebel into a modern context. Her most recent edited collection – *Early Childhood Practice: Froebel Today* (2012) – shows a knowing awareness of the difficulty of temporally translating centuries-old ideas, yet still makes a convincing case for the importance of the central principles and tenets of the kindergarten. As she tells us, 'a good framework transforms itself' (Bruce (Ed.) 2012: 6) and it is this adaptation as much as strength of numbers which have allowed educationally progressive ideas to flourish into the twenty-first century. By using such ideas as 'navigational tools' (Ibid) and not being dogmatic in their allegiance to historical principles, practitioners like Bruce have thus ensured that many of the ideas discussed within this book have retained their popularity and importance in the present. Much of this, as Chapter 4 made clear, has been undoubtedly aided by the sporadic attempts of governments and, more recently, external bodies to (re)introduce progressive ideas back into the mainstream. A case in point would be the recent Cambridge

Primary Review (2009) which, although dismissed by the authorities, received unofficial widespread support from practitioners in its calls for a raising of the school starting age, fewer examinations and homework and more autonomy for teachers.

This esteem is reflected not merely in ideological acceptance and transmission but from numbers upon the ground; recent statistics, for example, indicate that there are nearly 20,000 schools operating globally under the umbrella of Montessori, over 1,000 independent Waldorf-Steiner schools continue to flourish while kindergartens are to be found in almost every developed county in the world. Would this therefore indicate that progressivism has become the new orthodoxy? It is certainly true that many of the ideas historically seen as central to progressive discourse have become an accepted and implicit part of contemporary school practice. The increasing levels of informality between pupils and teachers acts as a good case in point. Whereas once a lack of firm discipline enforced by corrective and castigatory methods was the sole preserve of forward-thinking and progressive establishments (often those in the New Education Fellowship), today the beating and admonishment of children in educational settings is seen as unlawful and, in some quarters, sadistic. Where pupils are seen as 'difficult' – a contemporary manifestation of the 'juvenile delinquent' – they are today increasingly retained within schools, allowing them to feel part of the community and not excluded from their peers.

Likewise, the concept of 'play' has become one central to much recent educational discourse and initiative. The recent Early Years Foundation Stage (EYFS) pioneered by the New Labour government and recently updated by its coalition successor, for example, heavily emphasizes the importance and primacy of play. One of its four key priorities lists play as being 'at the heart of the EYFS, children need to play in order to have fun and in order to begin to understand the world around them' (EYFS 2008: 1). The equation of play with the concept of nothing more than 'fun' is one which may well have found support from past progressives keen to emphasize its liberating qualities while the notion of play as having a purpose in assisting and enhancing learning has a very long gestation going back to the proto-Romantics! Indeed many schools today, almost as a matter of course, readily acknowledge the Romantic attachment to nature by developing the school's exterior landscape often through the introduction of ponds and nature areas which can serve both an aesthetic and a didactic purpose. Likewise, many modern curricula have at their heart a basic recognition of the importance of learning through self-discovery and exploration particularly through attempts at creativity and self-expression.

Nevertheless, to suggest that education globally is today being driven by the imperatives of a progressive tradition is surely to be somewhat blinkered and naïve. Now, more perhaps than at any other time in history, education is being driven by the forces of the market and competition, with primacy given to results, league tables and quantifiable measures of achievement. Whatever the merits of such a system, undoubtedly it has meant a narrowing of the educational experience for many with subjects not seen as holding a high level of exchange value (typically vocational qualifications or those not seen as 'core') being shunned and relegated to a 'second tier' status. This has certainly been the case in Britain where the compulsory English, Maths and Science have been given primacy over the more artistic and creative subjects.

Nor is the existence of 'play' in curricula-speak and policy documents necessarily evidence of widespread practice; in a world where such qualifications and credentials are seen as central, there has been an increased tendency to see activities which lack a tangible benefit as both erroneous and irrelevant to the child's school experience.[1] The recent observations of Galton and Fogelman (1998) bear this out with the arts seemingly being squeezed out in the desire to promulgate a 'key' curriculum and single-subject teaching. Even where schools have been willing to embrace creativity and pupil self-expression, it tends only to be when receiving financial support and approval from governments and not when forced to rely on the impetus of their own steam. This has long been a perennial stumbling block and creativity generally has yet to become permanently embedded into the framework and ethos of British schools. While this continues to be less of a problem elsewhere, with Western Europe particularly more concerned over questions of didactics and educational transmission, the rise of international comparative data and the need to revive flagging economies in light of the recent recession may indeed mean an even greater return to a more 'knowledge-based' economy with education seen in light of what can be considered beneficial to the greater economic good.

These concerns have long been a feature of the crusade of the academic Sir Ken Robinson (1982 and 2001) who has tirelessly championed for play, creativity and self-expression as part of a balanced curriculum. Robinson argues that children are essentially creative beings and that recent educational policies, often driven by assessment, have served to blunt that natural tendency of spirit. In an amusing side note, he postulates why, given that we all have bodies, are not 'movement' subjects such as dance as integral to the curriculum as mathematics or science? While there is an element of throwaway flippancy in such a comment, it does raise serious questions as to the place or not of particular 'progressive' subjects within the context of a modern-day curriculum. Nor is Robinson arguing solely for 'play for plays sake'; much of his work additionally seeks to argue that creativity of this type can be as enhancing to the collective good as so-called 'hard' skills. After all, have not initiative, creativity and lateral thinking enhanced fields as diverse as architecture, business and sport? Is there not a strong element of imagination and novel problem-solving even within the more objective sciences? In many ways, Robinson's ideas echo those much earlier pioneering sentiments of Margaret McMillan in *Education through the Imagination* (1904) and her defence of the imagination which similarly sought to allay fears over its lack of instrumental value by yoking it to the cause of the 'national good'.

Furthermore, one of the problems with these systems of education is the very real impacts they have had upon communities of practices. With teachers being stripped of their autonomy through governmental control and inspectorate accountability, the plunging effects on morale which that has entailed[2] and the takeover of the sector by non-educational stakeholders, increasingly, schools themselves have become de-intellectualized places. Troublingly, education is seen as unproblematic, with the business of teaching reduced to a simple matter of didactics with academic research and expertize sidelined. This trend has been picked up by many of the thinkers working in the de-schooling movement explored in Chapter 8 and their belief that teachers themselves need, as a body *politick*, to be politicized and engaged in intellectual rumination upon the debates concerning educational transmission. Much of their writing, from Freire and Illich to Giroux and Apple, has therefore focused upon the teacher as a political agent and one who is capable of effecting change both outside and within the system. How they do this within systems which seek to dictate both what and how to teach and which therefore engenders attitudes of compliance may not always be apparently clear but perhaps this is where contemporary progressivism stands today. In many respects, the advances made by societies in terms of enfranchisement, health, parity between the genders and the understanding of children's minds means many of the more peripheral historical concerns of progressivism and its adherents have, within the Western context, perhaps been addressed. It is therefore this most modern formulation of progressivism – its more political orientation – which may be the most important in the twenty-first century as a vehicle in pushing for acceptance of alternative and long-established progressive concepts and ideas and in seeking to challenge those whose views about education may lack any rigorous intellectual frame of reference.

Ultimately, whether or not one chooses to subscribe to any or all of the ideas discussed here, it is undeniable that 'progressivism' and its adherents – from Locke onwards – sought to problematize education and challenge taken-for-granted assumptions about learning. Their education was never about the crude and ritualistic transmission of knowledge in an environment isolated and set-aside from its wider contexts. Often, advocating such ideas meant facing ridicule, dismissal, challenge and marginalization. Nevertheless, if one can take anything from these writers and their texts it is that there is a need to constantly be thinking about the practices of education both theoretical and practical and that these two facets should not, as John Dewey best made clear, be kept apart. While debates about the disappearance or curtailment of childhood in the modern age may rage, 'the child' in both ideological and practical terms has become today protected and recognized as fundamentally different from adults and unique in its own right. This is a result indisputably of many of the texts discussed here. If though we, as readers, academics, laymen or practitioners, are to preserve that notion and allow the natural expression of childhood, it surely serves us to at least engage with not only the questions posed throughout history but also, perhaps, the answers. Progressive thinkers have offered us a range of particular solutions and whether we agree with them or not, it must surely do us good to acknowledge their contribution and their conviction that the business of teaching and education more generally is neither simplistic nor driven solely by the constructions of adults. Let that be their greatest legacy.

Notes

1 This point was starkly illustrated by the furore surrounding an alleged cuff comment by the then Secretary of State for Education Charles Clarke, who dismissed the work of Medieval Historians as 'ornamental' and that such work should not be funded by the State. (Reported in the *Guardian*, 9 May 2003)

2 A recent (December 2012) survey of schoolteachers in England conducted by YouGov on behalf of the National Union of Teachers (NUT) found that 55 per cent considered their morale to be 'low' or 'very low'.

Bibliography

Introduction

Robin Alexander, *Culture and Pedagogy: International Comparisons in Primary Education*, (Oxford: Blackwell, 2000).

Robin Alexander et al., *Children, their World, their Education: Final Report and Recommendations of the Cambridge Primary Review* (London: Routledge, 2009).

—, *Curriculum Organisation and Classroom Practice in Primary Schools: A Discussion Paper* (London: Department of Education and Science 1992).

P. Ashton, P. Kneen, and F. Davies, *Aims into Practice in the Primary School* (London Hodder & Stoughton, 1975).

Robin Barrow, *Radical Education: A Critique of Freeschooling and Deschooling* (London Martin Robertson, 1978).

Kevin Brehony, 'From the Particular to the General, the Continuous to the Discontinuous: Progressive Education Revisited'. *History of Education* 30(5), (2001), 413–32.

Thomas Carlyle, *On Heroes, Hero-worship and the Heroic in History* (London: Chapman & Hall, 1888).

Sol Cohen, *Challenging Orthodoxies: Toward a New Cultural History of Education* (New York: Peter Lang, 1999).

John Darling, *Child-Centred Education and its Critics* (London: Paul Chapman Publishing, 1994).

Philip Gardner, *Hermeneutics, History and Memory* (London: Routledge, 2010).

Ian Grosvenor and Martin Lawn, Portraying the School: Silence in the Photographic Archives, in U. Meitzner, K. Myerts and N. A. Peim (eds), *Visual History. Images of Education* (Peter Lang: Bern, 2005), pp. 85–108.

Ian Grosvenor, Martin Lawn and Kate Rousmaniere, *Silences and Images: The Social History of the Classroom* (New York: Peter Lang, 1999)

Ian Grosvenor and Martin Lawn, Ways of Seeing in Education and Schooling: Emerging Historiographies. *History of Education* 30(2), 2001, 105–8.

William James, *The Will to Believe: And other Essays in Popular Philosophy* (New York: Longmans, 1897).

Keith Jenkins, *Refiguring History: New Thoughts on an Old Discipline* (London: Routledge 2003).

A. O. Lovejoy, *Essays in the History of Ideas* (Baltimore: John Hopkins Press, 1948).

Roy Lowe, *The Death of Progressive Education* (London: Routledge Press, 2007).

Gary McCulloch, *The Struggle for the History of Education* (London: Routledge, 2011).

Alun Munslow, *The Routledge Companion to Historical Studies* (London: Routledge Press, 2000).

Kari Palonen, *Quentin Sinner: History, Politics, Rhetoric* (Cambridge: Polity, 2003).

Melanie Philips, *All Must Have Prizes* (Boston, MA: Little, Brown & Company, 1996).

Quentin Skinner, 'Meaning and Understanding in the History of Ideas' *History and Theory*, 8 (1), (1969), 4–53.

—, *Meaning and Context: Quentin Skinner and his Critics*, (Cambridge: Polity, 1988).

William Richardson, Historians and Educationists: the History of Education as a Field of Study in Post-War England Part I: 1945–72. *History of Education* 28(1), 1999, 1–30.

Anthony Seldon, *An End to Factory Schools: An Education Manifesto 2010–2020* (London: Centre for Policy Studies, 2010).

Peter Silcock, *New Progressivism* (London: Falmer Press, 1999).

Robert Skidelsky, *English Progressive Schools* (Harmondsworth: Penguin, 1969).

Herbert Spencer, *The Study of Sociology,* With a new introduction by Michael Taylor. (London: Routledge, 1996).

W. A. C. Stewart, *Progressives and Radicals in English Education 1750–1970* (London: Macmillan, 1972).

Graham Vulliamy and Rosemary Webb, Progressive Education and the National Curriculum: Findings from a Global Education Research Project. *Educational Review* 45(1), (1993), 21–41.

Yoko Yamasaki, The Impact of Western Progressive Ideas in Japan 1868–1940. *History of Education* 39(5), 2010, 578–88.

Chapter 1 – Pioneering notions and practices

Philippe Aries, *Centuries of Childhood: A Social History of Family Life* (New York: Vintage Books, 1962).

James Axtell, *The Educational Writings of John Locke; A Critical Edition with Introduction and Notes* (Cambridge: Cambridge University Press, 1968).

Jan Amos Comenius, *Didactica Magna (Great Didactic)* (Göteborg: Daidalos, 1989).

John Darling and Sven Erik Nordenbo, Progressivism, in Nigel Blake, Paul Smeyers, Richard D. Smith and Paul Standish (eds), *The Blackwell Guide to the Philosophy of Education* (Oxford: Blackwell, 2003), 288–309.

Patrick Dillon, *The Last Revolution: 1688 and the Creation of the Modern World* (London: Jonathan Cape, 2006).

Peter Gay, Locke on the Education of Paupers, in Amélie Oksenberg Rorty (Ed.), *Philosophers on Education: New Historical Perspectives* (London: Routledge, 1998).

A. C. Grayling, *Descartes: The Life of René Descartes and its Place in his Times* (London: Free Press, 2005).

William Gilpin, *An Account of the Rev. Mr. Gilpin in William Gilpin, Memoirs of Dr. Richard Gilpin* (London: B. Quaritch, 1879).

Emily Grosholz, *Cartesian Method and the Problem of Reduction* (Oxford: Clarendon, 1991).

Deborah Harmon and Toni Stokes Jones, *Elementary Education: A Reference Handbook* (United Kingdom: ABC Clio, 2005).

Margaret King, *The Renaissance in Europe* (Boston, MA: Mcgraw-Hill Higher Education, 2003).

John Locke, *Some Thoughts Concerning Education* (London: A. and J. Churchill, 1693).

Alexander Meiklejohn, *Education Between Two Worlds,* With a new introduction by Lionel Lewis (New Jersey: Aldine Transaction, 2006).

Adam R. Nelson, *Education and Democracy: The Meaning of Alexander Meiklejohn, 1872–1964* (Madison: University of Wisconsin Press, 2001).

Nicholas Orme, *Medieval Children* (New Haven: Yale University Press, 2001).

Joy Palmer, *50 Major Tinkers on Education from Confucius to Dewey* (London: Routledge, 2001).

Jean Piaget, Jan Amos Comenius. *Prospects* XXIII(1/2), 1993, 173–96.

Neil Postman, *The Disappearance of Childhood* (New York: Vintage, 1996).

Margaret Puckett and Deborah Difilly, *Teaching Young Children: An Introduction to the Early Childhood Profession* (Clifton Park: Delmer Cengage Learning, 2003).

Jean-Jacques Rousseau, *Emile or On Education*, translated by Allen Bloom (New York: Basic Books, 1979).

Margurita Rudolph and Dorothy H. Cohen, *Kindergarten: A Year of Learning* (New York: Appleton-Century-Crofts, 1964).

W. A. C. Stewart, *Progressives and Radicals in English Education 1750–1970* (London: Macmillan, 1972).

Nathan Tarcov, *Locke's Education for Liberty* (Chicago: University of Chicago Press, 1984).

Chapter 2 – Romanticism

Lewis Anderson, *Pestalozzi* (New York: McGraw-Hill Book Co., 1931).

Philippe Aries, *Centuries of Childhood: A Social History of Family Life* (New York: Vintage Books, 1962).

Robin Barrow, *Radical Education: A Critique of Freeschooling and Deschooling* (London: Martin Robertson, 1978).

G. M. Blenkin, and A. V. Kelly, *The Primary Curriculum* (London: Harper and Row, 1981).

Herbert Bowen, *Froebel and Education by Self-Activity* (New York: Charles Scribner's sons, 1893).

Kevin J. Brehony, 'The Kindergarten in England 1851–1918' (2000) in Kindergartens and Cultures: The global diffusion of an idea (New Haven, CT: Yale University Press) by Roberta Wollons (Ed) pp. 59–87.

—, *The Origins of Nursery Education: Friedrich Froebel and the English System* (London: Routledge, 2001).

—, 'The Froebel Movement in England 1850–1911: Texts, Readings and Readers' 2006) in Perspektiven der Frobelforschung (Wurzberg: Konigshausen and Neumann by Helmut Heilund, Michel Gebel and Karl Neumann (Eds).

Norman Brosterman, *Inventing Kindergarten* (New York: Harry N. Abrams, 1997).

John Darling, *Child-Centred Education and its Critics* (London: Paul Chapman Publishing, 1994).

F. J. Darton, *Children's Books in England: Five Centuries of Social Life,* 3rd edition revised by Brian Alderson (Cambridge: Cambridge University Press, 1982).

Thomas Day, *The History of Sandford and Merton* (London: Bradbury, Agnew, & Co., 1783).

David Denby, *Great Books: My Adventures with Homer, Rousseau, Woolf, and Other Indestructible Writers of the Western World* (New York: Simon Schuster, 1996).

Richard Lovell Edgeworth, *Memoirs of Richard Lovell Edgeworth, Esq* (London: R. Hunter, 1820).

Friedrich Froebel, *The Education of Man,* translated from the German and annotated by W. N. Hailmann (New York: D. Appleton & Company, 1892).

—, *Mother-Play and Nursery Songs* (New York: Lee & Shephard, 1879).

—, *Pedagogics of the Kindergarten*, translated by Josephine Jarvis (London: Edward Arnold, 1897).

Andy Green, *Education and State Formation: The Rise of Education Systems in England, France and the USA* (London: Macmillan, 1990).

F. H. Hayward, *The Educational Ideas of Pestalozzi and Froebel* (New York: Greenwood Press, 1905).

Michael Heafford, *Pestalozzi: His Thought and its Relevance Today* (London: Methuen 1967).

Helmut Heiland, *Bibliographie Friedrich Fröbel: Primär- und Sekundärliteratur 1820–1990* (Hildesheim: Olms, 1990).

—, *Die Spielpädagogik Friedrich Fröbels* (Hildesheim: Olms, 1998).

Anne Higonett, *Pictures of Innocence: The History and Crisis of Ideal Childhood* (London: Thames & Hudson, 1998).

Peter Jimack, *Rousseau: Emile* (London: Grant & Cutler, 1983).

W. H. Kilpatrick, Pestalozzi as Educator, Introduction to *The Education of Man – Aphorisms*, (New York: Philosophical Library, 1951), vii–1.

Evelyn Lawrence, *Friedrich Froebel and English Education* (London: University of London, 1952).

Joachim Liebschner, *A Child's Work, Freedom and Play in Froebel's Educational Theory and Practice* (Cambridge: Lutterworth Press, 1992).

—, *Foundations of Progressive Education: the History of the National Froebel Society* (Cambridge: Lutterworth Press, 1991).

William Marsden, Contradictions in Progressive Ideologies and Curricula in England: Some historical perspectives. *Historical Studies in Education* 9(2), (1997), 224–36.

John Hope Mason and Martin Wokler (eds),, *Diderot: Political Writings* (Cambridge: Cambridge University Press, 1992).

Nicholas Orme, *Medieval Children* (New Haven: Yale University Press, 2001).

Steven Ozment, *Ancestors: The Loving Family in Old Europe* (Cambridge, MA: Harvard University Press, 2001).

Alice Paterson, *The Edgeworths: A Study of Later Eighteenth Century Education* (London: WB Clive, 1914).

Alan Richardson, *Literature, Education and Romanticism* (Cambridge: Cambridge University Press, 1994).

Johannes Ronge and Berthe Ronge, *A Practical Guide to the English Kindergarten* (London: A. N. Myers & Co., 1884).

Jean-Jacques Rousseau, *Emile or On Education*, translated by Allen Bloom (New York: Basic Books, 1979).

Michel Soetard, Johann Heinrich Pestalozzi (1746–1827). *Prospects: The Quarterly Review of Comparative Education* XXIV(1/2), (1994), 297–310.

Matthew Simpson, *Rousseau: A Guide for the Perplexed* (United Kingdom: Continuum International Publishing Group, 2006).

Kate Silber, *Pestalozzi: The Man and his Work* (London: Routledge & Kegan Paul, 1960).

Lawrence Stone, *The Family, Sex and Marriage in England 1500–1800* (London: Weidenfeld and Nicholson, 1977).

Daniel Trohler, Pestalozzi in *50 Major Thinkers on Education from Confucius to Dewey* (London: Routledge, 2001), 71–6.

Jenny Uglow, *Lunar Men: The Friends Who Made the Future 1730–1810* (London: Faber and Faber, 2002).

John Wesley, *The Works of John Wesley Volume 22 – Journal and Diaries V (1765–1775)* (Nashville, Tenn., Abingdon Press, 1993).

Peter Weston, *Friedrich Froebel: His Life, Times & Significance* (United Kingdom: University of Surrey Roehampton, 2000).

Chapter 3 – Gender

Anna Letitia Barbauld, *Selected Poetry and Prose,* edited by William McCarthy and Elizabeth Kraft (Peterborough: Braodview Press, 2001).

Susan Blow, *Educational Issues in the Kindergarten* (London: G. P. Putnam's Sons, 1908).

—, *Letter to a Mother on the Philosophy of Froebel* (New York: Appleton Press, 1899).

—, *Symbolic Education: The Mottoes and Commentaries of Friedrich Froebel's Mother Play* (London: Edward Arnold, 1895).

W. A. L. (Alan) Blyth, *English Primary Education: a sociological description* (London: Routledge & Kegan Paul, 1965).

Kevin Brehony, *The Origins of Nursery Education: Friedrich Froebel and the English system* (London: Routledge, 2001).

Marilyn Butler, *Maria Edgeworth: A Literary Biography* (Oxford: Clarendon Press, 1972).

Isabel C. Clarke, *Maria Edgeworth: Her Family and Friends* (New York: Hutchinson & Co., 1950).

Lawrence Cremin, *The Transformation of the School; Progressivism in American Education, 1876–1957* (New York: Knopf, 1961).

John Wilson Croker, Review of Memoirs of Richard Lovell Edgeworth. *Quarterly Review* XXIII, (July 1820), 510–49.

Maria Edgeworth, *Practical Education in Three Volumes* (New York: Woodstock Books, 1996).

—, *Practical Education* (*The Novels and Selected Works of Maria Edgeworth*, 12 vols: Vol.11. Susan Manly (Ed.) (London: Pickering & Chatto, 2003)).

—, *Harry and Lucy Concluded Volume 4 . . . being the last part of Early Lessons* (London: R. Hunter, 1825).

Elizabeth Eger, Introductory Note to Maria Edgeworth, *Popular Tales and Early Lessons* (London: Pickering & Chatto, 2003), pp. vii–xix.

Maria Falco, (ed.), *Feminist Interpretations of Mary Wollstonecraft* (University Park: Penn State Press, 1996).

James Fordyce, *Sermons to Young Women in Two Volumes* (London: printed for A. Millar and T. Cadell, J. Dodsley, and J. Payne, 1765 and 1766).

Lyndall Gordon, *Vindication: A Life of Mary Wollstonecraft* (London: Virago, 2005).

William Torrey Harris, 'Professor John Dewey's doctrine of interest as related to will'. *Educational Review*, 11, 486–93.

Mary Hilton, *Women and the Shaping of the Nations Young: Education and Public Doctrine in Britain 1750–1850* (United Kingdom: Ashgate Publishing, 2007).

Mary Hilton and Pam Hirsch (eds), *Practical Visionaries: Women, Education and Social Progress 1790–1930* (London: Longman, 2000).

Claudia Johnson, *Equivocal Beings: Politics, Gender, and Sentimentality in the 1790s* (Chicago: University of Chicago Press, 1995).

Cora Kaplan, *Sea Changes: Essays on Culture and Feminism* (London: Verso, 1986).

Gary Kelly, *Revolutionary Feminism: The Mind and Career of Mary Wollstonecraft* (Basingstoke: Macmillan, 1992).

Emily Lawless, *Maria Edgeworth* (London: Macmillan & Co., 1904).

Evelyn Lawrence, *Friedrich Froebel and English Education* (London, 1952).

Catherine Macaulay, *Letters on Education. With Observations on Religious and Metaphysical Subjects* (London: C. Dilly, 1790).

Susan Manley, Introductory Note to Maria Edgeworth, *Practical Education* (London: Pickering & Chatto, 2003), pp. vii–xxii.

William McCarthy, *Anna Letitia Barbauld: Voice of the Enlightenment* (Baltimore: The Johns Hopkins University Press, 2008).

Herbert McLachlin, *English Education under the Test Acts; Being the History of the Nonconformist Academies, 1662–1820* (United Kingdom: Manchester University Press, 1931).

Mitzi Myers, Reading Rosamond Reading: Maria Edgeworth's' Wee-Wee Stories' Interrogate the Canon, in Elizabeth Goodenough, Mark A. Heberle, and Naomi Sokoloff (eds), *Infant Tongues: The Voice of the Child in Literature* (Detroit, MI: Wayne State University Press, 1994), pp. 57–79.

—, Shot from Canons: Or, Maria Edgeworth and the Cultural Production and Consumption of the Late Eighteenth-Century Woman Writer, in Ann Bermingham and John Brewer (eds), *The Consumption of Culture, 1600–1800: Image, Object, Text* (London: Routledge: 1995), pp. 193–214.

Elizabeth Peabody, *Record of a School* (Bedford, MA: Applewood Books, 2007).

Mary Poovey, *The Proper Lady and the Woman Writer: Ideology as Style in the Works of Mary Wollstonecraft, Mary Shelley and Jane Austen* (Chicago: University of Chicago Press, 1984).

Virgina Sapiro, *A Vindication of Political Virtue: The Political Theory of Mary Wollstonecraft* (Chicago: University of Chicago Press, 1992).

Brian Simon, *Studies in the History of Education: [volume 1]: 1780–1870* (London: Lawrence & Wishart, 1960).

Ashley Smith, *The Birth of Modern Education: The Contribution of the Dissenting Academies 1660–1800* (London: Independent, 1954).

Hannah Swart, *Margarethe Meyer Schurz* (Wisconsin: Watertown Historical Society, 1967).

Claire Tomalin, *The Life and Death of Mary Wollstonecraft.* (New York: Penguin, 1992).

Sylvana Tomaselli, Introduction to *Mary Wollstonecraft, A Vindication of the Rights of Men and A Vindication of the Rights of Woman* (Cambridge: Cambridge University Press, 1995), ix–xxx.

Sarah Trimmer, *The Guardian of Education*, 5 vols. London, 1802–6. Reviews of *Practical Education* in I, no.8 (December 1802), 490–98; II, no.9 (January 1803), 30–43; no.10 (February 1803), 92–101; no.11 (March 1803), 163–71.

Mary Trouille, *Sexual Politics in the Enlightenment: Women Writers Read Rousseau*, (Albany: State of New York Press, 1997).

Mary Wollstonecraft, *A Vindication of the Rights of Woman with Strictures on Political and Morl Subjects* (London: Joseph Johnson, 1792).

—, *Thoughts on the Education of Daughters: With Reflections on Female Conduct, in the More Important Duties of Life* (Lodon: Joseph Johnson, 1787).

—, *Original Stories from Real Life with Conversations Calculated to Regulate the Affections and Form the Mind to Truth and Goodness*, (London: Joseph Johnson, 1788).

Jonathan Wordsworth, Introduction to *Original Stories from Real Life* (Oxford: Woodstock Books, 1990).

Chapter 4 – Psychology

Corelli Barnett, *The Audit of War; The Illusion and Reality of Britain as a Great Nation*, (London: Papermac, 1987).

Deanne Bealing, The Organization of the Junior School Classroom. *Educational Research* 14, (June 1972), 231–6.

Neville Bennett, Changing Perspectives on Teaching-learning Processes in the Post-Plowden Era. *Oxford Review of Education* 13(1), (1987), 67–79.

Basil Bernstein and B. Davies, Some Sociological Comments on Plowden, in R. S. Peters, (ed.), *Perspectives on Plowden* (London: Routledge & Kegan Paul, 1969), pp. 55–84.

Kevin Brehony, *The Origins of Nursery Education: Friedrich Froebel and the English System* (London: Routledge, 2001).

Peter Bryant, Piaget, Teachers and Psychologists. *Oxford Review of Education* 10(3), (1984), 251–9.

Gilbert Childs, *Education and Beyond: Steiner and the Problems of Modern Society* (Edinburgh: Floris Books, 1996).

Edouard Claparede, 'Preface' in Amelie Hamaide, *The Decroly Class: A Contribution to Elementary Education* (London: J. M. Dent & Sons), pp. xxi–xxvii.

Christopher Clouder and Martyn Rawson, *Waldorf Education: Rudolf Steiner's Ideas in Practice* (Edinburgh: Floris Books, 2003).

Ian Copeland, Special Education Needs, in Richard Aldrich (ed.), *A Century of Education* (London: Routledge Flamer, 2002), pp. 165–85.

Peter Cunningham and Philip Gardner, *Becoming Teachers: Texts and Testimonies 1907–1950* (London: Woburn Press, 2004).

Ovide Decroly, *Quelques notions sur l'évolution affective chez l'enfant* (Brussels: Lamertin, 1927).

Margaret Donaldson, *Children's Minds* (Glasgow: Fontana, 1978).

Francine Dubreucq, Jean-Ovide Decroly. *Prospects* 23(1), (1993), 249–75.

L. Francis Edmunds, *Rudolf Steiner Education: The Waldorf School* (London: Rudolf Steiner Press, 1987).

Mary Jane Drummond, Susan Isaacs: Pioneering work in Understanding Children's Lives, in Mary Hilton and Pam Hirsch (eds), *Practical Visionaries: Women, Education and Social Progress 1790–1930* (London: Longman, 2000), pp. 203–21.

Maurice Galton, Change and Continuity in the Primary School: the research evidence in *Oxford Review of Education* 13(1), (1987), 81–93.

Dorothy Gardner, *Susan Isaacs* (London: Toronto Methuen, 1969).

Judy Giles and Tim Middleton, *Writing Englishness, 1900–1950: A Introductory Sourcebook on National Identity* (London: Routledge, 1995).

Stephen Jay Gould, *The Mismeasure of Man* (New York: Norton, 1981).

Angelo Van Gorp, Ovide Decroly, A Hero of Education, in Marc Depaepe and Paul Smeyers (eds), *Educational Research: Why 'What Works' Doesn't Work* (Dordrecht: Springer, 2006), pp. 37–49.

Philip Graham, *Susan Isaacs: A Life Freeing the Minds of Children* (United Kingdom: Karnac Books, 2008).

Hadow Report, *Infant and Nursery Schools* (London: HMSO, 1933).

—, *Psychological Tests of Educable Capacity* (London: HMSO, 1924).

Granville Stanley Hall, *Adolescence: Its Psychology and Its Relations to Physiology, Anthropology, Sociology, Sex, Crime, Religion and Education* (New York: D. Appleton & Company, 1904).

Susan Isaacs, *The Educational Value of the Nursery School* (London: Headley Brothers, 1954).

—, *Intellectual Growth in Young Children* (London: Routledge & Kegan Paul, 1930).

—, *Social Development in Young Children* (London: Routledge & Kegan Paul, 1933).

Herbert Kliebard, *The Struggle for the American Curriculum, 1893–1958* (London: Routledge & Kegan Paul, 1986).

Rita Kramer, *Maria Montessori* (Chicago: University of Chicago Press, 1976).

Gary Lachman, *Rudolf Steiner: An Introduction to His Life and Work* (Floris Books: Floris Books, 2007).

Angeline Lillard, *Montessori: The Science Behind the Genius* (New York: Oxford University Press, 2005).

Jane Roland Martin, *The Schoolhome* (Cambridge, MA: Harvard Universiy Press, 1992).

Margaret Mead, *Coming of age in Samoa: A Psychological Study of Primitive Youth for Western Civilisation* (London: Cape, 1928).

Maria Montessori, *Dr. Montessori's Own Handbook*, 7th edition (London: William Heinemann, 1932).

—, *The Montessori Method: Scientific Pedagogy as Applied to Child Education in 'the Children's Houses'*, translated from the Italian by Anne E. George, with an introduction by Professor Henry W. Holmes (London: William Heinemann, 1912).

—, *The Secret of Childhood*, translated and edited by Barbara Barclay (London: Longmans, 1936).

Charles Murray and Richard Hernstein, *The Bell Curve: Intelligence and Class Structure in American Life* (New York: Free Press, 1994).

Thomas Percy Nunn, *Education; Its Data and First Principles* (London: E. Arnold, 1920).

John Paull, Rudolf Steiner and the Oxford Conference: The Birth of Waldorf Education in Britain. *European Journal of Educational Studies* 3(1), (2011), 53–66.

Plowden Report, *Report of the Central Advisory Council For Education (England) into Primary Education in England* (London: HMSO, 1967).

Bridget Plowden, 'Plowden' Twenty Years On. *Oxford Review of Education* 13(1), 119–124.

Michael Shapiro, *Child's Garden: The Kindergarten Movement from Froebel to Dewey* (University Park: Pennsylvania State University Press, 1983).

Brian Simon, *Education and the Social Order: British Education since 1944* (London: Lawrence and Wishart, 1999).

—, *Intelligence, Psychology and Education: A Marxist Critique* (London: Lawrence and Wlshart, 1971).

Robert Skidelsky, *English Progressive Schools* (Harmondsworth: Penguin, 1969).

Lydia Smith, *To Understand and to Help: The Life Work of Susan Isaacs* (Cranbury, NJ: Farleigh Dickinson, 1985).

E. M. Standing, *Maria Montessori: Her Life and Work* (New York: Penguin Putnam Inc, 1998).

W. A. C. Stewart, *Progressives and Radicals in English Education 1750–1970* (London: Macmillan, 1972).

Rudolf Steiner, *Human Values in Education: Ten Lectures Given in Arnheim (Holland) July 17–24, 1924*, translated by Vera Compton-Burnett (London: Rudolf Steiner Press, 1971).

—, *The New Art of Education: Thirteen Lectures Given at Ilkley,* authorized English translation/edited by H. Collison (London: Anthroposophical Publishing Co., 1928).

Kathy Sylva and A. H. Halsey, Plowden: history and prospect. *Oxford Review of Education* 13(1), (1987), 3–11.

William Van der Eycken and Barry Turner, *Adventures in Education* (Allen Lane: The Penguin Press, 1969).

John White, *The Aims of Education Restated* (London: Routledge & Kegan Paul, 1982).

Roy Wilkinson, *The Spiritual Basis of Steiner Education* (London: Sophia Books, 1996).

Jenny Willan, Susan Isaacs (1885–1948): Her Life, Work and Legacy. *Gender and Education* 23(2), (2011), 201–10.

Adrian Wooldrich, *Measuring the Mind: Education and Psychology in England, c.1860-c.1990* (Cambridge: Cambridge University Press, 1994).

Chapter 5 – Democracy: The New Education Fellowship

Louise Bates Ames, *Summerhill: For and Against* (New York: Hart, 1970), 64–84.

Kevin Brehony, A New Education for a New Era: creating International Fellowship through Conferences 1921–1938. *Paedagogica Historica* 40(5&6), (2004), 733–55.

W. F. Connell, *A History of Education in the Twentieth Century World* (New York: Teachers' College Press, 1980).

Jonathan Croall, *Neill of Summerhill: The Permanent Rebel* (London: Routledge & Kegan Paul, 1983).

Maurice Galton, Brian Simon and Paul Croll, *Inside the Primary Classroom* (London: Routledge & Kegan Paul, 1980).

Sheldon Glueck and Eleanor Glueck, *Unravelling Juvenile Delinquency* (New York: Commonwealth Fund, 1950).

Peter Gordon, The Writings of Edmond Holmes: A Reassessment and Bibliography. *History of Education*, 12(1), (1983), 15–24.

Peter Gordon and John White, *Philosophers as Educational Reformers: The Influence of Idealism on British Educational thought and Practice* (London: Routledge & Kegan Paul, 1979).

Deborah Gorham, Dora and Bertrand Russell and Beacon Hill School. *Russell: the Journal of Bertrand Russell Studies* 25, (2005), 39–76.

Fred M. Hechinger, *Summerhill: For and Against* (New York: Hart, 1970), 34–48.

Ray Hemmings, *Fifty Years of Freedom: A Study of the Development of the Ideas of A. S. Neill* (London: Allen and Unwin, 1972).

Eric Hobsbawm, *The Age of Extremes; The Short Twentieth Century, 1914–1991* (London: Michael Joseph, 1994).

Edmond Holmes, *What is and What Might Be: A Study of Education in General and Elementary Education in Particular* (London: Constable, 1911).

Susan Isaacs, Some Notes on the Incidence of Neurotic Difficulties in Young Children (Part 2). *British Journal of Educational Psychology* 11(2), (1932), 184–96.

Homer Lane, *Talks to Parents and Teachers* (London: G Allen & Unwin, 1928).

David Limond, 'All our Scotch education is in vain': The Construction of Scottish national identity in and by the early Dominie books of A. S. Neill. *History of Education* 28(3). 297–312.

Kevin Manton, *Socialism and Education in Britain, 1883–1902* (London: Woburn Press, 2001).

A. S. Neill, *A Dominie Dismissed* (London: Herbert Jenkins, 1917).

—, *A Dominie in Doubt* (London: Herbert Jenkins, 1921).

—, *A Dominie's Log* (London: Herbert Jenkins, 1916).

—, *Summerhill, A Radical Approach to Education* (London: Penguin Books, 1968).

—, *The Free Child* (London: Herbert Jenkins, 1953).

—, *The Problem Child* (London: Herbert Jenkins, 1926).

—, *The Problem Family* (London: Herbert Jenkins, 1948).

—, *The Problem Parent* (London: Herbert Jenkins, 1932).

—, *The Problem Teacher* (London: Herbert Jenkins, 1939).

David Newsome, *Godliness and Good Learning: Four Studies on a Victorian Ideal* (London, Murray, 1961).

F. Ivan Nye, *Family Relationships and Delinquent Behaviour* (New York: John Wiley & Sons, 1958).

Melanie Philips, *All Must Have Prizes* (Boston, MA: Little, Brown & Company, 1996).

J. Popenue, *Inside Summerhill* (New York: Hart, 1969).

Max Rafferty, *Summerhill: For and Against* (New York: Hart, 1970), 10–26.

James Scotland, *History of Scottish Education* (London: University of London Press, 1970).

R. J. W. Selleck, *English Primary Education and the Progressives, 1914–1939* (London: Routledge & Kegan Paul, 1972).

Chris Shute, *Edmond Holmes and 'The Tragedy of Education'* (Nottingham: Educational Heretics, 1998).

J. H. Simpson, *Schoolmaster's Harvest, Some Findings of Fifty Years 1894–1944* (London: Faber, 1954).

Robert Skidelsky, *English Progressive Schools* (Harmondsworth: Penguin, 1969).

H. Snitzer, *Summerhill: A Loving World*, (New York: Macmillan, 1964).

W. A. C. Stewart, *Progressives and Radicals in English Education 1750–1970* (London: Macmillan, 1972).

W. A. C. Stewart and W. P. McCann, *The Educational Innovators 1881–1967* (London: Macmillan, 1968).

Judith Stinton, *A Dorset Utopia: the Little Commonwealth and Homer Lane* (Norwich: Black Dog Books, 2005).

Margaret White, "The New Education Fellowship: An International Community of Practice." *New Era in Education* 82.3 (2001): 71–5.

W. David Willis, *Homer Lane, A Biography* (London: Allen & Unwin, 1964).

Chapter 6 – Democracy: Parker, Dewey and the American Tradition

Amos Bronson Alcott, *Observations on the Principles and Methods of Infant Instruction* (Boston: Carter and Hendee, 1830).

Robin Alexander, *Culture and Pedagogy: International Comparisons in Primary Education* (Oxford: Blackwell 2000).

Allan Bloom, *The Closing of the American Mind* (New York: Simon & Schuster, 1987).

Boyd Bode, *Progressive Education at the Crossroads* (New York: Newsome and Company, 1938).

Jack Campbell, *Colonel Francis W. Parker, the Children's Crusader* (New York: Teachers' College Press, 1967).

Max Cavitch, *American Elegy: The Poetry of Mourning from the Puritans to Whitman*, (Minneapolis: University of Minnesota Press, 2007).

Lydia Marie Childs, *The Mother's Book, 4th Edition* (Boston: Carter and Hendee, 1832).

John L. Childs, *American Pragmatism and Education* (New York: Holt, 1956).

Henry Steel Commager, *The American Mind* (New Haven: Yale University Press, 1950).

George S. Counts, *Dare the School Build a New Social Order?* (New York: John Day Co., 1932).

Lawrence Cremin, The Curriculum maker and His Critics: A Persistent American Problem. *Teachers College Record* 54(5), (1953), 234–45.

—, *The Transformation of the School; Progressivism in American Education, 1876–1957*, (New York: Knopf, 1961).

R. F. Dearden, *The Philosophy of Primary Education; An Introduction* (London: Routledge & Kegan Paul, 1968).

John Dewey, *Democracy and Education: An Introduction to the Philosophy of Education* (New York: The Macmillan Company, 1916).

—, *The Early Works of John Dewey, 1882–1898 volume 5 1895–1898* (Carbondale and Edwardsville: Southern Illinois University Press, 1972).

—, *Experience and Education* (New York: Kappa Delta Pi, 1938).

—, *How We Think: A Restatement of the Relation of Reflective Thinking to the Educative Process* (Boston: D. C. Heath and Co., 1933).

—, *The Public and its Problems* (London: Routledge, 1927).

—, *The School and Society* (Chicago: University of Chicago Press, 1899).

Kieran Egan, *Getting it Wrong from the Beginning:Our Progressivist Inheritance from Herbert Spencer, John Dewey, and Jean Piaget* (New Haven: Yale University Press, 2002).

Amy Gutmann, *Democratic Education with a New Preface and Epilogue* (Princeton, NJ: Princeton University Press, 2009).

E. D. Hirsch, *Cultural Literacy: What Every American needs to Know* (Boston: Houghton Mifflin, 1987).

William James, *Principles of Psychology* (London: Macmillan, 1890).

—, *Talks to Teachers on Psychology and to Students on some of Life's Ideals* (London: Longmans, Green & Co., 1899).

Ken Jones, *Beyond Progressive Education* (London: Macmillan, 1983).

W. H. Kilpatrick, The Project Method. *Teachers College Record* 19(4), (1918), 319–35.

Herbert Kliebard, *The Struggle for the American Curriculum, 1893–1958* (London: Routledge & Kegan Paul, 1986).

Herbert Kohl, *The Open Classroom: A Practical Guide to a New Way of Teaching* (United Kingdom: Taylor and Francis, 1969).

Alfie Kohn, *Beyond Discipline: From Compliance to Community* (Alexandria, VA: Association for Supervision and Curriculum Development, 1996).

—, *The Schools Our Children Deserve: Moving Beyond Traditional Classrooms and 'Tougher Standards'* (Boston: Houghton Mifflin, 2000).

Ellen Lagemann, Prophecy or profession? George S. Counts and the social study of education. *American Journal of Education* 100(2), (1992), 137–65.

Jay Martin, *The Education of John Dewey: A Biography* (New York: Columbia University Press, 2002).

Spencer Maxcy 'General Introduction' to *John Dewey and American Education Volume 1: The School and Society* (Thoemmes Press, Bristol, 2002) pp. ix–xxiv.

Katherine Camp Mayhew and Anna Camp Edwards, *The Dewey School; The Laboratory School of the University of Chicago, 1896–1903* (New York: D-Appleton-Century, 1936).

Louis Menand, *The Metaphysical Club* (London: Flamingo, 2001).

Douglas T. Miller and Marion Nowak, *The Fifties* (New York: Doubleday, 1977).

Wesley Null, *A Disciplined Progressive Educator: The Life and Career of William Chandler Bagley* (New York: Peter Lang Publishing, 2003).

Francis Parker, *Talks on Pedagogics: An Outline of the Theory of Concentration* (London: E. L. Kellogg, 1894).

Elizabeth Peabody, *Record of a School* (Bedford, MA: Applewood Books, 2007).

Daniel Perlstein, 'There is no Escape . . . from the Ogre of Indoctrination': George Counts and the Civi Dilemmas of Democratic Educators, in Larry Cuban and Dorothy Shipps (eds), *Reconstructing the Common Good in Education* (Stanford: Stanford University Press, 2000), pp. 51–68.

R. S. Peters (ed.), *The Philosophy of Education* (Oxford: Oxford University Press, 1973).

Diane Ravitch, *Left Back: A Century of Battles over School Reform* (New York: Simon and Schuster, 2001).

Alan Ryan, *John Dewey and the High Tide of American Liberalism* (New York: W.W. Norton, 1995).

I. Scheffler and V. A. Howard (eds), *Work, Education and Leadership: Essays in the Philosophy of Education* (New York: Peter Lang, 1995).

Michael Shapiro, *Child's Garden: The Kindergarten Movement from Froebel to Dewey*, (University Park: Pennsylvania State University Press, 1983).

John Shook and James Good, *John Dewey's Philosophy of Spirit, with the 1897 Lecture on Hegel* (New York: Fordham University Press, 2010).

Douglas J. Simpson and Sam F. Stack Jr. (eds), *Teachers, Leaders and Schools: Essays by John Dewey* (Carbondale: Southern Illinois University Press, 2010).

Charles J. Sykes, *Dumbing Down Our Kids: Why American Children Feel Good about Themselves But Can't Read, Write, or Add* (New York: St. Martin's Press, 1995).

Edward L. Thorndike's *Animal Intelligence:An Experimental Study of the Associative Processes in Animals* (New York: Macmillan, 1898).

Evelyn Weber, *The Kindergarten: Its Encounter with Educational Thought in America* (New York: Teachers' College Press, 1969).

Robert Westbrook, John Dewey (1859–1952). *Prospects: the Quarterly Review of Comparative Education* XXIII(1\2), (1993), 277–91.

Christopher Winch and John Gingell, *Philosophy of Education: The Key Concepts* (London: Routledge, 1999).

George Wood, *Time to Learn: How to Create High Schools That Serve All Students* (London: Heinemann Educational Books, 2005).

Chapter 7 – Social reform

John Siraj Blatchford, *Robert Owen: Schooling the Innocents* (Nottingham: Educational Heretics Press, 1998).

Elizabeth Bradburn, *Margaret McMillan: Portrait of a Pioneer* (London: Routledge, 1989).

Catherine Burke and Ian Grosvenor, *School* (London: Reaktion Books, 2007).

Malcolm Chase, *Chartism: A New History* (United Kingdom: Manchester University Press, 2007).

Thomas Cooper, *The Purgatory of Suicides: A Prison-rhyme in Ten Books* (London: J. How, 1845).

—, *The Life of Thomas Cooper Written by himself* (London: Hodder & Stoughton, 1872).

D'Arcy Cresswell, *Margaret McMillan: A Memoir* (New York: Hutchinson, 1948).

Ian Donnachie, *Robert Owen: Social Visionary* (Edinburgh: John Donald Publishers, 2005).

Michel Foucault, *The Archaeology of Knowledge* (New York: Pantheon, 1972).

Philip Greven, *Spare the Child: The Religious Roots of Punishment and the Psychological Impact of Physical Abuse* (New York: Knopf, 1991).

J. F. C. Harrison, *Robert Owen and the Owenites in Britain and America: The Quest for the New Moral World* (London: Routledge & Kegan Paul, 1969).

Harry Hendrick, *Children, Childhood and English Society, 1880–1990* (Cambridge: Cambridge University Press, 1997).

James Hole, *An Essay on the History and Management of Literary, Scientific, and Mechanics' Institutions, etc* (London: Longmans, 1853).

William Lovett and John Collins, *Chartism: A New Organization of the People* (London: J. Watson, 1840).

Albert Mansbridge, *Margaret McMillan: Prophet and Pioneer, Her Life and Work* (London: J. M. Dent & Sons, 1932).

Margaret McMillan, 'Voice Production in Board Schools'. *The Clarion*, 28 November 1896.

—, *Education through the Imagination* (London: Swan Sonnenschein, 1904).

—, *The Nursery School* (London: J. M. Dent & Sons Ltd, 1919).

—, *Nursery Schools; A Practical Handbook* (London: John Bale, 1920).

—, *The Life of Rachel* McMillan (London and Toronto: J. M. Dent & Sons, 1927).

Viv Moriaty, *Margaret McMillan: I Learn to Succour the Helpless* (Nottingham: Educational Heretics Press).

Robert Owen, *A Life of Robert Owen Written by himself* (London: E. Wilson, 1857).

—, *A New View of Society: Essays on the Formation of Character,* With an introduction by G. D. H. Cole (London: J. M. Dent & Sons, 1949).

Henry Pelling, *A History of British Trade Unionism* (Harmondsworth: Penguin, 1971).

Robert Pemberton, *The Happy Colony* (London, 1854).

Harold Perkin, *The Origins of Modern English Society 1780–1880* (London: Routledge, 1985).

Stephen Roberts, *The Chartist Prisoners: The Radical Lives of Thomas Cooper (1805–1892) and Arthur O'Neill (1819–1896)* (Oxford: Peter Lang, 2008).

Edward Royle, *Chartism, 2nd Edition* (London: Longman, 1986).

Harold Silver, *English Education and the Radicals, 1780–1850* (Lodnon: Routledge & Kegan Paul, 1975).

Brian Simon, *Studies in the History of Education: [volume 1]: 1780–1870* (London: Lawrence & Wishart, 1960).

—, *The Radical Tradition in Education in Britain* (London: Lawrence and Wishart, 1972).

Richard Simons, 'A Utopian Failure'. *Indiana History Bulletin* 18, (1941), 98–114.

Carolyn Steedman, *Childhood, Culture and Class in Britain: Margaret McMillan, 1860–1931* (London: Virago, 1990).

Dorothy Thompson, *The Chartists: Popular Politics in the Industrial Revolution* (New York: Pantheon Books, 1984).

E. P. Thompson, *The Essential E.P Thompson* (New York: The New Press, 2001).

Edward Vallance, *A Radical History of Britain: Visionaries, Rebels and Revolutionaries - The Men and Women Who Fought for Our Freedoms* (London: Little, Brown, 2009).

Chapter 8 – Critical pedagogy

Michael Apple, *Education and Power*, Second Edition (London: Routledge, 2011).

—, *Ideology and Curriculum*, Third Edition (London: Routledge, 2004).

Michael Apple, Luis Armando Gandin and Alvaro Moreira Hypolito, Paulo Freire, *50 Major Tinkers on Education from Confucius to Dewey* (London Routledge, 2001), 128–33.

Stephen Ball, *Global Education Inc: New Policy Networks and Neoliberal Imagery* (London: Routledge, 2012).

Robin Barrow, *Radical Education: A Critique of Freeschooling and Deschooling* (London: Martin Robertson, 1978).

Chet Bowers and Frederique Apffel-Marglin, *Rethinking Freire: Globalization and the Environmental Crisis* (London: Routledge, 2004).

Samuel Bowles and Herbert Gintis, *Schooling in Capitalist America: Educational Reform and the Contradictions of Economic Life* (New York: Basic Books, 1976).

Larry Cuban, *Hugging the Middle, How Teachers Teach in an Era of Testing and Accountability* (New York: Teachers' College Press, 2009).

Antonia Darder, *Reinventing Paulo Freire: A Pedagogy of Love* (Boulder, CO: Westview Press, 2002).

Kathryn Ecclestone and Dennis Hayes, *The Dangerous Rise of Therapeutic Education* (London: Routledge, 2008).

Paulo Freire, *Education for Critical Consciousness* (New York: Seabury Press, 1973).

—, *Pedagogy of the Oppressed, 30th Anniversary Edition* (New York: Continuum Published Company, 2000).

Francis Fukuyama, *The End of History and the Last Man* (London: Hamish Hamilton, 1992).

Henry Giroux, *Ideology, Culture and the Process of Schooling* (London: Falmer, 1981).

—, (with Stanley Aronowitz) *Education under Siege: the conservative, liberal and radical debate over de-schooling* (London: Routledge & Kegan Paul, 1986).

—, *Teachers as Intellectuals: Toward a Critical Pedagogy of Learning* (Granby, MA: Bergin & Garvey, 1988).

—, *Schooling and the Struggle for Public Life* (Boulder, CO: Paradigm, 2005).

Joe Marshall Hardin, *Opening Spaces: Critical Pedagogy and Resistance Theory in Composition* (New York: State University of New York Press, 2001).

Matt Hern, *Everywhere all the Time: A New De-schooling Reader* (AK Press, 2008).

Ivan Illich, *DeSchooling Society* (New York: Harper & Row, 1971).

W. Senteza Kajubi, New Directions in Teacher Education in East Africa. *International Review of Education* 17(2), 197–210.

Douglas Kellner, Multiple Literacies and Critical Pedagogies: New Paradigms. *Revolutionary Pedagogies: Cultural Politics, Instituting Education and the Discourse of Theory* (London: Routledge, 2000).

Joe L. Kincheloe and Peter McLaren, *Critical Pedagogy: Where are we Now?* (New York: Peter Lang Publishing, 2007)

Joe L. Kincheloe, *Knowledge and Critical Pedagogy: An Introduction* (Dordrecht: Springer, 2010).

Peter McLaren, *Cries from the Corridor: The New Suburban Ghettos* (New York: Methuen, 1980).

—, *Critical Pedagogy and Marxism* (New York: Continuum Published Corporation, 2013).

—, *Life in Schools: an Introduction to Critical Pedagogy in the Foundations of Education* (Boston, MA: Pearson, 2006).

J. Martin Rochester, Critical Demagogues. *Education Next* 3(4), (2003), 77–82.

Madan Sarup, *Marxism and Education* (London: Routledge & Kegan Paul, 1978).

Elizabeth Wood (ed.), *Play and Learning in the Early Years, from Research to Practice* (London: SAGE, 2010).

—, *The Routledge Reader in Early Childhood Education* (London: Routledge, 2008).

Conclusion: Methodological reflections

Robin Alexander et al., *Children, their World, their Education: Final Report and Recommendations of the Cambridge Primary Review* (London: Routledge, 2009).

Duncan Bell, *The Idea of Greater Britain: Empire and Future of World Order, 1860–1900* (Princeton, NJ: Princeton University Press, 2007).

—, Writing the World: Disciplinary History and Beyond. *International Affairs* 85(1), (2009), 3–22.

G. M. Blenkin, and A. V. Kelly, *The Primary Curriculum* (London: Harper and Row, 1981).

Kevin Brehony, 'From the Particular to the General, the Continuous to the Discontinuous: Progressive Education Revisited'. *History of Education* 30(5), (2001), 413–32.

Tina Bruce, *Early Childhood Practice: Froebel Today* (London: SAGE Publications, 2012).

Peter Cunningham, Innovators, Networks and Structures: Towards a Prosopography of Progressivism. *History of Education* 30(4), (2001), 433–51.

John Darling, *Child-Centred Education and its Critics* (London: Paul Chapman Publishing, 1994).

John Dewey, *Democracy and Education: An Introduction to the Philosophy of Education* (New York: the Macmillan Company, 1916).

John Dewey and Evelyn Dewey, *Schools of Tomorrow* (London, 1916).

Early Years Foundation Stage – *Everything you Need to Know* (Department for Children, Skills and Families, 2008).

Michel Foucault, *The Archaeology of Knowledge* (New York: Pantheon, 1972).

Maurice Galton and K. Fogelman, The Use of Discretionary Time in the Primary Classroom. *Research Papers in Education* 13, (1998), 113–39.

Philip Gardner, *Hermeneutics, History and Memory* (London: Routledge, 2010).

John Howlett and Paul McDonald, Quentin Skinner, intentionality and the history of education. *Paedagogica Historica* XLVII(3), (June 2011).

Robert Lamb, Quentin Skinner's Revised Historical Contextualism: A Critique. *History of the Human Sciences* 22(3), (2009), 51–73.

M. D. Lawson and R. C. Peterson, *Progressive Education; An Introduction* (Sydney: Angus and Robertson, 1972).

William Marsden, Contradictions in Progressive Ideologies and Curricula in England: Some historical perspectives. *Historical Studies in Education* 9(2), (1997), 224–36.

Jane Martin, 'Interpreting biography in the *History of Education*: past and present'. *History of Education* 41(1), (2012), 87–102.

—, *Making Socialists: Mary Bridges Addams and the Fight for Knowledge and Power, 1855–1939* (United Kingdom: Manchester University Press, 2010).

Margaret McMillan, *Education through the Imagination* (London: Swan Sonnenschein, 1904).

A. S. Neill, *Summerhill, A Radical Approach to Education* (London: Penguin Books, 1968).

Ken Robinson, *Out of our Minds: Learning to be Creative* (Oxford: Capstone Publishing, 2001).

—, *The Arts in Schools: Principles, Practice and Provision* (Calouste Glubenkian Foundation, 1982).

Quentin Skinner, *Visions of Politics, Volume 1: Regarding Method* (Cambridge: Cambridge University Press, 2002).

Index